THE FINAL MOVE BEYOND IRAQ

THE FINAL MOVE BEYOND IRAQ

MIKE EVANS

FRONTLINE

A Strang Company

Most Strang Communications/Charisma House/Siloam/FrontLine/Realms products are available at special quantity discounts for bulk purchase for sales promotions, premiums, fund-raising, and educational needs. For details, write Strang Communications/ Charisma House/Siloam/FrontLine/Realms, 600 Rinehart Road, Lake Mary, Florida 32746, or telephone (407) 333-0600.

The Final Move Beyond Iraq by Mike Evans
Published by FrontLine
A Strang Company
600 Rinehart Road
Lake Mary, Florida 32746
www.frontlineissues.com

Unless otherwise noted, all Scripture quotations are from the Holy Bible, New International Version. Copyright © 1973, 1978, 1984, International Bible Society. Used by permission.

Scripture quotations marked KJV are from the King James Version of the Bible.

Scripture quotations marked NASU are from the New American Standard Bible Updated Edition, Copyright © 1960, 1962, 1963, 1968, 1971, 1972, 1973, 1975, 1977, 1995 by The Lockman Foundation. Used by permission. (www.Lockman.org)

Cover design by Bill Johnson

Manuscript compiled by www.killiancreative.com

This book does not necessarily represent the views of any single person interviewed in its entirety.

Library of Congress Cataloging-in-Publication Data:
Evans, Mike, 1947–
The final move beyond Iraq / Mike Evans. -- 1st ed.
    p. cm.
Includes bibliographical references and index.
ISBN 978-1-59979-188-3 (trade paper)
1. Christianity and international affairs. 2. United States--Foreign relations--Iraq. 3. United States--Foreign relations--Middle East. 4. United States--Foreign relations--Israel. 5. End of the world. I. Title.
BR516.E93 2007
327.73056--dc22

2007005073

International Standard Book Number: 978-1-59979-188-3

First Edition

07 08 09 10 — 9 8 7 6 5 4 3 2 1
Printed in the United States of America

Dedication

This book is dedicated to the brave men and women who have paid the price in Iraq, and to their families, whose pride in America's new generation of heroes knows no bounds. More than 22,401 have been wounded and more than 3,000 have been killed while fighting the global jihadists in Iraq to secure our freedom from terror at home.

Acknowledgments

I wish to thank Stephen Strang, owner of Strang Communications, for his belief in this project; my publisher at Strang Communications, Tessie DeVore; and editor, Debbie Marrie. I am deeply appreciative for your immeasurable assistance in producing a quality manuscript.

To my dear friend Rick Killian, I can only say thank you for the hours invested in helping with this project. I wish to thank Arlen Young, whose assistance with this book was incalculable, and my executive administrator, Lanelle Young, for her invaluable assistance.

A very special thank you to Rick, Debby, and Clara Massey, who believed in this project from its inception, and especially to Rick, who traveled into battle with me in Israel during the Lebanon conflict so this story could be told. My sincere gratitude to Lee Roy and Tandy Mitchell, who hosted the first national event in support of the television special in their home.

My deepest gratitude to Israeli prime minister Ehud Olmert; former Israeli prime minister Benjamin Netanyahu; lieutenant general and former chief of staff to the Israeli Defense Forces, Moshe Ya'alon; advisor to the ministry of defense for Iranian affairs for the State of Israel, Uri Lubrani; ambassador Daniel Ayalon; former Israeli prime minister Ariel Sharon; ambassador for the State of Israel, Dore Gold; and to those who agreed to be interviewed, including Mr. James Woolsey, former CIA director; Gen. Hugh Shelton, former chairman of the Joint Chiefs of Staff; Gen. Yossi Peled, chief of the Northern Command of Israel; Gen. Dani Yatom, former director of Mossad, the Israeli intelligence service; Gen. Yaakov Amidror, former chief of Israeli Defense Forces intelligence; Lt. Gen. Tom , retired, U.S. Air Force; Capt. Chuck Nash, retired, U.S. Navy; Honorable Irwin Cotler, MP and former attorney general of Canada; professor Alan Dershowitz, Harvard Law School; Mort Zuckerman, owner and editor in chief of *U.S. News & World Report*; Tom Newman, executive director of the Jewish Institute for National Security Affairs; Isaac Herzog, minister of tourism for the State of Israel; Walid Shoebat; and J. R. Martinez, a U.S. soldier wounded in Iraq.

I am deeply grateful to the brave individuals who agreed to be interviewed in Iraq: Karim Sinjari, interior minister of the Kurdistan regional government; Adnan Mufti, speaker of the Kurdistan regional government parliament; Abdulla Ali Muhammad, head of Asiage, Kurdistan's "FBI"; Abdul Khaleed; Sheikh Ja'affra; Jafar Mustafa Ali, minister of state for Peshmerga affairs; Mizgeen Zabari, who fought with the U.S. Special Forces in Iraq; Douglas Layton; William Garaway; Col. Harry Schutte; Kosrat Resul, vice president of the Kurdish region; and Abdulbari al Zebari, member of the Iraqi Congress.

I also wish to thank Gen. Robert Huyser, commander in chief of U.S. Military Airlift Command; Maj. Gen. James E. Freeze, assistant deputy director for plans and policy, National Security; Gen. Jerry Curry, Department of Defense in the Pentagon; Gen. George Keegan, retired, chief of Air Force intelligence (1972–1977); Lt. Gen. Richard F. Schaeffer, retired, deputy chairman of NATO Military Committee (January 1974–June 1975); and countless others.

Finally, a book project of this magnitude demands a grueling work schedule. Most of all, I'm indebted to my beloved wife, Carolyn. Without her patience, compassion, encouragement, and sacrifice, there would be no possible way I could have achieved this.

Table of Contents

Introduction

Six days before the beginning of Operation Iraqi Freedom, I met with Mayor Rudolph Giuliani. He and I had been asked by the office of the mayor of Jerusalem to tape a segment to honor Ehud Olmert, who was leaving that post. As Mayor Giuliani and I talked, I asked him why he rejected the $10 million donation for disaster relief from Saudi Prince Alwaleed bin Talal.

He noted that when the prince had commented that the United States "should reexamine its policies in the Middle East and adopt a more balanced stand toward the Palestinian cause," thus suggesting that U.S. policies in the Middle East contributed to the September 11 attacks, Giuliani felt it would be morally irresponsible to accept the money.

He reiterated what he had commented to the media at the time: "I entirely reject [his] statement.... There is no moral equivalent for this act. There is no justification for it. The people who did it lost any right to ask for justification for it when they slaughtered...innocent people."[1]

I thought again about the words of Isser Harel, a good friend and founder of Mossad, Israel's intelligence agency. On September 23, 1980, I had dinner at Harel's home with Dr. Reuben Hecht, the senior advisor of Menachem Begin, the Israeli prime minister at that time. I asked Isser three questions, and I shall never forget his answers because all three came to pass just as he said they would.

"Who do you think will win the presidential election, Jimmy Carter or Ronald Reagan?"

"I know Carter is ahead in the polls, but the word on the street is Iran will have something to say about that. They are planning on releasing the hostages during the inauguration of Ronald Reagan to keep Carter from being reelected."

"Will President Sadat succeed with Jimmy Carter in pushing for human rights and democracy in Egypt?"

"We saved his life twice from radical Islamic terrorists. He will not always be there. I fear he will be killed."

"Will terrorism ever come to America?"

"America is developing a tolerance for terrorism. The United States has the power to fight terrorism, but not the will; the terrorists have the will, but not the power. But all of that could change in time. Oil buys more than tents. You in the West kill a fly and rejoice. In the Middle East, we kill one, and one hundred flies come to the funeral. Yes, I fear it will come in time."

"Where will it come to?" I asked him.

He thought for a moment. "New York is the symbol of your freedom and capitalism. It's likely they will strike there first at your tallest building, because it's your greatest fertility [phallic] symbol, and it is a symbol of your power."

As Giuliani and I talked, I kept thinking of statements I was hearing about Israel. I became convinced that Israel would once again be forced to pay the appeasement bill for the upcoming war, as it had during the first Gulf War. Once again they would be pressured into accepting a "land for peace" plan, just as they had at the Madrid Peace Conference in 1991. I remember it well since I had covered it at the Royal Palace of Madrid and was the first journalist to confront the then secretary of state James Baker during the event.

Since 2003, Tony Blair, prime minister of the United Kingdom, America's strongest ally, has pressured President Bush to push the "Road Map" plan that called upon Israel to relinquish Judea, Samaria, Gaza, and the West Bank, as well as East Jerusalem.

I write this book with a sense of urgency because "those who cannot remember the past are condemned to repeat it." This is precisely what is happening, once again, to appease racial and religious bigotry against the "Crusaders" and "Zionists"—the Christians and the Jews—but this time the stakes are much higher.

Iraq, Lebanon, and the Palestinian Authority (PA) are on the brink of exploding into a Shiite/Sunni Islamic revolution—a revolution that is spreading like an Ebola virus throughout the Middle East, a revolution that also has America in its crosshairs and hopes to spread to our shores. A volcano of terror is at the brink of exploding in Iraq. When it does, its destructive powers will spill over into Jordan and Israel if it is not stopped. This crisis is the greatest threat to the United States since the Civil War.

On December 6, 2006, James Baker and Lee Hamilton released the *Iraq Study Group Report* on what their bipartisan commission believes should be done in Iraq. In it they recommended that

- the Golan Heights be returned to Syria (a terrorist state);
- Judea and Samaria be given to a terrorist-led government (the Hamas-led Palestinian Authority);
- Iran and Syria be invited to the negotiating table as a "support group" with no preconditions and with UN resolutions against those two nations forgotten;
- right-of-return into Israel be given to Palestinians (terrorists) in Lebanon;
- Israel be required to return to pre-1967 borders (which would mean the dividing of Jerusalem);
- the UN be allowed to determine the destiny of Iran's nuclear program (which would, in my opinion, guarantee Iran with the bomb in a matter of a few years);
- amnesty be granted to terrorists (insurgents) who slaughtered American soldiers in Iraq.

On January 10, 2007, President George W. Bush addressed the nation concerning the Iraq crisis. He stated, "We benefited from the thoughtful recommendations of the Iraq Study Group."[2] He also said that he was immediately sending Secretary of State Condoleezza Rice to the Middle East.

This call to appeasement—just like Chamberlain's in the face of Nazi aggression in 1938—couldn't be clearer. My prayer in writing this book is that we will wake up before we find a sea of glassy-eyed human corpses (suicide bombers) strapped with dynamite and roaming our streets as they have done in Israel. I fear there will be another attack on American soil before the 2008 elections. Radical Islamic terrorists only step back when they fear us.

LOOKING BACK

When I sat down to write *Beyond Iraq: The Next Move*, it was in the midst of Operation Iraqi Freedom in 2003, and our troops were still pushing toward Baghdad. I was deeply concerned about the outcome of the war, and I remember writing:

- The war in Iraq would not begin until it had ended. The greatest threats to American troops would come after the war for Baghdad had been won.
- Iraq's future will be more mess than messianic.
- There will be an army of human corpses spread like a plague across Iraq in an attempt to weaken the resolve of the American people to win this war.
- Deposing Saddam Hussein would not end terrorism. Instead, Iraq would become the new Ground Zero. Terrorism in the Bible land would not end with the fall of Baghdad but rise to a new level.
- Syria and Iran would play the diplomatic card until the heat was off and then clandestinely go back to supporting terrorism.
- Every possible attempt would be made to start a civil war in Iraq. Islamic radicals would attempt to turn Iraq into another Lebanon.
- The war could not be partially won; the victor would be determined by who wins the last battle. We must see this war through to the end, or else the next time we have to fight terrorism it will be much worse.
- Can we lose the war on terrorism? We can, indeed, if we lose the battle for Iraq.

In October 2006, American troops in Iraq lived through their bloodiest month in over a year and a half—oddly coming right on the eve of our midterm elections where the war was a deciding factor for many voters. Those elections saw the Democrats decisively take over the House and capture a narrow majority in the Senate. The media called the election a mandate for the United States to get its troops out of Iraq.

Unfortunately, the talk was not about getting our troops out of Iraq after we have won, but about the quickest route to pulling them out without completely losing face in a kiss-and-run. Too many are willing to concede Iraq as another Vietnam because they can't stomach the cost of actually winning this fight. What they don't realize, however, is that if we don't win this fight now, the cost of the next one will be far greater.

An unrestrained Islamic revolution is spreading from Iran through Iraq, Lebanon, and the Palestinian territory as the world sleeps. The goal is to take over the Middle East and then the entire world. Many of us don't understand the true nature of what it will take to defeat this web of terror. We don't seem to understand that Iraq is not a war in itself, but only one of the first battles in the overall war on terrorism. Too many don't recognize the next World War has already started, and we are right in the middle of it. America needs to have the same resolve in dismantling the terrorists' worldwide network that we did in fighting the Axis powers.

Stabilizing Iraq is not a "Pottery Barn rule" about fixing what we have broken; it is only one of our first solid steps for victory in the war against the Islamofascists—a group even more dangerous than the Nazi Fascists of Germany of the 1930s and World War II. Too few Americans today realize that the "insurgents" we fight in the streets of Iraq are not disgruntled Iraqis caught in a cycle of incomprehensible ethnic intolerance, but terrorists sponsored by oil-rich countries like Iran—the current leader, financier, and exporter of world s—sent to sow civil war into the fledgling republic of Iraq with the same goals the Taliban had in fighting the Soviets in Afghanistan. They really believed that they defeated the Russians in Afghanistan and that it caused the collapse of the entire Soviet Union. They think that the same thing will happen if they defeat the United States in Iraq.

Just days after the release of the *Iraq Study Group Report*, the president of Iran, Mahmoud Ahmadinejad, intimated at his Holocaust-denying conference attended by David Duke, the grand wizard of the KKK, "The U.S., Britain, and Israel will eventually disappear from the world like the pharaohs. It's a divine promise."[3]

We fail to realize that we are fighting the newest world power set not on an ideology such as Communism or Nazism, but on a zealous, distorted form of Islam whose constituents are willing to both kill and die in the hope of spreading it worldwide. Their hope is to chase democracy and freedom from the Middle East, then from the world at large. Iran, the leader in this Islamofascism, is a regime with the mentality of a suicide bomber that is willing to go up in smoke as well, in the hope of wiping Judaism and Christianity off the map.

Iran's leadership is set on obtaining nuclear weapons and advancing its missile technology so that it has the power to destroy Israel and cripple the United States and Europe.

Ahmadinejad and his cohorts are willing to tell any lie and sign any treaty without the slightest intent of keeping it, simply to advance their cause—after all, one need not truthfully negotiate with "infidels." Just as Khomeini joined with and then ruthlessly turned on his allies in the Islamic revolution that transformed Iran into his own kingdom on Earth, so Iran now will cut any deal to get what it wants and then turn on those who helped them when it fits their greater purposes. Iran hopes to keep the international community at bay long enough to develop its own small nuclear arsenal—and once that is done, all previous bets will be off. President Mahmoud Ahmadinejad will be within one strike of doing what he has claimed for years ought to be done: wiping Israel "off the map" as the first step toward the world he envisions as ideal—a world without Zionism or America.[4] Most leaders do not believe he could ever really succeed, but they know that a dirty bomb the size of a refrigerator, planted in Tel Aviv or New York, could kill as many as a million Jews and Americans.

What we don't seem to understand most of all is that the road to victory in Iraq is not as much a matter of the Iraqis finally policing their own streets but of defeating the nuclear agenda and closing the terrorist-funding, petrodollar purse strings of Iran, which has $62 billion in reserves and believes it's on a mission from God.

The key to victory in Iraq is not promoting the agenda of Nuri Kamel al-Maliki, the Iraqi prime minister, but disarming the Islamofascist bigotry of Iranian president Mahmoud Ahmadinejad and the Supreme Leader of Iran, Grand Ayatollah Seyyed Ali Hossayni Khamenei. Right now the battle must not be over Iraq's stability or democracy but over ours. Regardless of how bad things look in Iraq, I would rather fight the worldwide Islamofascists in Iraq than in the streets of America.

They proved on 9/11 that their choice is to fight us on our own soil. We must never let it come to that again.

The world stands at a critical crossroads, but unfortunately it does so wearing politically correct blinders. Because of them, we see our friends—namely Israel—as the root of the problem, and our enemies—Islamists set to destabilize the democracies and moderate (in other words, "non-terrorist-supporting") governments of the Middle East—as misunderstood militants fighting for religious and political freedom. If we don't correct our view, we may soon abandon our friends to appease these "militants," only to find a nuclear knife in our backs as the reward.

If we don't find a way to turn the right corner in 2007, the road ahead may never again be as clear or as safe as it is now.

WHY WE FIGHT

Too few have seen the true costs of what we have to do in Iraq to win this crucial initial battle in what I call the "World War Against Terrorism." As a nation overall, we have been blinded by liberal rhetoric to the purpose of the war. It's time we set our blinders aside and acknowledge the truth.

We have only to look as far back as the presidency of Jimmy Carter to find a time when a Pandora's box was opened and the Islamic revolution was unleashed. Carter's worldview—as exemplified in his latest book, *Palestine: Peace Not Apartheid*—clearly articulates the belief system of the extreme Left. This ideology was alive and well during the time of the shah of Iran and leaves no question in my mind that it was responsible for the destabilization of Iran, a pro-Israel and pro-Western ally. Khomeini could never have succeeded with the birthing of the Islamic revolution without the assistance and support of President Jimmy Carter. Khomeini's Islamic revolution, in turn, birthed the onslaught of terrorism by which the entire world has been gripped and victimized.

We invaded Iraq for a number of reasons. The late Saddam Hussein's regime supported terrorism and had repeatedly used weapons of mass destruction (WMDs) against the Kurds of Iraq's northern regions and during the Iran-Iraq War. He murdered tens of thousands with chemical weapons during his time in power. Cleverly, however, as world pressure grew on Iraq to prove that they no longer had WMDs, many believe Hussein moved them into Syria before Operation Iraqi Freedom, and we have yet to hear the end of not finding them.

Still others believe that we invaded Iraq to set up a democracy there, but it was a democracy in Europe that voted Hitler into power, a democracy in Gaza that elected Hamas to control the Gaza Strip, and a democracy in Lebanon that gave Hezbollah seats in their parliament. While democracy is the hope for the future of the Middle East, as long as that democracy simply reinforces ethnoreligious prejudices, it won't matter. Until those in the Middle East are willing to follow the rule of law and allow freedom of religion for everyone, democracy there will only support mob rule and thugocracies. Besides, how can you have democracy in countries that are theocratic?

No, the United States went to Iraq to take the fight to the terrorists. In this we have been very successful. Every terrorist organization in the world is now in Iraq, and we are holding them at bay. The chaos in the streets is not a sign we are losing but a sign of a very difficult war fighting a type of warfare that we have never fought before. This war is not over, and we need to hold our resolve to see it through. Better we fight in the streets of Baghdad than in Washington, Los Angeles, or Dallas.

Can We Win?

Militarily, the United States is well poised to defeat any enemy world-wide. The U.S. Armed Forces defeated Hitler's Nazi machine in World War II. Ronald Reagan challenged Mikhail Gorbachev with, "Mr. Gorbachev, tear down that wall," and was credited with ending the Cold War. Even when faced with the possibility of taking on Iran, the United States is, by far, the better military technician, but appeasement will nullify that strength.

President Bush is trying to take down the wall that was built by family-owned corporations called countries—thugocracies—and the wall that was built by Islamofascists. The reality is that the family-owned corporations are like the Mafia; they are card-carrying cartels. The way the thugocracies keep the terror organizations from turning on them is by paying them off and by funding and fueling their causes. It is a "don't ask, don't tell" policy. In this light, Saudi Arabia continues to fund terrorist-Sunni rebels in Iraq, hoping to keep democracy as far from its borders as it can, even though the same tactic didn't work for them with Al Qaeda.

An enemy is needed in order to have an army. The Islamic world doesn't want the Palestinian crisis solved. The thugocracies and Islamofascists will do everything in their power to keep it from being resolved. If the Palestinian crisis were resolved there would be no enemy, and they need Israel to be the "Little Satan" of the Middle East in order to have someone to blame for their problems. The thugocracies and Islamofascists have models for Iraq: Afghanistan and Vietnam. The terrorists are depending on the antiwar liberals in America to rally behind and support their cause, and, in fact, they are.

The majority of Muslims are not opposed to democracy. There are more than seven million Muslims in America that are part of America's democratic system, and they are part of that system by choice. The majority of these men and women love democracy. The majority of Muslims are not Islamofascists—they want to live freely by the dictates of their own consciences just as the rest of the world does—but the Islamofascists do not, and they will do anything to keep even their own people from having freedom.

But the question begs to be asked: are our strengths and President Bush's policies enough? I am concerned that they are not. The United States certainly has the technology, but does it have the will to stay the course until victory is realized? Can the American people overcome the lack of will to win, the self-loathing, and the unconcern that seem to surround the war on terror?

The liberal Left has convinced many Americans that the war on terror cannot be won through military action and has fractured our will to win. The liberals point to the U.S. pullout in Lebanon, in Korea, and in Vietnam, or to the Soviet Union's withdrawal from Afghanistan to support their pronouncements. What these pundits do not seem to understand is that it was a military force that precipitated each decision to leave the field of combat—the Viet Cong, the North Koreans, Hezbollah, and the Afghan fighters. Were these not military victories for each of these groups?

Appeasement has been the offshoot of self-loathing. We hate war. General William Tecumseh Sherman said, "War is hell." Rather than believe that those who wage war against us are evil, we begin to see ourselves as evil for retaliating or, even worse, preemptively striking to prevent a sure danger to regional or world security. Self-loathing replaces righteous indignation—and begets appeasement. The desire to negotiate, no matter the cost, gives rise to those in the West who become unwitting cohorts to the jihadists. These individuals rationalize the presence of evil and attacks by terrorists based on their perception of our own past sins.

Daniel Pipes defines such concepts in these words:

> *Pacifism*: Among the educated, the conviction has widely taken hold that "there is no military solution" to current problems, a mantra applied in every Middle East problem—Lebanon, Iraq, Iran, Afghanistan, the Kurds, terrorism, and the Arab-Israeli conflict. But this pragmatic pacifism overlooks the fact that modern history abounds with military solutions. What were the defeats of the Axis, the United States in Vietnam, or the Soviet Union in Afghanistan, if not military solutions?
>
> *Self-hatred*: Significant elements in several Western countries—especially the United States, Britain and Israel—believe their own governments to be repositories of evil, and see terrorism as punishment for past sins. This "we have met the enemy and he is us" attitude replaces an effective response with appeasement, including a readiness to give up traditions and achievements.
>
> By name, Osama bin Laden celebrates such leftists as Robert Fisk and William Blum. Self-hating westerners have an outsized importance due to their prominent role as shapers of opinion in universities, the media, religious institutions and the arts. They serve as the Islamists' auxiliary mujahideen.
>
> *Complacency*: The absence of an impressive Islamist military machine gives many westerners, especially on the Left, a feeling of disdain. Whereas conventional war, with its men in uniform, its ships, tanks and planes, and its bloody battles for land and resources, is simple to comprehend, the asymmetric war with radical Islam is elusive.
>
> Box cutters and suicide belts make it difficult to perceive this enemy as a worthy opponent. Like John Kerry, too many dismiss terrorism as mere "nuisance."[5]

The result is unconcern, complacency, or lack of motivation—the disorder has many names. Whatever the name, it results in simply not taking the threat of terror attacks seriously. The first World Trade

Center attack in 1993 should have been a wake-up call; however, few have realized the import of that momentous explosion. It was a precursor to 9/11.

If we don't act now—and before terrorists have further access to nuclear weapons—for what will the 9/11 attacks be a precursor?

There is only one way to win in this clash of civilizations. Winston Churchill understood this when he spoke before Parliament on June 4, 1940, following the dark days of defeat at Dunkirk in which 338,000 Allied troops had to be evacuated to English shores:

> Even though large tracts of Europe and many old and famous States have fallen or may fall into the grip of the Gestapo and all the odious apparatus of Nazi rule, we shall not flag or fail. We shall go on to the end, we shall fight in France, we shall fight on the seas and oceans, we shall fight with growing confidence and growing strength in the air, we shall defend our Island, whatever the cost may be, we shall fight on the beaches, we shall fight on the landing grounds, we shall fight in the fields and in the streets, we shall fight in the hills; we shall never surrender.[6]

It was Winston Churchill who said that the world lacked the democratic courage, intellectual honesty, and willingness to act to stop Hitler's war machine in 1935.[7] If they had stopped him then, sixty-one million people would not have died.

The terror of 9/11 should have gotten our collective attention, but our attention span seems to be measured in nanoseconds rather than the years it will take to win this struggle. We tend to ridicule the ragtag armies of many of the world's superpower pretenders—Iran being a case in point. We refuse to admit that America, like Israel, could suddenly become a repository for suicide-belted jihadists intent on our destruction. We dismiss as a "nuisance" the threats made by the likes of Mahmoud Ahmadinejad. After all, what can these fanatical practitioners of Islam really have at their disposal?

- Weapons of mass destruction or the ability to obtain them
- Rabid religious fanaticism
- Funds flowing into their coffers from oil-rich Middle Eastern countries such as Saudi Arabia and Iran, among others

- Broad appeal—from beggars in the streets to university professors in the halls of academia; from Riyadh to Boston; from Tehran to Toronto
- Immigration and infiltration—legal immigrants to non-Muslim countries such as the United States, Great Britain, France, Germany, Canada, and Spain are well-versed in using the legal and political systems in those countries to further their agenda of ultimate domination.
- Sheer numbers—if the radical element of Islam measures only 10 percent of Muslims as a whole, the number is a staggering 125-million-plus. That is a sizeable army of radicals with only one ultimate aim: kill infidels wherever they may be found.

Will the lack of resolve, the self-loathing, and the lack of motivation cause the United States to end the war on terror? Will the West fall victim to disastrous losses of human life and goods? How long will it take to recognize the truth that no one, I repeat, no one—not a Christian, Jew, Hindu, Buddhist, or even a Muslim—is safe from the assault of the radical Islamist hatred? And the most pressing question of all: can the civilized world survive the onslaught of such fanaticism? What will it take to jar the West from its comfortable complacency?

THE ROAD AHEAD

When the 2006 elections took a left turn, it caused us not only to have to fight to bring peace to the streets of Iraq but also to prove to the liberals that the war was not only justified in the first place but also part of a much larger picture. Whatever form it takes, we will pay much more dearly down the road if we don't find a strategy for victory in Iraq.

We need to learn from what happened in the early 1980s in Lebanon. By pulling out because of the two suicide attacks, we left the country to Hezbollah and other terrorist organizations to do with it as they liked, and the result has been a war without end. Many are saying the same about Iraq, but the truth of the matter is that if we stay and finish the job, we can end it. If we pull out, we will only be setting up another, bloodier fight down the road. Had we stopped Hezbollah in Lebanon in the 1980s, winning this war might have been much simpler—or might never have had to be fought.

In the coming months, the United States must find a way to victory in Iraq—not appeasement and premature withdrawal of our troops. That will mean curbing Iran's influx of weapons and fighters into Iraq and its support of terrorist proxies, as well as disarming its nuclear ambitions. If we let the terrorists off now, they will only be that much stronger the next time we face them.

In the following pages we will explore why we are where we are today in the Middle East, the reasons for pushing forward with the moral clarity necessary to win the war on terrorism, and what the best road ahead will be. It is time for our nation to come together.

On March 30, 1863, in the midst of America's Civil War, Abraham Lincoln called the nation to prayer based upon 2 Chronicles 7:14:

> We have been the recipients of the choicest bounties of Heaven. We have been preserved, these many years, in peace and prosperity. We have grown in numbers, wealth and power, as no other nation has ever grown. But we have forgotten God. We have forgotten the gracious hand which preserved us in peace, and multiplied and enriched and strengthened us; and we have vainly imagined, in the deceitfulness of our hearts, that all these blessings were produced by some superior wisdom and virtue of our own. Intoxicated with unbroken success, we have become too self-sufficient to feel the necessity of redeeming and preserving grace, too proud to pray to the God that made us! It behooves us then, to humble ourselves before the offended Power, to confess our national sins, and to pray for clemency and forgiveness.[8]

President Ronald Reagan once told me, after I spoke briefly at the end of an event he hosted, that the greatest political body in America is not the Republican Party but the church. With a smile, he also said, "I am not as worried about the left wing or the right wing—I want God to heal the bird." Reagan was sworn in twice on 2 Chronicles 7:14—as he did the first time, the hostages were being released in Iran. During his second term, Communism fell.

I believe this is a battle between two books, two kingdoms, and two spirits—and that the key to victory lies more in the hands of the church in America crying out to God than it does in the politicians of

Washington DC. For that reason this book is designed as a twenty-one-day study tool, patterned after Daniel's twenty-one days of prayer told of in Daniel 10 that brought deliverance to his nation and his people. That is also why I have made available three weeks of messages for pastors and Bible teachers that are outlined in PowerPoint presentations you can find on our Web site at www.beyondiraq.com. In the back of this book is also a three-week Scripture-reading guide on Bible prophecy.

This book is designed as a companion reader for those twenty-one days of prayer and Bible study. God does answer prayer—indeed, America needs to become a purpose-driven nation again.

We have had a rude awakening—now we need a great awakening.

—MIKE EVANS

Etched into the main lobby wall of the original CIA headquarters were these words used to characterize the intelligence mission of a free society:

"And ye shall know the truth and the truth shall set you free."

PART ONE

THIS PRESENT STRUGGLE

Chapter One

A PROPHETIC STORM GATHERS

And then that day when we attack Israel, even the trees and the stones will have mouths. They will cry out. They will say, "There is a Jew hiding behind me. Come, O Muslim. Come, O slave of Allah. Come and kill him till not one male Jew is left."[1]

—WALID SHOEBAT,
former Palestinian terrorist
recounting the teaching he received as a child
and "terrorist-in-training" about Islamist eschatology

"Tell us, when will these things happen? And what will be the sign that they are all about to be fulfilled?"

Jesus said to them: "Watch out that no one deceives you.... When you hear of wars and rumors of wars, do not be alarmed. Such things must happen, but the end is still to come. Nation will rise against nation, and kingdom against kingdom. There will be earthquakes in various places, and famines. These are the beginning of birth pains....

"Brother will betray brother to death.... All men will hate you because of me, but he who stands firm to the end will be saved."

—MARK 13:4–5, 7–8, 12–13

The vast majority of students of prophecy have always believed that the end of the age would begin with a worldwide battle between Isaac, the Jew, and Ishmael, the Arab—a battle that would center on the Middle East, mainly Israel, and increase like a pandemic until it engulfed the entire globe. Only a deaf and blind man would not realize that this battle is, in fact, growing ever closer.

The apostle John received a vision on the Isle of Patmos in A.D. 95 that became the Book of Revelation. In that vision, John saw four riders on horseback galloping across the earth, bringing deceit, destruction, and devastation. Those four riders are commonly known as "The Four Horsemen of the Apocalypse." If you listen closely, you can hear the hoofbeats of those four horses across all the news channels and through-out today's newspapers and magazines.

The Book of Revelation begins with the unveiling of a scroll written on both sides and sealed with seven seals. Seals, in that day, were impressions made with wax, clay, or some other soft material that, when broken, revealed that an unauthorized person had tampered with the contents. The seals in John's vision had to be broken, one by one, to divulge the contents of what was inside. As John broke each seal, another portion of God's revelation about the final days of the earth was disclosed, each time divulging a worse horror than the revelation before.

Daniel, the prophet who lived in ancient Babylon (modern-day Iraq), wrote this of the mystery of the End Times in the twelfth chapter of Daniel. It begins:

> "At that time Michael, the great prince who protects your people, will arise. There will be a time of distress such as has not happened from the beginning of nations until then. But at that time your people—everyone whose name is found written in the book—will be delivered. Multitudes who sleep in the dust of the earth will awake: some to ever-lasting life, others to shame and everlasting contempt. Those who are wise will shine like the brightness of the heavens, and those who lead many to righteousness, like the stars for ever and ever. But you, Daniel, close up and seal the words of the scroll until the time of the end. Many will go here and there to increase knowledge." . . .
>
> I heard, but I did not understand. So I asked, "My lord, what will the outcome of all this be?"
>
> He replied, "Go your way, Daniel, because the words are closed up and sealed until the time of the end. Many will be purified, made spot-less and refined, but the wicked will continue to be wicked. None of the wicked will understand, but those who are wise will understand."
>
> —DANIEL 12:1–4, 8–10

On the Mount of Olives, Jesus's disciples asked Him what the sign of His coming and the end of the age would be. Jesus replied:

> You will hear of wars and rumors of wars, but see to it that you are not alarmed. Such things must happen, but the end is still to come. Nation

will rise against nation, and kingdom against kingdom....
    If those days had not been cut short, no one would survive.
    —MATTHEW 24:6–7, 22

As I write this, just such an apocalyptic time is threatening to arise from three modern-day Bible nations: Iraq, which was ancient Babylonia; Iran, which was Persia until 1935; and Israel, which was reborn in 1948 in the very land God promised to Abraham and his descendants in the Book of Genesis. Understanding the biblical backgrounds and cultures of these nations and peoples can be very enlightening for the days ahead.

FROM THE CRADLE OF CIVILIZATION

The kingdoms of Persia and Babylonia inhabited the region that played host to the world's earliest civilizations. They are thought by most archaeological scholars to contain the site named in the Old Testament book of Genesis as the Garden of Eden. Ur of the Chaldeans, the home of Abraham, was also a part of the region that was once Babylonia—later controlled by the Persians.

At its zenith, the Persian Empire encompassed the landmass from India to Greece, from the Caspian Sea to the Red Sea, and included the Arabian Sea. Its modern-day equivalent would be the countries of Pakistan, a portion of India, Afghanistan, Iran, Iraq, Syria, Turkey, Jordan, Israel, and Egypt—all combined into one vast empire.

For three millennia, Iran has maintained its existence as an autonomous territory and, as we have already noted, only changed its name from Persia in 1935. Unlike its neighbors, Iran is not Arab—it is Persian, or, more correctly, Indo-European. While the Iranians use Arabic script to write, the official language of the nation is not Arabic but Farsi. Unlike its neighbors, Iran's history is not rooted in Islam, but rather in the time when kings were gods and massive structures were erected in their honor. Even today, Iran celebrates No Ruz (meaning "new day" or "New Year"). This is not a tradition of Islam but rather of the days before Islam conquered Persia.

Cyrus the Great, the first Achaemenid emperor—and, incidentally, the first king to add "Great" to his title—established the Persian Empire by uniting two of the earliest tribes in Iran, the Medes and the Persians. He ruled the extensive empire from 550–529 B.C., when he was succeeded by his unstable son, Cambyses II.

Within four years of his ascension to the throne, Cyrus subjugated Croesus, the king of Lydia (of "rich as Croesus" fame), and controlled the Aegean coast of Asia Minor, Armenia, and the Greek colonies along the Levant (a large area in the Middle East bordered by the Mediterranean, the Arabian Desert, and Upper Mesopotamia). Looking eastward, Cyrus seized Parthia, Chorasmia, and Bactria. (For maps comparing ancient Persia with modern-day Iran, please see Appendix K.)

Cyrus ruled over one of the largest empires in early-recorded history. Though he conquered people after people, he was known for his unparalleled forbearance and charitable posture toward those whom he subjugated.

In 539 B.C., Babylon fell before the advance of Cyrus's army. He was greeted by roars of welcome from the Jews who had been carried captive to Babylon. Following his conquest of that great city, Cyrus permitted some forty thousand Jews to return to their homeland in Canaan. With such an unprecedented move, Cyrus displayed great deference toward the religious tenets and social mores of other peoples.

Let me stop here a moment and point out that under the leadership of Cyrus, the Persians exhibited great compassion in allowing the Jews taken captive by Nebuchadnezzar to return to Judah and to Jerusalem. What prompted the conqueror to allow the conquered to make their way home? None other than Jehovah God! God can move the heart of a king just as surely as he can move the heart of a pauper. As Proverbs 21:1 says:

> The king's heart is in the hand of the LORD;
> he directs it like a watercourse wherever he pleases.

Cyrus was lauded as "upright, a great leader of men, generous and benevolent. The Hellenes, whom he conquered, regarded him as 'Lawgiver' and the Jews as 'the anointed of the Lord.'"[2]

In biblical history, Cyrus is first mentioned in 2 Chronicles 36:22–23 and in Ezra 1:1–3. Both passages record that God "moved the heart of Cyrus king of Persia" in order to fulfill "the word of the LORD spoken by Jeremiah":

> In the first year of Cyrus king of Persia, in order to fulfill the word of
> the LORD spoken by Jeremiah, the LORD moved the heart of Cyrus king

of Persia to make a proclamation throughout his realm and to put it in writing:

"This is what Cyrus king of Persia says:

"'The Lord, the God of heaven, has given me all the kingdoms of the earth and he has appointed me to build a temple for him at Jerusalem in Judah. Anyone of his people among you—may his God be with him, and let him go up to Jerusalem in Judah and build the temple of the Lord, the God of Israel, the God who is in Jerusalem.'"

—Ezra 1:1–3

When King Nebuchadnezzar of Babylon captured Jerusalem in 604 B.C., every precious vessel was looted from the temple and carried away to Babylonia. When nations were conquered by the Babylonians, the idols worshiped by that people were placed in a position of subservience to Marduk, the idol worshiped by the Babylonians. The Israelites were an exception. They did not worship graven images; therefore, the vessels taken from Solomon's temple were likely placed in close proximity to, but not in subservience to, Marduk.

Daily food offerings were presented to the idol, and the food, blessed by being in the presence of their god, was then presented to the king. It was on such an occasion that Belshazzar, in a fit of drunken frenzy, demanded that the vessels from Solomon's temple be brought to the banquet hall.

Daniel 5:3–4 gives us this picture:

> So they brought in the gold goblets that had been taken from the temple of God in Jerusalem, and the king and his nobles, his wives and his concubines drank from them. As they drank the wine, they praised the gods of gold and silver, of bronze, iron, wood and stone.

The holy God of heaven was not amused by Belshazzar's antics. The banquet hall was silenced, and the king became a quivering mass as the fingers of a man's hand appeared and wrote a divine message on the wall:

> This is the inscription that was written:
> MENE, MENE, TEKEL, PARSIN
> This is what these words mean:

Mene: God has numbered the days of your reign and brought it to an end.

Tekel: You have been weighed on the scales and found wanting.

Peres: Your kingdom is divided and given to the Medes and Persians.

—DANIEL 5:25–28

Belshazzar didn't have long to wait for God to fulfill this indictment against him:

That very night Belshazzar, king of the Babylonians, was slain, and Darius the Mede took over the kingdom.

—DANIEL 5:30–31

Darius the Mede was later conquered by Cyrus the Great. (The Kurdish people in Kurdistan, from where I have written portions of this book, are descendants of the ancient Medes.)

It may startle you to know that God doesn't predict the future; He creates it. God foretells events to His prophets, who in turn prophesy to the people those things that God has revealed. God revealed His future plans to the prophets of old—Isaiah, Jeremiah, Daniel, Ezekiel, and others. Then in His perfect timing, He caused the prophesied events to become reality. He used ancient kings and kingdoms to chastise His errant children, the nation of Israel, and He used those same kings and kingdoms to return them to their rightful place.

As ruler of Persia, Cyrus was heir to all the vessels looted by the Babylonians from Solomon's temple in Jerusalem. Unlike other conquerors, Cyrus did something that was completely uncommon. Seventy years after the Jewish people were taken captive by Nebuchadnezzar, Cyrus allowed them to return home to Israel. (This is what Daniel had prayed for in Daniel 9:17–19.) Not only were they allowed to return, but also Cyrus provided everything they needed to rebuild the temple and the walls of the city. With their return to Jerusalem, he relinquished into their care the items that were taken from the temple.

Cyrus was unique, not only because he allowed the Jews to return to Israel, but also because his birth and his name were foretold by the prophet Isaiah almost one hundred fifty years before he was born. God also revealed Cyrus's mission to the prophet. Isaiah recorded that Cyrus would accomplish specific tasks under God's direction during his lifetime.

King Cyrus was destined to carry out God's plan as it related to His chosen people. It was through Cyrus that the Babylonian Empire and seventy years of Jewish captivity came to an end.

> Who says of Cyrus, "He is my shepherd
>   and will accomplish all that I please;
>   he will say of Jerusalem, 'Let it be rebuilt,'
>   and of the temple, 'Let its foundations be laid.'"
>
> —Isaiah 44:28

Although Cyrus was a practicing pagan, a worshiper of the god Marduk, he would achieve noble feats as an instrument in the hands of Jehovah God. He would contribute, albeit indirectly, to the coming of the Messiah, God's anointed One.

> Moreover, King Cyrus brought out the articles belonging to the temple of the Lord, which Nebuchadnezzar had carried away from Jerusalem and had placed in the temple of his god. Cyrus king of Persia had them brought by Mithredath the treasurer, who counted them out to Sheshbazzar the prince of Judah.
>
> —Ezra 1:7–8

> "However, in the first year of Cyrus king of Babylon, King Cyrus issued a decree to rebuild this house of God. He even removed from the temple of Babylon the gold and silver articles of the house of God, which Nebuchadnezzar had taken from the temple in Jerusalem and brought to the temple in Babylon.
>
> "Then King Cyrus gave them to a man named Sheshbazzar, whom he had appointed governor, and he told him, 'Take these articles and go and deposit them in the temple in Jerusalem. And rebuild the house of God on its site.' So this Sheshbazzar came and laid the foundations of the house of God in Jerusalem. From that day to the present it has been under construction but is not yet finished."
>
> Now if it pleases the king, let a search be made in the royal archives of Babylon to see if King Cyrus did in fact issue a decree to rebuild this house of God in Jerusalem. Then let the king send us his decision in this matter.
>
> —Ezra 5:13–17

> In the first year of King Cyrus, the king issued a decree concerning the temple of God in Jerusalem:
>
> Let the temple be rebuilt as a place to present sacrifices, and let its foundations be laid. It is to be ninety feet high and ninety feet wide, with three courses of large stones and one of timbers. The costs are to be paid by the royal treasury. Also, the gold and silver articles of the house of God, which Nebuchadnezzar took from the temple in Jerusalem and brought to Babylon, are to be returned to their places in the temple in Jerusalem; they are to be deposited in the house of God.
>
> —EZRA 6:3–5

History documents the birth, death, and achievements of Cyrus the Great. His name is recorded in the Bible over twenty times. *Encyclopedia Britannica* recognizes that "in 538 [B.C.] Cyrus granted to the Jews, whom Nebuchadnezzar had transported to Babylonia, the return to Palestine and the rebuilding of Jerusalem and its temple."[3]

It is ironic that the descendants of the very nation that were instrumental in returning the Jews to Jerusalem during the reign of King Cyrus now want them wiped off the map.

Darius I wrested the Persian kingdom from the descendants of Cyrus the Great, but the establishment of his rule was fraught by skirmishes with the surrounding provinces. Darius proved to be quite the tactician. His trusted generals used the small army of Medes and Persians to great advantage and were able to solidify Darius's rule over the entire Persian Empire.

Darius was a forward-thinking ruler whose legal expertise produced the "Ordinance of Good Regulations" used to create a uniform code of law throughout the empire. He created a system of mail transport much like the Pony Express. Darius built a system of roads that reached 1,500 miles from Sardis in Turkey to Shustar (the site of Daniel's overnight visit to the lions' den). Darius I was succeeded by his son, Xerxes I—also known as Ahasuerus—the king who took the Jewess Hadassah (better known as Esther) as his queen.

The story of Esther has all the elements of a modern-day love story: a beautiful young Jewish girl torn from her homeland and taken as a captive to Persia; a tyrannical ruler who banishes his queen from the royal throne—and initiates a search for her successor; and, of course, a dastardly villain, Haman, who desires to perpetrate genocide against the Jews:

Then Haman said to King Xerxes, "There is a certain people dispersed and scattered among the peoples in all the provinces of your kingdom whose customs are different from those of all other people and who do not obey the king's laws; it is not in the king's best interest to tolerate them."

—ESTHER 3:8

Esther's cousin, Mordecai, challenges the queen to approach the king (a move that could be punishable by death) and ask for the salvation of her people. In encouraging her to do so, Mordecai confronts Esther with these timeless words:

For if you remain silent at this time, relief and deliverance for the Jews will arise from another place, but you and your father's family will perish. And who knows but that you have come to royal position for such a time as this?

—ESTHER 4:14

Esther's response to Mordecai is magnificent:

Go, gather together all the Jews who are in Susa, and fast for me. Do not eat or drink for three days, night or day. I and my maids will fast as you do. When this is done, I will go to the king, even though it is against the law. And if I perish, I perish.

—ESTHER 4:16

With great trepidation, Esther approaches Ahasuerus and is granted an audience with the king. The plan for the destruction of the Jews by the foul villain, Haman, is thwarted, and Esther's people are allowed to live in peace in Shushan.

Many empires fall prey to the march of time. However, in Persia—or Iran—the Arab onslaught produced a cultural mix that was unique. Persia would forever be dramatically influenced by the armies of Muhammad, but so would the conquerors be influenced by their Persian subjects. Arabic became a new language in addition to Farsi, Islam became the new religion, mosques were built, and Islamic customs became the norm for the people of Persia.

Political correctness is not an invention of modern-day America; it has dictated the actions of people from the beginning of time. For many Iranian nobles, conversion to Islam was a politically correct move that enabled them to keep their vast holdings and coveted social position.

For others, the impetus for conversion was tax evasion. Their Muslim superiors had levied an exorbitant tax against all non-Muslims, which they wished to avoid. Some Jews living in Iran were forced, on forfeiture of their lives, to convert to Islam. Many, such as the Zoroastrian priests, simply fled the country.

Although the conquest of Iran by the Arab hordes was relatively violence-free, the ensuing struggle for leadership culminated in a bloody and lopsided battle. Hussein, the grandson of the Prophet Muhammad, and forces loyal to Caliph Yazid met on the plains of Karbala—today one of the holiest cities in Iraq. (It was to be a watershed event in Islam, for it was here that Hussein died, and it was here that the irreparable division between the Sunnis and the Shiites began.)

THE TEMPLE OF DOOM

Shia Islam was founded in A.D. 661 by Ali ibn Abi Talib. It was from his name that Shia evolved. It is literally a derivation of *Shiat Ali*—"partisans of Ali." As a descendant of Muhammad, Ali was thought to be the last of the true caliphs. He was wildly popular until he came face-to-face in a battle with the army of the governor of Damascus in A.D. 661. It is said that the Damascene soldiers attached verses from the Quran to the tips of their spears. When faced with fighting a force hiding behind the words of Muhammad, Ali's army declined to fight. Ali, left only with the option of negotiating with his enemy, sought appeasement. While he escaped death at the hands of his enemy in open combat, Ali was eventually killed by one of his own rabid followers.

When Ali died, the governor of Damascus, Mu'awiya, anointed himself caliph. Ali's son, Hassan, the rightful heir to the caliphate, died under suspicious circumstances, while the next in the line of succession, Hussein, agreed to do nothing until Mu'awiya died. He was soon disappointed yet again, however, when Mu'awiya's son, Yazid, appropriated the position of caliph and went to battle against Hussein. The bloody battle of Karbala that erupted resulted in the deaths of Hussein and his army. Only Hussein's baby boy survived the carnage, and he became the hope of reestablishing Ali's claim to the caliphate.

With the ascension of Mahmoud Ahmadinejad to the position of power in Iran, we have heard much about the last known descendant of Hussein, Muhammad al-Mahdi, or the *Mahdi*. Al-Mahdi was the Twelfth Imam in the line of Ali who disappeared down a well at the age of four. Refusing to believe that he was dead, his followers imbued him with timelessness. They declared him to be merely "hidden," and that on some future date he would suddenly appear to reestablish an Islamic caliphate worldwide. Their eschatology, however, proved problematic; it espoused an apocalyptic upheaval in order for the Mahdi, or Hidden Imam, to ascend to his rightful place of leadership. These "Twelvers" championed the belief that every individual, regardless of their religious belief, would one day bow to Islam—or die.

As time passed and the Mahdi failed to make an appearance, authority passed to the *ulema*, a body of mullahs endowed with the power to appoint a supreme leader. Perhaps one of the best-known imams was Grand Ayatollah Ruhollah Khomeini.

Notable among the various dynasties of Persia were the Safavids who ruled from 1501 to 1736. It was under this dynasty that Shia Islam became Iran's official religion. It was also during this time that Persia was united as a single sovereignty that became the bridge to what we now know as Iran.

It was the Afsharid leader Nadir Shah who first declared himself the shah of Iran in 1736. He invaded Khandahar in Afghanistan, and two years after assuming the throne in Iran, he overran India. He amassed great wealth, including the seizure of the renowned Peacock Throne and the 105-carat *Koh-i-Noor* (Persian for "mountain of light") diamond. (The magnificent diamond was presented to Queen Victoria in 1851 and is now part of the celebrated British Crown Jewels.) Nadir Shah was a tyrannical ruler; his reign ended with his assassination in 1747.

The Afsharid dynasty was followed by the Zand and Qajar dynasties. In 1906, Iran experienced a constitutional revolution that divided the power of rule between the shah and a parliamentary body called the *Majlis*. The last of the Qajar dynasty rulers, Ahmad Shah Qajar, was overthrown in a coup in 1921, and the Pahlavis—who sat on the Peacock Throne until 1979—took the power as shahs. Ahmad Shah Qajar died in exile in France in 1930.

It was the first Pahlavi, Reza Shah Pahlavi the Great, who in 1935 asked the world to stop referring to his nation as Persia and to use the name Iran instead. *Iran* means "land of the Aryans" and was the name the natives used in referring to their country.[4]

During more than twenty-five centuries of history, Persians have maintained their unique sense of identity. Though they converted to Islam, they have not always followed the accepted views of the religion. To an extent, Zoroastrianism, the religion of the early Persians, colors the Iranian variety of Islam.

Iran is now one of the largest countries not only in the Middle East, but also in the Islamic world. Because of past experiences, Iran has developed a thorny separatism. Invaded during both World Wars and later set upon by Iraq, Iran has reason to fear foreign influence.

The borders of Iran remained largely unchanged during the twentieth century, but the desire to recapture the glory of the vast Persian Empire has apparently lain dormant. Perhaps this pragmatism is the driving force behind Iran's seemingly sudden emergence as a budding player in the world's nuclear superpower game.

It was during the reign of the last shah of Iran, Mohammad Reza Pahlavi, that plans to bring Iran into the nuclear age began. Bushehr was to be the site of the first two reactors, and, indeed, building on the site began in 1975. While the shah was still in control, research and development on fissile material production was also initiated. This, however, as well as all of the shah's other ambitions, ended with the Islamic revolution of 1979.

BABYLON WILL RISE AGAIN

In my book *Beyond Iraq: The Next Move*, I discussed many of the biblical implications of the second Gulf War, including the fact that Saddam Hussein saw himself as Nebuchadnezzar reincarnate. It is odd to note that since the publication of that book, Hussein's end was very much like that of Nebuchadnezzar:

> Immediately what had been said about Nebuchadnezzar was fulfilled. He was driven away from people and ate grass like cattle. His body was drenched with the dew of heaven until his hair grew like the feathers of an eagle and his nails like the claws of a bird.
>
> —DANIEL 4:33

Daniel had just prophesied to Nebuchadnezzar that he was going to go insane, be driven from his kingdom, and end up in the field hiding, looking like a wild animal. Precisely what happened to Nebuchadnezzar happened to Saddam Hussein. On December 13, 2003, U.S. soldiers found him completely disoriented, hiding in a hole, his hair and fingernails grown out, and looking like a wild man. It was no different.

While Hussein's "Babylon" fell with him, the spirit of Babylon identified in the Book of Revelation did not. It is important to note that Persia is not mentioned in the Book of Revelation, while Babylon—likely the name used to represent the entire region around where the ancient city sat—is used several times as the head of the forces that rise against those represented by the city of Jerusalem—the Jews. In Scripture, Babylon is the seat of Satan's evil as much as Jerusalem is the seat of God's righteousness. They symbolize the two alliances that meet against one another in the final battle of Armageddon.

At the same time, however, the Book of Ezekiel describes the force that will rise against Israel during the End Times with these words, mentioning Persia and others by name:

> The word of the LORD came to me: "Son of man, set your face against Gog, of the land of Magog, the chief prince of Meshech and Tubal; prophesy against him and say: 'This is what the Sovereign LORD says: I am against you, O Gog, chief prince of Meshech and Tubal....Persia [Iran], Cush [other translations have Ethiopia or Sudan—possibly representing African Muslims] and Put [KJV: Libya]...[and] the many nations with you....
>
> "'...After many days you will be called to arms. In future years you will invade a land that has recovered from war [Israel's return to existence after WWII?], whose people were gathered from many nations to the mountains of Israel, which had long been desolate. They had been brought out from the nations, and now all of them live in safety. You and all your troops and the many nations with you will go up, advancing like a storm; you will be like a cloud covering the land.
>
> "'This is what the Sovereign LORD says: On that day thoughts will come into your mind and you will devise an evil scheme. You will say, "I will invade a land of unwalled villages; I will attack a peaceful and unsuspecting people—all of them living without walls and without gates and bars. I will plunder and loot and turn my hand against the resettled ruins and the people gathered from the nations, rich in livestock and goods, living at the center of the land."'"

"'…In that day, when my people Israel are living in safety, will you not take notice of it? You will come from your place in the far north, you and many nations with you, all of them riding on horses, a great horde, a mighty army. You will advance against my people Israel like a cloud that covers the land.'"

—Ezekiel 38:1–3, 5–6, 8–12, 14–16

Upon this assembly of nations against Israel, God declares He will pour out His wrath in what sounds very much like what happened in Hiroshima and Nagasaki:

"'When Gog attacks the land of Israel, my hot anger will be aroused, declares the Sovereign Lord. In my zeal and fiery wrath I declare that at that time there shall be a great earthquake in the land of Israel. The fish of the sea, the birds of the air, the beasts of the field, every creature that moves along the ground, and all the people on the face of the earth will tremble at my presence. The mountains will be overturned, the cliffs will crumble and every wall will fall to the ground….I will pour down torrents of rain, hailstones and burning sulfur on him and on his troops and on the many nations with him. And so I will show my greatness and my holiness, and I will make myself known in the sight of many nations. Then they will know that I am the Lord.'"

—Ezekiel 38:18–20, 22–23

Did ancient prophets predict Armageddon would end in a nuclear holocaust? Many biblical scholars have suggested that it will. Just read the following passages and see what you think:

Whoever flees at the sound of terror
    will fall into a pit;
    whoever climbs out of the pit
    will be caught in a snare.

The floodgates of the heavens are opened,
    the foundations of the earth shake.
The earth is broken up,
    the earth is split asunder,
    the earth is thoroughly shaken.
The earth reels like a drunkard,
    it sways like a hut in the wind;

so heavy upon it is the guilt of its rebellion
    that it falls—never to rise again.

—ISAIAH 24:18–20

This is the plague with which the LORD will strike all the nations that fought against Jerusalem: Their flesh will rot while they are still standing on their feet, their eyes will rot in their sockets, and their tongues will rot in their mouths.

—ZECHARIAH 14:12

By the same word the present heavens and earth are reserved for fire, being kept for the day of judgment and destruction of ungodly men....

But the day of the Lord will come like a thief. The heavens will disappear with a roar; the elements will be destroyed by fire, and the earth and everything in it will be laid bare.

Since everything will be destroyed in this way, what kind of people ought you to be? You ought to live holy and godly lives as you look forward to the day of God and speed its coming. That day will bring about the destruction of the heavens by fire, and the elements will melt in the heat. But in keeping with his promise we are looking forward to a new heaven and a new earth, the home of righteousness.

So then, dear friends, since you are looking forward to this, make every effort to be found spotless, blameless and at peace with him.

—2 PETER 3:7, 10–14

THE TRUE CALL OF BIBLE PROPHECY

While the exact players in End-Time events are not necessarily clearly outlined in Scripture, the present situation depicts all of the nations of the earth aligned either with Babylon or Jerusalem. Although Ahmadinejad and his belief in the rise of the Mahdi through an apocalyptic world struggle are terrifying in and of themselves, we are not without hope. Listen, for a moment, to the words of Jesus:

See to it that you are not alarmed. Such things must happen, but the end is still to come....He who stands firm to the end will be saved.

—MATTHEW 24:6, 13

We don't have the prophecies of Scripture so that we can cower and hide. While the Islamofascists are working to bring on Armageddon in a demonic frenzy, Jesus gave us another purpose as we head toward the Great Tribulation:

> Pray that your flight will not take place in winter or on the Sabbath. For then there will be great distress, unequaled from the beginning of the world until now—and never to be equaled again. If those days had not been cut short, no one would survive, but for the sake of the elect those days will be shortened.
>
> —MATTHEW 24:20–22

In other words, the severity of those last days—as well as the days we live in—depend greatly on the prayers and actions of Christians today. The Bible is not about trying to bring the end of the world as the Islamofascists hope to do, but about bringing salvation and God's love and mercy to a world going increasingly mad. It is not difficult to see who is behind these activities when Jesus plainly told us:

> The thief [the devil] comes only to steal and kill and destroy; I have come that they may have life, and have it to the full.
>
> —JOHN 10:10

It is up to Christians to face the present situation in the Middle East with moral clarity, to pray for the peace of Jerusalem, to oppose evil in this world, and to pray for justice and righteousness to prevail. It is time for the United States to remember its heritage in God, recalibrate its moral compass of right and wrong to God's way of thinking, and stand beside Israel, praying for her salvation both for this world and the world to come.

Chapter Two

RECALIBRATING AMERICA'S MORAL COMPASS

Every time the terrorists kill a civilian, they win. Every time the terrorists get the democracies to kill a child, they win. It's a win/win for the terrorists, it's a lose/lose for the democracies, and it's all because of the asymmetry of morality.[1]

—ALAN DERSHOWITZ

We can forgive you for killing our sons. But we will never forgive you for making us kill yours.[2]

—GOLDA MEIR

A wind of counter-revolution is blowing across the Middle East and directly into the faces of the Islamofascists and their hopes for spreading Khomeini's Islamic revolution worldwide. Both Iraq and Afghanistan have held democratic elections. President Bush was right in his decision to invade Iraq—he has established a base to inject the vaccination of democracy into the bloodstream of oil-rich, tyrannical regimes that suppress the human rights of the masses and confuse them with outlandish conspiracy myths about Israel and the West. The terrorists, however, are trying to destroy this move toward truth, freedom, and democracy—and the liberal Left in America is helping them succeed.

America is not hated by liberal leftists, appeasement states, and oppressive regimes because it is doing wrong but because it is doing right. The belief of these regimes is that a perfect world is a weak and anemic America that embraces the perpetrator and castigates the victim.

President Bush's plan, like that of Ronald Reagan toward the Soviet Union, will bring a new beginning to the Middle East. For the first time since the rebirth of their nation in 1948, the Israelis see the opportunity of a lifetime for a more democratic region. President Bush's battle for the soul of the Middle East is beginning to succeed, much to the chagrin of the liberal Left. In order for his course to continue, God-fearing Americans must unite and battle for the soul of America.

The foundational promise on which the return of Jesus Christ and all prophecy is contingent is found in Matthew 24:14:

> This gospel of the kingdom will be preached in the whole world as a testimony to all the nations, and then the end will come.

This doctrine is taught and believed by more than one billion Christians worldwide that consider themselves "evangelical."

The Middle East is the last frontier for the proclamation of our Judeo-Christian principles, fulfilling Jesus's last words on the earth:

> But you will receive power when the Holy Spirit comes on you; and you will be my witnesses in Jerusalem, and in all Judea and Samaria, and to the ends of the earth.
>
> —ACTS 1:8

The church will, in fact, respond to the words of Jesus, and in doing so will birth the greatest revival the Middle East—and the world—has ever known.

The basis for President Bush's conviction is this: good versus evil. It is a doctrine of the Bible from Genesis to the cross and to the very end of the age, as well as the foundational doctrine in President Bush's war on terror. As Edmund Burke's oft-quoted saying goes, "All that is required for evil to triumph is for good men to do nothing." It was the same doctrine Ronald Reagan used in defeating the so-called "Evil Empire" of the Soviet Union.

Why do followers of Christ feel a God-ordained call to wage war against evil and to support Israel? How is this mission based on the Bible, and how will it birth a great awakening in America and the Middle East, causing these believers to refocus their passions on confronting the root of all evil?

For example, how can Christians support a war when Jesus has said, "Love your enemies"? The New Testament clearly states that civil magistrates can wage war against all enemies, both foreign and domestic. Romans 13:1–4 (NASU) says:

> Every person is to be in subjection to the governing authorities. For there is no authority except from God, and those which exist are established by God. Therefore whoever resists authority has opposed the ordinance of God; and they who have opposed will receive condemnation upon

themselves. For rulers are not a cause of fear for good behavior, but for evil. Do you want to have no fear of authority? Do what is good and you will have praise from the same; for it is a minister of God to you for good. But if you do what is evil, be afraid; for it does not bear the sword for nothing; for it is a minister of God, an avenger who brings wrath on the one who practices evil.

Today, the battle of good versus evil is being fought from within. Liberals hate the America of which Christian presidents dream. They hate Israel, the Bible, and Christians in general. They subject Christians to scorn, ridicule, and discrimination. There is no attack on American culture more deadly than the secular humanists' attack against God in American public life.

The insults, verbal abuse, and attacks are so severe that anyone who contradicts them is labeled ignorant, evil, racist, and a bigot. The dumbing down of America has begun, and all in the name of political correctness and a new godless globalism.

The hippies of the '60s have become the establishment against which they once railed. Even though they run the culture, the media, the educational system, the courts, the arts, and so forth, they are still self-destructing. From the public and private sector, from mainstream Hollywood to the public schools, from Washington politics to local judges, from the arts to the sciences, they are self-destructing.

America, the noble experiment, is under siege. The tidal wave of evil is sweeping over our nation: the self-injuring, spirit-destroying, conscious-searing practices of pornography, abortion, homosexuality, and drug and alcohol abuse are being supported as they never have been before. There is a vicious moral and spiritual war raging in the hearts and minds of Americans.

THE COST OF DENYING THAT EVIL EXISTS

At the heart of liberalism is a belief that evil really doesn't exist, people are basically good, and thus individuals can't really be held accountable for the wrong they do. The liberal tactic is that it is better just to talk with people since we are basically all the same and reasonable at heart, rather than bringing criminals to justice or fighting to stop those committing crimes upon humanity.

The liberal crowd wants God and the Bible out of America. Our first president, George Washington, said, "Let us with caution indulge the supposition that morality can be maintained without religion.... Reason and experience both forbid us to expect, that national morality can prevail in exclusion of religious principle."[3] John Adams said, "Our Constitution was made only for a religious and moral people. It is wholly inadequate for the government of any other."[4]

Can the liberal secular humanists' hatred for all things Christian pass Natan Sharansky's "town square test"?

> Can a person walk into the middle of the town square and express his or her views without fear of arrest, imprisonment, or physical harm? If he can, then that person is living in a free society. If not, it's a fear society.[5]

The rights of Christians in America to express their views without fear of retaliation from liberal organizations are frequently challenged and are slowly being eroded.

I believe America is under attack from radical Islam because it is a Christian nation. Bush is hated because he is one of the most devoted Christian presidents in American history and because he applies Christian principles to every aspect of his policies. On the news of the first Bush election crisis in Florida, George Bush read in his daily devotional, "Son, remember your father's friends."[6] He picked up the phone, called James Baker, and asked him to fly to Florida to save the day.

President Bush has said, "When you turn your heart and your life over to Christ, when you accept Christ as the Savior, it changes your heart. It changes your life. And that's what happened to me."[7]

In his State of the Union address in 2002 (what is now called the "axis of evil" speech), President Bush drew a line in the sand for nations that he considers part of an axis of evil threatening the free world. On February 7, 2002, the president said, "Faith shows the reality of good and the reality of evil."[8]

George W. Bush began his second White House term with his freedom speech, as did Ronald Reagan with his speech about the threat of evil in the world and the hope of freedom. Reagan quoted John 3:16 (KJV) as his favorite verse: "For God so loved the world, that he gave his only begotten Son, that whosoever believeth in him should not perish, but have everlasting life." He explained his relationship with God in these words: "Having accepted Jesus Christ as my Savior, I have God's promise of eternal life in heaven."[9]

Reagan saw the evil of Communism not only as shutting down the churches, but also as threatening the eternal salvation of millions of people. He said of freedom:

> Above all, we must realize that no arsenal or no weapon in the arsenals of the world is so formidable as the will and moral courage of free men and women. It is a weapon our adversaries in today's world do not have. It is a weapon that we as Americans do have. Let that be understood by those who practice terrorism and prey upon their neighbors.[10]

Both Ronald Reagan and George W. Bush felt called to become president. Mother Teresa told me in Rome that she and her sisters stayed up two nights praying for Ronald Reagan after he was shot. She told me that she met with Mr. Reagan in June 1981 and said:

> You have suffered the passion of the cross and have received grace. There is a purpose to this. Because of your suffering and pain you will now understand the suffering and pain of the world. This has happened to you at this time because your country and the world needs you.[11]

She said that Nancy Reagan broke into tears. The president was deeply moved. Maureen Reagan, the president's daughter, told me that her father repeated the story often and said, "God has spared me for a reason. I will devote the rest of my time here on earth to find out what He intends me to do."

A PROPHECY

In October 1970, Pat Boone, Harald Bredesen, Herb Ellingwood, and George Otis, with Shirley Boone, had joined hands in a circle to pray with then governor Ronald Reagan. Otis said that as he prayed, his hands began to shake. (He was holding Reagan's hand.) Otis said, "Son, if you walk upright before Me, you will reside at 1600 Pennsylvania Avenue." The other three men who were present that day told me the same story.

I had the pleasure of meeting personally with Ronald Reagan several times at the White House during his presidency. He talked freely about spiritual matters. I was invited to the White House for a private dinner with the Reagan cabinet and eighty-six of America's top religious leaders shortly after his first inauguration and for the first Middle East national security briefing (on the sale of AWACS to Saudi Arabia) after Reagan's inauguration. I was also invited to speak briefly at the Republican National Convention in Dallas, Texas, in 1980.

Bush and Reagan were both greatly influenced by the writings of C. S. Lewis, and especially his book *Mere Christianity*, particularly book 1, which is entitled "Right and Wrong as a Clue to the Meaning of the Universe." The writings of Alexander Solzhenitsyn were also an influence. Solzhenitsyn addressed the Harvard graduating class in 1978 with a speech entitled "A World Split Apart." He characterized the current conflict for our planet as a physical and spiritual war that had already begun and could not be won without dealing with the forces of evil.

On January 20, 2005, after praying for guidance on the scripture he should choose as his inaugural scripture, George W. Bush placed his hand on his family Bible. He chose a scripture used by Ronald Reagan at the end of his famous "Evil Empire" speech at the Twin Towers Hotel in Orlando, Florida, on March 8, 1983. From Isaiah 40:31 (KJV), President Bush selected:

> But they that wait upon the LORD shall renew their strength; they shall mount up with wings as eagles; they shall run, and not be weary; and they shall walk, and not faint.

The real crisis we face today is a spiritual one; at root, it is a test of moral will and faith. Whittaker Chambers, the man behind one of the most divisive court cases of our time, the Hiss-Chambers case, wrote:

> The crisis of the Western world exists to the degree in which it is indifferent to God. It exists to the degree in which the Western world actually shares Communism's materialist vision, is so dazzled by the logic of the materialist interpretation of history, politics and economics, that it fails to grasp that, for it, the only possible answer to the Communist challenge: Faith in God or Faith in Man? is the challenge: Faith in God.[12]

For Chambers, Marxism-Leninism "is, in fact, man's second oldest faith. Its promise was whispered in the first days of the Creation under the Tree of the Knowledge of Good and Evil: 'Ye shall be as gods.'"[13]

The Western world can answer this challenge, he wrote, "but only provided that its faith in God and the freedom He enjoins is as great as Communism's faith in Man."[14]

Reagan's "Evil Empire" speech rocked the world. In it he said:

> Let us pray for the salvation of all of those who live in that totalitarian darkness. Pray they will discover the joy of knowing God. But until they do, let us be aware that while they preach the supremacy of the State, declare its omnipotence over individual man, and predict its eventual domination of all peoples on the earth, they are the focus of evil in the modern world.
>
> It was C. S. Lewis who, in his unforgettable *Screwtape Letters*, wrote: "The greatest evil is not done now in those sordid 'dens of crime' that Dickens loved to paint....It is conceived and ordered; moved, seconded, carried and minuted in clear, carpeted, warmed, and well-lighted offices, by quiet men with white collars and cut fingernails and smooth-shaven cheeks who do not need to raise their voice."...
>
> ...So in your discussions of the nuclear freeze proposals I urge you to beware the temptation of pride—the temptation of blithely declaring yourselves above it all and label both sides equally at fault, to ignore the facts of history and the aggressive impulses of an evil empire, to simply call the arms race a giant misunderstanding and thereby remove yourself from the struggle between right and wrong and good and evil.
>
> I believe we shall rise to the challenge. I believe that communism is another sad, bizarre chapter in human history whose last—last pages even now are being written. I believe this because the source of our strength in the quest for human freedom is not material, but spiritual. And because it knows no limitation, it must terrify and ultimately triumph over those who would enslave their fellow man. For in the words of Isaiah: "He giveth power to the faint; and to them that have no might He increased strength. But they that wait upon the Lord shall renew their strength; they shall mount up with wings as eagles; they shall run, and not be weary."[15]

Ronald Reagan's speech impacted the world. Natan Sharansky told me in Jerusalem that he remembers fellow prisoners tapping on the prison walls to communicate the American president's speech. Lech Walesa, the leader of the Solidarity movement in Poland, said the speech inspired him and millions of others.

A painting entitled "A Charge to Keep" hangs in the Oval Office. It was inspired by a favorite song from Charles Wesley. There is a determined rider ahead of two other riders urging his horse up a steep, narrow path. The rider bears a superficial resemblance to George W. Bush.

> A charge to keep I have,
> A God to glorify,
> A never dying soul to save,
> And fit it for the sky.
>
> To serve the present age,
> My calling to fulfill;
> O may it all my powr's engage
> To do my Master's will!

In November 1998, George W. Bush flew to Israel. The trip was sponsored by the National Coalition, a Republican-oriented, American lobby group that strongly supported the policies of then prime minister of Israel, Benjamin Netanyahu. Mr. Bush had dinner with Mr. Netanyahu on November 30, as well as meetings with other Israeli leaders. One of the highlights of the trip was a helicopter tour conducted by the foreign minister at the time, Ariel Sharon. Bush said to Mr. Sharon, "If you believe the Bible as I do, you know that extraordinary things happen."

When he and Ariel Sharon parted company, Mr. Bush shook his hand warmly and said, "You know, Ariel, it is possible that I might be president of the United States, and you the prime minister of Israel."

Sharon laughed and said, "It is unlikely that I, such a controversial figure in Israeli politics, would become the prime minister."[16] But Sharon did, in fact, become prime minister in a special election in February 2001.

During the last U.S. presidential election, Sharon was the first prime minister to refuse to meet with a presidential candidate, John Kerry. He would not even meet with Kerry's brother despite the fact that the majority of the Jewish community is Democratic. Sharon was willing to fall on his political sword for Bush. Had Bush lost, Sharon would have gone down with him.

George W. Bush has the opportunity to do to Islamofascism what Reagan did to Communism, but he needs our prayerful support. Now that the State Department is headed by Condoleezza Rice, it needs only to take the next step. As Ronald Reagan won the Cold War, so too can we win this war; however, we will never defeat Islamofascism without moral clarity! As Reagan said, "If we ever forget that we're one nation under God, then we will be a nation gone under."[17]

The church rallied around the movie *The Passion of the Christ* as a story about good versus evil. They did the same for the reelection campaign of George W. Bush. Christians saw the attacks against him as good versus evil. It is incumbent on the church to focus now on the source of all evil, Satan himself, and to pray for Christ to deliver us from that evil. I believe that if the church will make a commitment to 2 Chronicles 7:14 and to intercessory prayer, this passion for prayer and repentance will foment a Great Awakening in America that will spread throughout the world.

ONLY WITH MORAL CLARITY WILL WE FIND TRUE PEACE

In 1991, I was in the Royal Palace of Madrid for most of the sessions of the Middle East Peace Conference. I noticed that the Israel and Arab delegations were not making eye contact, and when they did, you could see their bitterness. There was a spirit of unforgiveness. During one of the breaks, I met the Syrian foreign minister and the Egyptian ambassador.

I turned to the Egyptian ambassador and said, "Why don't you forgive your brothers, as your most famous secretary of state and prime minister did?"

He looked at me, smiled, and said, "It never happened. We've never had such a man."

I opened my Bible to the Book of Genesis and read him part of the story of Joseph in Egypt who forgave his brothers.

Benjamin Netanyahu, whom I recommended for his first position in Prime Minister Begin's government in 1982, was shunned by President Clinton on numerous occasions because of Netanyahu's moral clarity and his great admiration for Ronald Reagan. As a member of the National Press Club, I had the occasion to hear Benjamin Netanyahu speak to that group. He mentioned Ronald Reagan, his policies, and his admiration for him. The members of the NPC laughed in derision.

I share these two stories with you to illustrate that far too few are guided by the moral truths of the Bible, or even understand them. This is where Christians need to stand up the most. We are in the current conundrum because of a lack of moral clarity and an inability to know who our friends are and who our enemies are.

We must know our enemies. We have two opponents, the irreconcilable wing of Islam and the evil power that inspires it. Once God's people see this clearly, we will plunder hell to populate heaven.

The basis for defeating the bigotry and despotism of Islamofascism is rooted in the Christian faith and moral clarity of George W. Bush, just as defeating Communism was rooted in the faith and moral vision of Ronald Reagan. Totalitarian regimes must be opposed. We must establish a biblical basis and principles for the battle that President Bush and America are fighting. This war cannot be won without this foundation. If we turn inward, relaxing in our own comforts, and stop promoting all the Judeo-Christian principles on which this nation was built, we too easily let evil have its way.

In the minds of Europe's leftist elite, Bush is a bloodthirsty, dim-witted cowboy. (Ronald Reagan was given a similar label, yet it was he who coined the term "Iron Triangle" to define the marriage between the liberal special interest groups, the politicians, and the media.) They mock Mr. Bush and impugn his Christian faith for seeing the world as black or white. They see his moral compass as a dangerous instrument. They have fallen in love with appeasement because they do not believe in evil and thus refuse to confront it.

On September 11, 2001, evil surfaced in America in a way never before seen. The nation rallied to confront evil in Afghanistan and Iraq. Since that time, our wounds have healed, our senses have been deadened, and our memories dulled. I believe we are on the brink of the greatest opportunity in history to confront the source of all evil. If we fail, the results will be catastrophic.

Liberals have a difficult time seeing moral issues clearly because most of them are moral relativists. They reject absolute standards of good and evil or right and wrong. In their worldview, man is perfectible, human nature is on a path toward enlightenment, and the concept of original sin is primitive.

These humanists invented Arafat as a peacemaker and gave him the façade of a freedom fighter, not a terrorist. In their eyes, those who blow up Jews are driven to such acts because of injustices. The victims of these crimes are seen as the causers of the problem, and the perpetrators are seen as the innocent and exploited. Those same humanists believe the lie that bad acts must be blamed on society or on psychological or economic circumstances. Moral relativists despise those who grasp the nature of evil. Victims are demonized and murderers are glorified. We saw that in September 1993 when Yasser Arafat was invited to the Clinton White House. Instead of being apprehended as a thug and murderer (there was an outstanding call for his arrest for ordering the brutal murders of ambassador Cleo Noel and *chargé d'affaires* C. Curtis Moore in Khartoum, Sudan, in 1973), he was welcomed like an international statesman.

President Bush, in his State of the Union speech following 9/11, said, "Evil is real, and it must be opposed."[18] President Bush was called "simplistic" because he did not see tolerance as a reasonable alternative. They wanted Bush to apologize for looking to his God and the Bible for guidance.

Secular humanists make excuses for evil, or worse, deny evil's existence and coddle it by refusing to confront it. Instead, they feed it. Jesus did not negotiate with evil; He did not sweet-talk it, nor did He compromise with it. Evil sees moral issues in shades of gray; moral clarity sees them in black and white. The reality of evil is rejected because the Bible is rejected as the gold standard of moral truth.

The Nazi Party referred to U.S. liberal ambassador Joseph Kennedy as Germany's best friend in London because of his open anti-Semitism. In their twisted minds, the Jews had provoked the war because they intended to destroy the German State. "Every Jew," wrote Nazi politician Joseph Goebbels, "is a sworn enemy of the German people."[19] He believed in the Jewish conspiracy myth called *The Protocols of the Learned Elders of Zion*. To the very end, the Nazis maintained plausible deniability about their injustices to the Jews. Adolf Eichmann—whose continued pleas that he was "just following orders" at the Nuremburg trials made him the poster child for abdication of conscience—was a prime example.

If the devil does exist, as the Bible says he does, there is no better proof of it than that those following his agenda seek first to destroy Jews, and then Christians. It is a lesson we should have learned in World War II and face again with the Islamofascists.

At the Harvard graduation ceremony in 1978, Alexander Solzhenitsyn shocked that august university and the nation with his speech, "A World Split Apart." Solzhenitsyn saw the effects of moral decay in America in the attempts to divorce God from its public squares and build a wall of separation between church and state, replacing God with the government as the creator of liberties. Having undermined her moral vision, America had lost her courage to confront evil in the world.

Solzhenitsyn noted that while engaged in occasional outbursts in dealing with weak governments, U.S. politicians became paralyzed when dealing with foreign powers and international terrorists. He characterized the current conflict for our planet as a physical and spiritual war that had already begun, and he identified the Soviet aggressors as the forces of evil. Solzhenitsyn knew millions of people had been killed in the Gulag prison camp system where he himself had suffered firsthand:

> How did the West decline from its triumphal march to its present sickness? Have there been fatal turns and losses of direction in its development? It does not seem so. The West kept advancing socially in accordance with its proclaimed intentions, with the help of brilliant technological progress. And all of a sudden it found itself in its present state of weakness.
>
> This means that the mistake must be at the root, at the very basis of human thinking in the past centuries. I refer to the prevailing Western view of the world which was first born during the Renaissance and found its political expression from the period of the Enlightenment. It became the basis for government and social science and could be defined as rationalistic humanism or humanistic autonomy: the proclaimed and enforced autonomy of man from any higher force above him....
>
> ...This new way of thinking, which had imposed on us its guidance, did not admit the existence of intrinsic evil in man nor did it see any higher task than the attainment of happiness on earth. It based modern Western civilization on the dangerous trend to worship man and his material needs.[20]

With those few words, Alexander Solzhenitsyn suddenly found himself a pariah. Once lionized by the media, now this great man was treated as though he didn't exist all because, within the rulebook of the intellectual elite, no one who believes in God is to be taken seriously. What's more, the late 1970s were supposed to be an era of détente, a time of lessening tensions; to issue moral judgments about Communism was seen as destructive to all chances for world peace. But Solzhenitsyn was never interested in lessening tensions. He knew that standing for the truth meant confronting the lie—confronting evil.

In his treatise "The Reagan Doctrine," Lee Edwards writes:

> Many conservatives consider Reagan's "evil empire" speech the most important of his presidency; a compelling example of what Czech President Vaclav Havel calls "the power of words to change history." When Reagan visited Poland and East Berlin after the collapse of Soviet communism, many former dissidents told him that when he called the Soviet Union an "evil empire," it gave them enormous hope. Finally, they said to each other, America had a leader who "understood the nature of communism."[21]

Ronald Reagan was a great admirer of Alexander Solzhenitsyn. Reagan agreed with his belief that the conflict between the Communist ideology and that of the free world presented a moral conflict. Unlike the liberal Left, Reagan did not accept the idea that Western democracy and a godless Communism could peacefully coexist. He believed that at some point, confrontation between the two superpowers was a certainty.

Reagan felt that every time relations between the two countries eased, the Soviets took advantage of the opportunity to take three steps forward in their plan for Soviet domination. It was his belief that the entire objective of the Soviet Union was to root out the seeds of democracy wherever they were planted and replace them with the tares of Communism.

The liberal Left had nothing but contempt for President Reagan's view of Communism. He was labeled as an "extremist" and compared to Joseph McCarthy, the rabid anticommunist of the late 1940s. And like President George Bush, he was labeled a Fascist. Liberals refused to believe that a totalitarian state was by definition evil in Reagan's day, and they still do not today.

Jesus's battle was between darkness and light! He taught us to pray that God would deliver us from evil. One hundred million people died in the twentieth century under totalitarian regimes. As a Jew, I am very aware of the Jews who died in the USSR and Europe, but that is only part of the heartbreak. I stood in Cambodia in the killing fields with a weeping pastor. We were surrounded by skulls and bits of clothing. The pastor took me to the tree in the park where the skulls of members of his church were crushed. Only six members of his church escaped death.

I echo the words of President Bush:

> I know that many Americans at this time have fears. We've learned that America is not immune from attack. We've seen that evil is real. It's hard for us to comprehend the mentality of people that will destroy innocent folks the way they have. Yet, America is equal to this challenge, make no mistake about it. They've roused a mighty giant.[22]

Chapter Three

WHAT THE FUTURE HOLDS

This new enemy seeks to destroy our freedom and impose its views. We value life; the terrorists ruthlessly destroy it. We value education; the terrorists do not believe women should be educated or should have health care, or should leave their homes. We value the right to speak our minds; for the terrorists, free expression can be grounds for execution. We respect people of all faiths and welcome the free practice of religion; our enemy wants to dictate how to think and how to worship even to their fellow Muslims.[1]

—PRESIDENT GEORGE W. BUSH

You withdraw when you win. Phased withdrawal is a way of saying, regardless of what the conditions are on the ground, we're going to get out of Dodge.[2]

—TONY SNOW,
presidential spokesman, responding to questions on
partitioning Iraq and withdrawing our troops,
October 19, 2006

On December 6, 2006, the Iraq Study Group—a bipartisan commission of politicians and lawyers cochaired by former secretary of state James Baker and former Indiana representative and 9/11 Commission vice-chair Lee Hamilton—released its report on the situation in Iraq. The report contained seventy-nine recommendations for what to do next in Iraq and began with these words: "The situation in Iraq is grave and deteriorating. There is no path that can guarantee success, but the prospects can be improved."[3]

The report was met with tremendous praise all across the Middle East. Abu Ayman, a senior leader of Islamic Jihad, said this of the report:

The report proves that this is the era of Islam and of jihad....
The Americans came to the conclusion that Islam is the new giant of the world and it would be clever to reduce hostilities with this giant.

In the Quran the principle of the rotation is clear and according to this principle the end of the Americans and of all non-believers is getting closer....

We hope that after chasing the occupation from Iraq, these jihad efforts and experiences will be transferred to Palestine, and yes, I mean that we expect these fighters will come to Palestine as part of a big Islamic army.[4]

Abu Abdullah, a senior leader of the "military wing" of Hamas, the Izzedine al-Qassam Martyrs Brigades, had this to say:

It is not just a simple victory. It is a great one. The big superpower of the world is defeated by a small group of mujahedeen (fighters). Did you see the mujahedeens' clothes and weapons in comparison with the huge individual military arsenal and supply that was carrying every American soldier?...

It is no doubt that Allah and his angels were fighting with them (insurgents) against the Americans. It is a sign to all those who keep saying that America, Israel and the West in general cannot be defeated on the ground so let us negotiate with them.[5]

Abdullah then added that following its withdrawal from Iraq, the United States would be defeated on its own soil.

Abu Nasser, the second-in-command of the Al Aqsa Martyrs Brigades, the so-called military wing of the Palestinian Authority, declared the report a victory for the insurgents:

The Iraqi victory is a great message and lesson to the revolutionary and freedom movements in the world. Just to think that this resistance is led by hundreds of Sunni fighters who defeated hundreds of thousands of Americans, British and thousands of soldiers who belong to the puppet regime in Baghdad. What would be the situation if the Shiites will decide to join the resistance?...

If Israel will not start negotiating its withdrawal we are ready to launch the new stage of the intifada.[6]

Mahmoud Ahmadinejad himself had this to say following the publication of the Study Group's report:

The oppressive powers will disappear while the Iranian people will stay. Any power that is close to God will survive while the powers who are far from God will disappear like the pharaohs....

Today, it is the United States, Britain and the Zionist regime which are doomed to disappear as they have moved far away from the teachings of God....

It is a divine promise.[7]

James Baker and Lee Hamilton couldn't have said it better had they waved the report before the terrorists as a white flag: America does not have the political will to win the war on terrorism.

Are we really on the edge of retreat?

CALLING OUR FRIENDS ENEMIES AND OUR ENEMIES, FRIENDS

What is the Baker-Hamilton report? It is an analysis of everything the Iraq Study Group believed the United States was doing wrong in Iraq. It is also an analysis of how and why the enemy is winning and why we are being defeated. It is a road map of how we should win the enemy over through appeasement.

Had someone written a report such as this on Nazism in the midst of World War II, it would have been labeled treason. The *Iraq Study Group Report* was not written as a national security document for the president and chiefs of staff to analyze; it was written for public scrutiny. The document was printed as a book with a media firm engaged to sell this doctrine of appeasement to the American people. By doing so, they have given the jihadists of the world a blueprint on how to ultimately defeat us.

One of the recommendations of the Iraq Study Group is to hold a Middle East peace conference with Iraq's neighbors to enlist their help in protecting Iraq's borders and do what they can to end the sectarian violence within those borders. Among those invited to the negotiating table would be Syria and Iran, and only one nation in the region would not be invited: Israel. Oh, and they thought Al Qaeda should not be negotiated with, either. What is the big carrot on the table to entice these nations to come? Israel would withdraw to its pre-1967 borders.

Why should we assume such a plan would work now? After all, it didn't work in Madrid after the first Iraq war, when Mr. Baker was secretary of state. Is it time to dust off the "Road Map" again?

As the Study Group itself said, there was really nothing new in their report. Instead, they collected what they felt were the best recommendations available and reported them to the president. The president was free to do as he wished with the results. Reading the report, one gets the feeling that it is a shotgun approach rather than a sharpshooter's. However, the mood of it is somber and has little good to say about how the war has been handled to date. It was as if they had written to fit the mood in the wake of the bloody outcome of the 2006 elections: *Iraq is a mess. Things are going from bad to worse there. We need to get our troops out. It is the Iraqis' problem to clean up their internal security issues, not ours. We have tried military action to make things better, but it hasn't worked; now it is time to turn it over to the diplomats—even if it means meeting with enemies who have shown a serious lack of good faith in the negotiations of the past. We've had too much war; now it's time to try some appeasement.*

As National Security Advisor Stephen Hadley responded:

> Here is Syria, which is clearly putting pressure on the Lebanese democracy, is a supporter of terror, is both provisioning and supporting Hezbollah and facilitating Iran in its efforts to support Hezbollah, [and] is supporting the activities of Hamas.... This is not a Syria that is on an agenda to bring peace and stability to the region.[8]

Regardless, the Baker-Hamilton committee seems to believe Syria is exactly the type of country we should try to woo to a regional security conference—and that we would be able to rely on them to work for peace, even though it has been the farthest thing from their agenda in over four decades.

In contrast, Defense Department officials are very uncomfortable with the idea of granting a role to Iran and Syria at the expense of Israel. In their view, such a strategy could well undermine Arab allies of the United States such as Egypt, Jordan, and Morocco:

> The regional strategy is a euphemism for throwing Free Iraq to the wolves in its neighborhood: Iran, Syria and Saudi Arabia.... If the Baker regional strategy is adopted, we will prove to all the world that

it is better to be America's enemy than its friend. Jim Baker's hostility towards the Jews is a matter of record and has endeared him to Israel's foes in the region.[9]

You would think there is a group of politicians in Washington that is more interested in its own political agenda than in finding a way for America to win.

A Petition for the President

In response to the *Iraq Study Group Report*, I drafted the following petition for President Bush:

Dear President Bush:

The crisis in Iraq is serious; however, I do not believe that the solution is to appease terrorist states, as proposed by James Baker and the Iraq Study Group (recommendation 55). The enemy has made Iraq the central front on the road to terror.

Mr. President, I fully support your 9/11 doctrine on terror: "If you harbor terrorists, you are a terrorist. If you train terrorists, you are a terrorist. If you feed a terrorist or fund a terrorist, you're a terrorist; and you will be held accountable by the United States and our friends."

The Baker-Hamilton report proposes that you reach out diplomatically to the terrorist state Iran as a support group member, while assessing no preconditions (recommendation 5). Mr. President, I do not support a terrorist regime becoming a support group member, especially one that is responsible for the murders of the majority of American troops in Iraq through improvised explosive devices (IEDs) and proxies, one that continues to enrich uranium, one that continues to proclaim that millions of Jews should be wiped off the map, and one that envisions a world without America. I do not believe that the UN Security Council—with France, Germany, Russia, China, and the United States as permanent members—should be the moral conscience to determine the future of Iran's nuclear program (recommendation 10).

The Baker-Hamilton Report also proposes that all militants and insurgents in Iraq (terrorists) that have killed Americans be granted amnesty (recommendations 31, 35). Mr. President, almost 3,000 Americans have been killed by terrorists. That is comparable to the number killed on 9/11. Another 21,000 have been seriously wounded. I do not support appeasing terrorists, nor do I believe that terrorists will stop killing Americans if we offer appeasement.

James Baker proposes that the entire crisis in Iraq is inextricably linked to the Arab-Israel conflict and that Israel must accept a terrorist regime as a partner in peace (recommendations 13, 14, 17). The report also states that land-for-peace is the only basis for achieving peace.

Israel is being asked, once again, to pay the appeasement price by allowing terrorists in Lebanon to return to Palestine; by giving a terrorist regime—the Palestinian Authority—land-for-peace, i.e., Judea, Samaria, and East Jerusalem; and by returning the Golan Heights with no preconditions (recommendation 16) to Syria, another terrorist state. The report also asks that Israel be excluded from a regional Middle East conference, while both Syria and Iran would be included (recommendation 3). I do not believe that appeasing racist regimes that refuse to recognize Israel's right to exist, that reject the Holocaust and want Jews wiped off the map, is the answer to our problems in Iraq.

I do not believe that terrorist states responsible for having murdered Americans and Israelis should be offered incentives (recommendation 51) or offered access to international bodies, including the World Trade Organization.

Neville Chamberlain proposed a similar appeasement plan to the Fascists; it cost the world 61 million deaths, including 6 million Jews. Winston Churchill said in 1931 that the world lacked the "democratic courage, intellectual honesty, and willingness to act."

We must not fail this test; if we do, the jihadists will head our way. The root of the rage is racial bigotry against Christians and Jews (Crusaders and Zionists).

Mr. President, I am praying for you. America and Israel are in harm's way. I humbly believe moral clarity and faith in God according to 2 Chronicles 7:14 will be the key in winning the war against Islamofascism, not appeasement.

IS IRAQ ANOTHER VIETNAM?

Though previously stated, it is worth repeating here: winning the war on terrorism means defeating the ideology of Islamofascism—it is not only about Iraq, but Iraq must be a first victory along the way. That victory has two centers of gravity: 1) maintaining Western civilization's political will to win this war; and 2) in the short term, stopping the flow of Iranian financial and arms support for terrorist groups in Iraq, while in the long term halting Iran's nuclear ambitions.

Just as Nazi Fascism rose in the 1930s from the ashes of a powerless, defeated nation in northern Europe to the point of threatening the world, a new totalitarianism in Islamofascism has arisen that promises an even greater challenge. This fanaticism is the central uniting principle of a world of disgruntled, underprivileged people who desire to bring down the nations who have, according to their distorted doctrines, exploited them for centuries. It is not a war to take what the West has, but to bring the West down to the level of the conquerors. It is more than Communism ever was, because it has added the zeal only possible in religious fervor; therefore, it is a greater threat to the world than anything we ever fought in the Cold War.

Liberals scoff at the idea that such military wimps as Iran could ever be a threat to our borders or existence as a nation. They seem to forget that if Islamofascists get the bomb, conventional military power will mean little. If the objective is simply to attack and disable the West with little fear of reprisals, there is nothing like having an entire regime with the mentality of a suicide bomber willing to hit the United States with a few carefully synchronized nuclear attacks. That would be better than an invasion. And just as I wrote in the prologue to my book *Showdown With Nuclear Iran*, Ahmadinejad's dream of wiping Israel off the map could be done with one nuclear strike centered on Tel Aviv.

Many liken the battle in Iraq to the war we fought in Vietnam but miss some key points of comparison. First of all, the Communists we fought in Vietnam were nowhere near being able to strike us with nuclear weapons. Some say the cost of Iraq is too high and point to Vietnam again in comparison. While I don't support the idea of one needless death among the sons and daughters who fight in the U.S. military, we need to realize that we have lost approximately three thousand soldiers in Iraq as compared with the roughly fifty-eight thousand who were lost in Vietnam.

While the cost of the war in Iraq is escalating, has anyone really stopped to consider the cost of retreat? If we don't win the war in Iraq and end the terrorist threat there, we will certainly have the chance to do it again when it "comes to a theater near you."

Have we been so quick to forget the lesson of *The Ugly American*? Perhaps we have, because today the term no longer refers to the hero of that book—a physically ugly but innovative man who went to Southeast Asia to use his inventiveness to raise the standard of living. Instead we use the phrase to refer to a bombastic, egomaniacal consumer of other cultures' resources so many in the world have come to see as the worst of American culture. Despite this, the main lesson of *The Ugly American* was that we lost the war in Vietnam not because of insurmountable odds but because Washington refused to let the military on the ground fight the war without being micromanaged by congressional committees and commissions. Those who called the shots refused to study the Viet Cong and Communists and counteract to their tactics. Traditional rules of firepower and the use of military strength to capture territory did little good in the jungle where lines meant nothing and guerrilla ambushes were easier than head-to-head clashes. The use of standard infantry techniques from World War I and II were constantly defeated in this chaos, and it is proving to mean even less in the streets of Baghdad. Do politicians again think they know better than military experts about how to win a war?

Isn't it interesting that there was not one active U.S. or Israeli general or even a specialist in Middle Eastern history and politics among the Iraq Study Group members? There was no one but politicians, lawyers, and diplomats. Oddly enough, the members decided the answers in Iraq were political and diplomatic, not military. What they provided was a way out, not a way to victory and to protect our troops. They suggested that untrustworthy regimes should be brought to the negotiating table with Israeli land offered to appease them.

Following the release of the Iraq Study Group's report, I debated the Iraq war with Al Sharpton on *Hardball With Chris Matthews*. The concensus of opinion from both Mr. Sharpton and Mr. Matthews was that Israel, not Iran, was the core of the problem.

Don't get me wrong, I would love to bring our troops home, but if we don't bring them home in victory, we would only be bringing home a fight to our own doorstep.

If we are fighting a war against covert, guerrilla forces, then we need to let our military experts in covert, guerrilla warfare direct the course to victory. We need to disarm militant groups such as al-Sadr's now possibly 60,000-strong Mahdi army; train the Iraqi forces to fight terrorism in their streets like the Israelis; let our special ops groups do what only they know how to do; and cut off the flow of weapons, finances, and soldiers from Iran and Syria to terrorists fighting in Iraq. We need to use our know-how and technology—things such as the Global Hawk, a long-endurance, high-flying, unmanned aerial vehicle—to watch the borders of Iraq and to close them to keep more terrorists and munitions from infiltrating the country.

At the same time, we need to continue to rebuild the infrastructure of Iraq's public services that our troops found barely functional when they entered the country. The tenets of life in a free society, such as schooling, medical treatment, transportation, freedom of religion, protection of the rights of minorities and women, and so on, must become "business as usual" in Iraq. This can only happen if the Iraqis find a new path to unity among the different ethnoreligious groups that were driven further apart by the Baath regime's oppression. Iraq must find a way to emerge from this conflict whole, or else it will only be fodder for its neighbors to pick apart later.

Sanctifying Civil War: The Proposal to Partition Iraq

While the Iraq Study Group argued against dividing Iraq into autonomous regions, many in the United States still believe it is the best path to getting our troops home sooner. In May of 2006, in response to the continued sectarian death squads and civil violence between Shiites and Sunnis, Democratic senator Joseph Biden Jr. and the president emeritus of the Council on Foreign Relations, Les Gelb, were the first to introduce the idea of dividing up Iraq as had been done in the Balkans. In a nutshell, they suggested partitioning Iraq into three regions along ethnic and religious lines, having each sovereignty police itself, dividing Iraqi oil revenues between the areas proportionate to the populations of each, and withdrawing the bulk of our troops by the end of 2008.

The argument behind much of this? Provisions were already made in the Iraqi Constitution for this kind of extreme federalist separation of power. The thought is that it would end ethnic fighting and reduce the need for U.S. troops in Iraq almost as soon as the borders between these regions could be set.

According to Peter Galbraith, a former State Department official and proponent of partitioning Iraq:

> Iraq's three-state solution could lead to the country's dissolution. There will be no reason to mourn Iraq's passing. Iraq has brought virtually nonstop misery to the eighty percent of its people who are not Sunni Arabs and could be held together only by force. Almost certainly, Kurdistan's full independence is just a matter of time. As a moral matter, Iraq's Kurds are no less entitled to independence than are the Lithuanians....And if Iraq's Shiites want to run their own affairs, or even have their own state, on what democratic principal should they be denied? If the price of a unified Iraq is another dictatorship, it is too high a price to pay.
>
> American policy makers are reflexively committed to the unity of Iraq, as they were to the unity of the Soviet Union and Yugoslavia. The conventional response to discussions of Iraq's breakup is to say it would be destabilizing. This is a misreading of Iraq's modern history. It is the holding of Iraq together by force that has been destabilizing. This has led to big armies, repressive governments, squandered oil revenues, genocide at home, and aggression abroad. Today, America's failed effort to build a unified and democratic Iraq has spawned a ferocious insurgency and a Shiite theocracy.[10]

Apparently, the majority of the American people view the war as a tragic mistake, and President Bush's approval ratings and the 2006 elections reflect the growing discontent. It seems more and more that a partitioned Iraq would permit the development of an exit strategy for the United States that an ongoing war cannot—but is that what we should do?

LOOKING CLOSER AT A PARTITION PLAN

While on the surface the idea of a partition plan looks reasonable, we don't have to scratch too deeply before we see the flaws and the reasons why the Bush administration is refusing the proposal. In essence, those that support this idea are admitting that the sectarian violence is more than we can handle and that Iraq is already in the middle of a civil war. If this is true, why leave our troops in the crossfire?

This proposal ignores the fact that the violence is being motivated by Tehran, not Iraqi citizens. Iran's goal is an Iraqi civil war between the Sunnis and the Shiites. If we are to keep Ahmadinejad from doing what he wants in Iraq, stabilizing Iraq becomes all that much more important.

While dividing the nation into regions according to ethnicity and religion looks easy on a map, Iraq's people do not just belong to three distinct groups. While the major groups are Shiite Arabs (55 to 60 percent), Kurds (17 to 21 percent), and Sunni Arabs (18.5 to 20 percent), the country has minorities of Assyrian, Chaldean, and Armenian Christians (roughly 3.5 percent), Turkomans (roughly 2 percent), and Mandians (roughly 0.5 percent).[11] As would be expected, there is a good deal of overlap between the areas where these ethnoreligious groups live, especially around Baghdad, where much of the trouble has occurred. Drawing lines between them would force migration or cause greater distress for minorities. Baghdad would have to become a shared region similar to Berlin at the end of World War II and before the fall of the Berlin wall.

At this moment, despite what is covered—or not covered—on the nightly news, the Kurdish north and Shiite south of Iraq are relatively peaceful and prospering. The Kurds insist on the constitutional right to run their own region, and Baghdad ministries are not permitted the right to open offices in the area. The area is so buzzing with new building by investors that a perpetual dust cloud of prosperous activity hangs over all the major cities.

The Shiite south is run by clerics, militias, and religious parties under the guise of municipal and government offices. For all practical purposes, it has become an Islamic state similar to Iran. An ongoing American presence in the Shiite southern regions would only serve to further aggravate relations with that sector. The coalition troops are a catalyst for ongoing attacks. With the exit of all coalition troops, there would be less likelihood of friendly-fire incidents.

It is the Sunni Arab heartland of Iraq that has become the battle-ground for American forces, terrorists, Shiite militias, and leftovers of those who supported the Baathists. Baghdad is a city divided into armed camps. Concrete barriers protect public buildings, hotels, and the homes of the rich and powerful. The wealthiest Iraqis fund their own private security forces, as do ministers and other government officials. Baghdad has come under a miasma of murders, kidnappings, robbery, and rape—a poster child for the breakdown of civil authority.

While Sunnis are a minority (roughly 32 to 37 percent of the nation including Arabs and Kurds), they have ruled Iraq—and none too kindly—since the Ottoman Empire began control of the area nearly five hundred years ago. As a result, tensions between the factions have not been dif-ficult to ignite.

The answer to ending Iraqi sectarian violence is not dividing Iraq into semiautonomous regions or states, but rather closing the spigot of Iranian and Syrian support of fractious militias and suicide bombers. It means securing the Iraqi borders so that the flow of terrorists and weapons into the country can be made much more difficult.

Again I say, since Syria is almost as much a puppet of Iran as Hezbollah, the road to victory in Iraq leads through Tehran. If we are to stop the fighting, we must squelch the hate-mongering flow of propaganda from the Islamofascists aimed at toppling the free world for their own agenda of Islamic domination. Eliminate the flame-throwers in Tehran, and don't be surprised when the fires in Baghdad suddenly get small enough for the Iraqis to handle themselves.

THE PROBLEM OF DIVIDING UP OIL REVENUES

According to conventional studies, Iraq now holds the third largest known oil reserves in the world at roughly 115 billion barrels (this is behind Saudi Arabia's 260 billion and Canada's 180 billion). However, oil experts also believe that the deserts of western Iraq—only about 10 percent of which have been explored—may hold as much as 100 billion barrels more, while others believe that it may prove to have even larger oil reserves than Saudi Arabia. It is a fact that seems to have Tehran and

Damascus salivating and hoping the United States cuts Iraq up to make the pickings easier.

Iraq's oil is also nearer to the surface than it is in other countries and therefore easier to extract, making it much more profitable. Estimates are that Iraq can produce oil at $1 to $1.50 a barrel, while it costs about $5 a barrel in other countries and as much as $12–16 a barrel in the North Sea. Analyst Mohammad Al-Gallani pointed out in the Canadian Press that of the 526 potential drilling sites in Iraq, only 125 have been opened.[12] However, despite its potential, much of Iraq's oil extraction infrastructure has been damaged in the wars of the last three decades, and it will take some time to get these fields efficiently productive again.

Iraq's major oil fields are in two locations: Kirkuk in the north and around Al-Basra in the south. Roughly 65 percent of Iraq's known oil reserves are in the Shiite south. Kirkuk holds roughly ten billion barrels but is also quite close to the other major fields of Bay Hassan, Jambur, and Khabbaz. If Iraq were divided in three regions, it is likely Kirkuk would be controlled by the Kurds and the southern fields in the south by the Shiites, leaving a disproportionately small amount to the central/western Sunni area.

While the Iraqi Constitution, as Senator Biden pointed out, allows for the formation of regions within Iraq, it was the Sunnis who showed the least support for the Constitution because of this. They knew there was an incredible risk of their being denied partial control of the oil production and revenues if Iraq were divided along ethnoreligious lines. Neither did the Sunnis want to be forced to rely on the good faith of their Kurdish and Shiite neighbors for financial support.

In my recent interview with former Navy captain Charles Nash, he told me that one of the reasons Iraq needed to stay together was that the different regions need each other if they are to succeed economically. While most of the oil is in the south, he noted that the south also has the most fertile soil for farming in all of the Middle East. The area could easily become the breadbasket of the entire region—something both the Kurds and Sunni Arabs could greatly benefit from with one exception: the Sunnis in the central region of Iraq have control of the greatest water supply in the Middle East, because of the courses of the Tigris and Euphrates Rivers. As one nation, Iraq has the potential to be a regional economic powerhouse; divided, it continues squabbling, and many in the Middle East stay hungry.[13]

A plan to give each region oil revenues proportionate to their populations seems fair, but again, the Sunnis would have no real control of the production in the other two regions and could not increase or decrease that production as demanded by their economy. It is a recipe for disaster. If there is a cause for civil war, it would be over that lack of control of its own destiny. Then borders dividing the Sunnis from these oil fields would serve as little more than Mason-Dixon lines.

ARE WE WILLING TO COMPROMISE OUR VALUES FOR THE SAKE OF GETTING OUT SOONER?

Another major problem with the idea of partitioning Iraq into three regions is the racial and religious segregation it would condone. Have we forgotten the point of the civil rights movement in the United States? After dismantling segregation at home and fighting apartheid in South Africa, are we now going to sanctify the sectarianism that is causing the strife in the streets of Iraq?

It is as if we learned nothing from fighting the previous two World Wars. World War I ended with too high a price exacted by the victors—a solution that only laid the foundations for World War II. Had we ended it instead by securing Germany's political future and solidifying its government before withdrawing, World War II might never have happened. Did we depose the Baath Party only to let Iraq fall into more dangerous hands? Did we end the rule of the Taliban in Afghanistan only to return it to the merciless tribal warlords who ruled it before them? If we do not replace the iron-fisted regimes with freedom-friendly governments, we will only face bigger problems down the road. Partitioning Iraq into three regions and then withdrawing our troops would weaken Iraq's future, put a stamp of approval on their racism, and make it easier for Iran and Syria to pick the country apart after our forces are gone.

In addition to this, it is also worth noting that partitioning countries has never led to lasting peace. Let's not forget it has been tried in Israel, India, Korea, Vietnam, Cyprus, and Bosnia—and those places are still political time bombs today.

BRINGING THE WAR BACK HOME

By bringing our troops home before Iraq is secure, we also turn the attention of terrorists back to their activities on U.S. soil rather than abroad. As terrorist responses to the Iraq Study Group plan have shown, the only thing terrorists are looking forward to more than winning in Iraq is being able to focus their attention once more on attacking Americans at home. As long as we keep them engaged in Iraq, attacks in the United States are much less likely. Should we withdraw our troops from Iraq before accomplishing all that they were initially sent to do—namely, deposing a terrorist-supporting regime and replacing it with one that will help us fight terrorism—then all we will have accomplished is to have strengthened their resolve to strike us again.

While it is unquestionable that we do not want to lose more lives to terrorist activities anywhere in the world—and that minimizing our military causalities is an important goal—who is better prepared to bear the brunt of such attacks: our military forces or our civilian population? In the end, the question should really not be one of withdrawing our troops to avoid harm but of the best way to reduce the risks of seeing them injured or killed. Perhaps the question should not be one of fewer troops but of more troops, or, as Daniel Pipes has suggested, concentrating our troops in less populated areas and getting them out of the crossfire between Sunnis and Shiites. While this is certain to allow more civil violence in Iraq, it would maintain the presence we need to keep the region stable, emphasize the need for Iraqis to police their own streets, and, as Pipes put it, "permit the American-led troops to carry out essential tasks (protecting borders, keeping the oil and gas flowing, ensuring that no Saddam-like monster takes power) while ending their non-essential work (maintaining street-level order, guarding their own barracks)."[14]

President Bush reiterated why we need our troops on the ground in Iraq in a press conference on October 25, 2006:

> Despite the difficulties and bloodshed, it remains critical that America defeat the enemy in Iraq by helping the Iraqis build a free nation that can sustain itself and defend itself.
>
> Our security at home depends on ensuring that Iraq is an ally in the war on terror and does not become a terrorist haven like Afghanistan under the Taliban....

...The fact that the fighting is tough does not mean our efforts in Iraq are not worth it. To the contrary; the consequences in Iraq will have a decisive impact on the security of our country, because defeating the terrorists in Iraq is essential to turning back the cause of extremism in the Middle East. If we do not defeat the terrorists or extremists in Iraq, they will gain access to vast oil reserves, and use Iraq as a base to overthrow moderate governments across the broader Middle East. They will launch new attacks on America from this new safe haven. They will pursue their goal of a radical Islamic empire that stretches from Spain to Indonesia....

If I did not think our mission in Iraq was vital to America's security, I'd bring our troops home tomorrow....

Our troops are fighting a war that will set the course for this new century. The outcome will determine the destiny of millions across the world. Defeating the terrorists and extremists is the challenge of our time and the calling of this generation. I'm confident this generation will answer that call and defeat an ideology that is bent on destroying America and all that we stand for.[15]

Unfortunately, such words of resolve are falling on deaf ears. Democrats and liberals are trying to convince America that the war was ill-conceived, that they were misled into supporting it, and that the cost has already been too great. Meanwhile they avoid the issue that pulling out now would guarantee an even greater and more costly conflict down the road. Again, their humanistic blinders are keeping them from seeing the true nature of the Islamofascists' doggedness and determination to end the dominance of Western democratic philosophy and replace it with Sharia law. Is that really so easily missed in Ahmadinejad's letter to President Bush?

Liberalism and Western-style democracy have not been able to help realize the ideals of humanity. Today these two concepts have failed. Those with insight can already hear the sounds of the shattering and fall of the ideology and thoughts of the Liberal democratic systems.[16]

Admitting Defeat

In his *NewsHour With Jim Lehrer* interview, Peter Galbraith advocated the division of Iraq into highly autonomous regions by saying it this way:

> Our ability to influence events in Iraq is extremely limited. I see no purpose for a continued U.S. presence in the Shiite southern half of Iraq.
>
> It is true that, if we withdraw, it will be theocratic. It will not apply the human rights provisions in the Iraqi constitution, and it will be dominated by Iran. But that's the case now, and we aren't going to do anything to change it.[17]

This pretty much summed up Galbraith's comments overall. For Democrats like him and Senator Biden: things are bad now and there is nothing we can really do to change them, so why not pull out and cut our losses? They speak as if leaving Iraq in the hands of Iran is something that will save U.S. lives in the long run. The liberals are too ready to surrender to the terrorists, blame the loss on the Republicans, and think afterward they can laugh themselves all the way to the White House in 2008 with little thought as to what that president will face because of their short-sightedness.

I wonder how it made the Democratic winners feel to have Al Qaeda celebrate their November 2006 midterm victories. Shortly after those elections Abu Hamza al-Muhajir said on an Internet audio, "The American people have put their feet on the right path by...realizing their president's betrayal in supporting Israel. So they voted for something reasonable in the last elections."[18] Al-Muhajir sounded as if he were gladly welcoming new allies into the U.S. Congress. I pray to God he was wrong, but liberals are going to need to wake up. If they continue on the path they are on at present, they will be just the allies for whom al-Muhajir is hoping.

We need to get back to winning this battle, as I have already outlined, and set our resolve to accept nothing short of clear victory in Iraq. If we don't find the moral clarity to fight this evil until it is soundly defeated, all we will be doing is importing the war back to U.S. soil and facing a far bloodier war down the road. Is that what we really want to do?

Chapter Four

THE CENTERS OF GRAVITY

There is no way, either to stabilize the situation in Iraq, or to solve any kind of conflict around us—the Israeli/Palestinian conflict, all other conflicts—without dealing today with this Iranian regime....The center of gravity to deal with the problem today is Iran.[1]

—LT. GEN. MOSHE YA'ALON,
former Israeli Defense Forces chief of staff,
now a fellow at the Washington Institute for
Middle East Policy

I believe that the Iranians are a very politically aware group of folks—as are the folks that are running Al Qaeda, who are the Sunni extremists. All of these people at the top leadership of these countries and these organizations understand that the center of gravity in the war against them is the will of the American people to fight.[2]

—CAPT. CHARLES NASH,
retired U.S. Navy pilot of more than twenty-five years
and member of the Iran Policy Committee

For the American people in late March and April of 2003, Operation Iraqi Freedom seemed a textbook example of what modern warfare could be. In less than six weeks, U.S.-led coalition forces took on Saddam Hussein's defiant regime as an initial step in the war on terrorism that began in response to the attacks of September 11, 2001. Our air raids were surgically precise, losses were at a minimum, civilians were spared as much as possible, and Iraqis celebrated in the streets and toppled statues of the dictator in what looked like the tearing down of the Berlin wall. Americans read into President Bush's May 1, 2003, proclamation of the end of major combat operations[3] nothing short of complete victory. A "Mission Accomplished" banner hung proudly behind him from the USS *Abraham Lincoln* as he made this speech—and on that day no one was willing to say otherwise.

A JUST WAR?

Why was Operation Iraqi Freedom necessary in the first place? It has been an issue of some debate in the years since President Bush gave that speech aboard the USS *Abraham Lincoln*. It's now a mantra of preference among liberals that the United States was tricked by oil-greedy Republicans to invade Iraq and that we never should have toppled Hussein's Baathist regime in the first place.

The seeds of the second Gulf War were sown in the late 1990s in Somalia. Jihadist forces, under the command of Ayman al-Zawahiri— a suspected instigator of the August 7, 1998, bombings of U.S. embassies in Dar es Salaam, Tanzania, and Nairobi, Kenya—were aided and funded by Iraq through Sudan. The union was solidified in 1998–1999 with the realization between Saddam Hussein and Osama bin Laden that cooperation was vital in order to humiliate the "Great Satan" of the United States and its "Little Satan" Middle Eastern ally, Israel. While courting bin Laden, Hussein was also paying homage to Yasser Arafat, supporting the Palestinian Authority's terror network by showering monetary awards on the families of suicide bombers attacking Israel. The plan was to create total disarray in the Middle East, thereby jeopardizing the interests of the United States and its regional allies, which also include Saudi Arabia, Egypt, Kuwait, and Jordan.

When terrorists struck at the heart of America on 9/11, what had been the possibility of a war on terror became a grim reality. Noting the response to the attacks, Hussein was persuaded that after Afghanistan, Iraq would be first on President Bush's list of terrorist-harboring, terrorist-supporting nations and that an attack was imminent. Hussein began to plot a possible guerrilla defense against a U.S. invasion.

One of the most prolific providers of information to the West on Saddam Hussein's war plan was Lt. Col. al-Dabbagh. He spent in excess of seven years spying on Hussein, in persistent fear for his life. Al-Dabbagh's reports were delivered through Dr. Ayad Allawi, cofounder of the Iraqi National Accord, an exile group that opposed Hussein's regime, and the man who would serve as the first interim president in the new Iraqi government after Hussein's fall.

One of the documents forwarded to London by al-Dabbagh was the minutes of a Hussein meeting in December 2001. The gathering of top military commanders focused on how Iraq would defend itself against an almost inescapable U.S. attack. Aware of the impossibility of winning a conventional war, Hussein ordered large caches of weapons to be deposited at various locations throughout Iraq. According to the document, Hussein was concerned with "how to sustain the continuation of war after occupation."[4]

According to Lt. Col. al-Dabbagh, it was at about this time that he and other senior commanders were informed that Saddam intended to deploy his WMD arsenal to defend the country against an American-led attack. Dr. Allawi said of this information from al-Dabbagh:

> Yes, we passed this information on to the British and Americans. It was part of a constant stream of intelligence we passed on to both intelligence agencies. And I still believe it is true. You must remember the dedicated efforts that were undertaken by Saddam and his institutions to hide and conceal [WMDs] was gigantic.[5]

The locations of Hussein's guerrilla war supplies were said to be at GPS coordinates known only to his son, Qusay, and his private secretary, Abid Hamid Humud. In their book, *Endgame: The Blueprint for Victory in the War on Terror*, retired Air Force lieutenant general Thomas McInerney and retired Army major general Paul Vallely commented that while few weapons of mass destruction have yet been found in Iraq, "what already has been found in Iraq is an astonishing amount of conventional weapons in stockpiles throughout the country."[6]

The necessity of stopping Saddam Hussein's terror network became even more apparent when the Israelis captured three men trying to cross the Jordan River into the Palestinian Territory in September 2002. Following interrogation, the Israelis learned that the three were graduates of the Hussein-trained Arab Liberation Front. The three, along with Iraqis and terrorists from other Muslim countries, had received special training by the infamous Unit 999 commissioned by Hussein specializing in hijacking, explosives, sabotage, and assassination.

The three infiltrators revealed that others in the unit, including members of Al Qaeda, were trained in handling chemical weapons and poisons, especially ricin. Following training, they moved to join Ansar-al-Islam, a Kurdish wing of bin Laden's Al Qaeda. The three were exported to Israel specifically to target civilian aircraft with shoulder-fired missiles at Tel

Aviv's Ben-Gurion Airport. They were also to target Americans en route to Iraq.

Clusters of the trainees were dispatched to Turkey, France, and Chechnya. This was later confirmed by Turkish Security Forces who arrested two Al Qaeda operatives with instructions to attack the U.S. air base at Incirlik with chemical weapons.

Armed with intelligence reports such as those indicating that Iraq was supplying WMDs to bin Laden's terrorists, the United States began to put together a coalition to stop Saddam Hussein in Iraq. For President Bush, this was a vital step in fighting the war on terror.

Since the end of Desert Storm in 1991, Hussein had been defying UN weapons inspectors and the UN Security Council in a game of cat and mouse about Iraq's WMD programs. Iraqi antiaircraft batteries and missiles had from time to time locked onto and even fired upon coalition fighters running routine missions to enforce the northern and southern no-fly zones that had been set up at the end of the first Gulf War. In 2002, regime change in Iraq became a major goal of the Bush administration because of Hussein's continued human rights violations, support of terrorist organizations, and lack of evidence that he had put an end to his WMD programs. On October 10–11, 2002, Congress over-whelmingly approved taking military action against Iraq by approving the Iraq War Resolution with a vote of 296–133 in the House and 77–23 in the Senate.[7] Public opinion also greatly favored the move; roughly 79 percent of the American population supported the war by May 2003.[8]

No Cooperation From the Arab World

As the Bush administration worked diligently to put together a coalition similar to that of the first Gulf War, it rapidly became apparent that the Arab world would sit on the sidelines of this engagement. The fear of retaliation by rabidly radical Muslims within their ranks could not be overcome by persuasion or diplomacy. A confrontation with the various terrorist factions operating in the Middle East could well mean internal upheaval, death, and destruction, not to mention the violent overthrow of existing rulers in a 1979-style Islamic revolution by extremists against moderate Arab states.

Vulnerable Arab countries feared that a U.S. attack on Iraq would prove to be the glue that would cement the various terrorist networks into a cohesive force that would severely punish anyone seen to be cooperating with the American-led coalition. There was a very real fear that, instead of liberating Iraq for democracy, it would become a haven for brutal terrorist groups to plan and execute a takeover of the entire Muslim world. Having successfully run the United States out of Lebanon following the bombing of the Marine barracks in Beirut in 1983, terrorist organizations did not tremble in fear at facing allies of the "Great Satan."

There was also anxiety at the thought that the expansive Sunni-controlled reservoirs of oil in the southern part of Iraq would be overrun by the Shiites in Iran. Such an event could give rise to a situation similar to that in Lebanon where Iran's proxy, Hezbollah, is firmly in control of the south and could just as suddenly control the lion's share of Iraqi oil.

Egyptian political analyst and writer Ayman El-Amir was certain that the planned invasion of Iraq had nothing to do with terror and everything to do with oil. He cautioned against creating an upheaval in the region:

> The US is now embracing a change-of-leaders doctrine and in a rela-
> tively short time the justification for such changes will be as varied as
> harboring terrorism, suppressing political dissent, or endangering US
> economic interests by, say, enforcing an oil embargo.
>
> Any large-scale invasion of Iraq is a risky proposition. The chaos
> it will create in the delicate, multi-ethnic balancing act that is
> Iraq, and its ramifications in the Arab world, may far outweigh the
> benefits.... Should the ouster of President Saddam Hussein be as swift
> and surgical as the US military would like it to be, leaders in the region
> and elsewhere may soon find themselves added to President Bush's
> laundry list.[9]

King Fahd in Saudi Arabia was particularly disturbed by the direction events were taking in Iraq and Afghanistan. Osama bin Laden was a Saudi citizen with quite a following in his homeland. The king was understandably concerned that he and/or his country could become bin Laden's next target. It did not take long for this fear to translate into a refusal to allow American troops to use bases in Saudi Arabia to launch attacks on Iraq.

RIPPLES IN THE POOL

The Saudi royal was not the only head of state concerned about an invasion of Iraq. Both Syria and Iran could see the handwriting on the wall. Would the overthrow of Saddam Hussein be like a pebble tossed into a pond? Would the ripples spread out to encompass both of Iraq's neighbors? Syria and Iran could readily be classified as terror-harboring and terror-supporting states, both of which President Bush promised to target following the events of 9/11. Not only that, but if the United States invaded Iraq, Iran would have U.S. troops on both its eastern and western borders with the U.S. presence already in Afghanistan. Fearing a Western-style democracy in Iraq, governments in Damascus and Tehran began to plot their course to thwart the United States at every turn.

A long-standing friendship between Hussein's sons and Syria's al-Assad made him the perfect cohort to assist in hiding Iraq's supply of WMDs. Syria acted as the go-between for the purchase of military equipment for Iraq from Russia, Yemen, and other black market suppliers in Africa. The country's defense minister, Mustafa Tlass, was culpable in the illegal sale of Iraqi oil in order to pay for the various arms purchases.

With Hussein's acquisitions list in hand, Syria went shopping for munitions, replacement parts for tanks, planes, antiaircraft artillery, and the like. It was not a stretch for Syria to want to acquire such material, but it was far more revealing when the purchasing agent began to inquire about parts of a Kolchuga radar system manufactured in the Ukraine, or for Russian-made Kornet antitank guided missiles. That raised a few eyebrows. Convoys from Syria to Iraq transported thousands of the Russian-made missiles, as well as several hundred shoulder-fired antiaircraft missiles, to Iraq. Not all of the armaments left their storage facilities in Syria for Iraq, though. To protect against U.S. bombing runs, large numbers of parts and munitions stayed behind in the safety of Syria.

Ever defiant, Bashar al-Assad also pursued strategic alliances with the other two members of what President Bush had labeled the "axis of evil"—North Korea and Iran. Even though Iran and Iraq had been bitter enemies in the 1980s, Iran's mullahs placed the perseverance of the region's radical Islamic footprint above any past differences. Such alliances were designed to intimidate the United States into backing down from any plans to confront Iraq. After all, would the United States risk retaliation against Israel and other U.S.-friendly Arab states by the triumvirate of evil in order to unseat Saddam Hussein? Would President Bush be willing to alienate the Saudi Arabian royals by endangering the precarious balance among the Gulf States? Would he chance estrangement from U.S. allies in the West by ignoring their specific warnings against an invasion, especially since most gave little credence to the fact that Al Qaeda terrorists were receiving training in chemical weapons and other poisons in Iraq?

When faced with the almost-certainty of an incursion into Iraq, radical Islamic leaders and representatives made a beeline to Damascus to consult with the powers-that-be. The line was a "who's who" of radicals. First on the agenda was Ayatollah Mahmoud Shahroudi from Iran. Following a tête-à-tête with al-Assad and members of his entourage, Shahroudi issued a warning against invading Iraq. He felt that an invasion would cause irreversible chaos in the region.

Shahroudi went from that meeting to confer with Hezbollah leader Sheikh Hassan Nasrallah to lay the groundwork for the next step in the holy war against both Israel and the United States, or what Ayatollah Khomeini in 1979 called the "occupier Zionist regime." With Hezbollah firmly entrenched in Lebanon, al-Assad could be assured of having a tactical partner well-positioned to play a primary role in exporting terrorism to Israel.

Another in line to visit al-Assad was the president of North Korea's Supreme People's Assembly. His interest in Syria was basically one of economics. North Korea was a prolific purveyor of technology and information to both Syria and Iran. Such staples as the various stages of the Shahab missiles were produced in North Korea and exported to Iran and Iraq. A steady stream of North Korean technology was also instrumental in Iran's quest for nuclear arms. Iraq, Iran, Syria, and North Korea pledged among themselves to defend against a pro-Western Iraq and determined to do everything possible to prevent such a turn.

North Korea made its presence known in the equation when, in December 2002, the *So San* was boarded in the Arabian Sea by sailors from American and Spanish ships. When Navy SEALs searched the ship, they discovered that underneath a supposed cargo of cement bags lay the real payload: fifteen complete Scud missiles, fifteen conventional warheads, twenty-three containers of nitric acid fuel, and eighty-five barrels of unidentified chemicals.[10] Intelligence sources speculated that the ship, bound for Yemen as its next port, would ultimately finish its voyage in Iraq.

One unidentified spokesperson said that if the United States invaded Iraq, the Iraqis would strike military targets, while the United States would be accused of targeting civilians. I'm reminded of a comment that professor Alan Dershowitz made during my recent interview with him:

> Countries like Israel and the United States will do anything to avoid killing children, whereas the tyrannical regimes of terrorism will do anything to kill children—they figured out this cruel arithmetic of death. [11]

Overtures of an alliance between Iraq and Iran began to surface in 2002. Saddam Hussein's son Qusay took a delegation of upper-echelon Iraqis to Tehran on a weapons-buying mission. Of particular interest to them was the acquisition of Iran's staple, the Shahab-3. The group also hoped to induce the Iranians to return dozens of military aircraft, including a number of F-1Es, captured during the Iran-Iraq War. So desperate were the Iraqis for war materials that they ultimately offered to buy and then return the aircraft to Iran when no longer needed to battle the United States.

A major concern of Iran was that the aging weapons sold to Iraq would be turned against them at some point later. As part of the agreement, Iraq pledged safe passage for military equipment across its country to Iranian proxies in Syria and Lebanon. The outcome of Qusay Hussein's trek to Iran was a pledge of ammunition and spare parts only.

The one thing the Hussein regime may have overlooked was the tendency of the Shiite population of Iraq to side ideologically with Iran against Saddam. Of course, the Iranians could easily see how Saddam's removal by the U.S. military could benefit their plan for regional domination. Tehran would be prepared for the eventuality with trained infiltrators ready to slip into Iraq when the opportunity arose. Shiites already living in Iran were natural allies in Iran's postwar plan. Among the first infiltrators across the border were card-carrying members of the Islamic revolutionary Guard Corps under the direction of Iranian colonel Hosni Merza Khalil. This either went unnoticed by Iraq or Saddam turned a blind eye to the incursion by his former enemy in appreciation for the help against the United States.

Iran's preparations for what was a certain invasion of Iraq by American and coalition troops were ongoing. In what had the appearance of a politician in a cross-country stumping trip, Iranian Revolutionary Guard commander Yahya Rahim-Safavi visited al-Assad in Syria to review that country's preparations for a U.S. attack on Hussein's regime. From there, he met with Hezbollah and Hamas representatives in Lebanon.

Safavi then met with Fatah to discuss Yasser Arafat's plans to extract payment from Israel for the invasion—even though Israel was once again not permitted to participate in the military exercise against Iraq. Israel was targeted by Saddam during the first Gulf War in retaliation for the coalition attack. There was no reason to believe that it would escape Hussein's wrath during another incursion.

PREPARATIONS FOR AN EVENTUAL INTIFADA AGAINST THE WEST

As it became more obvious that war would be the result of Saddam Hussein's defiance, radical Islamists began to assemble in Iraq training camps in preparation for attacks against nations, both Western and Arab, that joined the coalition to unseat the Iraqi dictator. Both Iran and Syria funneled terrorists from Palestine, Jordan, and other Arab countries. Part of their audacious plan was to create situations that would force Israel into a confrontation with both Syria and Lebanon. (This plan came to fruition when Hezbollah crossed into Israel in July 2006, kidnapped Israeli soldiers, and began lobbing Katyusha rockets into Northern Israel.) The fear was also that Iran would be surrounded by pro-American regimes in Afghanistan and Iraq, a notion that frightened the controlling mullahs. The response of the leaders in Tehran was to plan a series of saber-rattling war games designed to impress the Americans with their ability to repel any imminent threat from that quarter. An American presence in Iraq was perceived by the tyrannical Tehran mullahs to be an obvious threat to the survival of Iran's theocratic government.

In a move designed to take the spotlight off Tehran, two Iranian proxies—Hezbollah and Hamas—planned an all-out intifada against Israel if called upon to launch such an attack. The plan was welcomed by Nasrallah in Lebanon and by Arafat in the Palestinian Authority, who was particularly eager to forestall any attempts by the United States to democratize the PA. Arafat reportedly founded a new terrorist organization comprised of his most elite to bolster Iraq.

Deputy Secretary of State Richard Armitage was among the seemingly few that readily recognized the threat imposed by Hezbollah. In an interview with *60 Minutes,* Armitage expressed his concern: "Hezbollah may be the 'A-Team of Terrorists,' and maybe Al Qaeda is actually the 'B' team. And they're on the list and their time will come."[12] According to the CBS report, Florida Democrat Bob Graham believed that Hezbollah had a global network of radical Islamic supporters, with enough operatives in the United States to pose a terrorist threat here. Said Graham, "It has a significant presence of its trained operatives inside the United States waiting for the call to action."[13] Graham, aware that Hezbollah's funding came from Iran and Syria, mentioned the "blood debt" dating back to the bombing of the Marine barracks in Beirut in 1983.

In March 2002, Bashar al-Assad made his intentions toward Israel perfectly clear in a television address:

> As far as an occupier is concerned, there is no distinction between soldiers and civilians.... There is a distinction between armed and unarmed, but in Israel everyone is armed. In any case, we adopted the following concept: resistance to occupation is a legitimate right.[14]

By October 2002, Syria and Iran had an organized plan of attack to disrupt any significant U.S. progress in Iraq should President Bush go ahead with plans for an invasion. The DEBKA*file* reported that:

> Syria's Bashar [al-] Assad shares Tehran's conviction that the installment of a pro-American regime in Baghdad is extremely dangerous, a direct threat to the Ayatollahs in Tehran, the Baath regime in Damascus, the freedom of operation of the Syria-based Palestinian terror groups, and the very existence of the Lebanese Hizballah, Tehran's primary arm for overseas operations and intelligence.[15]

Although the two countries were apparently taking every precaution to prevent a second war in Iraq, neither was proactive at the outset of the actual conflict. However, both countries soon made their presence felt as pipelines for terrorists flooding into Iraq from Arab nations around the world. Iran would go a step further and provide military-grade improvised explosive devices (IEDs) to the terrorists.

Also on the drawing board was an alliance between Iran, Syria, and Hezbollah. The "Party of Allah" was to bear the primary responsibility for causing interference with what stability there might be in the region. Nasrallah, the prime instigator of trouble in South Lebanon, would see his clout increase to a more provincial role. His cooperation with Iran and Syria was paramount in intensifying the current jihad and taking it to the next level.

Following directives from their mentors, Iran and Syria, Hezbollah terrorists repeatedly tested Israel's resolve and defenses. Katyushas were fired into Northern Israel from outposts in Southern Lebanon, roadside bombs targeted Israeli Defense Forces (IDF) patrols inside Israel, attempted kidnappings were regular occurrences, Israeli Arabs were kidnapped and interrogated to obtain information about Israel, sniper attacks were common, and Israeli civilians were murdered.[16] Hezbollah had no lack of armaments made available by Iran and Syria: heavy artillery as well as thousands of missiles and rockets, including the longer-range Fajr-3 and Fajr-5. The Fajr rockets are manufactured in Syria, thus eliminating the possibility that Syria could claim ignorance in the jihad against Israel. Supplies transported into Lebanon also included the Zelzal-2 with a range that would allow attacks on Tel Aviv. Not only did the rockets have longer-range capabilities, the warheads were larger. There was also an influx of Revolutionary Guard–trained fighters and longtime Al Qaeda members.

Syria and Iran were ready should the United States attack Iraq—not to join in the immediate fray but to step in and create chaos and confusion following the removal of Saddam Hussein. The plan to humiliate the United States and drive coalition forces out of Iraq would allow Syria to carve out the Sunni region for itself and Iran to take possession of the Shiite region and either to overrun the Kurds or allow them self-governance. Given their past hatred of one another, the question of how to turn an Iraq devastated by war into a pro-Iranian entity would still be a challenging one. In preparation for such an eventuality, three Iraqi opposition leaders met in Tehran in December 2002. Massoud Barzani of the Kurdistan Democratic Party (KDP), Ahmad Chalabi of the INC (INC), and Ayatollah Mohammad Baqer al-Hakim of the Supreme Council for Islamic Revolution in Iraq (SCIRI) held meetings with each other and with top Iranian leaders.[17] Chalabi's overtures to the Iranians were a surprise for the Bush administration, as they had initially handpicked him as the Iraqi leader to replace the soon-to-be ousted Saddam Hussein.

In discussing how to fashion a postwar Iraq into a country that would most benefit Iran and Syria, Supreme Ayatollah Seyyed Ali Khamenei and then Iranian president Mohammad Khatami determined that a government in Iraq must be easily persuaded to support Iran's regional interests. The two reached one conclusion: Iraq was unsuitable for a Khomeini-type upheaval and a Shiite-dominated theocracy. In *The Secret History of the Iraq War*, Yossef Bodansky wrote at length about Khamenei's rhetoric leading up to the Iraq confrontation. Khamenei was certain that:

> The arrogant and imperialist United States has not realized its objectives in Palestine and Afghanistan, and its stupendous financial and human outlays have brought it nothing but loss. It will be the same story in the future, God willing.[18]

Bodansky says, "In mentioning 'neighboring nations,' Khamenei for the first time alluded to Iran's direct role in confronting the United States [in Iraq]."[19]

Apparently, the two Iranians were convinced that Ahmad Chalabi would implement Iran's plan for a speedy election in Iraq once the United States had disposed of its archenemy, Saddam Hussein. It would be in Iran's best interests to have a pro-Iranian Shiite such as Chalabi in a position of power. In fact, according to a *Newsweek* report:

> Before the U.S. invasion of Baghdad, Chalabi's Iraqi National Congress maintained a $36,000-a-month branch office in Tehran—funded by U.S. taxpayers. INC representatives, including Chalabi himself, paid regular visits to the Iranian capital. Since the war, Chalabi's contacts with Iran may have intensified: a Chalabi aide says that since December [2005], he has met with most of Iran's top leaders, including supreme religious leader Ayatollah Ali Khamenei and his top national-security aide, Hassan Rowhani. "Iran is Iraq's neighbor, and it is in Iraq's interest to have a good relationship with Iran," Chalabi's aide says.[20]

Chalabi, the golden boy, became tarnished and would, ultimately, be investigated for fraud. Charges were later dropped due to lack of evidence.

Israel's Role

While the United States was hard at work building a coalition in advance of a possible attack in Iraq, Israel was making war preparations at home. During the first Gulf War, Saddam Hussein had hinted at including payloads of chemical weapons in his Scuds targeting Israeli cities. This time Israel would be prepared to retaliate at the first sign of a missile launched in its direction. Having been asked to keep a low profile, as in 1990, Israel provided assistance in other ways. According to *USA Today*, Israeli commandos provided intelligence services to the United States, as well as:

> ...conducted clandestine surveillance missions of Scud missile sites in Western Iraq....Infantry units with experience in urban warfare...helped train U.S. Army and Marine counterparts...for possible urban battles in Iraq.... [Israel also] "reserve[d] the right to defend itself against an unprovoked attack."[21]

As defense preparations continued, new concerns arose; the Palestinian Authority's leader, Yasser Arafat, had a new toy. He became enamored of toy airplanes—literally. The Iraqis had allegedly taken toy airplanes, operated by remote control, and retrofitted them to carry explosives. A gleeful Arafat ordered that toy stores order large supplies of the model planes, bound ostensibly for children in hospitals in the PA. Not surprisingly, no child received a toy airplane. The planes were said to have been paid for by funds designated for humanitarian projects. The planes were converted into mini-bombers capable of carrying explosives—another means to kill innocent civilians in Israel.[22]

Israel's hopes of being able to defend itself were dashed when, on December 22, 2002, senior officials in the Bush administration "told Israeli Defense Minister Shaul Mofaz that the U.S. has decided that Israel will not be involved in the war against Iraq even if Iraq launches a missile attack against Israel."[23] Mofaz also reassured the Israeli people that the Israeli Air Force was prepared to defend the country. In fact, by January 2003, the Israeli Air Force was flying reconnaissance forays over parts of Iraq.

In an attempt to sidetrack the United States from its focus on Iraq, Saddam Hussein pushed his Palestinian allies to launch a series of attacks against Israel. The *Jerusalem Post* reported that one major suicide attack was thwarted when police discovered a car filled with gasoline canisters and 300 kilograms of explosives. The vehicle was successfully detonated with no harm to anyone. Hezbollah stepped up attacks as well, sending a barrage of antitank missiles and mortar rounds into the Mount Dov region. Not to be outdone, Hamas jumped into the melee with Qussam rocket attacks into southern Israel.[24]

The increased activity caused Israeli officials to question whether or not the United States possessed a contingency plan based on all possible worst-case scenarios in Iraq. A *New York Times* article outlined some of the same concerns and nightmarish possibilities expressed by the Israelis:

> In the last war Saddam Hussein blew up almost all of Kuwait's oil wells; in the next he could blow up Saudi Arabian wells, with significant repercussions for the international economy... [or if he] goes after Israel with the chemical or biological weapons...Israel...will retaliate, perhaps even with nuclear weapons. Just over the horizon lies Pakistan, a Muslim country armed with nuclear weapons and permeated by extremists. Pervez Musharraf...is unlikely to survive politically should there be a nuclear attack by an American ally on Iraq's Muslims. Islamists...would take control of Pakistan's nuclear arsenal; lacking the ability to launch missiles that would reach Israel, they would turn on India, their more proximate enemy. A nuclear attack would set off global chaos.[25]

Whether or not the United States had these plans in place, it was on March 17, 2003, that President Bush gave his final ultimatum: "Saddam Hussein and his sons must leave Iraq within 48 hours. Their refusal to do so will result in military conflict commenced at a time of our choosing."[26]

On March 20, 2003, at approximately 02:30 UTC, explosions were heard in Baghdad. The "shock and awe" air campaign to cripple Iraq's defenses had begun. Within roughly twenty days, coalition forces captured Baghdad and were greeted by Iraqis cheering and pulling down a statue of Hussein, whose twenty-four-year rule had come to an end. By April 15, Tikrit, Hussein's hometown, was under coalition control. At that time it appeared the major fighting of the invasion was effectively over. On May 1, President Bush declared the cessation of major combat operations, and the occupation of Iraq, with the aim of establishing democratic self-rule, began.

Who would have imagined that in the next forty-two months we would suffer nearly twenty times as many casualties as during the time of the major combat operations? Little did anyone think at the time that over three years later, there would still be no end in sight to the major U.S. presence in the country, except perhaps the forces Hussein had enlisted to fight the real war in Iraq—the terrorist/guerrilla war that would be born the same day the occupation began.

Chapter Five

THE REAL BATTLE FOR IRAQ BEGINS

They intended to spread Islam and in the rhetoric of Ahmadinejad, you can see that. He thinks there is going to be a second coming and that before that second coming can happen there has to be a clash of civilizations.[1]

—CHRIS HAMILTON,
senior fellow of Counterterrorism Studies,
Washington Institute for Near East Policy

Since the revolution by Khomeini, the view of Iran is to try to spread the Muslim revolution all over the world. To ruin whatever smells democratic, to ruin whatever seems democratic, and on the remnant of those democratic walls to build a new entity—an extreme Islamic regime that will be operated according to the Sharia Law which is the Islam leaders' codex of laws. What they want to see is a new world where Islam is in control, and all entities will be like Iran, meaning they will be controlled and ruled by the ayatollahs, by the spiritual leaders, the clerics.[2]

—GEN. DANI YATOM,
former head of the Israeli intelligence service Mossad
and chief of staff under Prime Minister Ehud Barak

Once it became apparent to Hussein that his bravado was not going to deter the U.S.-led coalition from an attack, he began to order the disbursement of trainees from the various terrorist training camps around Iraq, most notably in Nasiriyah and Fallujah. The trainees were provided money, arms, explosives, and transportation. Teams of terrorists were assigned the job of penetrating Saudi Arabia's borders with the assignment to carry out terrorist attacks. One team was able to murder a Saudi judge, Abdul Rahman al-Suhaybani, known for combating subversive activities in his province. The team members then went underground to join the vast terror networks—Al Qaeda, al-Muwahhidun, Hezbollah, and others—so that they could one day emerge to kill again.

With the U.S. air and ground offensives in full swing and coalition troops steadily advancing on Baghdad, Hussein began to lose confidence in the outcome of the war. It is thought that Hussein began to put into effect several possible escape plans. One involved calling in markers from his friends in Belarus. Hussein asked for charter flights to transport cargo and members of his family out of Iraq. A plane identified as a Belarusian IL-76 transport allegedly took off from Saddam International Airport and traversed Iranian airspace on its flight to Minsk, Belarus. There was initial speculation that both Hussein and his sons were on board the flight.[3] Another exile-of-choice location was Paris, and indeed a group of Hussein's handpicked scientists were among the first to be transported from Iraq to Paris via Damascus. This was yet another example of French cooperation with Saddam Hussein's regime.

Another arrangement involved Hussein joining a convoy of Russian diplomats from Baghdad to Damascus. When it was suggested that there might be a safer route through Amman, the Russian delegation declined and insisted on going to Damascus. With the convoy was Russian ambassador to Iraq, Vladimir Titorenko. It has been reported that Hussein donned a disguise and joined the convoy carrying some twenty-five Russians. Just outside Baghdad, the convoy came under fire; five diplomats were wounded, some seriously, said Russian foreign ministry spokesman Alexander Yakovenko. Although the U.S. Central Command maintained that there were no coalition forces near where the attack occurred, Secretary of State Colin Powell contacted Russian foreign minister Igor Ivanov to express his sincere apology for the incident. Powell did not admit any U.S. culpability, though.[4]

As the ground fighting around Baghdad began in earnest, Lt. Gen. John Abizaid, CENTCOM deputy commander, reported, "Regular Iraqi army units seemed to vanish as the coalition advanced. Low numbers of Iraqi prisoners indicated that the regular army units were avoiding the fight.... Regular Iraqi forces [along with senior officers] 'have just melted away.'"[5]

With coalition troops entering Baghdad, the city fell into chaos. Various Iranian-armed and funded militia groups began to make their presence known in the city. The Shiite faction was, from all accounts, the most well armed and organized of the groups. The popularity of the anti-American, anti–Saddam Hussein groups grew as it became known they could provide food and medicine to the neighborhoods they controlled. One such area became known as Sadr City, a low-income suburb of Baghdad and home of some two million Shiite Muslims.

It looked as though advance preparations by Iran and Syria to make Iraq virtually uncontrollable were in full swing. The rage and antipathy of the Muslim world was directed at the "Great Satan." Decree after decree and fatwa after fatwa were issued, calling for jihad against the United States. One came from Dr. Muhammad Sayyed Tantawi, sheikh of Al-Azhar. He rallied the Iraqi people to continue their *"Jihad* in defense of religion, faith, honor, and property, because *Jihad* is a religious ruling of Islam aimed at opposing aggressors," and encouraged Arab and Islamic volunteers to travel to Iraq, "to support the *Jihad* of their oppressed brethren there, because resistance to oppression is an Islamic obligation, whether the oppressor is Muslim or not."[6]

In meetings between Iran's Khamenei and Khatami and Syria's al-Assad, the leaders determined that the United States should be met with violent resistance from the various Iraqi factions and from jihadists imported for the purpose of creating pandemonium for the coalition troops. The men called on the radical Islamic forces in the region to oppose an American occupation by every means possible. Again, Yossef Bodansky reported that Majlis (Iranian parliament) deputy Majid Ansari, in a briefing prior to the summit between Khamenei and al-Assad, outlined Iran's position:

> Even if they [the Americans] succeed in capturing Iraq...they will still face difficulties....We [the Iranian leadership] are hoping that the Americans would be bogged down in Iraq and fail to realize their expansionist politics....Even if America were to become victorious in Iraq for a short time...such a victory will be the beginning of serious problems for America's warmongering and expansionist politicians.[7]

Both leaders were well aware that they were unable to forestall an American attack but could create havoc within Iraq once Saddam Hussein was deposed. The call for Islamic fanatics—terrorists, all—went forth and was answered by volunteers from Algeria, Saudi Arabia, Egypt, the Palestinian Territory, Yemen, Pakistan, Afghanistan, Chechnya, Iran, and Syria, among others. The question for the coalition troops now became one of how to identify peaceful Iraqi citizens from the influx of terrorists bent on killing them in any way possible.

Outside Baghdad, Shiite enclaves that had been suppressed under Saddam Hussein's Baathist regime welcomed liberation by the coalition troops. In al Najaf, a long-repressed Iraqi leader and exile, Abdul Majid al-Khoi, was among the first to return to throngs of ecstatic townspeople. It was al-Khoi who first contacted Grand Ayatollah Ali al-Sistani and persuaded him to issue a decree to the Shiite population not to resist the American troops.

Iran was incensed, and retribution soon followed. Al-Khoi was attacked outside the Grand Imam Ali mosque by a death squad, his body hacked to pieces. It was widely intimated that the attack was carried out by a squad of the Mahdi army controlled by Iran-supported Sheikh Moqtada al-Sadr, whose family represents itself as the champion of the Shiite majority.

All the meetings, the conversations, and the proposals flying between Tehran and Damascus were for one purpose only: to stop the spread of democracy in the Muslim world. Tehran specifically saw the tide of democratic change as a direct threat to the continuance of its Islamic revolution. At that time, no Middle Eastern country—particularly Iran—possessed the weapons to effectively challenge the United States. Furthermore, if the United States could not be stopped in Iraq, would Iran be next in the crosshairs of democracy? The mullahs were desperate to find ways to further advance Iran's interests.

Spurred on by Iran's influence, and in direct defiance of Ali al-Sistani, "another Iraqi exile in Iran, Kadhem al-Husseini al-Haeri, issued a religious edict urging Iraqi Shiites 'to seize the first possible opportunity to fill the power vacuum in the administration in Iraq.'"[8] Indeed, as coalition troops withdrew from largely Shiite towns and villages, Iranian proxies were rapidly filling the void. It was not difficult to trace the point-of-origin of some of the infiltrators, especially when a Syrian missile (Syria, of course, being Iran's "axis of evil" compatriot and the homebase of Iranian proxy Hezbollah) was used to bring down an Air Force A-10 over Baghdad.

The United States began to realize the seriousness of Syrian involvement in the continuing upheaval in Iraq and began to make plans to put a stop to it. Some in the Bush administration made conciliatory comments denying a possible move against Syria, and Britain's Tony Blair assured al-Assad that he would not support such a move.

Faced with a growing certainty that it would be next in America's sights, Syria pled with Saudi Arabia to intercede. Backed by Saudi promises to persuade al-Assad to relinquish Iraqi henchmen that had fled to Syria, the leaders in Riyadh successfully averted a Syrian invasion that would have been on the coattails of the Iraqi one.

"ALLIES" AND ALLIANCES

Although some participated in the 1990–1991 Gulf War, many of America's so-called allies sat on the sidelines during the Iraq invasion of 2003. However, once the coalition troops marched into Baghdad and began pulling down the idol-like images of Saddam Hussein, the Europeans began to line up for a piece of the postwar building program. They were eager to share in the bounty that was sure to result from the pillaging of Saddam's palaces and storehouses. France and Germany began to try to ingratiate themselves with the United States to secure a role in future Iraq projects. They, along with other United Nations members, wanted a central role in the process. Even as France's smooth-talking then foreign minister Dominique de Villepin was encouraging the Bush administration to let bygones be bygones, a French delegation was winging its way to Tehran to meet with leaders from Iran and from the Iraqi resistance.

Meanwhile in Iraq, Iranian-supported factions were spreading the jihad much like Typhoid Mary spread her murderous disease across New York in the early 1900s. Moqtada al-Sadr and his cronies spread "Shiite-controlled Iraq" propaganda, while other clerics encouraged their followers to defy American troops in open hostility. The southern Iraqi city of Kut rapidly became a stronghold for Iranian-backed forces determined to spread Grand Ayatollah Khomeini's Islamic revolution to Iraq, and Tehran infused Sadr's Mahdi army with new blood, raising their numbers to five thousand men. (As of the end of 2006, estimates of the Mahdi army's size have grown to around sixty thousand.) These death squads assumed the duties of the local police while emulating the Iranian style of dress and driving vehicles supplied by Iran.

One of the ways the Iraqi Shiites made their presence known following the collapse of Hussein's government was to celebrate Ashura, a holy day set aside to display the might of the Shiites. A part of the ritual surrounding Ashura Day is the use of chains for self-flagellation. It was during Ashura that the Iranian-backed forces made their presence known near Karbala and al Najaf, two of the holiest Shiite cities in Iraq. It is estimated that some two million people began the march toward the two cities, rapidly joined by millions from nearby cities, all "protected" by forces loyal to Iran. Intelligence services surmise that the march to and from Karbala and al Najaf was a means to transport weapons, explosives, munitions, and money throughout Iraq, as well as a means to transport and embed Iranian agents.

By the end of April 2004, coalition forces were already beginning to sit up and take notice of all the activity sponsored by neighboring Iran. In one of my meetings with Lt. Gen. Moshe Ya'alon, he stated that more than 85 percent of the improvised explosive devices used in Iraq were furnished by Iran.

The coalition troops were becoming more and more vulnerable to suicide attacks carried out by terrorists crossing the border from Iran. To compound the problem, Hezbollah forces remaining in Iraq after Saddam's fall were joined by more forces slipping across the border from Syria. It was estimated that some twenty-five thousand to thirty thousand Iranian forces were actively fighting coalition forces in Iraq. This was a surprising turn of events for the Bush administration. The *Washington Post* reported they had "underestimated the Shiites' organizational strength... [and were] concerned that those sentiments could coalesce into a fundamentalist government [in Iraq]."[9]

True to Israeli concerns expressed before the war, it appeared that the administration had a clear entry strategy but were unprepared for the task of stabilizing Iraq and dealing with the various factions in the country. Like the Energizer Bunny, France was too eager to jump on the bandwagon to encourage the United States to seek Iran's assistance in the region. The French foreign minister de Villepin was one of the first to openly endorse asking Iran to join in providing assistance in the rebuilding of Iraq. What neither France nor the United States could know was that Iran was preparing to unchain the terrorist forces of Islamic radicals in Iraq. This, apparently, was in response to Iran's fear that, given the opportunity, the United States would stop the Shiite majority in Iraq from controlling that country.

Equally staunch in making Iraq a case study for dealing with terrorist states, President Bush, in his speech aboard the USS *Abraham Lincoln* on May 1, 2003, had issued this warning:

> Any person involved in committing or planning terrorist attacks against the American people becomes an enemy of this country, and a target of American justice.
>
> Any person, organization, or government that supports, protects, or harbors terrorists is complicit in the murder of the innocent, and equally guilty of terrorist crimes.
>
> Any outlaw regime that has ties to terrorist groups and seeks or possesses weapons of mass destruction is a grave danger to the civilized world—and will be confronted.[10]

To add to the Islamic radical frenzy, Osama bin Laden reared his head via an audiotape from Pakistan and challenged the terrorists racing toward Iraq not only to attack American troops but to turn their hatred on moderate Arab countries that dared support the United States, such as Pakistan, Afghanistan, Bahrain, Kuwait, and Saudi Arabia. On the tape, unveiled in a CBS news report, bin Laden called for every segment of Islamic society to support suicide bombers. With repeated calls for martyrdom, bin Laden expressed his support for "those martyrs who sacrificed their lives for the sake of Islam."[11]

IRAN RISES

With Tehran's encouragement, resistance from the Shiites in Iraq was growing daily. U.S. and British patrols in principally Shiite cities were greeted with chants and barrages of rocks thrown from rooftops.

Initially, the Shiites in Iraq assumed the role of peacemaker. They seemed to be willing to support the United States during the invasion, certain that when the dust settled, the United States would back a Shiite-majority government. As sure as the Iraqis were that this would happen, Tehran was equally sure that an American-friendly, democratic Iraq would not be in their best interest. Ayatollah Baqir al-Hakim, the leader of the Iranian-sponsored Supreme Council for Islamic Revolution in Iraq (SCIRI), intensified his call for a Baghdad regime much like that in Iran. Al-Hakim was certain that the future of Iraq lay in an Islamic theocracy, not a Western-style democracy. In early May 2004, al-Hakim took his well-practiced, middle-of-the-road, democracy-for-Iraq rhetoric to al Najaf. Of course he knew, as did Iran, that a democratic election in a Shiite-majority Iraq meant control of the government for that faction. He preached security for Iraq with the inference that it could only be achieved by the groups that were armed and funded by Iran.

Unbeknownst to many, this also included Al Qaeda radicals ready and willing to enter the terrorist-driven battle against the United States. Just how far was Iran willing to go to achieve its aims in Iraq? Tehran was willing to provide a safe haven for Osama bin Laden and his cronies. In fact, it was widely reported that Al Qaeda personnel, including bin Laden (who is a Sunni Muslim), were entertained by Iranian government officials. Cooperation between the Sunnis and Shiites, as well as a base in Iran, would provide bin Laden with a launching pad for future attacks against other U.S.-friendly Arab regimes such as his own home country, Saudi Arabia. And it would allow Iran to more rapidly take on the role of "Terror Central." This was not surprising, since Iran had been instrumental in providing safe and undocumented passage for the hijackers responsible for the 9/11 attacks.

The knots in the noose of terror encircling Iraq were being formed with residual Al Qaeda operatives in Afghanistan, Pakistan, and Iran as well as Syrian Hezbollah with ties to Al Qaeda in Syria and Lebanon. How long would it be before the various factions began to pull on the rope, strangling coalition troops and forcing the United States to abandon its commitment to stay the course in Iraq?

Iran, leery as it was of a Western influence, was equally wary of one of Iraq's most respected ayatollahs, Grand Ayatollah Ali al-Sistani. They feared that his more lax form of Islam practiced around al Najaf would not look favorably on Iran's overtures. Iran began to accelerate the only plan that it knew with any certainty might work—terror attacks against American troops. Tehran was certain that a sustained flood of terror would demoralize the U.S. military and the American people and therefore influence the Bush administration to bow to pressure from Congress to withdraw the troops as quickly as possible.

The go-ahead to launch terror attacks on U.S. troops in Iraq further emboldened Osama bin Laden to call his troops together to plan new attacks, not only against the government in Riyadh but against the British, Israelis, tourists, and politicians. In fact, anyone who was pro-West would become an open target for bin Laden's troops. At the top of his list were the same nations that topped Tehran's list of Islamic traitors—Egypt, Jordan, Morocco, Saudi Arabia, and other Arab states with Western leanings.

Bin Laden's first targets were compounds that housed Western interests in Riyadh. In the early morning hours of May 12, 2003, five vehicles eased their way through the city. Three of the vehicles were packed with explosives; the other two carried assault teams. As the sun peeked over the edge of the city, massive blasts rocked three Western compounds, killing twenty-six people, nine of them Americans, and wounding more than one hundred sixty people. These explosions were followed days later with similar blasts in Casablanca that claimed the lives of thirty-three civilians and injured more than a hundred. According to a *Washington Post* report, Iran was complicit at least in the Riyadh bombings:

> Saad bin Laden [Osama bin Laden's son] and other senior Al Qaeda operatives were in contact with an Al Qaeda cell in Riyadh, Saudi Arabia, in the days immediately prior to the May 12 suicide bombing there that left 35 people dead [this number also counts the nine suicide bombers],…European and U.S. intelligence sources say. The sources would not divulge the nature or contents of the communications, but the contacts have led them to conclude that the Riyadh attacks were planned in Iran and ordered from there.[12]

Prominent Al Qaeda member Ayman al-Zawahiri joined the call for vicious, worldwide attacks against Americans and Jews. In a harangue delivered in May 2003, he ranted:

> The crusaders and the Jews do not understand but the language of killing and blood. They do not become convinced unless they see coffins returning to them, their interests being destroyed, their towers being torched, and their economy collapsing. O Muslims, take matters firmly against the embassies of America, England, Australia, and Norway and their interests, companies, and employees. Burn the ground under their feet, as they should not enjoy your protection, safety, or security. Expel those criminals out of your countries.…Learn from your 19 brothers who attacked America in its planes in New York and Washington and caused it a tribulation that it never witnessed before.[13]

The powers-that-be in Iran were convinced that America had a two-fold plan for the Middle East: regime change where necessary and democratization of other Arab states. Tehran had learned by studying American involvement in other regions that the Americans were good at quick response but had a very poor track record when it came to defending prolonged occupations; perfect examples could be found in Vietnam and in Lebanon. Given these two options, and fearing American incursion, the Iranians came up with a third plan: rather than be dominated by the United States, Iran would dominate. How would they achieve their plan? As the world would soon see, it would pick up the pace on Iran's nuclear program and succeed through nuclear blackmail.

Tehran believed that Iran—not Iraq—had always been the ultimate goal of an American invasion. A foothold in that country would place American troops in two countries surrounding Iran's borders: Iraq and Afghanistan. An invasion of Iran seemed to be the next logical step in what was seen as a U.S. bid for regional domination. U.S. efforts, or so Tehran believed, were focused only on preserving the Zionists that had usurped land from the Palestinians, and in order to do that, Iranian influence had to be curbed. Therefore, in the minds of the mullahs in control, the only answer was a U.S. invasion of Iran and an end to Khomeini's Islamic revolution. In June 2003, a power play designed to showcase Iran's presence in the Persian Gulf unfolded. The Iranian Coast Guard stopped two boats carrying four U.S. soldiers and five civilians. The occupants of the two boats were blindfolded and interrogated by the Iranians before being released, according to U.S. Central Command.[14]

Just a few days before the incident in the Persian Gulf, Secretary of Defense Donald Rumsfeld had subtly warned Iraq's neighbors against interference in that nation's liberation. Said Rumsfeld in a *Wall Street Journal* article: "Assistance from Iraq's neighbors will be welcomed. Conversely, interference in Iraq by its neighbors or their proxies— including those whose objective is to remake Iraq in Iran's image—will not be accepted or permitted." Rumsfeld went on to say that the transition to democracy would "take time" and that the "ultimate political outcome must be decided by the Iraqi people." The end result in Iraq should not be made to "replicate any other system [of governance]."[15] All the political pundits had to figure out now was how to keep the Shiite majority from controlling Iraq and linking arms with Iran.

OPEN-ENDED OCCUPATION

America was now firmly entrenched in Iraq, but the unanswered question was, "For how long, and toward what end result?" Protests, not only from factions in Iraq but also from the entire Muslim world, were increasing. Terrorist organizations seemed capable of humiliating and/ or killing American troops at will. Rather than reinforcing the Bush administration's war on terror, the terrorists in Iraq were sucking the life and the will to win out of Operation Iraqi Freedom. Coalition troops were faced with an increasingly bold guerrilla war fought by jihadists.

The Iraqi resistance movement was compared to the Palestinian resistance against the Israelis. It was also heralded as an infusion of new life into the Lebanese and Palestinian intifada against the Jews. With all eyes on Iraq, both Iran and Syria could take advantage of the opportunity to build forces in Lebanon and in Gaza, Israel's closest neighbors.

However, just as the Madrid Peace Conference following the first Gulf War ran through Jerusalem, so a resolution to this war would as well. The first entity to benefit from the defeat of Saddam Hussein was the Palestinian Authority. In fact, the two coalition leaders, George W. Bush and Tony Blair, agreed even before the outbreak of hostilities on the link between the war on Iraq and the Israeli-Palestinian conflict. Indeed, the entire European political establishment tied the defeat of Saddam Hussein to a renewed peace process between Israel and the Palestinians.

In an address to Parliament before the war began, Blair started the campaign to link the Palestinian question to the war in Iraq. He reassured his listeners that peace between the Jews and the Palestinians was of paramount importance. It was the beginning of a push for what was to become known as the Road Map for Peace that would be unveiled in June 2003.

Following a meeting at Camp David between the president and Mr. Blair, President Bush stated:

> History requires more of our coalition than a defeat of a terrible danger. I see an opportunity, as does Prime Minister Blair, to bring renewed hope and progress to the entire Middle East. Last June 24th, I outlined a vision of two states, Israel and Palestine living side-by-side in peace and security. Soon, we'll release the road map that is designed to help

turn that vision into reality. And both America and Great Britain are strongly committed to implementing that road map.[16]

Blair responded by noting a date for the public debut of the Road Map:

> We both share a complete determination to move this forward. It is, indeed, often overlooked that President Bush is the first U.S. President publicly to commit himself to a two-state solution, an Israel confident of its security and a viable Palestinian state. And I welcome the decision announced recently to publish the road map as soon as the confirmation of the new Palestinian Prime Minister is properly administered.[17]

The Road Map plan included sponsorship by the UN, the EU, and Russia—none of which supported the war with Iraq. According to sources in Jerusalem, Israel accepted the Road Map in principle but had a number of reservations. This could well have been a sign that Israel learned a valuable lesson post-Madrid. It learned that it cannot afford to make unilateral concessions. Israel recognized that a new Middle East could not evolve in response to a UN Security Council resolution or to a well-executed public relations campaign by the EU, even if Arafat and the various factions could be successfully lured to the bargaining table.

For the moment, at least, Israel was satisfied with being relegated to the background, comfortable with helping Washington without public recognition. It must have created quite a shock wave in the Knesset when their staunch political ally, George W. Bush, announced the Road Map with its steps to a two-state solution. The entities resident in the Palestinian Authority met the news with their usual response: a suicide bomber detonated a backpack of explosives inside an Israeli pub, killing three and wounding twenty. And still, Israel was pressured to turn a blind eye on the daily threats of terrorism by Hamas, Fatah, Hezbollah, and a plethora of terror organizations in deference to the new peace process, the Road Map. Knesset member Uzi Landau wrote:

> If the Quartet's road map is accepted, Yasser Arafat will win the greatest victory of his life. Despite the blatant violation of all his commitments in the Oslo agreements and his responsibility for the murder of more than 1,000 Israelis—nearly 800 of them during the last two years of terror—he has not been punished. On the contrary, he...will get...the establishment of a state...without negotiation.[18]

While the Quartet (the UN, EU, Russia, and the United States) was pushing the Road Map, Iran's President Khatami was looking for a few good friends in Syria, Lebanon, and Yemen, all states known to fund and harbor terrorists. In Syria, Khatami deliberated on how the two countries could resist what they saw as the U.S. intentions to occupy the region without antagonizing Washington. Of particular interest was American support for Israel and how to pursue terror activities against that country without retaliation by the United States. Despite these concerns, Hezbollah continued its dogged pursuit of Israeli civilians with rocket fire into Northern Israel.

Sadly, President Bush's attempts to gain unilateral Arab support for its liberation of Iraq by tossing out another two-state carrot were met with disdain. The Muslim world recognized long ago that a two-state solution was not the real answer to the "Jewish problem." The only answer that would suffice would entail pushing the Jews into the Mediterranean, or, as President Ahmadinejad would later opine, wiping Israel "off the map."

THE HOPE FOR PEACE

Coalition forces spent the summer of 2003 still searching for the remnants of the Iraqi government, including Hussein's two sons, Uday and Qusay, who were killed in gunfire on July 22. In the months following the cessation of major combat, more than two hundred top Baath Party officials were either killed or captured. Saddam himself was eventually found hiding in a spider hole near Tikrit on December 13. Again, many thought these were signs that victory and Middle East peace were well within reach.

However, the months that followed would paint the war as far from over.

How was it that the butcher of Baghdad, the rebuilder of Babylon, the supreme leader of Iraq was found cowering in a spider hole in Iraq? Apparently Saddam had set up a meeting with two trusted allies, the brothers al-Omar. Saddam was to meet them and be taken to his next safe house. At the designated spot, Hussein was either taken captive or drugged, then deposited in the spider hole, where he was later discovered by American troops.

In the perfect "how the mighty are fallen" scenario, the cringing dictator had been unceremoniously dumped into a six-foot-deep hole in the ground with no sanitation and barely room to move about. His hole was well supplied, however, with $750,000 in one hundred dollar bills and stacks of documentation on the Iraqi resistance. For all of his money, he had little food, few clothes, and no way to communicate with the outside world.

What led the American troops to an isolated farmhouse looking for Saddam Hussein? Days before his capture, army intelligence sources had captured a senior security officer from Hussein's retinue. After inter-rogation, the officer, Mohammed Ibrahim Omar al-Musslit, revealed Hussein's whereabouts. Operation Red Dawn was launched with a con-voy of more than thirty armored vehicles and six hundred troops. Special Forces groups searched the two farmhouses indicated by al-Musslit, only to come up empty-handed. They were preparing to depart when a soldier noticed a crack in the ground. Quick reconnaissance revealed the hiding place of the most wanted man in all of Iraq, Saddam Hussein.

Islamic radicals quickly responded to Hussein's capture by jockey-ing for positions of importance in Iran. Al Qaeda was the first to jump on the "Saddam is gone, and we're taking over" bandwagon. Bin Laden was eager to let the Americans know that he was responsible for the murderous suicide attacks throughout Iraq. He wanted bragging rights for the numbers killed and wounded. He wanted the credit for the anti-American guerrilla warfare that was so rampant in the coun-try. Bin Laden's lieutenant, Ayman al-Zawahiri, was quick to add that American soldiers were cowards and that Al Qaeda would pursue them even into the United States.

The Iraqi resistance movement was next to step up to the plate to alert the Iraqi people that the capture of Saddam Hussein was simply a photo op to ensure President Bush's reelection. The Baathists invited all Iraqis to join in the struggle to repel the American invaders. All of the groups urged that the resistance against the U.S. occupation continue in full force. However, it was not the urging of the jihadists that encour-aged Iraqis under the umbrella of the radical Islamists; it was the deep dissatisfaction with the political process, the lack of basic services, and the failure to stop the murder and mayhem in the streets of the cit-ies. Faced with what might best be described as anarchy, Washington continued to paint a rosy picture on events in Iraq, going so far as to reiterate that Iraqi resistance was ebbing.

An announcement that the United States would begin withdrawing from Iraq in mid-2004 was met with skepticism, especially when it was made clear that troops would remain in Iraq for some time. The problem for the coalition leaders would be how to ensure that Iraq didn't immediately fall into the hands of the Shiite majority, rather than become a democratic government for all the people. As soon as the discussions began, Ayatollah al-Sistani issued yet another fatwa calling for a one-man/one-vote system. The resulting stalemate threatened the entire political process for which the United States–led coalition had fought.

One London correspondent summed up the situation in Iraq very succinctly when he wrote:

> In this miasma of inaction, the lead roles of the national drama are being filled by an assertive handful of self-interested parties keen to fix things in their favour. The low-level, often inter-ethnic, conflict that bedevils Iraq is as much about staking a claim to post-coalition power as driving the infidels from the country.
>
> And just as they watched passively for years while Saddam Hussein's brutal ultimate in nanny states made every decision for them, so Iraqis are watching and waiting now.[19]

As the fledgling democracy of Iraq entered 2004, it was obvious that, far from ebbing, the resistance was becoming a flood that threatened to consume everything in its path. Shiites, Sunnis, Kurds, Turkmen, and Islamic terrorists from around the world were overtly or covertly planning ways to achieve their goals. The reaction from the Iraqi tribes and sects was a surprise to Washington. Far from welcoming the Americans as liberators, the Iraqis welcomed the deposing of Saddam Hussein and then quickly wanted the "infidels" out of their country. It was apparent that a Bush strategy to respond unilaterally when threatened, or even preventatively, would not be welcomed with open arms.

The Bush administration never questioned that it would be able to put together a strike force that would be totally successful against Hussein. The hope that a democratic Iraq would become a certainty was slowly becoming a battered dream. What no one took into account was the ideology behind the Muslim culture. Americans are born with freedom of choice; it is difficult to understand how a person steeped in the tradition and mores of Islam would be reluctant to embrace democracy and freedom of choice. Washington was unprepared to deal with the harsh truth that was found in Iraq. Like a child caught in the throes of the terrible twos, unable to understand the meaning of the word no, the Washington intelligence community forged ahead despite obvious signs that the majority of the Iraqi people were not eager to accept Westernization. Therefore, President Bush was not sufficiently warned about the prospect of failure.

It is apparent that the Bush administration vastly underestimated the enemy—no, not Saddam Hussein, but the government in Iran. With the challenge of "Bring 'em on" issued by President Bush, the jihads worldwide did just that.

When the president attempted to negotiate with the Sunni Arabs on controversial issues regarding federalism and the removal of the Baathist influence, he was thanked politely. He was severely handicapped by not having been prepared in advance for the idiosyncrasies of the Muslim ideology. The Bush administration really did not understand the various divisions in the Muslim society and was working at a great disadvantage.

It was not the president but his ambassador to Iraq, Dr. Zalmay Khalilzad, who was responsible for bartering an agreement between the Kurds and Shiites that would prove to be the foundation of Iraq's new constitution. Khalilzad was immediately faced with the challenge of finding common ground among the Shiites, Kurds, and Sunni Arabs. The Kurds feared losing their independence, the Shiites wanted a more self-serving constitution, and the Sunnis objected to everything proposed by the Shiites and the Kurds.

The Sunni delegation had been infiltrated by members of Hussein's Baath Party, which further complicated matters for Khalilzad. The spokesman for the group, Saleh al-Mutlaq, was the former translator for Saddam Hussein and a Sunni Arab, and, as such, offended the Kurds and Shiites.

By insisting that this particular group be included in the formulation of the constitution, and although its adherents did not participate in the general election, the Bush administration conferred authenticity upon them.

The Shiites wanted an Islamic state—Sharia law to replace the secular civil code—that would lead to rule by Shiite ayatollahs recognized by the constitution and a constitutional court based on Islamic law. Such a court would be able with impunity to overrule civil laws enacted by the parliament and government. This was in line with the authority that had been conferred upon Grand Ayatollah Khomeini as the Supreme Leader in Iran. Secular Arabs recognized the path down which such an arrangement would take Iraq; the Bush administration seemed to be in a state of denial.

According to the resulting constitution, Iraq is a moderate Islamic state. Officially, Islam is the state religion and *a* basic source of legislation, not *the* basic source desired by the Shiites.

To the secular Arabs in Iraq, all the factional divides are incomprehensible. Religion had never before been a big factor in politics in Iraq, and, indeed, that aspect may take a backseat in time. That remains to be seen. I certainly feel that as long as Iran has a direct influence on the Shiites in Iraq, it will continue to stir civil strife between the Shiites and the Sunnis. The drive for a democratic Iraq has released emotions in the nation that had long been suppressed. Only time will tell whether or not the various sectarian groups will be able to hammer out a viable working relationship.

Not only was President Bush misinformed regarding the ideology of the Muslim culture, he was misinformed about the presence of quantities of WMDs in Iraq. As far back as 1998, a task force comprised of members of the House released a paper, "The Iraqi WMD Challenge: Myths and Reality." The paper outlined the inequities between the production of and the possession of WMDs. It indicated that Hussein possessed small quantities of WMDs and even had the means to disburse the chemicals. However, it outlined the fact that production had been delegated to Sudan, Libya, and Algeria, a fact that escaped many in the intelligence community in Washington. The evidence that Iraq had the capability to deliver WMDs via unmanned aircraft was the deciding factor for some who voted to pursue Operation Iraqi Freedom.

The question remains: where are the WMDs, tanks, armored vehicles, jet fighters, and gunships that Saddam was so eager to display in giant parades and was willing to risk his dictatorship to protect? Like the battalions of soldiers that just melted away before the U.S. invasion, so it seems did his armaments. The most logical explanation offered is that they have been secreted below ground in massive bunkers or exported to Syria and Iran. The Bush administration miscalculated the wiliness of Saddam Hussein. Were his delaying tactics simply to insure that his war matériel was moved to safer locations? Perhaps Hussein is the only one with all the pieces to the puzzle, and of course, he's not sharing that information with anyone now.

Chapter Six

THE WORLD WAR AGAINST TERRORISM

I see the threat posed to the United States and Israel as the beginning of a one-hundred-year war. You can call it World War III. You can call it the beginning of a new type of warfare....I would rather not use analogies to World War I and World War II and just think of this as a new kind of warfare that the West is clearly disadvantaged by. The asymmetry of morality makes it very hard for us to fight groups that have no morality.[1]

—ALAN DERSHOWITZ

We are in dire need of you....The field of jihad can satisfy your scientific ambitions, and the large American bases [in Iraq] are good places to test your unconventional weapons, whether biological or dirty, as they call them.[2]

—ABU AYYUB AL-MASRI,
leader of Al Qaeda in Iraq,
in a call for experts in the fields of
"chemistry, physics, electronics, media and all other sciences—
especially nuclear scientists and explosives experts"
to join the terror group's holy war against the West

Near the beginning of 2006, in addition to targeting coalition and, in particular, American troops, the tactics again seemed to take a new direction. A new level of violence began arising between the Shiites and the Sunnis. On February 22, 2006, two bombs exploded in the Shiite Al Askari mosque, severely damaging its golden dome and interior. The mosque is powerfully significant to Shiite Muslims because it is the burial place of Ali Al-Hadi and his son, Hassan Al-Askari, the Tenth and Eleventh Imams. They are the immediate predecessors of the Twelfth, or Hidden, Imam, Muhammad Al-Mahdi, the one known as *the* Mahdi for whom al-Sadr's Mahdi army is named, who disappeared down a well in Iran in the tenth century and would one day return to triumphantly spread Islam to the world. It is believed his apocalyptic return from a well in Jamkaran, Iran, will bring the world under control of a new Muslim caliphate that will lead Islam to world supremacy.

One of those responsible for this bombing had been wearing an Iraqi military uniform. Shiites responded by attacking and destroying Sunni mosques. Several Sunni imams were summarily executed by al-Sadr's Shiite militia. Shiite mobs in other Iraq cities stormed jails and executed inmates. In retaliation, groups of Sunnis attacked Shiites, dragging them from vehicles to be murdered. As many of the U.S.-trained and armed Iraqi police force looked on in fear, others simply joined the assailants. Not even a curfew imposed on Baghdad could stop the slaughter. Bodies were dumped on Baghdad streets, handcuffed, and shot execution-style. In all, 184 Sunni mosques either lay in rubble or were vandalized, and more than one thousand Shiites and Sunnis were murdered.

In the ensuing months, sectarian death squads roamed the streets killing thousands. Someone was trying to sow the seeds of ethnic violence in the hope of starting a civil war.

DESCENT INTO ANARCHY

With cries that the resistance would not end until the infidels were driven from Iraq, new recruits joined daily. Intelligence sources indicate a new cooperation among heretofore antagonistic factions. Some Shiite groups are consorting with Sunni groups; Baathist brigades work alongside the fedayeen (Arab commandos) to take out coalition troops and bring down American aircraft. The United States is caught in the crosshairs of every terrorist organization in operation in Iran, Iraq, and Syria and can do little to stop the resulting bloodshed. The disorganized Baathist forces that fell so rapidly under the initial assault are regrouping as guerrilla warriors with only one intention: to strike the coalition forces at every turn.

The Muslim world did not see this as a war to curb Saddam Hussein's terror activities, but rather as another attack by "Crusaders" against Islam. One of the most respected analysts in the Arab world, Abdul Bari al-Atwan, made a further comparison:

> The U.S. forces have not liberated Iraq; they have humiliated it, occupied it, torn it apart, and subjugated its sons. The United States is now preparing to subjugate the rest of the Arabs in the same way and by the

same destructive operation; therefore, it will not meet with anything except resistance and hatred....This means that the aggression will not stop at the borders of Iraq, exactly the same as when Hulagu [a Mongol leader] occupied Baghdad, looted it, enslaved its inhabitants, and destroyed it as a springboard to occupy the entire region.[3]

To a seriously affronted Muslim world, the infidels—this time American soldiers rather than Mongols—had again ridden into Baghdad to pillage and humiliate the Iraqi people. Osama bin Laden issued the call to jihad against the invaders. And now, Mahmoud Ahmadinejad has donned the mantle of Ayatollah Khomeini, taken up bin Laden's call, and is fostering an Islamic revolution that is aimed at the bloodiest clash of religious ideologies the world has ever seen between Islam, Judaism, and Christianity.

In the rush to prepare for certain invasion by American and coalition troops, Saddam Hussein set out to cover his tracks and eliminate all threats. In a move designed to prevent the coalition forces from interrogating one of the world's most brutal and prolific terrorists, Hussein's elite troops entered an Iraqi upper-class stronghold in Baghdad and assassinated Abu Nidal along with four of his henchmen. Nidal was responsible for the deaths of hundreds in terror attacks worldwide. Although Hussein had ordered the murder of Nidal, he was reacting to pressure from Hosni Mubarak in Egypt and Yasser Arafat, who did not want Nidal's secrets exposed to Western scrutiny. With intelligence supplied to Hussein by Russian leader Vladimir Putin, Nidal had received overtures from the CIA and was considering disclosing confidential information in exchange for asylum. Hussein made sure that didn't happen.[4]

Perhaps the biggest challenge for the United States is the renewed battle against Saddam's secret weapon: the parallel underground force trained by North Korea in the art of carrying out a prolonged guerrilla war. To provide further safeguards for himself, Hussein established a parallel government with outposts around Iraq as a firewall against a U.S. invasion. The warriors inside this parallel Saddam Hussein–induced network were trained to create civil upheaval and insurrection against invading forces. To facilitate the fighters, Hussein engaged China and North Korea to build a series of underground bunkers almost completely undetectable from the air. These bunkers were thought to house his stockpile of weapons, including the elusive WMDs.

It was no wonder that as Operation Iraqi Freedom advanced, coalition troops found themselves under constant bombardment from a variety of terror cells and networks hard at work to create civil strife. With Syria's help—as a backer of terror activities and a shelter for terrorists, as well as an open pipeline for incoming jihadists—it was no wonder that the United States was finding it more and more difficult to police Iraq. And, although they had no formal agreement to cooperate, Syria became a recruiting ground for Iran to enlist the aid of Hezbollah fighters in and around Baghdad.

U.S. forces found it increasingly difficult to identify friend from foe among the Iraqis. As Lt. Col. Eric Schwartz told a *New York Times* reporter:

> I don't believe there is a single organized group.... The information that we have is that it may be a collection of folks. It may be Iraqis. It may be Syrians. It may be Palestinians. We believe that Al Qaeda is possibly in there.[5]

Spurred on by influential ayatollahs whose Friday sermons were filled with anti-American, hate-filled oratory and the offering of food and spending money, young Muslims in surrounding Arab countries—Syria, Saudi Arabia, and Palestine, among others—were eager to join the fight to expunge the infidels from Arab land. It didn't hurt the cause that there was also a promise of paradise and young virgins, should a recruit become a suicide bomber.

One of the most vocal proponents of the rebellion has been Moqtada al-Sadr, who has made no secret of his ties with Iran. During the height of resistance in July 2003, al-Sadr made a four-day visit to Iran for meetings with Rafsanjani, the former Iranian president, and senior leaders in Ayatollah Khamenei's office. There he received an appointment as an official emissary of Iran's Ayatollah Haeri. Al-Sadr committed to pursue the Iranian plan for Iraq: a theocratic government that wed the political and the religious. It was his assignment to denigrate Ayatollah al-Sistani in Iraq, to undertake assassinations, and to foment resistance in any way possible. In return, he would be supplied with expert assistance from Hezbollah and the elite Qods force of Iran.[6]

Al-Sadr's mentor eased the way for success for his protégé by issuing a fatwa aimed at Saddam's Baath Party members. He decreed that they were open targets for Moqtada's death squads, thus giving him a permit to murder. Even as al-Sadr was issued his license to incite rebellion, a decree was issued to Iranian-supported cells to engage British troops near Basra, as they were thought to be easier targets for cells trained in Iran. A group of pro-Iranian militant agitators whipped a local group in Majar al-Kabir into a killing frenzy. The result was the mob killing of six Royal Military Police troops. A second attack targeted the British 1st Battalion of the Parachute Regiment. The third British detachment to come under fire was the crew of a Chinook helicopter while attempting to rescue a detail of British soldiers under small arms and grenade fire. Iran was determined to do the very thing that it chastised the United States for doing: interfering with the government in Iraq.

In July, al-Sadr introduced his Mahdi army to the people of al Najaf. His announcement was made to a group of followers garbed in shrouds, ostensibly to indicate their readiness to die as martyrs. Their rallying cry was reminiscent of that introduced by Khomeini: "Death to America" and "Death to Israel."

Al-Sadr was confident of the support that he would receive from his Iranian sponsors. He had at his fingertips a network of terrorists, some from Lebanon and others from Iran and Syria. Their only purpose was to kill the invaders and anyone associated with them. Iran's noose was tightening on Iraq. The path of the jihadists was crowded with those willing to be martyred for the resistance.

With so many willing to take on the Americans and their colleagues, attacks against the troops escalated to as many as twenty-five daily. The weapons of choice grew more sophisticated. Missile launchers and hand grenades, as well as rocket-propelled grenades (RPGs) and military-grade IEDs, became the norm.

CIVIL WAR?

What was published early on as a decisive victory in Iraq has rapidly descended into anarchy, with the various factions warring against each other and against the coalition troops. Death squads roam the streets of Baghdad, Sunnis fight Shiites, ayatollahs fight ayatollahs for predominance, and, in the background, Iran continues to arm and support groups loyal to Tehran.

Local militia groups sometimes open fire on police or coalition forces, resulting in gunfights that last for days. Offensives have been mounted to disarm and drive out these militants. In these bloody street battles, it is often hard to tell civilians from rebels, and slowly the surgical-accurateness of the U.S. attacks has begun to be called into question. Due to protests from the newly formed Iraqi Governing Council and media pressure, assaults are halted short of their goals and truces are negotiated. For every two steps forward, it seems U.S. efforts are forced to take three back.

Ambushes, suicide bombings, kidnappings, and murders have become the order of the day during the occupation. Roadside bombs using IEDs target anyone who happens to get in the way. Suicide bombers attack coalition checkpoints and other gathering places with regularity. Of the explosive devices used to kill U.S. personnel, retired Navy captain Charles Nash noted that they had changed in recent months, though were still coming from the same source:

> When I was in Baghdad, I actually held one of those explosive devices—IEDs—in my hand. At the time it was the latest threat—a brand new generation. It actually forms a projectile when it blows up that pierces armor plate. You have to manufacture these things. It's not rocket science, but somebody has to know how to do it to make them effective.
>
> Iranians have been doing that. We know they've been doing that.[7]

This "latest threat" in that IEDs have significantly upgraded near the end of 2005 also proves Iran is more openly supporting the insurgents.

By the end of 2006, a new name was being given to these devices: EFPs, which stands for "explosive-formed penetrators." Unlike regular roadside bombs, EFPs remain intact as they explode. The steel tubes with curved metal seals form a kind of super-shrapnel that can go directly through a tank's or Humvee's armor. The explosion turns the caps into molten jets of metal. Other than keeping a low profile, U.S. troops have little defense against these better-engineered booby traps. Again, evidence suggests these are being smuggled across the Iranian border.[8]

In a recent interview with former CIA director James Woolsey, he said this of Iran's involvement in Iraq:

Iran is playing a very important role in Iraq by smuggling in improvised explosive devices and the technology for them, by helping militias such as Moqtada al-Sadr's brigades attack Sunni, and troubled survivability of the government in Iraq. Iran has a long border with Iraq. It's been infiltrating money, terrorists, various, I think, operational gear, and weapons for some time. It's one of the biggest problems in Iraq.[9]

One thing has become abundantly clear: those we are fighting are not a ragtag band of disgruntled Iraqis; we are facing a professional, full-frontal assault by well-armed terrorists. Iraq is headed down the slippery slope toward civil war, and at present the United States seems impotent to halt the slide.

REBUILDING THE INFRASTRUCTURE

It was obvious to all the American leaders in Iraq that Saddam had not spent his oil money on the infrastructure in his country. In what would become another finger pointed at U.S. inefficiency, it had failed to restore public utilities to the major cities, to stop looting, to prevent rampant crime in the streets of Baghdad, to halt sabotage to oil facilities, and to provide basic protection to peaceful citizens. This differed widely from what the Iraqis saw as the United States providing for its own military and civilian staff. The United States was criticized for grabbing the best buildings and for quickly providing amenities to their own. This only led to further disillusionment, as well as fueling the rumors that the Americans were there to stay, not to relinquish control to the Iraqis as soon as possible.

Efforts to restore services were hampered by roaming resistance groups that targeted Iraqi civilians hard at work on repairing the infrastructure and providing the basics. The workers suffered verbal harangues at best, beatings and public execution at worst. As U.S.-trained Iraqi police began to patrol the cities, they became immediate targets for the terrorists. They were murdered on the streets, in training facilities, and in police stations; they were killed where they ate and where they slept. Is it any wonder that nothing constructive can be accomplished in Iraq, or why the Americans are blamed for all the ills that have befallen the nation since the removal of Hussein?

This violence only added to the difficulties that the United States faced daily in Iraq. The news that Saddam's sons had been killed elicited a surprising backlash among the Muslim media. The Hussein sons were quickly elevated to martyr status, which all but negated the horrific crimes perpetrated by the two under their father's tutelage. This only served to swell the ranks of willing martyrs for the cause. The one to benefit least from the release of the Iraqi people from the repressive Hussein regime was the United States. The invasion was declared to be the best thing that had ever happened in inspiring the Islamist cause.

ENTER IRAN, AGAIN

At this point in the war, even Arab-friendly states were beginning to back away from America's involvement in Iraq. Egypt's Hosni Mubarak signed on with Iran to send Egyptian extremists imprisoned in Iran to Iraq as fighters. Mubarak, concerned about the rise of fanatical Islam in the Middle East and how it may affect Egypt, wanted to jump on the support bandwagon. He acknowledged the role of Hamas and other Palestinian forces in an effort to prevent an incursion into his country. Mubarak pledged funds and arms in support of the Islamic groups in close proximity of Egypt. After meetings between Iran's intelligence chief, Ali Yunesi, and Mubarak's envoy, Gen. Omar Suleiman, Iran agreed to a pact with Egypt that would protect Mubarak's empire.

Not content with only creating an anti-American revolution in Iraq and a Sunni-Shiite civil war, Tehran also set about to create civil war between the ranks of the U.S.-friendly Kurds and Turkmen. Communities rose against each other, clashes with United States troops became more common, and a warning was issued against trying to disarm the Kurdish soldiers. As the unrest grew, the door was opened for infiltration into Kurdish ranks by bin Laden's Al Qaeda terrorists and others from Syria and Iran. The United States was in grave danger of losing another ally in Iraq.

The Islamic radical offensive against American forces escalated as the year neared an end. On October 26, 2006, in the midst of Ramadan, suicide bombings escalated in the heart of Baghdad. An American Black Hawk helicopter was downed near Tikrit, a first for the terrorists in this conflict. The Al-Rashid Hotel in Baghdad was hit by rockets fired from launchers disguised as generators. The targets were American VIPs, including Deputy Defense Secretary Paul Wolfowitz. Killed during the attack was an American colonel. A number of American civilians and military personnel were wounded. It was later determined that the rockets used were modified versions of rockets originating in France and the old Soviet Union.

The attack was followed by what the Islamic radicals deemed to be a symbolic withdrawal of Americans from the Al-Rashid Hotel to the safety of the green zone and to protected sites outside the city. The Americans were on the run, albeit not very far.

Following closely on the heels of the attack on the Al-Rashid on October 27 were car bombing attacks on targets in Baghdad, the Red Cross headquarters, Iraqi government offices, police stations, and a fourth attack that failed when the car bomb did not explode on contact with a cement barrier outside a second police compound. The driver responsible for the failed mission carried a Syrian passport.

On October 28, revolutionaries targeted a tank north of Baghdad, shot a Baghdad deputy mayor—an American ally—in the head at a café in Baghdad, attacked an Iraqi military police convoy, bombed a shopping area serving Iraqis working for the government, and blew up an American supply train near Fallujah. The attackers didn't stop there. October 30 saw the dawning of another day of intense terror activities: U.S. military patrols were attacked, roadside bombs detonated, police stations strafed with gunfire, American bases hit by mortar fire, and an American patrol ambushed. The attacks spilled over into the next day with attacks on Americans in Mosul and Abu Ghraib. As October gave way to November, the attacks intensified, both in power and superiority.

Once the terrorists became aware that they possessed the capability to bring down a Black Hawk, an all-out campaign to rid the skies of helicopters and troop transport planes began anew. With an arsenal of rockets and machine guns, the insurgents were able to hit the engine of a Chinook helicopter. The crash killed sixteen and injured twenty on board. Another attack on a Black Hawk near Tikrit resulted in the deaths of all six crewmembers. Yet another Black Hawk, hit by machine-gun fire, rolled violently and crashed into another helicopter, bringing both down. Seventeen were killed and five wounded.

November saw an increase in the number of strikes and a new round of assassination attempts aimed at those thought to be in collusion with the United States. Car bombings increased as American patrols were decreased to protect the troops. American commanders instigated new evasive actions designed to safeguard American units, and the terrorists took advantage of their absence.

Meanwhile, Osama bin Laden had not been idle. He was busy setting up training camps in remote locations to provide on-the-job training for the insurgents flooding into Iraq. The objective was to whip out small cells in a short period of time, equip them with arms and funds, and send them forth to create murder and mayhem at will. The CIA determined that bin Laden had a pool of some ten thousand Saudi radicals ready and willing to join his cause—a situation that could ultimately signal trouble for the House of Saud. Why? A number of his commanders had joined him straight from the ranks of important tribes in Saudi Arabia.

However, just as the terrorists had their training network, so did the United States. Once again the armed forces called on the Israelis, long submerged in combating antiterrorism and urban fighting. The intifada had served as an excellent training ground for the Israeli Defense Forces. They were, in turn, able to share their knowledge acquired in the trenches with U.S. troops. Special combat units were sent to Israel to train, and in return Israeli commanders were invited to the United States to provide instruction for their U.S. counterparts.

The Israelis were also able to provide information on special operations and knowledge of the particulars of dealing with the kind of social structure the Americans were encountering in Iraq. The United States even went so far as to clandestinely import Israeli instructors into Iraq to provide on-the-ground indoctrination.

IRAN'S BURGEONING NUCLEAR AMBITIONS

Meanwhile, it was revealed that Iran had put itself back in the race for nuclear power. After the revolution of 1979, Iran's nuclear program was all but defunct. Contractors who had been working with the shah's government canceled all nuclear contracts, including finishing the Bushehr nuclear power plant whose two reactors were partially completed. The facility was further decimated in repeated attacks during the Iran-Iraq War of the 1980s. In 1995, Iran contracted with Russia to rebuild one of the reactors at Bushehr, much to the chagrin of the United States, but little evidence existed to prove that Iran's nuclear capabilities would produce anything more than electricity.

Then in 2002, Alireza Jafarzadeh, a member of the dissident People's Mujahedin of Iran (also known as Mujahadeen-e-Khalq, or for short), revealed that Iran had two secret facilities aimed at something more than just powering cities: a partially underground uranium enrichment site at Natanz and a heavy water facility in Arak.

Thus began the cat-and-mouse game I outlined in detail in *Showdown With Nuclear Iran* that I will not recap here. Iran, because of the extremism of its worldview, saw no reason to play things straight with outside infidels. Needless to say, this issue came to a head again in the summer of 2006 with two new events.

The first was that a package of incentives was offered by the EU3 (Great Britain, France, and Germany) and the United States to Iran to stop its uranium enrichment programs. Iran promised a response to this by August 22, 2006. The second was Iranian talks with world leaders that took place in early July before the G8 Summit in Russia on July 15–17. At these talks, Iran was told that pressure to verify that its nuclear program was peaceful would be a major point of discussion at the G8 Summit.

To this, Iran's response was twofold as well. As Israeli minister of tourism Isaac Herzog told me:

> Mr. Ali Larijani, who was the head of the National Security Council of Iran, completed his negotiations with Javier Solano, on behalf of the G8 in Europe, and instead of flying back home, landed in Damascus. He landed in Damascus [on] the morning of the abduction [of two Israeli soldiers on July 12 near the Israel-Lebanon border]. Now tell me if that's not a coincidence?

Shortly after those kidnappings, Hezbollah began firing Katyusha rockets on Israel's northern cities. The result was the Israeli-Hezbollah conflict that saw Israel push deeply into Lebanon with the hope of disarming Hezbollah. A UN ceasefire proposal brought the hostilities to an end on August 11, 2006, but despite suffering the destruction of most of their rocket launchers and armaments, much of the world media proclaimed Hezbollah the true winner of the fighting. During this time, the G8 Summit had come and gone, and the press paid little attention to Iran and its uranium enrichment. On July 31, however, the UN Security

Council had set an August 31 deadline for Iran to stop its enrichment activities or face sanctions. The deadline came and went with no further action.

Regarding the first event, the UE3 and U.S. incentive program for August 22, Iran responded with a long document that said they would gladly return to the negotiating table but refused to stop their enrichment activities, which had, of course, been the prerequisite set forth in the incentive plan for negotiations to resume. On August 31, President Ahmadinejad boldly stated via Iranian television, "They should know that the Iranian nation will not yield to pressure and will not let its rights be trampled on."[10] On October 23, Ahmadinejad announced, "The enemies, resorting to propaganda, want to block us from achieving (nuclear technology)...but they should know that today, the capability of our nation has multiplied tenfold over the same period last year."[11] Then on October 27, Iran announced that it had doubled its nuclear enrichment capabilities. "We are injecting gas into the second cascade, which we installed two weeks ago," an unidentified Iranian official reported.[12] An Iranian official also announced Iran would add three thousand new centrifuges to the facilities at Natanz by March 2007 of the type that a BBC expert said could be used to enrich uranium to weapons grade.[13]

Obviously Iran has no intentions of stopping its nuclear pursuits just because we've asked them nicely.

According to all sources, Iran is very close to its determined plan of possessing nuclear weapons capabilities. Pakistan, North Korea, and even Russia can be thanked for the advances in nuclear technology enjoyed by this rogue nation bent on destruction. While the world's eyes were turned on Israel and Lebanon in the summer of 2006, Iran's nuclear pursuits slipped under the radar of world leaders. One can but wonder how much additional technological progress was made by the scientists at the enrichment facilities scattered across Iran as Hezbollah lobbed shrapnel-laden missiles into the midst of Israeli cities.

In an interview on CNN in May 2006, Ehud Olmert, the Israeli prime minister, said, "The technological threshold [for Iran to make a nuclear weapon] is very close. It can be measured by months rather than years."[14]

Of course, the estimates of when Iran might possess the technical capabilities to produce a nuclear device have ranged from the end of

2006 to the prognostications of Director of National Intelligence John Negroponte. He told BBC Radio's *Today* program that "Tehran could have a nuclear bomb ready between 2010 and 2015."[15]

IRAN'S PROXY WARS

Although the kidnappings and missile attacks in the summer of 2006 heightened U.S. awareness of Iran's threat to worldwide freedom, this had become clear to me as early as 1983. It was a little past 6:00 a.m. in Beirut, and I was standing on a beachhead along the beautiful Mediterranean, talking to a group of marines.

The U.S. Marines stationed at Beirut's International Airport were just beginning a new day. One marine sentry at the airport gate looked up to see a big, yellow Mercedes truck barreling down on the security gate. The sentry reportedly stated that the driver of the truck smiled at him as he crashed through the gates. The truck was on a course for the lobby of the barracks. The sentries, armed only with loaded pistols, were unable to stop the speeding vehicle.

The Mercedes carried explosives equal to six tons of TNT. The driver rammed into the lower floor of the barracks and discharged his deadly cargo. The explosion was so great that the four-story building collapsed in a heap of rubble. Many of the 241 dead were not killed by the blast itself but were crushed beneath the cinder-block building as it fell in on itself.

Not since the first day of the Tet Offensive in Vietnam (January 31, 1968) when 243 were killed had America recorded such a deadly one-day toll on its military. It remains the deadliest post–World War II attack on Americans overseas.[16]

In order for the "Great Satan" to be eradicated so that an Islamic divine culture might emerge, violence is condoned. It was Iran's proxy Hezbollah—the Party of Allah—that attacked the United States' Eighth Battalion of Marines in their barracks in Lebanon in 1983.

Little did I know at the time that Iran would push America out of Lebanon through its terrorist organizations and would orchestrate a scenario so diabolical that the president of the United States would provide protection for the world's then most fearsome terrorist organization, the PLO. More than ten thousand terrorists were allowed to board ships for Tunisia as Israeli general Ariel Sharon was told to stand down. This, despite the fact that he and his forces had Yasser Arafat in the crosshairs with a chance to severely cripple terrorism for years to come. Instead, victory was taken from them, and the terrorists gained ground. Israel has suffered the consequences in the form of repeated attacks by Iran's proxy suicide bombers and Katyusha rocket attacks. In the years since the fight in Lebanon in the 1980s, we have done little but encourage the use of terrorist tactics over and over again. We shake our fists, but in the end withdraw before any real victory.

Today, Iran stands all the stronger for our lack of resolve and inability to truly curb its ambitions. Alan Dershowitz had this to say about Iran's threat:

> One of the reasons I personally was against the war in Iraq—for me it was a very close question, but I came out against it—was because I thought it would divert attention away from Iran, which posed a much more serious threat because religious extremism is always more danger-ous than secular extremism. I also worried about the rule of unintended consequences—that the tyranny of Saddam Hussein would be replaced by a tyranny of radical Islamists—and unfortunately those fears have come to fruition.[17]

Yes, Iran is serious—deadly serious. Their intentions can neither be taken for granted nor minimized. Iran seeks converts to its fanatical lifestyle from every nation, not just among the Arabs. Remember, after all, Iranians are not Arabs but Persians. Theirs is not a racial war but a religious one. Iran wants nothing more than that every knee on earth should bow to Allah and believes that there will be no real peace in the world until the world is Muslim. If you doubt this, just look at the tenor of President Mahmoud Ahmadinejad's letters to President Bush and the American people that are included in Appendices A and B of this book. If I were to put the message of each into a nutshell, they are both basically saying, "Become Muslim and we shall all live at peace."

Oddly, President Ahmadinejad's letters feel strangely parallel to letters the prophet Muhammad sent to his neighbors, and I was told about this by Walid Shoebat, a former Palestinian terrorist, in a conversation I had with him recently:

When the prophet Muhammad sent his letters of warning to all the people around him, there's two words used at the beginning of the letter, *"Aslim, Tuslim."* ...*Aslim* means "Become a Muslim" or "Submit to Islam." ... *Tuslim,* "then you will be at peace." So, "Submit to Islam, thou shall then be at peace."

If you do not submit, then we have to deal or wage war, because it's not permissible in Islam to wage war unless you warn your enemy and offer Islam to him. This is the message throughout the jihad and the Muslim world: "We come to represent the Lord of the worlds, this world, and the underworld. Become Muslim or die."[18]

It seems hard to believe in our politically correct society today when talk of religion in government is so looked down upon, but we are facing a religious zeal in Ahmadinejad and his followers that is like nothing we have ever seen. Perhaps his hero, the founder of the Islamic revolution, Ayatollah Ruhollah Musavi Khomeini, said it best: "I say let Iran go up in smoke, provided Islam emerges triumphant in the rest of the world."[19]

The Islamization of Palestine was orchestrated through Iran. Palestinians were secular nationalists, not Islamic fundamentalists, before Iran's influence held sway. It was the Iranian mullahs that indoctrinated the children of Palestine with the dogma of the Islamic revolution and persuaded them to become human bombs.

Hamas, which controls the Palestinian Territory today, is another proxy of Iran, getting much of its financial support and weapons from Tehran, as is Hezbollah in Lebanon with its ten thousand missiles. The world saw Iran's true intentions the day Israelis intercepted a Palestinian ship, the *Karine-A,* in the Red Sea on January 4, 2002. The ship was loaded with Katyusha rockets with a maximum range of twelve miles, as well as assault rifles, antitank missiles, mines, ammunition, and explosives. Most of the weapons were Iranian, and all were bound for Iran's proxies entrenched in Gaza and Lebanon.

HAMPERED BY TUNNEL VISION

Tunnel vision has plagued Operation Iraqi Freedom almost from the beginning. The desire to depose and capture Saddam Hussein overshadowed the reality of conducting a war to liberate people who really don't know how to handle liberation. Many, having never been free, don't know what to do with a freedom that flies in the face of their Islamic theology. It appeared that being controlled by a Muslim madman was preferable to being handed independence by infidels.

An epidemic of violence now grips Iraq, and the prospect of having no vaccine to combat it is demoralizing. Like sharks in a feeding frenzy, the various terrorist organizations, sects, tribes, and Islamic factions feed not only on the chum, but also turn on each other with disastrous results. In the final analysis, it seems that civil war is inevitable and that nation-building in Iraq is not working.

The outcome of the march into Baghdad, and the resulting brouhaha in congressional halls, was that President Bush had lost the ability to deal with other, more outrageous Muslim leaders, such as Ahmadinejad in Iran and al-Assad in Syria. Iran poses a grave nuclear threat, not only to the region but to the world. Peaceful Muslims worldwide are slowly being hijacked by the more radical elements. Iran is becoming a central player in the Shiite versus Sunni sects of Islam, and unfortunately, America, the "Great Satan," has become the unifying force that all love to hate. Iran rejoiced when, under the tutelage of Ayatollah Khomeini, the American embassy in Tehran was overrun and Americans were held hostage for 444 days. The jubilation continued when Iranian proxies in Lebanon struck a deadly blow to the marine compound that resulted in the United States packing its bags and going home. Today, Iran has focused on Iraq with every intention to drive coalition troops out of that country just as they did Lebanon and create a unified Shiite state from the Persian Gulf to the borders of Syria, and perhaps beyond.

APPROACHING HOOFBEATS

As I write this it is as if four sets of hoofbeats—like the coming together of fronts into a storm of prophetic proportion—are descending on the Middle East. On one front, the coalition forces of Operation Iraqi Freedom struggle to keep a foothold against terrorists and ethnoreligious violence descending toward civil war. On another, Al Qaeda and its other Sunni terrorist brotherhoods shower destruction and death wherever they can, hoping Iraq descends into chaos. From another, Iran, Hezbollah, and al-Sadr's army brings its own Shiite hope that the present fighting will escalate to apocalyptic proportions, thus ushering forth the Mahdi—"the perfect man"—to spread throughout the world a Golden Age of Islam. And, meanwhile, in the west, Israel stands by, watching quietly and preparing to defend itself once more against any and all threats.

The fact is, while all eyes seem focused on the battle for Iraq, the real danger is Iran, which—with the help of Russia and probably North Korea—stands on the brink of becoming a nuclear power, an accomplishment few in the world—and especially Israel—are willing to let happen peacefully. So, as the diplomatic struggle to end Iran's nuclear agenda grows increasingly fruitless, Israel's elite troops practice for an assault on Iran's underground sites. Helicopters, F-15s, snipers, and trained bomb-carrying dogs have drilled for months in preparation to halt Iran's ability to use nuclear weapons to attempt to realize their dream to wipe Israel off the map.

The point of no return for Israel will come when Iran has within its grasp the ability to produce a nuclear weapon—the point at which they have finally overcome the technical difficulties in refining natural uranium to include roughly 4 percent uranium-235. Once that point is reached, Iran's scientists just need to repeat the process enough times to produce the purity of uranium-235 considered weapons grade— something that would be made much easier by the three thousand centrifuges Iran has reported it will be installing at Natanz by March 2007.

If diplomacy with Iran to stop its refinement of nuclear materials continues to prove futile as 2007 progresses, the inevitability of an Israeli strike on key development facilities in Iran will grow. Such an attack could set the stage for every nation in between—Israel, Lebanon, Syria, Jordan, Saudi Arabia, Iraq, Kuwait, and Iran—to become the battleground for World War III that France, Great Britain, Russia, and Germany were in World War II. Certainly if Israel is forced to attack, the skirmish we saw between Hezbollah and Israel in the summer of 2006 will seem like children shooting off bottle rockets in comparison.

Israel has reiterated that it will not allow "atomic ayatollahs" to point their nuclear weapons at Jerusalem. That fear is multiplied by America's nightmare that nuclear weapons will fall into the hands of Iranian-sponsored terror squads. For this reason, America continues to seek ways to diplomatically persuade Iran to abandon its nuclear program, but the clock is on Iran's side. The longer Tehran stalls, the closer they get to the knowledge they need to produce weapons-grade uranium—a point that the West cannot let Iran reach, unless, of course, we are all willing to convert to Iran's form of Islam at the barrel of a nuclear silo. To be sure, while the United States and Europe might possibly delay too long, Israel will not.

Still others sit watching, some more interested than others. The moderate states of Jordan, Saudi Arabia, Egypt, and Kuwait are anxious for peace in the region and know they would also be targets of a nuclear Iran because of their friendliness with the West. North Korea pushes forward with its own nuclear program and missile tests, flexing its muscles threateningly toward the Far East and the world. War and genocide rage along ethnoreligious lines in Sudan, where hundreds of thousands have died. Meanwhile, the Taliban is doing everything it can to reemerge in Afghanistan in skirmishes that draw little attention in light of the fighting on the other side of Iran.

It is fair to say that no U.S. president in the history of our nation has faced such pressure in the international arena with troops in Iraq and Afghanistan, nuclear threats from Iran and North Korea, a war on terrorism that is losing its focus in the eyes of the American people, and midterm elections that seriously divided his support in Congress. While the last two two-term presidents made tremendous strides in foreign policy in their last couple of years in office—Reagan by seeing the fall of the Soviet Union and Clinton with the end of the war in the Balkans—the last two years of George W. Bush's presidency will not only define him in the eyes of history, but could also define the future of the United States and Western democracy.

2007 Is the Critical Year

The 1960s produced the television series *Lost in Space*. While much of that series may have been forgettable, except to today's cult following, one catchphrase resurfaces from time to time. One of the characters was a child named Will Robinson. His companion was a robot whose attitude toward young Will was always protective. When threatened with peril, the robot would intone, "Danger, Will Robinson! Danger!" While the robot could warn of danger, Will was the one responsible to take the proper evasive action to protect himself and/or his family.

Today, we in America are being warned repeatedly about the danger we face from Iran and its headlong rush to acquire nuclear weapons. In late October 2006, at a fund-raiser hosted by Lee Roy Mitchell, founder of Cinemark Corporation, and Norm Miller, of Interstate Batteries, for my *Final Move Beyond Iraq* television special, Lt. Gen. Moshe Ya'alon, former IDF chief of staff, gave a keynote speech. As he had done in our previous meetings, Ya'alon issued yet another warning of the danger posed by the Iranian government. Among his comments, he said, "Iran is now the center of gravity. The only nation that can shut down 100 percent of Iran's nuclear program and neutralize their ability to retaliate is the United States." He went on to say, "It cannot be done in 2008; it will be too late."[20]

In talking with Ya'alon, his rationale was clear. Sometime in 2007 or 2008, Iran will reach the point of no return in its nuclear program. Once they do that, even if they are set back somehow immediately afterward, they can always proceed to produce nuclear weapons in secret later on because they will already have the knowledge of how to do so. Iran must never be able to reach this point in its nuclear research.

If Iran is to be stopped before this, the United States must act decisively in 2007. If we wait until 2008, elections will be too distracting to Congress to be able to rally support for such an effort—an effort that may necessitate military action. With the Bush administration's policies and plans concerning the war on terror already under tremendous fire at home, it is unlikely those vying for political office will have the courage to do what is right in the face of Iran's nuclear threat.

Lt. Gen. Ya'alon is only one of many who have cried, "Danger, America! Danger!" And, like young Will Robinson, the decision to act to protect our nation and our families is ours to make, and the plan is ours to execute. The safety of future generations is in our hands. The questions now are: What will we do with this deadly knowledge? How much time do we have to act? Do we have the resolve to win the war on terror regardless of what it takes? Or do we allow ourselves to be swallowed up in the tsunami of terrorism that is certain to engulf the shores of America if the Islamofascists are not stopped?

PART TWO:

THE FINAL
SOLUTION WHILE
THE WORLD SLEEPS

Chapter Seven

FUMBLING OUR ALLY, IRAN

Ayatollah Khomeini will "eventually be hailed as a saint."[1]
—UN AMBASSADOR ANDREW YOUNG

Khomeini is a "Gandhi-like" figure.[2]
—WILLIAM SULLIVAN,
U.S. ambassador to Iran

The lavish 2,500th anniversary celebration in 1970 of the founding of the Persian Empire from the time of Cyrus the Great, with its $200 million price tag, was the single most breathtaking display of how seemingly out of touch the shah was with the people of Iran. Many mark it as the beginning of the end of his reign. The occasion succinctly symbolized the Western leanings of the shah that infuriated the Shiite Muslim majority of Iran, few of whom gained any benefit from the millions collected from Iran's oil revenues—something that only fueled their hatred of him all the more when they saw hundreds of millions spent on foreigners for the three-day anniversary celebration.

The oil boom of 1974 did nothing to alleviate this, either, as instead of Iran again becoming the great civilization Shah Pahlavi promised Iranians it would become through his progressive programs—it was his dream to make Iran the fifth most powerful nation in the world before he died—Iranians experienced alarming inflation and could only sit by as the gap between rich and poor grew all the more exaggerated. The black market thrived as bureaucracy, bottlenecks, shortages, and inflation hampered legitimate businesses. Meanwhile, tens of thousands of jobs went to foreign workers. Many of these were to help operate the expensive, high-tech U.S. military equipment the shah bought to bolster his army and dream of becoming a world power.

One of the organizing forces in this growing dissatisfaction with the shah's Western leanings—and one that was greatly underestimated—was Ayatollah Ruhollah Khomeini, who had been exiled in 1964 for his opposition to the shah's White Revolution, a series of reforms to modernize Iran, including, among many other modernizations, voting rights for women, land reforms abolishing feudalism, changes in the laws to allow the election of religious minorities, and civil code changes that gave women legal equality in marital issues—a move that would break up property owned by some Shiite clergy.

Khomeini had begun his career as a respected religious figure in the Iranian city of Qom. After Khomeini went public with his criticisms and personal attacks against the shah, he was arrested on June 5, 1963. A three-day riot broke out in protest and ended with Khomeini being kept under house arrest for eight months and then released, only to attack the Pahlavi government again. In November of 1964, he was arrested a second time and deported to Turkey in exile. He was later allowed to move to Iraq, where he spent the next thirteen years of his life. In 1978, Khomeini ran afoul of then vice president of Iraq Saddam Hussein and was forced to flee. From Iraq, the ayatollah traveled to Neauphle-le-Château in France.

During these years Khomeini refused to be silent and continued his influence in Iran by building a formidable support network through the power of the spoken word. His weapon of choice was not the sword, the gun, or the suicide bomber at that time, but simple cassette tapes of his recorded sermons. The tapes were smuggled into Iran by pilgrims returning from pilgrimages to the holy city of al Najaf in Iraq. The tapes were duplicated over and over and passed among the masses that were eager to see the shah deposed. He, among others, fueled Muslims' disdain for what was called *Gharbzadegi*, "the plague of Western culture," and teachers like Khomeini found many willing to embrace their more leftist interpretations of the Shiite faith. Khomeini's influence grew as the Pahlavi dynasty waned. At the same time, the United States became a symbol of the West that mullahs and clerics felt was corrupting Iran because of the shah's close ties and obsequiousness to it.

DEMOCRACY UNDERMINED

It is worth noting here that the shah was not only seen as a Western puppet because of his friendliness with the United States, but also because it was the 1953 coup by the United States and Great Britain that first propelled him into a position of power. During the first half of the twentieth century, Iran (still known to the West as Persia until 1935) became increasingly important on the international stage because of the discovery of oil there under the Qajar dynasty in May of 1908. As industrialization gripped the globe, the discovery of this coveted commodity would prove to be one of Iran's greatest bargaining chips on the world market, both in the twentieth and twenty-first centuries.

In 1921, Reza Khan, Pahlavi's father (also known as Reza Pahlavi and later as Reza Shah), a military leader, staged a coup d'etat against the Qajar ruler. He marched his troops into Tehran and seized the capital almost unopposed. His demand that the government resign was met, and his cohort, Seyyed Zia'eddin Tabatabaee, was declared prime minister of Iran. Reza Khan was named commander of the army and took the name Reza Khan Sardar Sepah.

In 1923, Reza Khan was officially named prime minister by Ahmad Shah Qajar before he was exiled to Europe. The *Majlis* (Iranian parliament) declared Reza Khan the shah of Persia on December 12, 1925. His son, Mohammad Reza Pahlavi—the man Khomeini would help depose in 1979—was named crown prince.

It was at that time Reza Khan adopted the title of Reza Shah, and he ruled Iran for more than sixteen years. His accomplishments were many. Under his leadership, the Trans-Iranian Railway from Tehran to the Caspian and Persian Seas was completed. He also set about to improve the educational system. Between 1925 and 1940, Reza Shah expanded the education budget in Iran from $100,000 to $12 million. To encourage studies, he exempted secondary school students from military service. He founded Tehran's university in 1934[3] and many other universities in the years following. He also sought to diminish the power and influence of traditional religious schools. He instituted a law of uniform dress, which made European-style attire for every man mandatory, with the exception of religious students. Religious students had to take a government examination before they could exercise this exemption. Numerous Iranian students received European educations because of his progressive programs.

During most of this time, the world at large still referred to the lands governed by Reza Shah as Persia, which came from the Greek name

Persis. On March 21, 1935, the shah requested that the public worldwide henceforth use "Iran" as the official name of the nation.

World War II brought a change in leadership for Iran but not a change in the ruling house. Fearing that Reza Shah's refusal to allow British troops to be stationed in Iran would lead to an alliance with Nazi Germany, the UK and the USSR joined hands to force Reza Shah to abdicate the Peacock Throne. His son, Mohammad Reza Pahlavi, assumed the throne on September 16, 1941. Reza Shah went into exile first to the Island of Mauritius, then to Johannesburg, South Africa. He died there in 1944.

Mohammad Reza Shah Pahlavi began his reign apparently with every intention of following the dictates of a constitutional monarchy (the form of democratic government in Great Britain and the form Iran had taken in 1906). Though he was the monarch, the shah took a hands-off approach to domestic politics and generally yielded to the wishes of the Iranian parliament. Pahlavi predominately occupied himself with the affairs of state and either openly defied the prime ministers or impeded the legislative process in such matters. Prone to indecision, however, Pahlavi relied more on manipulation than on leadership. He concentrated on reviving the army and ensuring that it would remain under royal control as the monarchy's main power base.

In 1951 a strong rival to Pahlavi's power emerged when Mohammed Mossadegh, a nationalist, was elected prime minister of Iran. In spite of Pahlavi's British connections, Mossadegh secured the votes necessary in parliament to nationalize the British-controlled Anglo-Iranian Oil Company (AIOC) in what became known as the Abadan Crisis. This cut off British profits from and control of Middle Eastern oil. In response, Great Britain decided to depose Mossadegh and his cabinet and solidify power in Pahlavi. When they asked Harry Truman to help with the coup in 1951, he refused, but when they asked Dwight Eisenhower shortly after his election in 1953 for U.S. support and help in their plans, Ike agreed.

So it was that a military coup headed by former minister of the interior and retired army general Fazlollah Zahedi, with covert support by British intelligence and the CIA (code-named Operation Ajax), finally forced Mossadegh from office on August 19, 1953. Zahedi became the new prime minister, authority was pulled from the democratically elected wing of the government and redeposited in the throne of the shah, and Mossadegh was tried for treason. In return, the shah agreed to let an international consortium of 40 percent British, 40 percent American, 14 percent Dutch, and 6 percent French companies run Iranian oil production for the next twenty-five years. Profits were to be split fifty-fifty with Iran, but Iran was never allowed to audit the books to see if this was done fairly, nor were any Iranians allowed to be on the board of directors of any of these companies. It was at this time that the Anglo-Iranian Oil Company became the British Petroleum Company, one of the root companies of British Petroleum (BP) today.

It was the first time in history that the United States had helped to undermine a democratic government—a decision we would pay for in 1979 when the United States made another costly mistake in turning our backs on the very shah we had first brought to power.

ENTER JIMMY CARTER

When Jimmy Carter entered the political fray that was the 1976 campaign, America was still riding the liberal wave of anti-Vietnam emotion. In fact, a group labeling itself the Institute for Policy Studies (IPS) was determined to inject liberal politics into every arena. Their network included many of what were labeled "alternative media outlets." The IPS-controlled liberal Left was determined that Democratic front-runner Jimmy Carter would adopt the platform written by Marcus Raskin, one of the founders of IPS. Raskin and his henchmen were able to wrest a promise from Carter that he would, if elected president, cut spending by the military and contest the production of the B-1 bomber, among other things.

Iran was an early bone of contention among Carter's staff selections. In truth, Carter's transition team asked for an in-depth report on Iran even before he assumed the reigns of government. In reevaluating the Carter presidency, John Dumbrell wrote that Walter Mondale and his aide, David Aaron, had links to the Iranian resistance based in the United States. They were persuaded that the shah was not entitled to rule Iran and determined he needed to be restrained. Others in Mondale's periphery simply wanted the ruler removed from the throne. According to Congressman David Bower, "Opportunists in the State Department were trying to out-Carter Carter."[4] Once in office, the president's liberal Left supporters felt justified in redoubling efforts to remove the shah from the Peacock Throne.

When James Earl Carter took office in January 1977, he inherited the well-ingrained policies of Richard Nixon and Henry Kissinger. During the five years preceding Carter's inauguration, the shah had purchased some $10 billion in U.S. military matériel. Nixon and Kissinger had set in motion an agenda for the next several decades. The U.S. government's presence in the Persian Gulf region and its supply of oil from that area were contingent on the good will of the shah. The United States looked to the shah for the economic survival of Western industry, and the shah relied on the United States for the arms and assistance to implement his vision for Iran's future. Failure on the part of either entity could cause unimagined economic and political upheaval.

In the mid-70s, the shah had morphed from an insecure young leader to one who was fully in control of the bureaucracy in Iran, who was working to bring the country into the twentieth century, and who was not looking for advice or direction, not even from his mentor, the United States government. When Jimmy Carter arrived in Washington DC, he was the recipient of the years-earlier Richard Nixon–Henry Kissinger arms sales policies that placed the security of one of the world's richest regions in the hands of a monarch whose determination to bring social and economic change to Iran did not take into account the smoldering fires of Islamic unrest.

The shah had enjoyed a prolonged political association with the Republican administrations of Nixon and Gerald Ford. He was understandably wary of Carter, whose campaign platform stressed both human rights issues and reduced arms sales. This was a major concern, as the shah's regime had been criticized for the actions of its secret police, the SAVAK, and had a long-standing relationship with U.S. arms suppliers.

Pahlavi's personal confidant, Asadollah Alam, wrote in his diary about the shah's concerns over Carter's election: "Who knows what sort of calamity he [Carter] may unleash on the world?"[5] In September of 1976, Alam met with Uri Lubrani, Israel's representative in Iran, and asked for his assistance to help improve the shah's image with the American people.

In that same year that Jimmy Carter was inaugurated, Islamic leader Ali Shariati died, and a huge potential rival to Ayatollah Khomeini was removed, thus solidifying Khomeini's support in Iran more than ever. In October of that year, Khomeini's son Mostafa died of what was apparently a heart attack, but antigovernment forces pointed the finger at SAVAK and Mostafa was proclaimed a martyr. While there were various factions opposing the shah's regime—leftists, the People's Mujahedin of Iran (MEK), communists, and other groups—Khomeini had suddenly become the most popular opponent to Pahlavi's rule.

At the same time, with the hope of improving the image of the United States as the benevolent superpower to the post-Vietnam world, Jimmy Carter created a special Office of Human Rights, and the shah emerged high on the agency's list. Washington put pressure on the shah to relax his control and allow more political freedom. This prompted the release of more than three hundred political prisoners, relaxed censorship, and overhauled the court system, which had the unforeseen side effect of allowing greater freedom for opposition groups to meet and organize.

Carter's secretary of state Cyrus Vance was the first in the administration to visit Iran. Vance was in the country for a meeting of CENTO, the Central Treaty Organization, to discuss security in the region. While traveling with Vance, an "unidentified spokesperson" for the State Department leaked the information that the United States was pleased with the shah's human rights efforts and was therefore willing to sell him AWACS aircraft.[6] In July, President Carter informed Congress that it was his objective to sell seven AWACS planes to Iran. After months of congressional wrangling and intense debate, the sale was approved. The final package included an additional $1.1 billion in spare parts and instruction.

While the shah's internal changes were making an impression on Carter, young men and women in Iran were swarming to radical Islam. Iran had never seen anything like this before in its history. University students gathered at Islamic study centers to debate the imams of Shia Islam. Young women clothed themselves in the *chadors* (long black veils) that had been outlawed by the shah. This new, radical Islam exploded on the campus of the University of Tehran in October 1977. A group of students calling for the isolation of women on campus rioted, leaving behind a trial of burned-out buses and broken windows.

While the ultimate aims of different groups opposing the shah varied greatly—some wanted a return to constitutional monarchy, others a socialist/communist government, and the imams and clerics an Islamic republic—Khomeini artfully united these groups against the shah by avoiding the specifics of what would happen beyond toppling the

Peacock Throne. As a result, opposition groups that would normally have been contending with one another instead grew more unified—a remarkable feat by Khomeini that accelerated the revolution in Iran and later proved to be a deadly mistake for all but the Islamists.

CARTER, PAHLAVI, AND KHOMEINI

On November 15, 1977, Mohammad Reza Shah Pahlavi and Empress Farah flew to the United States for a visit to President Carter and the First Lady in Washington. As the two couples stood on the south lawn of the White House, they were met by hundreds—some say thousands—of Iranian students who had congregated in Lafayette Square. (At that time, the United States boasted an Iranian student population of over sixty thousand.) In a move to control the crowd, Washington police lobbed tear gas canisters into their midst. Unfortunately, the tear gas blew across the White House lawn and into the eyes of the Carters and their visiting dignitaries. With faces streaming with tears, the Carters were forced to cut their greetings short and retreat into the White House.

The two men were to meet again about six weeks later in Tehran. President Carter had been in the Middle East to promote a peace plan between Israel and her neighbors. He and Rosalynn planned a brief visit to Tehran to spend New Year's Eve with the shah and his wife. Before leaving the States, Carter was presented with a declaration signed by a number of well-known Iranian activists. Rather than present the declaration to Pahlavi, Carter rose to the occasion and toasted the shah with:

> Iran, under the great leadership of the shah, is an island of stability in one of the more troubled areas of the world. This is a great tribute to you, Your Majesty, and to your leadership, and to the respect, admiration, and love which your people give to you.[7]

With these words, Jimmy Carter reinforced the pro-shah stance that had long been American policy. However, in just months, Iran would be gripped by bloody riots as the shah struggled to quell the radical Islamists and other groups bent on deposing him.

During Ramadan in August 1978, large demonstrations erupted all across Iran. Curfews were imposed in some cities following days of mass rioting. The city of Abadan was the site of a mass murder said to have been staged by Islamic radicals. The doors of a theater hosting an Iranian film were barred while the building was torched; 477 people died in the conflagration. The shah's attempts to suppress the rioting were rejected by his enemies and supporters alike. His enemies saw it as a weak attempt at appeasement, and his supporters just saw it as weakness, period.

All the while the shah was desperately trying to regain control in Iran, Ruhollah Khomeini had been in Iraq fomenting revolution. In his book *The Spirit of Allah: Khomeini and the Islamic Revolution*, Amir Taheri wrote of the charges that Khomeini's underground network leveled at the shah. He was randomly charged with being a womanizer, a homosexual, a Jewish convert, a drug addict, and a Catholic. He was also labeled the "American shah" and "Israel's shah." Even the Empress Farah did not escape Khomeini's twisted defamation. She was maligned as an adulteress and linked to none other than Jimmy Carter.[8]

Khomeini's rhetoric was designed to incite fear in the lower classes in Iran—the have-nots who were forced to do without while witnessing the overindulgence of the upper classes. It trumpeted what was seen as the shah's collusion with Israel and the United States. The intellectuals, the political vanguard in Iran, initially took a wait-and-see attitude, but it was not long before they joined forces with the oppressed and poverty-stricken who took to the streets in protest of the shah's policies. With the help of PLO-supplied weapons, trained terrorists, and the murders of Iranian demonstrators as a means to incite the mobs in the streets, the mayhem spread. No wonder Yasser Arafat was hailed as a friend by Khomeini after he seized control of Iran. (Arafat's reward was the Israeli embassy in Tehran with a PLO flag flying overhead.)

In an attempt to repress Khomeini's influence, the shah appealed to the newly elevated president of Iraq, Saddam Hussein, to clamp down on the ayatollah's activities. In an aborted attempt to flee Iraq, Khomeini and his entourage became stranded at the Kuwait border when that country would not grant him entry, and he was refused reentry into Iraq. Finally, the ayatollah was granted permission to return to Baghdad where, on October 6, he was deported to France. Far from halting his interference in Iran, his exile only fired the passions of the Islamic radicals in that country.

Things were only beginning their downward spiral.

Chapter Eight

THE RISE OF ISLAMOFASCISM

What is Islamofascism? Islamofascism is radical Islam combined with undemocratic institutions in such a fashion that it creates a threat to the neighborhood, and in concentric circle fashion. A threat to the extent to which Iran develops a missile envelope that goes outward, and all of a sudden it begins to encapsulate the American-European allies [in the Middle East] and eventually [sets its aims on] the United States itself.[1]

—PROFESSOR RAYMOND TANTER

We have a phenomenon we are witnessing now that is the emergence of a kind of transnational, global, totalitarian, political Islam—and again I want to make it clear that I'm not, in any way, being critical of Islam as a religion—on the contrary, I think this is a usurpation and highjacking of Islam...whereby one seeks a form of world domination. That is why the phrase "Islamofascism" has been used to characterize the totalitarian and political character of this transnational, radical Islam, which is operating now in the mosques, in the media, in the schools, and training camps.[2]

—DR. IRWIN COTLER,
Canadian MP and former minister of justice
and attorney general of Canada

In November 1978, President Jimmy Carter appointed George Ball, an undersecretary of state in the Kennedy and Johnson administrations, to study the situation in Iran and make policy recommendations. Ball's eighteen-page communiqué was strongly critical of Nixon's Iranian policies. He inferred that the rule of the shah was at an end and encouraged Carter to begin dialogue with Khomeini.

It was also in November that Ambassador William Sullivan telegraphed the White House to report that the shah's support was rapidly eroding, including that from the military. Sullivan encouraged the administration to adopt a transition policy that would support a takeover by the military and the mullahs. In his report, Sullivan called Khomeini a "Gandhi-like" personage, a moderate, and a centrist who would not personally involve himself in the politics of Iran.[3] James Bill, a leading expert on Iran, proclaimed in a *Newsweek* interview on February 12, 1979, that "Khomeini is not a mad *mujtahid* [high-ranking clergyman]...but a man of impeccable integrity and honesty."[4] Somehow, these learned men totally missed the fact that Khomeini and his fellow militants viewed the revolution as a struggle between an oppressed Iran and the "Great Satan" superpower of the United States.

Carter's national security advisor, Zbigniew Brzezinski, advised the president to reject George Ball's report, although Ball likened the shah's regime to that of Humpty Dumpty in the sense that it was irreparable. Brzezinski's counsel was that Carter should send a high-level military liaison to Iran in support of Iran's armed forces. Carter chose Gen. Robert "Dutch" Huyser, deputy commander in chief of the U.S. European Command under Alexander Haig. Huyser's personal interaction with Iranian military leaders for over a decade made him the obvious choice. It was Huyser to whom the shah expressed his concerns that he would alienate President Carter by not moving quickly enough to institute sweeping human rights changes to appease the administration.

In Huyser's own words, he was charged by President Carter:

> ...to convey [President Carter's] concern and assurances to the senior military leaders at this most critical time. It was of vital importance to both the Iranian people and the U.S. government that Iran have a strong, stable government which would remain friendly to the United States. The Iranian military was the key to the situation.[5]

In my book *Showdown With Nuclear Iran*, I wrote of a meeting I had with Robert Huyser:

> Huyser was a man of principle and moral clarity and believed that his mission was to support prime minister Shapour Bakhtiar and Iran's generals. Carter promised that the U.S. would protect and provide all assets needed to shore up the government, which was increasingly endangered by violent protests against the regime of the shah, Mohammed Reza Pahlavi. Despite a history of support going back to World War II, Carter had no desire to see a pro-shah regime in power. The comparison made sense to a point: the ayatollah opposed the shah, who had a terrible

record of human rights abuses. But that's where the comparison breaks down. Gandhi was nonviolent. The Ayatollah was anything but.[6]

In Huyser's assessment of the situation in Iran, he opined that the United States should have learned the importance of the "need to stand by one's friends."[7] He felt that by abandoning the shah, a long-time partner in the region, the United States had "lost a close and sturdy ally which could have provided stability for Western interests in the Persian Gulf."[8] General Huyser said of the Carter administration:

> The administration obviously did not understand the Iranian culture, nor the conditions that prevailed in the last few months of the shah's reign. I believe that Washington should have recognized the seriousness of the situation early in 1978. If the real intent was to support the existing government, much could have been done to bolster the shah's lagging confidence and resolve....
>
> The President could have publicly condemned Khomeini for his interference. He could have solicited the support of our allies, and in conjunction with them he could have given material support to the Bakhtiar government.[9]

Unfortunately for the United States, these were not all of the ills suffered as a result of electing the Georgian peanut farmer to the presidency. History will ultimately define Carter's White House years by

- the Soviets invading Afghanistan (Carter's response was to boycott the 1980 Olympics in Moscow) and the birth of Osama bin Laden's terror organization;
- recession, high inflation, high interest rates (21.5 percent), gas lines, and rationing;
- the fall of the shah of Iran, the inception of the Islamic revolution, and the rise of Islamic fundamentalism;
- the loss of U.S. stature worldwide;
- the American hostage crisis that ultimately cost him reelection;
- extreme micromanagement;
- the alienation of Congress;
- the stripping of U.S. missiles in South Korea and Carter's offer to remove all troops;

- reduction of the defense budget by $6 million;
- emasculation of the CIA by cutting 820 intelligence jobs;[10]
- praise of such heinous dictators as Tito, Ceaușescu, Ortega, and, following his presidency, Kim il-Sung of North Korea;
- the rise of Marxism in Nicaragua;
- the relinquishing of control of the Panama Canal to a dictator. (Hutchison Whampoa Ltd., a front for the Chinese military, now controls entrance and egress points at either end of the canal.)

AN AMERICAN ALLY DEPOSED THROUGH NEGLECT

As the defiance against the shah's regime grew, Iran's prime minister Shapour Bakhtiar persuaded the monarch and his wife to leave the country. Ostensibly, Bakhtiar's plan was to try to pour oil on Iran's troubled waters. He disbanded SAVAK, freed all political prisoners, and allowed the shah's nemesis, Ayatollah Ruhollah Khomeini, to return to Iran.

In February 1979, Khomeini boarded an Air France flight to return to Tehran. Barely off of the plane in his return, he voiced his opposition to Prime Minister Shapour Bakhtiar's government, pledging, "I will kick their teeth in." He appointed his own competing interim prime minister and defied any to oppose him, stating that such an act would be a "revolt against God."[11] On March 30 and 31, a popular vote nationwide endorsed the establishment of an Islamic Republic. With the establishment of the Islamic Republic of Iran, Khomeini became Supreme Leader (*Vali-e Faqeeh*). On April 1, 1979, the greatest April Fools' joke of all time was played on the people of Iran: Ayatollah Khomeini proclaimed the "first day of God's government" and established himself as the Grand Ayatollah. He awarded himself the title of "Imam" (the highest religious rank in Shia). The events following that proclamation have had a lasting effect not only on Iran, but on the entire Middle East and the world.

The newly crowned Grand Ayatollah had showed the rest of his Arab brethren how to unify secular, social, and religious groups in their hatred for the shah and the United States, and used it as a political and military tool to overthrow the government. Then, once he was back in Iran, he rewarded those who had supported his revolution with a swiftness and brutality that even SAVAK couldn't have mustered.

A killing spree followed, targeting former officials of the shah's government as well as those who had been looking for something other than an Islamic republic with Khomeini as its supreme leader for life. Even fleeing Iran wasn't enough. In the decade following the Islamic revolution of Iran, at least sixty-three Iranians abroad were killed or wounded, including the man who had allowed Khomeini to return, former prime minister Shapour Bakhtiar. In the months following the coup, dozens of newspapers and magazines opposing Khomeini's government were shut down, and a cultural revolution began as universities were closed for two years to cleanse them of Western influence. Thousands in the government and military lost their positions because they were seen as too Western-leaning. Groups such as MEK found themselves outsiders and targets of the very government that they had helped to put into power.

CARTER TRIES TO MAKE FRIENDS WITH A VIPER

The Carter administration scrambled to assure the new regime that the United States would maintain diplomatic ties with Iran. Even as that message was being relayed to the ambassador in Tehran on February 14, the embassy was besieged by a mob of Islamic militants, many wearing the headpieces that identified them as Palestinian fedayeen (those ready to sacrifice their lives). This was further proof of Khomeini's reach in the Islamic world. Rather than return fire on the intruders, Ambasssador Sullivan surrendered the embassy after a scramble to destroy sensitive electronic devices and classified documents. In the midst of the chaos that followed, Khomeini's personal representative, Ibrahim Yazdi, arrived in the embassy. Yazdi and another mullah were able to turn the crowd back, thus ensuring the safety of the occupants of the embassy.

At this juncture, Ambassador Sullivan attempted to reassure Khomeini that the United States had accepted the inevitability of the uprising and would not intervene in Iranian affairs. However, another seed sown through Operation Ajax was that the United States embassy was seen as a den of spies gathered to overthrow Iran as it had done in 1953. As a result, extremists saw it as a target that needed clearing out in order to protect the fledgling Islamic republic rather than as a voice to be trusted.

Khomeini could not have defeated the shah of Iran on issues that interested the mullahs alone. Either the Iranian or U.S. armed forces could easily have taken out the rebel forces, but Carter knew little of the effective use of military power—regardless of the fact that he had no will to use it—and viewed Khomeini as more of a religious holy man in a grassroots revolution than a founding father of modern terrorism. Thus the United States failed to act on behalf of its longtime ally, the shah. At the same time the Iranian national armed forces chose a stance of neutrality "in order to prevent further disorder and bloodshed,"[12] so it did not act, either. With the declaration that the military would remain impartial in the struggle, Khomeini realized his dream: Iran was his, and the process of total Islamization could begin.

The shah of Iran left his country a broken and ailing man, his body wracked by cancer. His first stop was a visit to his good friend Anwar el-Sadat in Egypt. From there he moved briefly to Morocco, then to the Bahamas, and then Mexico. Despite his long association as a key United States ally, the shah was initially denied entry into our country. However, as his cancer—non-Hodgkin's lymphoma—grew worse and needed more sophisticated medical treatment, the door finally opened for him to enter the United States on October 22, 1979.

Before departing Mexico City for New York, the shah wrote in his personal journal:

> Clearly, I was a very sick man....Nine months had passed since I left Iran, months of pain, shock, despair, and reflection. My heart bled at what I saw happening in my country. Every day reports had come of murder, bloodshed, and summary executions....All these horrors were part of Khomeini's systematic destruction of the social fabric I had woven for my nation....And not a word of protest from American human rights advocates who had been so vocal in denouncing my "tyrannical" regime...the United States and most Western countries had adopted a double standard for international morality: anything Marxist, no matter how bloody and base, is acceptable.[13]

AN EMBASSY UNDER SIEGE

It was not necessarily the shah's arrival in New York that sparked what was to later become known as the "Second Revolution." It was, rather, a string of innocent contacts from well-wishers that would incite the hostile takeover of the U.S. embassy in Tehran mere weeks later. A videotape of the shah receiving such visitors as Henry Kissinger, David Rockefeller, several former Iranian officials, and other dignitaries was shown in Iran.

For those in Iran who were paranoid that the shah might attempt to return, this was proof of the duplicity shared by both the shah and Washington. Coupled with reports of counter-revolutionary forces taking up residence in Iraq and in Iran, little else was needed to fuel the fires of another anti-American backlash. They soon began to suspect the United States of plotting to deprive them of the fruits of their victory and the desire to restore American influence in Iran in a new form.[14]

On November 4, 1979, a group of student dissidents who had adopted the moniker "Imam's Disciples" entered the U.S. embassy in Tehran for the second time, again with little resistance. Although Khomeini denied any knowledge of the impending takeover of the U.S. embassy, it was likely his vitriolic anti-American oratory that gave the mob of some three to five hundred young Iranians the impetus to seize the compound. Khomeini had denounced the U.S. government as the "Great Satan" and "Enemies of Islam."[15] Khomeini's ploy was to cast the United States as evil and himself as the defender of righteousness.

When the dust settled, sixty-six captives were in the hands of their Iranian captors. Their ordeal was to last 444 days. The jailers were determined not to release their prisoners until the shah was sent back to Tehran to stand trial and return billions of dollars he had allegedly appropriated from the people of Iran.

Carter never understood it! Khomeini said, "The West who killed God and buried Him is teaching the rest of the world to do so." He went so far as to openly accuse the United States of being the fountain of all the world's evil. When the head of the French Secret Service, the Count of Maranche, suggested to Carter in 1980 that Khomeini be kidnapped and then bartered for an exchange with the hostages, the president was indignant. "One cannot do that to a holy man," he told the French super-spy.[16] In fact, the Carter-appointed ambassador to the UN, Andrew Young, asserted that the ayatollah would "eventually be hailed as a saint."[17] It was Young who proudly identified with the Iranian militants, because it reminded him of the civil rights struggles in the United States.

Public support and sympathy for Jimmy Carter eroded as time passed, and he remained indecisive on how to handle the hostage crisis. Negotiations, both overt and covert, were not productive, and there were no indications that the captors were relenting. Finally, in April 1980, Carter approved a risky rescue mission. The plan was doomed almost from the start. Three of the helicopters vital to the plan malfunctioned, eight servicemen lost their lives, and three were wounded when on take-off their chopper crashed into a C-130 transport plane. The aborted attempt only added fuel—and video footage—to the Iranians' gleeful assertion that the "Great Satan" was impotent—a toothless tiger.

In a renewed effort to secure the release of the hostages before the newly elected president, Ronald Reagan, took office, the Carter administration entered into negotiations with the Iranians to release assets frozen by the U.S. government when the embassy was overrun and the hostages taken. Warren Christopher and a small contingent of State and Treasury Department officials flew to Algiers for face-to-face negotiations with an Algerian team representing the Khomeini government.[18] When a final agreement was reached, the Carter administration relinquished $7.977 billion to the Iranians. According to one source, the transfer required fourteen banks and the participation of five nations acting concurrently.[19]

Although negotiations continued into the wee hours of January 20, 1980, Carter's efforts to secure the release of the hostages on his watch remained fruitless. In fact, an ABC television crew documented Carter's futile "all-night effort to bring the 52 hostages home before the end of his term."[20] (The captors had released 13 hostages shortly after the initial seizure, plus an additional hostage the following July for medical reasons.)

President Harry S. Truman's desk in the Oval Office sported a sign that said, "The buck stops here." Perhaps the same could be said of Jimmy Carter's involvement in fomenting the Islamic revolution that has plagued the world in general and America in particular since the rise of Khomeini. It was truly the birth of the Islamofascist ideology we fight today in the war on terror. President Carter excelled in other areas but was always at a distinct disadvantage when confronted with American foreign policy, having been a Washington outsider before being elected president. Jimmy Carter's intelligence did not disguise the fact that he could not fully assimilate the situation in Iran.

CARTER'S LIBERAL LEGACY

Jimmy Carter had originally crept into the White House with a campaign emphasis on the word *faith*. It was a theme that appealed both to conservative Christians and liberal Democrats disenchanted with the Johnson and Nixon White House years. This tactic gave Carter a slight edge with the American public, and that—coupled with his popularity in the South—won the election. He may have pulled the wool over the eyes of southern conservatives, but it wasn't long before he divorced himself from their influence, and since leaving office he has broken with his Southern Baptist tradition, as well. In fact, Carter said of one-time supporter Rev. Jerry Falwell, "In a very Christian way, as far as I'm concerned, he can go to hell."[21]

It apparently was no surprise to Southern Baptist Theological Seminary president R. Albert Mohler Jr., who wrote in the *Atlanta Journal-Constitution*, according to Michael Foust, that "the former president actually began distancing himself from the Southern Baptist Convention years ago.... 'On issues ranging from homosexuality and abortion to the nature of the gospel and the authority of Scripture, the former president is out of step with the majority of Southern Baptists.'... The theological divide between Carter and mainstream Southern Baptists is vast."[22]

The Carter presidency can, perhaps, be summed up with two words: wretched ineptitude. America's thirty-ninth president was he-of-the-overly-inflated-ego. Said ego was responsible for Carter's early alienation of Congress and, in fact, from his own Democratic party. House Speaker Thomas "Tip" O'Neill was shunned as early as Carter's inaugural dinner when he found his table on the far fringes of the event. Ned Rice of the *National Review Online* described Carter as "the Barney Fife of American presidents: alternatively bumbling, then petrified, then egomaniacal, then back to bumbling, and so on for four long, surreal years. One of history's true buffoons."[23] It is interesting to note that 1976 was a banner year for future presidential hopefuls: Carter was elected president, William Jefferson Clinton became attorney general in Arkansas, and Albert Gore won a place in the Tennessee House of Representatives.

Carter's government might best have been classified by the word *pacifism*, an ideology that was clearly expressed in his choice of Cabinet members. His appointment of Cyrus Vance as secretary of state sounded the alarm through the halls of Congress and set the stage for a dovish administration. (Vance resigned in protest of the aborted hostage rescue attempt.) Henry Kissinger said of the Carter administration:

> [It] has managed the extraordinary feat of having, at one and the same time, the worst relations with our allies, the worst relations with our adversaries, and the most serious upheavals in the developing world since the end of the Second World War.[24]

Carter all but ignored congressional suggestions regarding appointments to various posts and continued to select pacifists and near-pacifists to populate upper-level posts.

Many of those who were recruited to implement Carter's newly adopted globalism policies were selected from the George McGovern fringe. Some were tagged "the Mondale Mafia" after Carter's vice president, Walter Mondale. In fact, a number of Carter appointees, including Anthony Lake, Richard Holbrooke, and Jessica Tuchman, went on to serve in the Clinton White House. During the early days of the Carter administration, the triumvirate of Cyrus Vance, Zbigniew Brzezinski, and UN Ambassador Andrew Young had comparable input into foreign policy decisions.

The agenda, as put forth by Carter's liberal leftist advisors, embraced what came to be called *regionalism*. It eschewed military intervention in favor of social reform and human rights issues. Historian J. A. Rosati wrote, "The Carter administration attempted to promote a new system of world order based upon international stability, peace, and justice."[25] To the detriment of future generations, Iran became the test case for Carter's new prototype.

Author Steven Hayward characterized the Carter doctrine as "a sentimental, neopacifist view of the world [that] has come to define the core ideology of Democratic party liberalism today... [and] the philosophical view that your good intentions outweigh the practical consequences of your actions and words—and left-wing Christian pacifism that believes the use of force is always wrong."[26]

Carter's legacy of liberalism has had a definite and continuing impact, not only on the Democratic Party of Hillary Rodham Clinton and John Kerry, but on the world as a whole. It is a universalistic, one-size-fits-all approach. Jimmy Carter became all things to all people in order to impress all. He became a champion of human rights and, by so doing, introduced the world to one of the most heinous regimes in history in the new Islamic Republic of Iran. He climbed into bed, figuratively, with Yasser Arafat and the PLO in order to establish a legacy as a "peacekeeper." Far from protecting America's foreign policy interests, Carter made whatever concessions necessary to be seen as the president of peace.

Had Jimmy Carter adopted a slightly more hawkish stance and been more prone to protect American interests overseas—and certainly in Iran—the world might well have been a safer place today. The fall of the shah of Iran opened the door to the rise of Islamic radicalism in Iran and throughout the Arab and Muslim countries. It also led to the assassination of Anwar Sadat in Egypt. This is not the footprint of a peacemaker.

Carter's belief that every crisis can be resolved with diplomacy—and nothing but diplomacy—now permeates the Democratic Party. Unfortunately, Mr. Carter is wrong. There are times when evil must be openly confronted and defeated. Without a strong military backup with a proven track record of victories, diplomacy can be meaningless. As Theodore Roosevelt liked to put it, "Speak softly and carry a big stick."[27]

In his book *Failing the Crystal Ball Test*, Ofira Seliktar says of the situation with Iran:

> Although the Carter administration bears the lion's share for the policy failure, the role of Congress in the Iranian debacle should not be overlooked...the Democratically controlled Congress was responsible for turning many of the [Carter] imperatives into applied policy, most notably in the realm of foreign aid, military sales, human rights, and intelligence...leftist and liberal members of Congress strove to put the United States on the "right" side of history. To do so, they had to stop American anticommunist interventions around the world and terminate relations with right-wing authoritarian regimes, many of which faced leftist insurgencies.[28]

While Jimmy Carter has done good things in his life, most notably his association with Habitat for Humanity, his foreign policy decisions as president of the United States have led to more turmoil in just about every region where he tried to intervene. Carter seemed to think that it was enough to talk people into a stupor, and then entice them with treaties and incentives.

Mr. Carter and his fellow pacifists have yet to understand the impossibility of reasoning with the unreasonable. It is never advisable to sell one's soul to the devil in order to keep him at bay. Sooner or later, evil demands the supreme sacrifice and will achieve its goals, not through compromise but through terror and coercion. This is one lesson that James Earl Carter has never learned.

The former president's connections with Yasser Arafat and the PLO are legendary. Some believe that it was through Carter's machinations that Arafat, the godfather of world terrorism, was knighted with the Nobel Peace Prize. It is general knowledge that the Carter Center is underwritten by funds from Palestinian sources. Perhaps that is why he described the PLO in glowing terms as "a loosely associated umbrella of organizations bound together by common goals, but it comprises many groups eager to use diverse means to reach these goals."[29] How benevolent! It sounds nothing like the organization responsible for the intifada against the Jews and the murder of hundreds of innocent civilians.

Although Yasser Arafat has departed the scene, Carter has continued to court the good will of terrorists, madmen, and leftists, all the while criticizing the Bush administration to any and all who would listen. Perhaps it was a reflection of Jimmy Carter's own divisiveness that caused the chair of the Nobel awarding committee to use the presentation ceremony as an opportunity to criticize the Bush administration.[30]

In 1986, Carter defied restrictions imposed on Syria for the attempted bombing of an American airliner by filing a false travel plan before departing for Damascus.[31] He felt that he was somehow exempt from the laws of the land that governed other American travelers. His actions made it apparent to all that he supported al-Assad's regime and, as such, was treated to a hero's welcome.

It was not long after leaving office that the world would begin to see Carter's real legacy. As early as 1984, he was suggesting that Russian ambassador Anatoly Dobrynin support Ronald Reagan's opponent, Walter Mondale, in the upcoming presidential election. He also felt it incumbent as an ex-president to write a letter to the regimes in Syria, Saudi Arabia, and Egypt, asking them to stall the invasion of Iraq in 2003.[32]

However, it was Bill Clinton who elevated Carter to the role of infallible elder statesman. With Clinton's approval, the former president traveled to North Korea for discussions on that nation's nuclear ambitions.

One reporter wrote that Carter agreed to give North Korea:

> ...500,000 metric tons of oil, tons of grain, and a light-water nuclear reactor....The unverifiable agreement Carter designed allowed North Korea to develop as many as half-a-dozen nuclear weapons—which he now blames on George W. Bush.[33]

The former president's interference with foreign policy did not end there. He wrote a speech for Yasser Arafat and certified the "election" of Venezuela's Castro-clone, Hugo Chavez.[34] In a trip to Cuba in 2002, the erudite Mr. Carter called UN Ambassador John Bolton a liar for daring to insinuate that Castro was developing biological weapons, reports of which, by the way, first surfaced during the Clinton administration.[35] In the ultimate kudos, the man from Plains, Georgia, James Earl Carter, was himself awarded the Nobel Peace Prize in 2002.

In his most recent book, *Palestine: Peace Not Apartheid*, the former president equates Israel's battle to combat terrorism within its borders to the hateful South African practice of apartheid. The reader would be hard put to uncover actual instances of the dreadful terrorism suffered by the Israelis mentioned in the book. It says little about the fact that Israel has already given away land in failed attempts to achieve peace with its neighbors, or the ensuing missile attacks and kidnappings initiated from the very land that was given away. Apparently, Mr. Carter has also forgotten Munich and the massacre of the Israeli Olympic team and the murder of Leon Klinghoffer aboard the *Achille Lauro*, among other such atrocities committed in the name of Palestinian liberation. In fact, throughout the book, he champions the PLO and denigrates Israel.

Among the inequities in Mr. Carter's discourse is

- the deliberate misrepresentation that Israel was the aggressor in the 1967 war;
- a failure to reveal the threat against Israel that precipitated the destruction of Iraq's nuclear reactor at Osirak in 1980;
- the exoneration of Yasser Arafat for walking out of the peace talks with Ehud Barak.

He gives no credit to Israel for decades of attempts to establish a peaceful relationship with the Palestinian Authority, and in fact faults them for the ills of the region.

Harvard law professor Alan Dershowitz says of Carter's book:

> It's obvious that Carter just doesn't like Israel or Israelis....He admits that he did not like Menachem Begin. He has little good to say about any Israelis—except those few who agree with him. But he apparently got along swimmingly with the very secular Syrian mass-murderer Hafez al-Assad. He and his wife Rosalynn also had a fine time with the equally secular Yasir Arafat—a man who has the blood of hundreds of Americans and Israelis on his hands.[36]

The first executive director of the Carter Center—as well as its founder of a Middle East program—Kenneth Stein, was openly critical of Jimmy Carter's latest book. In a letter to the *Atlanta Journal-Constitution*, Mr. Stein wrote:

> President Carter's book on the Middle East, a title too inflammatory to even print, is not based on unvarnished analysis; it is replete with factual errors, copied materials not cited, superficialities, glaring omissions, and simply invented segments.
>
> Aside from the one-sided nature of the book, meant to provoke, there are recollections cited from meetings where I was the third person in the room, and my notes of those meetings show little similarity to points claimed in the book.[37]

Palestine: Peace Not Apartheid is an outrageous misrepresentation of events in the Middle East, but certainly no more outrageous than Carter's leftist manipulation of events in Iran. Carter did everything in his power to weaken the shah and to prop up Khomeini. Mr. Carter has remained consistent since that time—consistently wrong. He articulates a worldview of the liberal Left.

I am reminded of the debate between vice presidential hopefuls Dan Quayle and Lloyd Bentsen. After comparing his tenure as a U.S. senator with that of John F. Kennedy, Dan Quayle was met with this response from Senator Lloyd Bentsen: "Senator, I served with Jack Kennedy, I knew Jack Kennedy, Jack Kennedy was a friend of mine. Senator, you are no Jack Kennedy."

Jimmy Carter has taken credit for being the architect of peace between Egypt and Israel. He can, indeed, take the credit, but he is not the one directly responsible; it was Menachem Begin. Begin and I had many discussions about the meetings at Camp David and matters relating to Anwar Sadat. Menachem Begin told me that the idea to pursue an accord with Egypt came to him while on a visit to Romania. Begin said he mentioned to Nicolae Ceauşescu that he would like to have direct talks with Sadat. This was not an unusual move for Begin. In his first pronouncement as prime minister of Israel, he called on Arab leaders to meet him at their earliest opportunity.

Later, when Sadat visited Romania, Ceauşescu told him of Begin's wish to meet with him. According to the prime minister, an exchange of views took place there, and then later between the two men. Nicolae Ceauşescu confirmed his role when he remarked in a speech in Bucharest that year that he had acted for the settlement of the Middle East peace issues through negotiations. Sadat used a public occasion to indicate that for the sake of peace, he would be ready even to travel to Israel to speak to the people of Israel from the rostrum of the Knesset.

Immediately, Menachem Begin countered by inviting the Egyptian leader to Jerusalem. He extended the invitation in a speech to a delegation of members of the American Congress Armed Forces Special Committee touring the Middle East, which was proceeding to Cairo the next day. When he heard that Sadat later told the same committee he had not received an official invitation, Begin immediately broadcast a special appeal in English directly to the Egyptian people; he followed that with a formal invitation transmitted through the American ambassador.

In his speech to the people of Egypt appealing to Anwar Sadat to meet with him, of which he gave me a copy, he said:

> Citizens of Egypt, this is the first time that I address you directly, but it is not the first time I think and speak of you. You are our neighbors and will always be. For the last twenty-nine years, the tragic and completely unnecessary conflict continued between your country and ours. Since the time when the government of King Farouk ordered to invade our land, Eretz Yisrael, in order to strangle our newly restored freedom and democracy, four major wars have taken place between you and us.

Much blood was shed on both sides, many families were orphaned and grieved in Egypt and in Israel.... You should know we have come back to the land of our forefathers. It is we who established independence in our land for all generations to come. We wish you well; in fact, there is no reason whatsoever for hostilities between our people.... Your president said two days ago that he was ready to come to Jerusalem to our Knesset in order to prevent one Egyptian soldier from being wounded. I have already welcomed this statement, and it will be a pleasure to welcome and receive your president with the traditional hospitality you and we have inherited from our common father, Abraham.

I, for my part, will be ready to come to your capital, Cairo, for the same purpose: No more war, but peace, real peace, forever.[38]

I asked Prime Minister Begin if he was really that eager to go to Egypt. With a smile and a twinkle in his eye, he replied, "Yes, I would really like to see the pyramids. After all, our ancestors built them. But I will assure the Egyptians that we will not ask for compensation."

For years, Mr. Carter has accepted the accolades of those who thought him to be directly responsible for the meetings between Sadat and Begin. Mr. Carter's perception is his reality; he really believes he was the instigator of the Peace Accords between Egypt and Israel. That same perception permeates his new book, *Palestine: Peace Not Apartheid*.

Jimmy Carter is, in truth, one of the few ex-presidents to openly and maliciously attack a sitting U.S. president, and his criticisms are not limited to Ronald Reagan or George H. W. Bush—Carter is equally free with his criticism of President George W. Bush. His spiteful comments rival those of any of the self-appointed spokespersons for the liberal Left, all of whom are "world citizens" loyal to no particular nation. The former president cautions against a strong, unilateral policy in the Middle East. He seems to favor any world political group that is anti-United States and/or anti-Bush. It was this Carter ideology that so pleased the Nobel Peace Prize committee. However, it does absolutely nothing to strengthen U.S. ties worldwide.

On August 15, 2006, Carter was interviewed by *Der Spiegel* magazine. It was yet another opportunity for him to spew his hateful rhetoric against President Bush. But then, the American public is becoming accustomed to the liberal Left's attacks from the likes of John Kerry,

Al Gore, and, of course, Howard Dean. Carter not only attacked the president, but he also castigated Israel for their:

> …massive bombing of the entire nation of Lebanon. What happened is that Israel is holding almost 10,000 prisoners, so when the militants in Lebanon or in Gaza take one or two soldiers, Israel looks upon this as a justification for an attack on the civilian population of Lebanon and Gaza. I do not think that's justified, no.[39]

Mr. Carter seemed to have conveniently forgotten that Hezbollah (a terrorist organization) invaded Israel, killed eight Israeli soldiers, and *then* kidnapped two others. It seems also to have escaped his attention that the prisoners being held by Israel are *terrorists* with one agenda—to kill innocent Jewish civilians.

Apparently, as a card-carrying member of the liberal Left, Mr. Carter has sided with the enemy of the United States at every available opportunity. In her book *Treason,* Ann Coulter writes:

> Liberals unreservedly call all conservatives fascists, racists, and enemies of civil liberties…malign the flag, ban the Pledge, and hold cocktail parties for America's enemies.…Liberals attack their country and then go into a…panic if anyone criticizes them.…Every once in a while, their tempers get the best of them and…liberals say what they really mean.…Their own words damn them as hating America.[40]

She further defines liberals by saying:

> Liberals demand that the nation treat enemies like friends and friends like enemies. We must lift sanctions, cancel embargoes, pull out our troops, reason with our adversaries, and absolutely never wage war— unless the French say it's okay.…Democratic senators, congressmen, and ex-presidents are always popping up in countries hostile to the United States—Cuba, Nicaragua, North Korea, Iraq—hobnobbing with foreign despots who hate America.[41]

It has been said repeatedly that Jimmy Carter's term in office was America's lowest possible point in history. Indeed, his foreign policy decisions continue to plague the United States today.

Publisher William Loeb said of the Carter presidency: "Reelecting President Carter would be the equivalent of giving the Captain of the Titanic an award as Sailor of the Year."[42]

There is a general consensus, especially among conservatives, that Jimmy Carter is the worst president in U.S. history. For the past twenty-five years, Carter has behaved badly toward his successors. Sadly, there has been no outcry regarding his boorishness. His acerbic tirades against Reagan and the two Presidents Bush—in front of foreign audiences, yet—have been insolent and discourteous, to say the least. Still there are those who overlook his behavior simply because he has worked with Habitat for Humanity.

Many of Carter's pronouncements have been misleading and, in some instances, totally erroneous. He made the protection of "human rights" the basis of his entire presidency (and its afterlife). Carter saw change sweeping over the world. In *Our Endangered Virtues*, Carter wrote of his desire to see "democratization" spreading into areas worldwide. The only thing that spread during Carter's administration was hatred for all things Western—*especially* all things Western. His domestic policy blunders were only equaled, and possibly surpassed, by his foreign policy blunders.

President Jimmy Carter left office scorned by political liberals and conservatives alike. Syndicated columnist R. Emmett Tyrrell Jr. summed up Jimmy Carter's White House years this way:

> In social policy he was strictly New Age liberal. He even expressed a belief in UFOs....In foreign policy he was a pompous procrastinator, lecturing Americans on their "inordinate fear of Communism."
> ...Carter began his political career welcoming the support of the Ku Klux Klan. He adjusted his appeal to the dominant forces in the Democratic Party of the 1970s....He is another howler voice in the chorus of the Angry Left.[43]

In his post–White House years, James Earl Carter is still a pompous howler bent on blackening the United States wherever he's allowed to travel as an ambassador of "good will."

EXPORTING THE ISLAMIC REVOLUTION

Soon after seizing power during the Carter administration, Ayatollah Ruhollah Khomeini began to realize that he had no use for Iraq's Baathist-led government. Having taken refuge in al Najaf after being expelled from Iran, Khomeini had seen firsthand Hussein's repression of the Shiite Muslims in that country. To add insult to injury, Hussein had deported Khomeini from Iraq at the request of the shah in 1978 just as his influence was growing.

So it was that Khomeini encouraged the Shiites across the border to remove Saddam from power and establish an Islamic Republic like that in Iran. In response, Hussein had Grand Ayatollah Muhammad Baqir al-Sadr arrested, his sister raped and murdered in front of him, and then al-Sadr himself brutally killed. Five days later, Hussein declared war on Iran.

The bombing of Iranian airfields and military outposts in September 1980 signaled the beginning of the Iran-Iraq War. While Hussein's initial raid into Iran resulted in the capture of territory that included the port city of Khorramshahr and oil facilities in Abadan, it soon became apparent that Iran had the advantage. Iran's population was concentrated far from the border with Iraq, while the majority of the Iraqis lived near Iran's eastern border, easy prey for air attacks.

Throughout the war, both Hussein and Khomeini continued attempts to incite the inhabitants of the other's country to rebel—Hussein the Sunnis in Iran and Khomeini the Shiites in Iraq. Few from either group seemed willing to submit to the pressure, however.

As the war dragged on and trained military personnel dwindled in Iran, Khomeini induced young Iranians to volunteer for suicide missions. He conscripted youngsters as early as twelve years old to become living minesweepers. The children were manacled together, and each was given a red plastic key with which to open the gates of paradise. Then they marched off across the fields to clear the way.[44]

Hussein could raise only disinterested Shiite conscripts and Kurds with no interest in fighting against Iran. When the Iraqi military became severely depleted in 1983, Saddam brought out his supply of chemical weapons, including mustard gas. It was one of several nerve agents used by Saddam during the war.

America, for the most part, stood on the sidelines as the two countries battled for supremacy in the region. Under Ronald Reagan's administration, Donald Rumsfeld was appointed special emissary to Iraq. In meetings with Hussein, Rumsfeld explored Iraq and American hostility toward both Iran and Syria but failed to confront Hussein's use of chemical weapons. He did discuss that fact with Saddam's deputy prime minister Tariq Aziz, but not with the dictator. It was a clear signal that the Reagan administration would not pursue justice for Iraq's use of chemical weapons against its enemy. In fact, the administration actually opposed a UN resolution that condemned Hussein's use of such weapons.

Reagan had a valid reason for supporting Iraq during the war with Iran: a winning Iran would result in its controlling the oil reserves of both countries, as well as the Persian Gulf. It would present an unparalleled opportunity for Khomeini's Islamic revolution to spread. There was also the fact that the Reagan administration actually saw Hussein as both a political and economic ally in the Middle East.

In the mid-1980s, however, the Reagan administration did a sudden about-face and began a clandestine program to arm Iran. The resulting Iran-Contra scandal sent the Reaganites scrambling to repair the damage and caused a further tilt toward Hussein's regime in Iraq. In May 1987, the USS *Stark* was hit by two missiles fired from an Iraqi warplane. The two Exocet missiles killed thirty-seven American sailors. The administration accepted Iraq's explanation that the attack was an accident.

In March 1988, Iraqi planes dropped gas-filled canisters over the Kurdish city of Halabja, which at the time was held by Iranian troops. Accustomed to taking shelter underground from Iranian warplanes, the families in Halabja took refuge in basements across the city. What they could not know was that the gas would seek the lowest places in the city. The basements literally became death chambers for those seeking asylum. It is estimated that more than five thousand residents of Halabja perished as the gas spread over the city and from the complications of inhaling the foul concoction.

The U.S. Senate reacted to the horror that was Halabja by passing the Prevention of Genocide Act. The House, however, passed an emasculated version of the Senate proposal. The administration, still believing that

Hussein might become a viable ally in the region, was prone to overlook this and similar acts that killed the Kurds in northern Iraq.

The Iran-Iraq War would last more than eight years with neither side ever really gaining much of an advantage. Millions of Iraqis and Iranians died in the conflagration, at least two million were injured, and the two nations spent a combined total of over $1 trillion. The war was ever a stalemate, neither side being able to defeat the other, nor being able to agree with the other on conditions for a truce. The fighting only finally ended in response to UN Resolution 598 that called for a ceasefire, but even that was ignored for over a year as each side made one final attempt at victory.

Much like the war in Iraq today, the war between the two neighboring nations was a war of ideologies and divergent civilizations. Hussein saw himself as the Arab leader who would defeat the Persians. Khomeini saw it as an opportunity to export his Islamic revolution across the border to the Shiites in Iraq, and then beyond that to other Arab countries. Though this dream for Khomeini would prove unattainable during his lifetime, it never died. It was revived and revitalized with the election of Mahmoud Ahmadinejad to the presidency of Iran in 2005.

Chapter Nine

THE NUCLEAR BOMB OF ISLAM

It is the duty of Muslims to prepare as much force as possible to terrorize the enemies of God.[1]

—OSAMA BIN LADEN

The Iran crisis is serious because the clock is ticking. Iran is trying to develop a complete nuclear fuel cycle, going from uranium mining to converting the uranium ore to uranium gas, compressing that gas into yellow cake and then creating a feed stock which can be enriched... into nuclear fuel which would go into a bomb. Marry that fuel with a delivery system like a missile and you have a threat not only to Israel and Saudi Arabia, but probably to portions of Southern Europe.[2]

—PROFESSOR RAYMOND TANTER

Iran's president Mahmoud Ahmadinejad is either mad as a hatter or wily as a fox. He has managed, during his presidential tenure, to discomfit and confound political analysts with a rabid determination to achieve his nuclear ambitions. Today, Iran is well on its way to becoming a nuclear power, and its target is none other than what Ayatollah Khomeini first dubbed "The Great Satan," America, and "The Little Satan," Israel.

Ahmadinejad has a zealous belief that he is an instrument of Allah's will and that all infidels deserve at best to be placed in subservient roles in his society, or, in many cases, killed outright. In the words of James Woolsey, former CIA director, Ahmadinejad's extremist arm of Islam consists of "theocratic, totalitarian, and anti-Semitic genocidal fanatics."[3]

Iran's president believes he was placed in his position to finish the work of his hero, Ayatollah Khomeini, and bring about an apocalyptic event that would result in the spread of the Islamic revolution far beyond the boundaries of Iran. He will use whatever means are at his disposal— suicide bombers with conventional dynamite-laden backpacks, dirty bombs, and/or missiles carrying nuclear payloads—in order to achieve his goals.

With the exception of the two attacks on the World Trade Center in 1993 and 2001, America has, thus far, escaped the barrage of suicide bombers that have long plagued Israel—but for how long? While Ahmadinejad and his volunteer army of jihadists might see the "dirty bomb" approach as being the most effective against the United States, Israel, on the other hand, is well within range of Iran's missiles—any one of which could be armed with a nuclear warhead that would wreak untold devastation on that tiny country.

And which nations will step into the fray and take the initiative to call a halt to Iran's nuclear objectives? France? Germany? Spain? Great Britain? We simply cannot depend on our so-called Western allies to face down the likes of Ahmadinejad and his fanatical backers. Our only real ally in this Middle East mess is Israel, a tiny David in the midst of a sea of Goliaths. How long will Israel sit by and allow the giant, in this case Iran, to hurl epithets across the barren desert before she reaches into her arsenal and fells this deadly antagonist?

Not long enough for it to arm itself with nuclear weapons, that is for sure.

There are no countries other than the United States and Israel that seem willing to take on the likes of Iran's mad mullahs. It appears more and more likely that the United States, not Israel, will be the one to go it alone in order to stop the snowballing process of nuclear enrichment in Iran—and its decision to do so will more than likely have to come in 2007.

Even while American and European diplomatic sources try new and improved ways to dissuade Iran's nuclear ambitions, Israel prepares for the worst: the need to attack Iran's nuclear facilities just as it took out Iraq's Osirak facility in 1981.

Is such a thing really a possibility? As one Israeli security source said, "If all efforts to persuade Iran to drop its plans to produce nuclear weapons should fail, the US administration will authorise Israel to attack."[4]

According to that same source, "Iran's nuclear future is under construction on a spit of land…150 miles east of Kuwait. The Bushehr nuclear site is the home to a nearly completed Russian-built plant that will be capable of producing a quarter of a ton of weapons-grade plutonium a year—enough, say nuclear experts, to build 30 atomic bombs."[5] And this is only one of a line of nuclear-based facilities around the country. Some are so deeply buried as to be virtually impossible to penetrate. These include sites such as Saghand, Ardekan, and what will probably be Israel's first target: Natanz, an enrichment facility.

The obstacles to a successful attack by Israel are enormous and daunting. Israeli planes would have to fly over Turkey, American coordination would be absolutely necessary, retaliatory assaults would be swift and certain, and the targets are many—some number them around one thousand—and perhaps not all yet identified. Israel's F-15 pilots, however, will be ready and waiting for the signal. And, while the mission may be hazardous, Israel knows it must act to preserve itself, just as it did at Entebbe and later at Osirak. Israel will not permit its existence to be jeopardized, especially by regimes that have never quieted about their desire to give Israel's land to the Palestinians.[6]

THE GREATEST EQUALIZER

In 1945, after months of agonizing fighting in the Pacific theater, U.S. president Harry S. Truman finally issued orders to drop two atomic bombs on Japan in an attempt to end World War II more quickly. On August 6, "Little Boy" fell on Hiroshima with a payload whose explosive power was equivalent to 15,000 tons of TNT. Three days later, "Fat Man" was released over Nagasaki and carried a 23-kiloton (23,000-ton) punch. Approximately 130,000 people were instantly vaporized and more than 340,000 would die from the effects of those two blasts over the next five years.

Several survivors of the blast recalled their horrific experiences:

> When the blow came, I closed my eyes but I could still feel the extreme heat. To say the least, it was like being roasted alive many times over....I noticed that the side of my body was very hot. It was on fire. And I tried to put it out. But it would not go out so easily....You could hardly recognize me, my lips and my face were all popped up like this and my eyes, I had to force my eyes open with my fingers in order to see. (Testimony of Takehiko Sakai)[7]

> The blast was so intense, it felt like hundreds of needles were stabbing me all at once. (Testimony of Yoshito Matsushige)[8]

> People...had no hair because their hair was burned, and at a glance you couldn't tell whether you were looking at them from in front or

in back....I can still picture them in my mind—like walking ghosts. (Testimony of a grocer who escaped into the street)[9]

There were lots of naked people who were so badly burned that the skin of their whole body was hanging from them like rags. (Another witness)[10]

A tremendous blast wave struck our ship....Observers in the tail of our ship saw a giant ball of fire rise as though from the bowels of the earth, belching forth enormous white smoke rings. Next they saw a giant pillar of purple fire, 10,000 feet high, shooting skyward with enormous speed....Awe-struck, we watched it shoot upward like a meteor coming from the earth instead of from outer space....It was a living thing, a new species of being, born right before our incredulous eyes....It was a living totem pole, carved with many grotesque masks grimacing at the earth. (War Department press release)[11]

I looked at the face to see if I knew her. It was a woman of about forty. A gold tooth gleamed in the wide-open mouth. A handful of singed hair hung down from the left temple over her cheek, dangling in her mouth. Her eyelids were drawn up, showing black holes where the eyes had been burned out. (Testimony of Fujie Urata Matsumoto)[12]

A blinding flash swept across my eyes. In a fraction of a second, I looked out the window toward the garden as a huge band of light fell from the sky down to the trees. Almost simultaneously a thunderous explosion gripped the earth and shook it....There seemed no alternative to death as the earth heaved. (Testimony of Hideko Tamura Friedman)[13]

One U.S. naval officer said of Nagasaki: "Like the ancient Sodom and Gomorrah, its site has been sown with salt and Icabod is written over its gates."[14]

J. Robert Oppenheimer had been absolutely correct. While witnessing the first nuclear test at Alamogordo, New Mexico, on July 16, 1945, Oppenheimer was reminded of a line from the *Bhagavad Gita*, the Hindu scripture: "Now I am become Death, the destroyer of worlds."[15]

In their book *Endgame*, Lt. Gen. Thomas McInerney and Maj. Gen. Paul Vallely have this to say when discussing the threat of weapons of mass destruction being used in a terrorist attack:

Many of the scenarios about terrorism concern "weapons of mass destruction," otherwise known as nuclear, chemical, and biological weapons....As grave as the threats posed by biological and chemical weapons are, however, they are not as grave as that posed by nuclear weapons....A biological attack would not destroy the infrastructure that our country depends upon. Telephone lines would be working. Electricity would be generated and transmitted. Highways and railroads would remain open. Computer networks would remain functioning. However frightening a biological attack might be in theory, it is unlikely to achieve much in fact....

Even if terrorist groups were given chemical weapons from the arsenal of a country, there is no guarantee that they would be able to transport them safely to the target cities or gather them in sufficient quantities to kill and injure large numbers of people....

Chemical weapons, like biological weapons, do not destroy buildings or bridges or any other vital infrastructure or interfere seriously in the operation of the government.

From a military perspective, therefore, using nuclear weapons just makes more sense. Mounting a terrorist operation using weapons of mass destruction would be expensive, even if the most expensive item— the weapons themselves—were "donated" by Iran or North Korea. If would be extremely wasteful for the web of terror to expend immense manpower on an operation that would not deliver a crushing blow to the United States.[16]

Today even a relatively small atom bomb—say, 20 kilotons, roughly the explosive power of what was dropped on Nagasaki, though now capable of being transported in a much more compact container—would kill hundreds of thousands almost instantly, and many more would die from the radiation exposure in the days following. Millions would suffer the effects of the blast for the rest of their lives. Were such a bomb strategically placed—say, in the Library of Congress, for example—the blast would destroy the Capitol Building and the Supreme Court as well as a great number of governmental office buildings, including the Department of Health and Human Services—the very office that would have otherwise organized the rescue and emergency care operations for just such an attack. Thousands of key government officials would be dead in a split second. When the attacks of 9/11 took place, the entire U.S. economy shuddered—what would happen after a nuclear attack in Washington? Or what if the attack hit Wall Street instead? Or even both?

According to former CIA director James Woolsey:

Hassan Abbasi—I believe his name is—a chief of strategy for Ahmadinejad—said sometime…that there were twenty-nine sites in America and the West that if they were destroyed—and he knew how to destroy them—they would "bring the Anglo-Saxons to their knees." And that once that was done, nobody else would fight.[17]

In a meeting with Harvard law professor Alan Dershowitz in 2006, I asked him about Iran's threat to the United States. Dr. Dershowitz said:

Iran is a major, major threat to the United States. Iran, if it's not stopped, will get a nuclear bomb, and it will use that nuclear bomb to blackmail America and other countries….A nuclear weapon, whether used or hung, is the sword of Damocles—it changes the entire structure and balance of power….You can deter people who don't want to die—but many of Iran's leaders welcome death. They are part of the culture of death. They see life on earth as only a segue to Paradise with their seventy-two virgins—or whatever the rewards are going to be—and it's very hard to deter a culture that welcomes death. So Iran would be a great threat to the United States.

As Tom Friedman once said, "If terrorists are not stopped in the Middle East, they're coming to a theater near you"—and they're coming to the United States, to Europe…[even] Western European countries are vulnerable to an Iranian nuclear threat.[18]

Former prime minister of Israel Benjamin Netanyahu had this to say:

Up until now, nuclear weapons have been in the hands of responsible regimes. You have one regime, one bizarre regime, that apparently has them now in North Korea. [However,] there aren't a billion North Koreans that people seek to inspire into a religious war. That's what Iran could do. It could inspire the two hundred million Shiites. That's what they intend to do—inspire them into a religious war, first against other Muslims, then against the West.

…It is important to understand that they could impose a direct threat to Europe and to the United States—and to Israel, obviously. They don't hide it. They don't even hide the fact that they intend to take on the West.[19]

In June 2002, following the destruction of the World Trade Towers in New York City, Suleiman Abu Gheith, bin Laden's press secretary, made a terrifying announcement on a defunct Internet site: "We have the right," said Abu Gheith, "to kill four million Americans—two million of them children—and to exile twice as many and wound and cripple hundreds of thousands." In the perverted and warped minds of these fanatics, the four million represented the number that needed to be killed to balance the scales. In effect, Abu Gheith was saying that America was responsible for the deaths of four million Muslims. The number would be equal to forty-nine hundred 9/11 attacks.[20]

When Tom Ridge, secretary of homeland security under President George W. Bush, was asked to define his greatest nightmare, he replied, "Nuclear."[21]

THE SUICIDE REGIME

Iran is certainly not constrained by what was called the "MAD deterrent" (mutual assured destruction) during the Cold War of the twentieth century. The theory behind this policy is that each superpower engaged in the Cold War—i.e., Russia and the United States—was sufficiently armed to destroy the other several times over in the event of an attack. The outcome of such an event would bring about the near total destruction of both countries and the world.

This theory was directly responsible for the nuclear arms race that was unleashed during the late 1940s, and lasted through the mid-1980s. Both nations had sufficient incentive not to engage in a direct nuclear conflict, and both were content to employ proxy wars around the world. Could it have been this "proxy war" concept that gave Iran the idea of stationing groups such as Hezbollah and Hamas in Lebanon and Gaza, and to send proxies into Iraq to foment upheaval in that country?

Perhaps the most pressing question after all is not when will Iran have the bomb, but rather, will the mad Ahmadinejad be deterred by "mutual assured destruction"?

Gen. Yossi Peled, the commander of Israel's northern divisions in the recent fighting between Israel and Hezbollah, said this about Iran's having nuclear weapons:

> If this moment comes that Iran has nuclear ability, let's say they decide to make a move in the Middle East to free it from the bad influence of the West. They would take [on] Egypt, Israel, Lebanon—it's against the interests of the Western world and against the United States. Don't you think it will limit the reaction of the United States? Everything will change. I wish to be wrong, but I don't feel so.
>
> The second point is that they think in a different way than you and me and most of the Western world. Maybe they will be ready to sacrifice half of the Islamic world to destroy half of the Western world. It's possible because they think a different way, have a different religion, live according to a different mentality. And already, they are strong enough to convince their people it is okay to sacrifice a million to achieve control.[22]

Professor Raymond Tanter, a national security advisor under Reagan/ Bush and one of the founders of the Iran Policy Committee, sees Islamofascist extremism and nuclear weapons as a mix the West truly can't sit by and let happen:

> What difference does it make if an Islamofascist regime gets nuclear weapons? It would be a huge boost to the government of Iran in terms of its...diplomatic ability to coerce the neighbors; it would accelerate the arms race in the Middle East where Saudi Arabia, Egypt, and Israel will either acquire or make explicit their nuclear weapons. The threat from Iran is a huge destabilizing factor in U.S.-European relations.
>
> So what then is the nation prepared to do? I say go ahead and try diplomacy but realize that when you are dealing with an Islamofascist regime, diplomacy is unlikely to work. Why not? Because the Islamofascist regime is not a normal regime where you make cost benefit calculations, where you make proposals and counter-proposals, [where] you make compromises. This regime doesn't negotiate in the same manner that a western government would negotiate. Hence you should try diplomacy, but be prepared for diplomatic failure and have options other than military options. That's what I call regime change; by empowering the Iranian people through their opposition groups.[23]

The power of Khomeini's radical Islamic belief system brainwashed into the mind of every Islamic fanatic has never been more apparent than in the various attacks around the world that have killed American soldiers, civilian bystanders, and even fellow Muslims. The Iranian-backed death squads in Iraq have no compunction about blowing themselves up in crowded marketplaces, outside schools, in busy city centers, all the while shouting, *"Allah akbar!"*—"Allah is supreme!"

According to former Palestinian terrorist Walid Shoebat:

> [Ahmadinejad] would sacrifice his whole country. When somebody reaches to the tyranny of Islamic fundamentalist like Ahmadinejad, his people don't matter, just like Hitler. The people do not matter. They're just elements to establish a goal. With Islamic fundamentalism and Nazism, two things are very similar. The end justifies the means, and there is no respect for borders.[24]

Apparently in the fanatical Islam mind-set, it is OK to kill Muslim brothers, for they will attain heaven; the hated infidel will, however, go to their reward in hell. For the radical jihadists, the end justifies the murders of innocent Muslim passersby because, after all, they will attain their reward that much sooner. Sadly, young Iranian students are literally brainwashed by textbooks found in their schools. The youngsters are taught that to sacrifice themselves as martyrs for the "cause" is the ultimate goal, and they must be ready at all times for the opportunity to attain that goal.

John R. Bolton, then undersecretary for arms control and international security, said in August 2004:

> What we ask for is not much—only what is necessary to protect our security and to prevent Iran from developing nuclear weapons and other WMD. All that Iran must do is to abide by the treaties it has signed banning weapons of mass destruction and stop its program to develop ballistic missiles. We cannot let Iran, a leading sponsor of international terrorism, acquire the most destructive weapons and the means to deliver them to Europe, most of central Asia and the Middle East, or beyond.[25]

Without serious, concerted, immediate intervention by the international community, however, Iran will reach that goal.

AHMADINEJAD: NOT YOUR ORDINARY MADMAN

We must understand that Mahmoud Ahmadinejad is not your run-of-the-mill madman. He firmly believes in the soon return of the Twelfth Imam, a character in Iranian mythology that can only be resurrected through an apocalyptic struggle. His grasp of this concept has spilled over into his speeches, including an address to the United Nations where he boldly called for "the emergence of a perfect human being who is heir to all prophets and pious men. He will lead the world to justice and absolute peace."[26] It is at the core of his writings and is taught in Iranian schools. This belief has shaped the life vision and the presidency of Mahmoud Ahmadinejad.

In discussing Ahmadinejad, Dr. Irwin Cotler, member of the Parliament of Canada and former minister of justice and attorney general of Canada, had this to say when I spoke to him recently:

> I think that Ahmadinejad is a greater threat than bin Laden....Bin - Laden at this point is a fugitive from justice and people are seeking to find bin Laden, but Ahmadinejad is a world leader in the sense that he is invited by the United Nations to address the general assembly and it confers an immunity upon him if not a legitimacy....
>
> I think Ahmadinejad is a kind of global threat to anyone who does not share his apocalyptic vision of the universe, and therefore he is not only a threat to Israel and the Jews. I know another lesson of history is that while it may begin with Jews, it doesn't end with Jews. We learned that in the Second World War....I think that the threat here is, in fact, global—that it encompasses even those Muslims who in any way would seek to make peace with Israel. He's made that intention clear by saying that those Muslims who would recognize Israel will burn in the *Uma* of Islam. Ahmadinejad is a global threat, and his criminality is global in its intent.[27]

Ahmadinejad has already laid the groundwork for an attack on Israel by spewing his ire at every opportunity. He has said, repeatedly, that Israel should be wiped "off the map," that the Holocaust is a myth perpetrated by the Jewish people as a justification to give them Palestine, and that the Jews should be relocated to a colony in Europe, or perhaps Alaska. He chaired a conference in Tehran in October 2005 called, "A World Without Zionism and America."

During the conference, Ahmadinejad quoted Ayatollah Khomeini and then added, "Anybody who recognizes Israel will burn in the fire of the Islamic nation's fury [while] any [Islamic leader] who recognizes the Zionist regime means he is acknowledging the surrender and defeat of the Islamic world."[28] He would not hesitate to launch an attack to obliterate Israel, even if it meant taking out the Palestinians, too. Of course, such an attack would mean immediate counterstrikes by Israel that would decimate Iran.

While such tactics might give the Palestinians and perhaps even the Iranian population pause for thought, Ahmadinejad would count it as the ultimate in martyrdom, and thus the ultimate in self-glory. The indoctrination of the martyr complex has become so ingrained in the radical Islamic psyche that human life has no value except for how the person dies; not even the lives of wives and children, mothers and fathers, friends and neighbors matter next to the chance to go out in a glorious explosive strike at the infidels.

One of Ahmadinejad's heroes is Grand Ayatollah Khomeini. It was he who said:

> I am decisively announcing to the whole world that if the world-devourers [i.e., the infidel powers, meaning anyone that dared to disagree with him] wish to stand against our religion, we will stand against their whole world and will not cease until the annihilation of all of them. Either we all become free, or we will go to the greater freedom which is martyrdom. Either we shake one another's hands in joy at the victory of Islam in the world, or all of us will turn to eternal life and martyrdom. In both cases, victory and success are ours.[29]

With this in mind, the idea of mutual assured destruction is not a restraint that will work with the ilk of Ahmadinejad and his cronies.

The current ruling mullahs in Iran fully believe that Allah has pre-ordained their success; they are determined to tread the path he has laid out for them. And they believe that they will triumph, that they will truly establish an Islamic caliphate worldwide, and that every knee will bow to Islam and every Christian and Jew will be enslaved.

When Ayatollah Khomeini made his triumphant return to Tehran in 1979, the religious fanatics were convinced they would win. Why? They saw Americans as weak. They saw America as having the weapons, but not the will, not the determination, not the resolve to carry out a prolonged war of attrition. The Grand Ayatollah reiterated the belief that the United States lacked the fervor necessary to challenge the Islamic revolution that was willing to fight for centuries if necessary to reach its aims.

Khomeini laid out the plan: eradicate the nation of Israel; rid the Middle East of the Jews. He convinced his compatriots that the elimination of Israel was a divine edict from Allah's mouth. He, and then his successors, concluded that, when push comes to shove, the United States and its Western allies would abandon Israel rather than go to war on its behalf.

While Khomeini was a hero to Ahmadinejad, his true mentor is Ayatollah Mohammad Taghi Mesbah Yazdi. It is this man who has shaped much of Ahmadinejad's worldview. Yazdi is the director of the Imam Khomeini Education and Research Institute in Qom. He is also a member of the Iranian Assembly of Experts. Reputedly, the hard-liner Yazdi believes, "If anyone insults the Islamic sanctity, Islam has permitted for his blood to be spilled, no court needed."[30]

In my interview with James Woolsey, he touched on the subject of Yazdi and his influence over Ahmadinejad:

> Ahmadinejad believes that the Twelfth Imam, the Hidden Imam, the Mahdi, went into occlusion, as he would put it—disappeared in the eighth century—and is waiting to come back....
>
> [Ahmadinejad] goes off every week or two to sort of commune with the Hidden Imam and get his instructions.... [Ahmadinejad's] mentor is an Ayatollah named Mesbah Yazdi, who runs a school in Qom, in the holy city in Iran. The reason Mesbah Yazdi was exiled there in 1979 by the Ayatollah Khomeini was because Khomeini thought he was too radical. So Ahmadinejad's mentor was too radical for Khomeini.
>
> The beliefs that surround their worldview have to do with working hard to get a lot of people killed as quickly as possible. So the prize of pain will summon the Mahdi. And then they also believe once the Mahdi comes, the world will only exist for a brief period of time. So Ahmadinejad is effectively on a campaign to see if he can't get the world to end.[31]

What weapons are effective against an enemy such as this? Will those Muslims that do not share this Iranian president's worldview be enticed to take up arms against him? Can we even convince them that they are in as much danger as any infidel on the globe? Or will we simply sit idly by and allow the madmen, Mahmoud Ahmadinejad and the mullahs in Iran who support him, to take the world by nuclear storm?

HOW POSSIBLE IS A TERRORIST NUCLEAR ATTACK?

In 1999, as I was reading the chapter on the opening of the scrolls in the Book of Revelation, I became inspired to write a novel, *The Jerusalem Scroll*. In chapter eight of the novel, I described a meeting in the Soviet Union between the Russian Mafia and an Islamic terrorist organization. The purpose of the meeting? The Islamic terrorist organization was negotiating the purchase of suitcase nuclear bombs:

> "Both of us know the United States is the Great Satan," Khaled continued. "Remove these obstructionists and we can eradicate the Zionists instantly. In one great sweep, our armies will dispatch these pests." He gestured as if swinging a sword in the air. "Of course, your help is essential for our victory, my brother."
>
> "Yes. Yes." Ivan's smile never changed. He held a Cuban cigar between his thumb and index finder and kept popping it into the black forest above his fat lower lip. The former KGB agent chewed his cigar, but said nothing more.
>
> "We would have no problem transporting the bomb south through Afghanistan and then into Iran," Khaled continued. "Our friend, Osama bin Laden, has already made his facilities in the Kandahar region available to us." He crossed his arms over his chest confidently. "No problem anywhere along the way." He laughed. "The CIA trained and armed his people to fight you in Afghanistan. Now we both win. It's payback time."
>
> The bomb was to be purchased for twenty million dollars.
>
> Avraham studied the man across from him. Tanned, graying, slightly over-weight, the prime minister had more determination and sheer guts than one might have thought. Avraham would have to reevaluate his opinion of the leader.
>
> "The gravity of this policy ought to cause the Western nations to be a bit more temperate toward us and a great deal more supportive of our position."

For a moment Avraham pondered his response. The right words were everything in a conversation of this magnitude. "What if, God forbid, one of those bombs went off in New York City or Los Angeles? I'd think there would be a radical change in perspective." He shook his head.[32]

Unfortunately, just such a scenario seems all too easy for terrorists to instigate and all too easy for them to pull off.

In September 2003, Yossef Bodansky and I spoke at the World Conference on Terrorism in Jerusalem. As director of the Congressional Task Force on Terrorism and Unconventional Warfare in 1998, Bodansky stated:

> The Afghans have sold seven to eight billion dollars of drugs in the West a year. Bin Laden oversees the export of drugs from Afghanistan. His people are involved in growing the crops, processing, and shipping. When Americans buy drugs, they fund the jihad.[33]

When Osama bin Laden left Sudan at the insistence of the United States in 1996, he arrived in Jalalabad on a Hercules C-130 cargo plane specifically outfitted for him. One hundred fifty Al Qaeda associates and his children and wives accompanied him.

Bin Laden was not the wealthy terrorist that most people had pictured him to be in 1996. The Saudi government revoked his citizenship and froze his assets in 1994. He was in desperate need of a new source of revenue. In 1997, the poppy harvest in Afghanistan had sold 3,276 tons of raw opium, and revenues began to pour into the coffers of Al Qaeda at a rate estimated to be between $5 and $16 billion per year.[34]

Bin Laden's cut was somewhere between $500 million to $1 billion per year. His decision to secure suitcase nuclear bombs and nuclear technology from the Russian Mafia cost bin Laden $30 million in cash and two tons of refined heroin.[35] As a matter of fact, the United States filed court papers in an extradition hearing in December 1998 charging a senior bin Laden deputy with attempting to purchase "enriched uranium for nuclear weapons."[36]

Is it possible to launch a suitcase-sized nuclear device with a grenade or rocket launcher? Yes. These weapons of terrorism could also be triggered in shopping malls, theaters, or sports stadiums in metropolitan areas. The death tolls would be astronomical.

In 1998, more than seven hundred reports of nuclear material sales were received at the Russian Defense Ministry. These materials were reportedly being sold to various buyers within and outside the Russian borders.[37]

In that same year, Boris Yeltsin's security secretary, Alexander Lebed, met behind closed doors with members of the U.S. House of Representatives. Lebed reported that as many as 40 nuclear-laden suitcase bombs were missing from the Russian arsenal. He surmised that they could be in the hands of Muslim radicals. Lebed could account for only 48 of the 132 suitcases that had been produced by the Russians and had no idea what had happened to the missing 84 nuclear devices.[38]

Reporter Steve Kroft interviewed Lebed for a segment of *60 Minutes* in 1997 and asked him how easy it would be to steal a suitcase bomb. Lebed's response was frighteningly clear. According to Lebed, since each bomb is actually made in the form of a suitcase, it would be easy to walk down any street in Moscow, Washington, or New York City with one of these bombs and never raise an eyebrow.

Kroft went on to ask Lebed about detonation. Lebed's response to this question was even more threatening than the first: no secret codes from the Kremlin are needed, and the detonation could be prepared in as little as twenty minutes. Only one person is required to trigger this nuclear weapon.

Admitting that the bombs could be in Georgia, the Ukraine, the Baltic countries, and beyond, Lebed went on to say: "More than 100 weapons out of the supposed number of 250 are not under the control of the armed forces of Russia. I don't know their location. I don't know whether they have been destroyed or whether they are stored or whether they've been sold or stolen. I don't know."[39]

In an appearance on *Meet the Press* in December 1991, Dick Cheney made this observation: "If the Soviets do an excellent job at retaining control over their stockpile of nuclear weapons—let's assume they've got 25,000 to 30,000; that's a ballpark figure—and they are 99 percent successful, that would mean you could still have as many as 250 that they were not able to control."[40]

When asked about the propinquity of a nuclear threat, Yossef Bodansky said:

> We don't have any indication that they are going to use [the nuclear weapons] tomorrow or any other day. But they have the capability, they

have the legitimate authorization, they have the logic [for using them]. One does not [make] the tremendous amount of expenditures, effort, investment in human beings, in human resources, to have something that will be just kept somewhere in storage.[41]

In November 2001, bin Laden granted an interview to Pakistani editor Hamid Mir. Mir pointedly asked if bin Laden had obtained nuclear devices. Bin Laden responded, "It is not difficult, not if you have contacts in Russia and with other militant groups. They are available for $10 to $20 million." Al-Zawahiri, bin Laden's chief strategist, interposed, "If you go to BBC reports, you will find that thirty nuclear weapons are missing from Russia's nuclear arsenal. We have links with Russia's underworld channels."[42]

There is absolutely no doubt that in 1993, bin Laden began his search for nuclear devices in an attempt to build a viable nuclear arsenal. His first attempted purchase was enriched uranium from South Africa.[43]

Bin Laden's hunt for nuclear weapons concluded with purchases of forty-eight nuclear suitcases from the Russian Mafia. He added between twelve and fifteen kilos of uranium-235 from Ukrainian arms dealer Semion Mogilevich.[44]

What might bin Laden's target be? Consider Times Square in New York. A ten-kiloton bomb disguised in a suitcase or other everyday guise could kill as many as one million people in seconds and devastate Manhattan Island, some of the most precious real estate in America. And, if one is not enough, how many are too many? Two? Three? Four? We already know Osama bin Laden will not be satisfied with one million dead. If placed in the largest U.S. cities across the nation, it would be a simple matter to meet Al Qaeda's horrific objective of killing four million Americans.

It is impossible to know how many Al Qaeda members have been recruited since 9/11. This fanatical and deadly organization could be ten times bigger—or more—than it was before 9/11. There is no question that Osama bin Laden is being protected in Pakistan. Three times as many Pakistanis trust Osama bin Laden to do the right thing than they do President Bush.[45]

Saudi Arabia supplied much of the funding to Dr. Abdul Qadeer "A. Q." Khan to further Pakistan's nuclear program. Saudi defense minister Prince Sultan was given the grand tour of Pakistan's nuclear enrichment facilities in 1999. The prince invited Dr. Khan to visit Saudi Arabia. In the past ten years, Riyadh has bestowed roughly $1.2 billion worth of oil annually on Islamabad. The Saudi government has not been paid in return.[46]

U.S. intelligence agents intercepted a cargo ship bound to Libya from Malaysia in October 2003. The cargo hold contained boxes marked "Used Machinery." Inside the boxes the agents discovered quantities of centrifuge parts used in the enrichment of uranium. The shipper: A. Q. Khan. The purchaser: Muammar al-Qaddafi.

This one incident revealed the reprehensible by-product of the international black market, the prolific trade in nuclear materials and technology. The head of the International Atomic Energy Agency, Mohamed El Baradei, has referred to this as the "Wal-Mart of private-sector proliferation."[47]

What was it that persuaded Muammar al-Qaddafi to open Libya to American intelligence officials and international weapons inspectors? Fear may have been the deciding factor. It is thought that al-Qaddafi was intent on avoiding retaliation, not if, but when terrorists use suitcase nuclear bombs against America. Al-Qaddafi would certainly have been on America's short list of targets.

AN AMERICAN HIROSHIMA?

One month after terrorists flew fuel-laden passenger jets into the World Trade Center and the Pentagon, President Bush was presented with an even more diabolical scenario. George Tenet, CIA director, informed the president at the daily intelligence briefing that "Dragonfire," a CIA agent, relayed information that Al Qaeda operatives were in possession of a ten-kiloton nuclear bomb, apparently stolen from the Russian arsenal. "Dragonfire" was convinced that the nuclear device was not only on American soil, but was, in fact, in New York City.

> "It was brutal," a U.S. official told *Time*. It was also highly classified and closely guarded. Under the aegis of the White House's Counterterrorism Security Group, part of the National Security Council, the suspected nuke was kept secret so as not to panic the people of New York. Senior FBI officials were not in the loop. Former mayor Rudolph Giuliani says he was never told about the threat. In the end, the investigators found nothing and concluded that Dragonfire's information was false. But few of them slept better. They had made a chilling realization: if terrorists

did manage to smuggle a nuclear weapon into the city, there was almost nothing anyone could do about it.[48]

Why is the thought of a terrorist organization possessing a nuclear weapon so frightening? America's entire nuclear defense has always been based upon the premise of MAD, or the hope of intercepting intercontinental ballistic missiles in flight through something like the "Star Wars" program of defense satellites. No country with nuclear weapons would dare attack America because they knew immediate retaliatory annihilation would result. However, a terrorist organization with no physical address, no telephone number, and no zip code would not fear such retaliation.

During the Dragonfire incident, President Bush's first order was to Vice President Dick Cheney. He was dispatched from Washington DC to an unnamed site. Cheney would spend several weeks at the secret location. The president's second order was to a group of Nuclear Emergency Support Team specialists (NEST). They were sent to New York City to hunt for the suspected weapon. (The operation was so top secret that no one, not even Rudolph Giuliani, mayor of New York City, was notified.) In another development, the CIA Counterterrorism Center had intercepted dialogue on Al Qaeda channels about an "American Hiroshima."[49]

The defining thought about a nuclear terrorist attack in the United States is that only about 5 percent of the ten million cargo containers entering U.S. ports each year are thoroughly inspected.

It is highly probable that Israel will attack Iran to destroy the country's nuclear reactor before it is activated, just as it did in Iraq in 1980. The serious threat of a Muslim country with access to a nuclear weapon is a valid concern. The truth: Pakistan, a Muslim country, already possesses approximately fifty nuclear weapons, as well as materials for making at least that many more.

American military minds are deeply concerned about a nuclear attack in America. And Warren Buffet, well-known financier, says, "It will happen. It's inevitable. I don't see any way it won't happen."[50]

Not if—but when.

Chapter Ten

THE BATTLE FOR THE SOUL OF AMERICA

The first Muslim elected to the United States Congress is a Democrat from Minneapolis with ties to an Islamic group....

Minnesota's new Representative in the House, Keith Ellison, was endorsed and partly financed by the Council on American-Islamic Relations (CAIR), a massive U.S.-based organization that avidly defends Osama bin Laden and other militant Islamic terrorists and considers U.S. action against terrorists anti-Islamic.[1]

—CORRUPTION CHRONICLES,
a *Judicial Watch* blog,
November 8, 2006

We cannot just allow [our moral values] to be frittered away because we're unwilling to defend them. This, I think, is absolutely critical...our moral values will sustain us. Our values as a civilization, our religious values, will sustain us because they are civil values; they are tolerant values, and this, it seems to me, is the kind of thing that will enable all of us to pull together and sustain whatever efforts it takes to resist this attack on us.[2]

—MORT ZUCKERMAN,
editor-in-chief of *U.S. News & World Report*
and publisher/owner of *New York Daily News*

The battle for the soul of America began with three terrorist attacks of the 1960s, the assassinations of three men: John F. Kennedy, Robert Kennedy, and Martin Luther King Jr. The murders of these three men were as devastating to that generation as was the attack on Pearl Harbor on December 7, 1941, or the attack on the Pentagon and the World Trade Center towers on September 11, 2001.

Just as the attack on Pearl Harbor plunged the United States into a global fight for freedom, the assassinations in the '60s signaled the end of the age of innocence that had been enjoyed by the American people.

Almost overnight, we went from *I Love Lucy, Leave It to Beaver,* and *Father Knows Best* to the proclamation that God was dead and Woodstock. Social revolution in the arts that initially seemed harmless—the Beatles, Mick Jagger and his Rolling Stones, the LSD craze—soon became a full frontal assault against traditional family values and an American culture steeped in the tenets of the Bible.

The Bible says, "You will know the truth, and the truth will set you free" (John 8:32). Rather than create freedom, the social revolution of the '60s enslaved. People became addicted to drugs, sex, pornography, and strange philosophical/"spiritual" beliefs. Values based on Judeo-Christian mores were left behind as people turned to Eastern religions and New Age practices for answers to life's biggest questions. Ouija boards supposedly provided insight for the searcher, Satanism saw a rise in practitioners, and we were subjected to the likes of Charles Manson and his demonic cult with a morbid fascination.

"Behold, I Stand at the Door . . ."

Most can remember the classic painting of Jesus standing outside a door waiting to be allowed entry. That poignant portrayal of Christ on the outside, wanting to fellowship with His creation, has never been more powerful than it is today. Prayer has been excised from schools, suits have been filed to force Congress to remove "under God" from the Pledge of Allegiance, displays of the Ten Commandments have been removed from public buildings, and the motto "In God We Trust" is in danger of extinction. Teachers have been forbidden even to carry a personal Bible in view of students, Christian literature has been removed from library shelves, religious Christmas carols have been banned from school programs, and "spring break" has replaced the Easter vacation.

We can but ask ourselves: Are we better off today than we were in 1963 when, following a suit filed by Madalyn Murray O'Hair, the U.S. Supreme Court in an eight-to-one decision voted to ban "coercive" prayer and Bible-reading from public schools in America? Are our schools safer? Are fewer kids on drugs? Are fewer kids engaged in promiscuous sex? Are fewer crimes committed by school-age children?

Battle after battle has slowly stripped Christians in America of their rights. On July 19, 2004, after a lengthy fight, a 5,300-pound monument of the Ten Commandments was removed from the Alabama courthouse rotunda. Judge Roy O. Moore, who had championed the cry to leave the monument in place, was removed from office—all in the guise of the separation of church and state. The American courts that espouse such movements as "gay rights," "abortion rights," and even "animal rights" are now pursuing the right to be godless. I wrote in *The American Prophecies:*

> We have rejected the foundation of our culture that has traditionally held us together—God and the Holy Scriptures—and as our culture drifts away from that center, we...no longer hear His voice. As a nation, our innocence is being drowned. Things are falling apart. In our halls of justice, in our pulpits, and in the political arenas, those who would speak for God not only lack the conviction to be effective, they are being systematically silenced because of a perverted interpretation of "separation of church and state." First Amendment rights are denied to those who would speak for God, while those who fight for self, special interest, and immorality are passionately intense...as the "spirit of the world" takes over....We have witnessed this spirit being more active in our world than ever before through the "isms" of Fascism, Nazism, Communism, and terrorism—the greatest threats to human liberty we have ever faced.[3]

When the first Continental Congress set out to write the document that would govern the fledgling United States, not one time did they adopt the words "separation of church and state." It's not there! Read it for yourself:

> Congress shall make no law respecting the establishment of religion, or prohibiting the free exercise thereof.[4]

In the twenty-first century, the courts of our land protect perversion while chastising the church. The writers of the Constitution would likely be amazed at the interpretation of the document over which they shed blood, sweat, and tears, and appalled at the lack of moral clarity in America today. The men who approved the purchase of Bibles with congressional funds, the men who regularly called for national days of prayer and fasting, the men who appointed Senate chaplains, would mourn the path down which succeeding Congresses and Supreme Courts have taken this once-proud nation.

The social revolution of the '60s echoed Nietzsche's declaration, "God is dead." John Lennon proclaimed that the Beatles were more popular than Jesus. *TIME* magazine reporter John T. Elson wrote, "There is an acute feeling that the churches on Sunday are preaching about the existence of a God who is nowhere visible in their daily lives,"[5] and questioned the dedication of professing Christians. According to Elson's article, God had been replaced by science, and the church had become "secularized."

With the lack of moral clarity in the secularized church, is there any wonder that the malaise has spread to the governing bodies of this nation? The bedrock foundation of the faith of our fathers has been replaced with shifting sands. The sacrifices of those who have gone before, from the War of Independence that birthed this nation to the war on terror birthed on 9/11, have been diminished. The blood of dead soldiers, patriots from the past, cries to us from battlefields around the world. These men and women sacrificed all to insure freedom for all. Perhaps Dr. James Dobson summed it up most succinctly when he admonished: "We're at a pivotal point in the history of this country. Be a participant. Don't sit on the sidelines while our basic freedoms are lost."[6]

DARKNESS DESCENDS

We all vividly remember the horrifying pictures of New York City following the World Trade Center attack on 9/11. Clouds of black smoke rushed through the cement canyons of that vibrant city, leaving death and destruction in their wake. The vision of people jumping from the windows of the burning and collapsing buildings will be forever etched in our minds.

Natural disasters in recent years have produced equally nightmarish memories—the wall of water in the tsunami that devastated parts of South Asia in December 2004; Hurricane Katrina, which ravaged the Gulf Coast in August 2005. But none can compare with the amoral blanket of darkness that has settled over America. We see it in movies, television, magazines, and on billboards; we hear it in music that seems to possess the listener; we shoot it into our veins, smoke it in a pipe, or down it from a bottle. It's the epitome of evil.

The "anything goes" sexual revolution of the '60s was fueled by such "scientific studies" as the Kinsey Report—a man who sexually abused children in the name of science—and fed by the likes of Hugh Hefner's "Playboy philosophy." The advent of the Internet only served to make the sexual revolution more readily available.

Internet pornography alone is a $57 billion industry worldwide, $12 billion in the United States alone. According to *Internet Filter Review*, "U.S. porn revenue exceeds the combined revenues of ABC, NBC, and CBS (6.2 billion)."[7] The average age of a child exposed to pornography on the Internet is eleven years old, and a staggering 90 percent of eight- to sixteen-year-olds have viewed pornography online (most while doing homework).

Another favorite pastime of the morally decadent is to try to bring God down to their level. Taking the constitutional edict that "all men are created equal," they have applied it to religion and have declared that all religions are the same. "We are all going to the same place," they say. "We're just taking different roads to get there." Sin has been banished from our vocabulary, the cross of Christ has been reduced to costume jewelry (the gaudier the better), and the blood of Christ has been counted as worthless. Religions that once elicited horror, Satanism and witch-craft, are accorded equality with Judaism and Christianity, and are, in fact, featured in the religion sections of the newspaper. And who would have thought that Anton LeVey's *Satanic Bible* would have become a collector's item, sometimes selling for as much as $1,000 per copy?

It has often been said that human beings have a God-shaped hole in their hearts, a place that can only be filled by a relationship with their Creator. It is a spiritual law written on a tablet of flesh. Those who try to fill that void with everything imaginable—drugs, sex, pornography, alco-hol, perversion, pagan religions—are only lying to themselves.

There is neither time nor space to fully discuss stem cell research, the divorce plague, fatherless families, the "feminism mystique" of Gloria Steinem, child abuse, and other such issues. All, however, have played a part in secular America's slide into depravity and debauchery. And the starkest reality of all is that the secularized church has often concurred. Isaiah 5:20 says:

> Woe to those who call evil good
>   and good evil,

> who put darkness for light
>   and light for darkness,
> who put bitter for sweet
>   and sweet for bitter.

We have clearly reached the point that the apostle Paul expressed in his first letter to Timothy:

> The Spirit clearly says that in later times some will abandon the faith and follow deceiving spirits and things taught by demons. Such teachings come through hypocritical liars, whose consciences have been seared as with a hot iron.
>
> —1 TIMOTHY 4:1–2

No? When did you last weep for an abuse victim, mourn the senseless death of an innocent and defenseless child, reach out to a battered wife, or donate to a clinic that offers an alternative to abortion?

The genie of evil has been let out of the bottle. America has sown the wind and is reaping the whirlwind. Babies die daily, aborted, sacrificed on the altar of self-interest. Abortion has become a valid means of birth control for many women. Have a one-night stand, get pregnant—no problem! Take a morning-after pill or run down to the abortion clinic on the corner. After all, it's only "tissue," not a real baby. It's a fetus, not a child fearfully and wonderfully made. Is there any wonder that Dr. Billy Graham said that if America failed to repent of her evil, God would have to apologize to Sodom and Gomorrah?

A TOLERANCE FOR EVIL

On September 11, 2001, America met evil head-on when nineteen Islamic fanatics commandeered four American airliners and piloted two into the World Trade Towers and a third into the Pentagon. The fourth airliner, likely headed for a target in Washington DC, was retaken by passengers and crashed into a field in Pennsylvania. It was our first taste of the hatred of jihad as preached by radical Islamic clerics.

Immediately following the attack, the politically correct were hard at work to avoid calling a terrorist a terrorist. Some objected to the use of the words *Islamic* or *Muslim* in describing these mass murders.

Others objected to the use of the word *terrorist*. While the American public was traumatized and paralyzed by the horrific events, members of the American press were locked in a debate over how not to offend a particular segment of society. A memo from Reuter's news department written by Stephen Jukes admonished his department not to use the word *terrorist*. He wrote, "One man's terrorist is another man's freedom fighter."[8] Never mind that Osama bin Laden had issued an edict calling on every *Muslim* to kill Americans.

Before the dust had settled over New York City and the fires were extinguished at the Pentagon, these spin doctors were outlining their campaign to thwart any attempt to hunt down those responsible for the carnage. What followed in the weeks after 9/11 was a succession of antiwar demonstrations reminiscent of the Vietnam era, a series of peace vigils, and other protests. America was declared guilty of aggression, having deserved the attacks due to some perceived ill against Islam and/or its adherents. Those not blaming the United States found another scapegoat in Israel. Why was it so hard to place the blame precisely where it belonged, on a group of radical Islamofascists spouting a hate-filled ideology and killing innocent people?

Lesbian writer Susan Sontag wrote in defense of those who called the hijackers "cowards":

> And if the word "cowardly" is to be used, it might be more aptly applied to those who kill from beyond the range of retaliation, high in the sky, than to those willing to die themselves in order to kill others. In the matter of courage (a morally neutral virtue): whatever may be said of the perpetrators of Tuesday's slaughter, they were not cowards.[9]

Not cowards? Nineteen men sauntered aboard four airlines loaded with passengers—men, women, and children—took control of those giants of the air, murdered not only the passengers but thousands of other innocent bystanders without ever looking them or their families in the eyes—and that is not a cowardly act?

Yet another writer took Americans to task for the upsurge in patriotism and the number of American flags that were raised in the days immediately following the terrorist attack. The flag was purported to be a visual symbol of bigotry, criminality, hatred, and even homophobia in America.

The novelist Barbara Kingsolver jumped into the mêlée with this liberal, enlightening pronouncement:

> Patriotism threatens free speech with death. It is infuriated by thoughtful hesitation, constructive criticism of our leaders and pleas for peace. It despises people of foreign birth. It has specifically blamed homosexuals, feminists and the American Civil Liberties Union. In other words, the American flag stands for intimidation, censorship, violence, bigotry, sexism, homophobia and shoving the Constitution through a paper shredder. Whom are we calling terrorists here?[10]

President Bush was repeatedly denounced for having stated unequivocally that America would hunt down the perpetrators and punish the planners of the attack on America. The president was careful to explain that any strike would be specifically directed at the organizations that funded and harbored terrorists worldwide. In an address to the joint session of Congress on September 20, 2001, President Bush precisely identified the target:

> Our enemy is a radical network of terrorists, and every government that supports them.
>
> Our war on terror begins with Al Qaeda, but it does not end there. It will not end until every terrorist group of global reach has been found, stopped, and defeated.[11]

The president warned the American people not to expect the war on terror to be concluded swiftly:

> Americans should not expect one battle, but a lengthy campaign, unlike any other we have ever seen. It may include dramatic strikes, visible on TV, and covert operations, secret even in success. We will starve terrorists of funding, turn them one against another, drive them from place to place, until there is no refuge or no rest. And we will pursue nations that provide aid or safe haven to terrorism. Every nation, in every region, now has a decision to make. Either you are with us, or you are with the terrorists. From this day forward, any nation that continues to harbor or support terrorism will be regarded by the United States as a hostile regime.[12]

And so, the war against bin Laden and the Taliban in Afghanistan was launched. In two short months, the Taliban had been routed, and a new leader, Hamid Karzai, was in place. During his State of the Union address in January 2002, President Bush was able to tell the viewing audience that America had "rid the world of thousands of terrorists, destroyed Afghanistan's terrorist training camps, saved a people from starvation, and freed a country from brutal oppression."[13]

Attention quickly turned from bin Laden and Afghanistan to other countries that harbored and funded terrorists—namely Iraq. Saddam Hussein was clearly pleased with the overt attack on Americans in their own homeland. Hussein had for decades provided a safe house for international terrorists. He gave sanctuary to Abu Abbas, the mastermind of the *Achille Lauro* hijacking in 1985, and Abu Nidal, a terrorist mercenary said to be responsible for the deaths of as many as nine hundred people. He also provided safe harbor for the lone escapee from the 1993 World Trade Center bombing, Abdul Rahman Yasin. Hussein doled out large sums of money to the families of suicide bombers that died in attacks against the Jews in Israel. It seemed only natural to turn the attention in the war on terror to Saddam Hussein.

It is interesting to note that the focus on Saddam Hussein began not with President George W. Bush but with former president Bill Clinton in 1998. In 1998, Hussein ousted the UN weapons inspectors in clear violation of the ceasefire agreement following the first Gulf War. The Clinton administration requested that Congress draft what was called the Iraqi Liberation Act. The act proposed that a regime change be sought. The bill, as signed by Clinton, stated that "it should be the policy of the United States to seek to remove the Saddam Hussein regime from power in Iraq, and replace it with a democratic government."[14] Furthermore, the Senate approved the use of force in order to achieve that objective. It was overwhelmingly supported by a majority in both the House and the Senate.

With such a show of support for regime change in Iraq, it was only natural that President Bush might expect the same kind of support from Congress when Saddam Hussein began to openly defy UN calls for weapons inspections. The president appealed to the UN to call a halt to Hussein's game playing. In his speech, he reiterated that all of the sanctions and incentives to tempt Hussein to comply had been in vain. A toothless UN was impotent against the "butcher of Baghdad."

Across the country, murmurs of dissent became a roar of antiwar protests. Even Jimmy Carter entered the fray on the side of the dissenters. He averred that Baghdad posed no threat to America. Carter's declaration was soon accompanied by a similar statement from the ubiquitous Al Gore. The cacophony grew as senators Tom Daschle and Ted Kennedy joined in the debate. It seemed that many could not quite understand how a brutal dictator that had at various times invaded both Iran and Kuwait, committed mass murder with WMDs against his own countrymen, and opened his borders to avowed terrorists could possibly pose a threat to anyone.

As the countdown to an Iraq invasion proceeded, the number of antiwar protestors grew, not just in the United States but worldwide. Were they protesting the attack on America by Al Qaeda? Were they protesting Hussein's brutal attacks against his own people? No, the targets of the demonstrations were the United States and Israel. America was labeled a "terrorist state" and President Bush equated to Adolf Hitler. The Washington protest crowd included the likes of Representative John Conyers and Charles Rangel, and New York City councilman Charles Barron. In his comments, Barron cast the United States into the same "axis of evil" category with Iran, Iraq, and North Korea.

Unfortunately, not every liberal in America agreed with talk show host Alan Colmes, of *Hannity & Colmes* fame. In his book *Red, White, and Liberal*, the very liberal Mr. Colmes wisely said, "The time to debate going to war was before the fact. Once American men and women were in harm's way that debate was over and lost by those of us who opposed the intervention."[15]

Conversely, a professor of anthropology at Columbia University, Nicholas de Genova, gave this rousing speech at what was cavalierly called a "teach-in":

> Peace is not patriotic. Peace is subversive, because peace anticipates
> a very different world than the one in which we live—a world where the
> U.S. would have no place.... The only true heroes are those who find
> ways that help defeat the U.S. military. I personally would like to see
> a million Mogadishus.[16]

Oddly enough, Dr. de Genova made these comments in reference to:

...the ambush of U.S. forces by an al-Qaeda warlord in Somalia in 1993. The Americans were there on a humanitarian mission to feed starving Somali Muslims. The al-Qaeda warlord was stealing the food and selling it on the black market. His forces killed 18 American soldiers and dragged their bodies through the streets in an act designed to humiliate their country.[17]

The hateful rhetoric aimed at American troops engaged in life and death battles did not lessen when American troops marched into Baghdad on April 9, 2003; indeed, the hue and cry to bring the soldiers home only rose. Even as Hussein's heinous prisons were emptied and his monstrous torture chambers taken apart, even as tons of humanitarian aid flowed into Baghdad to feed the hungry and provide much-needed medication to the ill, the liberal Left was condemning the U.S. incursion into Iraq. Like de Genova, the most open and voluble of the detractors were among America's university elite.

ISLAMOFASCISTS: NOTHING NEW

There has long been a fascination in the Islamic world with all things Hitler. In fact, the Arab states of Syria and Iraq, both Baath Party regimes, were patterned after Hitler's Fascist concepts. Just as Hitler's vision was a world under the domination of his Nazi regime, so the vision of today's radical Islamic clerics is a world under the domination of Islamic, or Sharia, law.

This was never more apparent than when Ayatollah Ruhollah Khomeini launched his Islamic revolution even as the shah of Iran was fleeing the country. As I stated earlier, it was Khomeini who dubbed America "The Great Satan" and tagged our closest ally, Israel, "The Little Satan." Truthfully, these are the only two nations with the ability and the hope of the moral clarity needed to quench the flame of Islamic revolution before it ignites across the globe.

The liberal Left in America took up the banner of the oppressed and downtrodden in Iran and ran with it. What followed was a litany of charges leveled against America for her support of the shah's regime, for supporting Israel locked in a life-and-death struggle with the Palestinians, for bombing Hiroshima and Nagasaki at the end of World War II, for Vietnam, and so on. Palestinian terrorists became "freedom fighters," and the innocent victims of their atrocious acts became the instigators simply for daring to live in Israel. Suicide bombers who brought devastation to buses, restaurants, busy shopping malls, and even schools were given the religious designation of martyr.

Radical Islam has given birth to a weapon that truly cheapens human life: the suicide bomber. But this will be as nothing compared to the weapons of mass destruction under preparation in radical Islamist states—weapons whose targets may begin with Israel but ultimately are aimed at the world's greatest democracy.

The secular, liberal Left refuses to accept the very serious threat posed by the Islamic radicals. They refuse to accept the fact that every American, place of origin not withstanding; every Jew, wherever found; and every Muslim who disagrees with the particular philosophy of the Islamic fanatics is a target. University professors will not be spared simply because they have supported the radical any more than the leftists siding with Khomeini were in deposing the shah; erudite philosophers will not be spared because of their education, and the religious Left will not be spared simply because of their worldview on religion. While their support is now welcomed and heralded worldwide by terrorist organizations, once the terrorists reach their goals, they will turn their guns on these as infidels just as they did following the Islamic revolution of 1979. No, everyone will be required to conform to the doctrines and dictates of the mad mullahs who have hijacked an entire religion—or else.

In fact, on February 26, 1993, Yigal Carmon, counterterrorism advisor to the prime minister of Israel, warned the Pentagon that, in his estimation, radical Islam was an imminent threat to America. At the end of his briefing, he was told by smirking critics that they did not consider religion to be a threat to national security.

Following his address at the Pentagon, Carmon flew to New York City, where, while having lunch at 12:18 p.m., a huge explosion took place nearby: Islamic terrorists had attempted to blow up the World Trade Center; one thousand were injured and six killed.

Islamic terrorists finished the job on September 11, 2001, and still no one wants to admit *why* we were attacked—just by whom. But Osama bin Laden is just the vanguard of a religious hatred that will engulf the entire world if not stopped.

Days before the 9/11 attacks, the UN sponsored a World Conference against Racism, Racial Discrimination, Xenophobia, and Related Intolerance. Hidden behind that grand title was a hate-filled attack against Western democracy in general and the United States and Israel in particular. Charges such as racism, slavery, and colonialism were leveled against these two democracies. It was not surprising that the Muslim regimes still using these practices escaped such criticism. No mention was made of the genocide in Rwanda or Iraq; no condemnation was levied against Iran's use of children as minesweepers during the Iran-Iraq War; nor was there a mention of the suppressive regimes in Saudi Arabia or of Syria's subjugation of the Lebanese people.

In attendance at the conference were such stalwart liberals as Jesse Jackson and Julian Bond and ten members of the U.S. Congressional Black Caucus. In a world forum, the group took its own country to task and called for the United States to pay trillions of dollars in compensation for the slavery that had been abolished in the United States in 1865. No such demands were made against other states, including those African nations that willingly participated in the trafficking of human beings. Although Cuba is said to have imported more slaves than the United States, favorite son Fidel Castro escaped condemnation unscathed. This only served to underline the double standard practiced by the UN.

As the rhetoric inside the conference became more bitter and the conference deteriorated into a blatant anti-Semitic attack against Israel, President Bush, Secretary of State Colin Powell, and the Israeli delegation exited the proceedings in protest. Some conference-goers took to the streets to parade vile posters with swastikas and pictures of Jews with fangs that dripped blood. Richard Heideman, president of B'nai B'rith International, in an open letter to all Jewish community leaders, said of the Durban Conference:

> We and other delegates have been bombarded by Nazi-like propaganda, by caricatures, by hate material, by physical and verbal assaults and by intimidation. And all within sight of U.N. officials, all in clear and open violation of the charters, conventions and declarations which define the very purpose of the world body.[18]

The British representative of the World Jewish Congress, Lord Greville Janner, said it "was the worst example of anti-Semitism I've ever seen."[19]

The conference was attended by a number of nongovernmental organizations (NGOs) funded by the Ford Foundation and drawn from the ranks of the American Civil Liberties Union, the NAACP, the National Lawyers Guild (labeled by J. Edgar Hoover as a subversive organization and possibly a cover for the Communist Party), and the pro-Castro Center for Constitutional Rights (CCR).

Leftist groups that had once focused on social justice turned their focus almost entirely on Palestine and Iraq. These two terrorist-harboring and supporting states became the darlings of the liberals worldwide. Countries and organizations that differed ideologically became frightful enemies. Their venom focused on one group in particular, the World Trade Organization, whose projects were deemed to be a major cause of environmental concerns worldwide.

The hatred for this organization and its participants congealed into one of the largest protests, some 50,000 strong, ever seen in Seattle, Washington. Anarchy ruled as streets were blocked, Molotov cocktails destroyed local businesses, and chaos reigned. Successive meetings of the World Trade Organization in Czechoslovakia, Canada, and Italy were also disrupted by demonstrators. From these protests was born the World Social Forum, a group whose professed aim is to "mobilize solidarity for the Palestinian people and their struggle for self-determination as they face brutal occupation by the Israeli state." Simply put, this world coalition of leftist liberals has one aim: the emasculation of the United States and the destruction of Israel.

PALESTINE: THE CATALYST

The various wars that have occurred in the Middle East are over what is perceived to be skirmishes on the periphery of the current war on terror and therefore completely separate from the jihad declared on the United States. It is easier, then, to view the terrorists as despairing victims and not the murderers and hate-mongers they are.

When the original UN partition plan was drawn for Palestine, the Jews and Palestinians were to occupy 20 percent of the Palestine Mandate initiated by the League of Nations in the 1920s. Great Britain was entrusted with the execution of the mandate. The League of Nations and Britain determined in September 1922 that a homeland for the Jews would not include any of the land east of the Jordan River, three-fourths of the territory outlined in the mandate. That area would ultimately become the Hashemite Kingdom of Jordan, an area with a Palestinian majority. Jews were banned from settling anywhere in that area.

In 1937, a royal commission of inquiry was given the directive to try to resolve the differences between the Palestinians and the Jews. A plan was put forth to divide the territory into two separate states. This was rejected by the Arabs because it called for the creation of a Jewish state in which some Palestinians would live. The Jews resisted the plan because it only allotted them approximately 1,900 of the available 10,310 square miles in the territory. They, however, agreed to negotiate, while the Arabs refused.

Again, in 1939, the British tried to persuade the Arabs to agree to a state in Palestine, and a limitation on the number of Jews that would be allowed to immigrate. This was also declined by the Arabs. How can one explain, then, the vilification of the Jews that has resulted simply because they occupy 1 percent of Arab lands in the Middle East and only 10 percent of the entire Palestine Mandate?

The Middle East conflict is not about land or the establishment of a state for the Palestinian people. This has been offered and rejected various times—at Oslo in 1939, at Camp David, and in Washington DC. The conflict is about the destruction of the State of Israel and the annihilation of the Jewish people. The Palestinian Authority doesn't want a portion of Jerusalem, but rather all of Jerusalem. They do not simply desire to occupy the West Bank, but all of Israel, from the Jordan River to the Mediterranean Sea. It is not a matter of "land for peace"; it is a matter of using any means possible to rid the Middle East of the Jewish population altogether. They do not wish the subjugation of the Jewish people; they wish their destruction. This was Egyptian leader Gamal Abdel Nasser's agenda. It was Yasser Arafat's agenda. It is the agenda of Bashar al-Assad of Syria and Mahmoud Ahmadinejad of Iran.

Perhaps Yasser Arafat condensed the Arab-Israeli conflict into the most succinct statement of all when he said: "We shall oppose the establishment of this state to the last member of the Palestinian people, for if ever such a state is established it will spell the end of the whole Palestinian cause [the obliteration of Israel]."[20]

Unfinished Business

Political pundits are quick to point out that the war in Iraq is President Bush's war, when, in fact, it is an unfinished chapter in the presidency of Bill Clinton. When the World Trade Center was bombed in 1993, Clinton was in office. It was under his watch that Americans were targeted by Islamic radicals. It was the Clinton administration that failed to hold the regimes responsible for the attack. It was in 1998 that Saddam Hussein defied the UN and expelled the weapons inspectors. Clinton went so far as to call for a regime change and launched air and missile strikes against Iraq, but considered nothing further. Former CIA director James Woolsey had this to say about the effectiveness of the missile strikes:

> In '93, Saddam [Hussein] tries to kill former President [George H. W.] Bush in Kuwait with a bomb. And President Clinton launches two-dozen cruise missiles against an Iraqi intelligence headquarters in the middle of the night so it would be empty. And has his secretary of state explain that we did it in the middle of the night so there wouldn't be anyone there. I don't know what we had against Iraqi cleaning women and night watchmen, but I would not have called that an effective response.[21]

When President Bush picked up the gauntlet thrown down by Saddam Hussein and began his campaign to pursue terrorist-supporting and terrorist-harboring states, he was strongly supported. Even his previous opponent in the run for the White House, Al Gore, strongly supported the action. However, once the troops were committed to engage Hussein's forces, the detractors began to rise to the surface. Democratic leaders were urged to abandon Bush and resist the call for the invasion of Iraq.

A petition signed by thousands, including Al Sharpton, Jesse Jackson, Gloria Steinem, and a host of Hollywood celebrities, caused the political Left to rethink their commitment. Suddenly Al Gore, once a proponent of the war in Iraq, began to criticize President Bush when he saw that doing the right thing might be politically dangerous to his agenda. He was soon joined by former president Jimmy Carter, who seemed to have conveniently forgotten that President Bush had sought the help of the UN Security Council. He also seemed to have forgotten that Democratic president Bill Clinton had approved strikes against Afghanistan and Iraq, among others, without prior UN sanction.

Carter and Gore proved to be just the tip of the iceberg of quick Democratic opposition to the war. House minority leader Nancy Pelosi made her dissatisfaction known just as quickly in a press conference soon after American forces entered Baghdad. Said Pelosi, who voted against going to war with Iraq, "I have absolutely no regret about my vote on this war.... The cost in human lives, the cost to our budget, probably $100 billion. We could have probably brought down that statue [referring to the toppled statue of Saddam Hussein] for a lot less."[22] (Following the 2006 elections, Ms. Pelosi was elected House majority leader.)

Before the war began, the liberal Left set a course to defame, denigrate, and malign President Bush with no thought for the thousands of troops stationed in and around Iraq. They had no regard for the newly elected Iraqi officials who have struggled to build a stable government on the rubble of Saddam Hussein's evil dictatorship. The president's credibility, veracity, and ideologies have been questioned. He was accused of having conducted a pointless and independent war, devoid of allies such as Russia and France.

It was pointed out time and again that Saddam Hussein possessed no weapons of mass destruction, as the president had led the American people to believe—despite the fact that Hussein had used chemical weapons in the war with Iran, and again to murder scores of his own people in the Kurdish north. No credence was given to the proposal that Hussein had ample time before the beginning of the conflict to move those weapons across the border into Syria and entrust them to al-Assad. And the fact that some twenty-five million Iraqis had been freed from the control of the vicious Hussein was casually overlooked.

The liberal Left continues to obsess over weapons of mass destruction while, at the same time, infecting the nation with "weapons of mass deception." I doubt that few, if any, of these "bleeding-heart liberals" have visited the mass graves of the Kurds gassed by Saddam Hussein. Even as I write this, I am looking into the faces of Kurds who experienced Hussein's unspeakably horrific acts against the Kurdish people. The sadness reflected on their faces is heartbreaking.

The presidential election of 2004 was an all-out assault against the Iraq war, the Bush doctrine on terror, and the American people who strongly supported the president. It proved the truth of the adage that if you're told a lie often enough, it becomes believable. Howard Dean, a rabid war critic, tossed his hat into the candidate ring, then Al Gore, Dick

Gephardt, and John Kerry. The candidates vied for the honor of producing the most hateful campaign rhetoric against the war in Iraq. It was even suggested that the war on Iraq was conceived before the attack on America on September 11, 2001.

At the end of a bitter and divisive campaign during which Senator Kerry proffered that the war on terror was simply a police action and could easily be handled by occasional military intervention and accused the White House of assaulting the basic freedoms of the American people, George Bush was reelected to another term as president. The liberal Left, however, remains firmly committed to the agenda of appeasement and apathy.

ATTACK OF THE LIBERALS

Attacks against America's spiritual and moral foundation have been ceaseless during the past decades. Yet according to the Barna report, 47 percent of American adults attend church in a typical weekend, 71 percent believe in God described as the all-powerful, all-knowing, perfect Creator of the universe who rules the world today, and 54 percent of all Americans identify themselves as Christians. Americans, in general, are still church attendees. Witness the success of the Left Behind series by Tim LaHaye and Jerry Jenkins, *The Purpose Driven Life* by Rick Warren, and Mel Gibson's *The Passion of the Christ.* The Bible is still an all-time national best seller.

Why, then, has a largely Christian nation allowed the marketplace and the political arena to be stripped of everything godly? Why has abortion flourished? Why has God been taken out of schools, while the distribution of condoms is allowed? Everything anti-Christian is promoted, and Christians are ridiculed. The desire to fit in has reduced the average Christian to a spineless jellyfish, afraid to speak up for fear of derision.

Many churches, once strongholds of everything good and right, have become just another club where people gather to socialize. They, too, have fallen prey to the corruption of the secular and have become watered-down versions of their former self, palatable to all and effective for none. Christians have become indistinguishable from the nonbeliever down the street. Researcher George Barna had this to say about Christianity today:

If Jesus Christ came to this planet as a model of how we ought to live, then our goal should be to act like Jesus. Sadly, few people consistently demonstrate the love, obedience and priorities of Jesus. The primary reason that people do not act like Jesus is because they do not think like Jesus. Behavior stems from what we think—our attitudes, beliefs, values and opinions. Although most people own a Bible and know some of its content, our research found that most Americans have little idea how to integrate core biblical principles to form a unified and meaningful response to the challenges and opportunities of life. We're often more concerned with survival amidst chaos than with experiencing truth and significance.[23]

Even so, the church remains America's last hope in a hopeless world. And who, in this truth-challenged, politically correct world will dare to stand up and deliver the unadulterated truth according to God's Word? As I ask this question, I'm reminded again of the scripture in Romans 1:25 KJV that speaks of those *"who changed the truth of God into a lie."*

A new translation of the Bible launched in 2004, called "Good as New" and endorsed by the British Archbishop of Canterbury, has done just that—changed the truth of God into a lie. Ruth Gledhill, a religious correspondent for the *London Times*, wrote, "Instead of condemning fornicators, adulterers and 'abusers of themselves with mankind,' the new version of his first letter to Corinth has St. Paul advising Christians not to go without sex for too long in case they get 'frustrated.'"[24] It further encourages everyone to have a "regular partner."

In the King James Version, the passage in 1 Corinthians 7:2 reads, "Nevertheless, to avoid fornication, let every man have his own wife, and let every woman have her own husband." In the Good as New version, that verse reads, "My advice is for everyone to have a regular partner."[25]

In modern-day America, churches in general have moved more and more to the left, too often becoming not a lighthouse for the lost but a lobby for liberals. The church has become more a launching pad for numerous political candidates rather than a sacred sanctuary of redemption. Organizations such as the National Council of Churches cater to the secularist agenda rather than truly representing millions of evangelical Christians in America today.

Perhaps most disturbing is that the National Council of Churches receives funding from a variety of leftist organizations such as:

> ...$100,000 from the Ford Foundation [in 2000]; $149,400 from the Annie E. Casey Foundation in 2000–2001; $150,000 from the Beldon Fund in 2001; $500,000 from the Lilly Endowment in 2002; $50,000 from the Rasmussen Foundation in 2003 and $75,000 from the Rockefeller Brothers Fund that same year.
>
> ...[Such support] has done little to counter the contention of critics that the NCC, far from doing God's work, serves as little more than a vehicle to advance the left-wing interests of its leaders.[26]

Another trademark of the NCC is its condemnation of Israel as an aggressor and violator of human rights. Little, if any, acknowledgement is given to Israel's constant bombardment via missiles and suicide bombers from the countries that surround this strong American ally. In fact, members of the NCC have voted at various times to divest holdings associated with Israel in an attempt to cripple the economy of that tiny nation.

THE EVANGELICAL RIGHT

The evangelical Right in America has become, at various times, a scapegoat, the butt of jokes, a laughingstock, and a frequent target of the liberal media. Evangelicals are portrayed as trying to impose their outdated theology on an enlightened population. In response, the church has become paralyzed, hypnotized, and ostracized by the very people who most need to connect with it in order to hear the story of the saving grace of God.

It sometimes seems that the church has given up and is content to sit idly by and watch a world doomed for hell, while placidly waiting for the remnant to be raptured. The church has abandoned the Great Commission in favor of "the Great Omission," taking on many of the characteristics of the church in Laodicea as described by the apostle John:

> So, because you are lukewarm—neither hot nor cold—I am about to spit you out of my mouth. You say, "I am rich; I have acquired wealth and do not need a thing." But you do not realize that you are wretched, pitiful, poor, blind and naked.
> —REVELATION 3:16–17

John W. Chalfant, author of *Abandonment Theology*, describes it this way:

> Clergy and their followers have been teaching, preaching, and saturating the media and their church members with the doctrine of surrender and political non-involvement. They are not teaching us to surrender to Christ through obedience to the commandment of God. Rather, they tell us that America is finished, that the collapse of our heritage and our freedoms has been predetermined within a definable near-future time frame and is therefore beyond our control.[27]

The highly respected theologian Dr. Francis Schaeffer penned a sobering book just before his death. In *The Great Evangelical Disaster,* Schaeffer issued a somber and concise overview of the twentieth-century church. He wrote:

> Here is the great evangelical disaster—the failure of the evangelical world to stand up for truth as truth.... The evangelical world has accommodated to the world spirit of the age.... To accommodate to the world spirit...is nothing less than the most gross form of worldliness.... We must say, with exceptions, the evangelical church is worldly and not faithful to the living Christ.[28]

What a tragic indictment, yet how true.

Rather than walking God's way, many demand their own way, throwing tantrums like wayward children when challenged by what the Bible really says. True to Isaiah 53:6, "Each of us has turned to his own way."

The desire for acceptance has replaced the hunger to draw close to Christ. Doubt has replaced determination, fear has overcome faith, conformity to the Word has been replaced with conformity to the world, and the voice of one "crying in the wilderness" has been replaced by a cacophony of celebrity-seekers. Separation from the world has evolved into separation of church and state, and the consequences of removing God from the political process has had dire results for the true church.

The good news is that there is a remnant. Not all Christians have bought into the secular, liberal leftist agenda. It is because of these men and women, unnamed giants of the faith, prayer warriors all, that there is still hope. It is because they firmly hold to the truth in 2 Chronicles 7:14:

> If my people, who are called by my name, will humble themselves and pray and seek my face and turn from their wicked ways, then will I hear from heaven and will forgive their sin and will heal their land.

America doesn't have to reap the whirlwind; we do not have to get what we deserve. God has graciously made a way of escape. The answer is in humility: "Humble yourselves, therefore, under God's mighty hand, that he may lift you up in due time" (1 Pet. 5:6). We, like the apostle Peter after his denial of Christ, must become broken before the Lord in order to find forgiveness and restoration. Integrity must triumph over deception; the desire to do what is right must overcome the desire to conform to the mores of this world.

The church must undergo the scrutiny of the light. No longer can the church tolerate the incursion of darkness; evil must be acknowledged and defined as such. The church still has a choice. The words of Joshua ring in my spirit: "But if serving the LORD seems undesirable to you, then choose for yourselves this day whom you will serve.... But as for me and my household, we will serve the LORD" (Josh. 24:15). The choice is yours.

Epilogue

TUESDAY, JANUARY 30, 2007, NORTHERN IRAQ

As I sit here in Iraq, finishing the research for this book, my mind is spinning with memories of my time here during the Persian Gulf War. I think about how much has changed since that visit. Like a snake charmer, the fragrance of the untapped oil reserves beneath the fields of Kirkuk has seduced Turkey and Iran into an insane obsession.

I reflect on the landscape around me. Iraq is a small country about the size of California, yet two-thirds of it is not inhabited; it is simply desert. The majority of the population lives in Central and Northern Iraq.

I can't sleep. I keep thinking about the events that unfolded through-out Iraq the day before my arrival.

January 29, 2007, had begun like many others, with time slowly sift-ing away like the sands in an ancient, apocalyptic hourglass. Despite the familiarity, it was not just a normal day; it was Ashura, the holiest day on the Shiite calendar, commemorating the seventh-century death of the martyr-saint Imam Hussein, the son of Ali, the Prophet Muhammad's cousin. Like dry leaves on the wind, millions of pilgrims had blown into Iraq from Iran and Muslim countries worldwide to honor this day.

In al Najaf to the north, hundreds of thousands of men vowing to become martyrs had beaten themselves with chains and cut themselves with swords in an attempt to feel the pain of Imam Hussein—a common practice during Ashura. Their blood flowed like a river, mixing with the blood of hundreds of thousands throughout Iraq. With joy, they cried out to their fallen and martyred Imam.

Suddenly, chaos had erupted as Sunni Arab gunmen and Shiite fol-lowers of Ahmed Hassani al-Yemeni, a vanguard of the Mahdi, attacked. The battle began as terrorists moved closer toward al Najaf with plans to kill Grand Ayatollah Ali al-Sistani, the most powerful cleric in Iraq. His followers believe that he speaks for Allah. Sunni terrorists wearing the headbands of martyrdom that declared them to be "Soldiers of Heaven" opened fire on the pilgrims. It was the perfect storm—a conspiracy timed to coincide with the climax of Ashura.

High-level Iraqi intelligence leaders later told me that it was an opera-tion by Iran coordinated with the Mahdi army under the leadership of Sheikh Moqtada al-Sadr in an attempt to drive the last nail in President George Bush's coffin. The plan was to kill al-Sistani, since he is a mod-erate, and blame it on the Sunnis. Al-Sistani is the enemy of the radical al-Sadr, who believes al-Sistani to be a traitor to the Islamic revolution. Without a quick response from the U.S. and Iraqi military, the murder would have taken place.

The day wore on with maniacal screams of "Bush, the infidel's great-est Satan" reverberating through neighborhoods, interspersed with cries mocking Christians and Jews as monkeys, pigs, and infidels. As the daylong battle continued, many wondered if it would spark an Islamic revolution.

Then U.S. troops rushed in and averted the holocaust that the murder of al-Sistani would have ignited. Red flames from U.S. Abrams tanks and Black Hawk helicopters lit up the dark sky near al Najaf. Suddenly, a burst of machine-gun fire hit its mark, and a trail of black smoke followed one of the helicopters as it crashed to the ground. The streets of Iraq were cov-ered with more U.S. blood as ground troops and armored vehicles poured into the city. Some two hundred people were arrested and three hundred were killed during the attack.

Today, in the wake of yesterday's violence, we stopped in an Iraqi village. I looked into the eyes of Iraqi widows whose shy smiles are tinged with pain. The weapons of mass destruction of Saddam Hussein killed every living thing in their village. These women in black mourn the deaths of their husbands, fathers, sons, and brothers. The pictures of their loved ones are their only link to the past.

In tears, they told me, "We hear the American media asking, 'Where are the weapons of mass destruction?' Tell them to come here; we will show them. These weapons of mass destruction are in our blood and in our souls. We will take you to the mass graves." Tomorrow, we will go with them. Many, however, do not even have a gravesite to visit. The bod-ies of their loved ones were completely destroyed, preventing the widows, young and old, from remarrying.

While they spoke, I looked around at a countryside where entire vil-lages had been exterminated, erased from the map as if they never existed. Every living thing was destroyed—dogs, cows, but especially the men. It mattered not whether they were six months old or sixty years old.

I considered how this genocidal barbaric atrocity has been erased from the minds of the people and from the newspapers of the world. It is as if it never happened. But it *did* happen...as the world slept.

Iraqi weapons of mass destruction killed more than one million Iranians and almost two hundred thousand Iraqi Kurds. Still, the anti-war liberals scream about an unjust war because the WMDs could not be found. Iraqi intelligence officials tell me that they were shipped to Syria. They also readily tell me that Saddam's top leaders smuggled billions into Syria and are now working with Iran to defeat "the Great Satan" in Iraq.

Earlier today, I met with the Speaker of the House in Kurdistan, Adnan Mufti. With us was U.S. Col. Harry Schutte. I asked Mufti to tell me about terrorist attacks in Erbil, one of Iraq's largest cities and the city over which he presides.

"Terrorist attacks?" smiled Mufti. "This city has not had a terrorist attack in over one and one-half years."

Colonel Schutte spoke up. "The U.S. media will not tell you that. [The city is so safe] our airport has over eighty flights per week."

"I read the *Iraq Study Group Report* that criticized your region for not flying the Iraqi flag," I said.

Mufti responded, "Yes, they did. This was the same flag planted in over five thousand villages that were gassed. We have a constitution, and our region is democratic. Why must we fly the Iraqi flag? Would the U.S. ask the Jews that suffered in the Holocaust to fly the Nazi flag? We refuse to honor the 'Hitler' who gassed our people; we want the new flag approved by our constitution."

Mufti also rejected the Iraq Study Group's proposal that two terror states, Iran and Syria, "meddle in [their] affairs."

"Why," he asked, "did no one from the Iraq Study Group come here? They ask where the proof is that the Bush policy is succeeding in Iraq. We are the proof. Your nation saved us from extermination. We are a stable region that is a model of everything the United States wants for Iraq. Why is it being kept hidden?"

I was reminded as I looked into his eyes that he was the target of a bomb attack by fanatic Muslims because of his strong support for America and was poisoned by Saddam Hussein and almost died.

Mufti placed a letter in my hands to deliver to President Bush and

Vice President Cheney. He said, "I sent it through diplomatic channels via the U.S. ambassador but did not hear back." I promised
I would do my best to get it into the hands of the president.

Now as I sit here writing, the final moments of Ashura have already
passed into history. I reflect on the Kurdish people I have met so far on my
trip. I found the Kurds to be very tolerant of other religions. They enjoyed
telling me their history, which traces back to the Medes, from the story
of Daniel in the lions' den and the conversion of the Mede king, Darius,
to the appeal of the Jewish orphan, Esther. They told me of the Magi, the
wise men who followed the star and presented gifts to the Christ child,
and of the Medes who were converted on the Day of Pentecost.

They told me about Christians by the tens of thousands that had fled
north out of Sunni and Shiite strongholds toward the Valley of Nineveh,
a few miles from Erbil. The horrible story of a fourteen-year-old being
crucified for sharing his faith broke my heart as I thought of the innocence of my own precious grandchildren. I heard of a pastor who was
beheaded for sharing the gospel and of women having had acid thrown
in their faces for going to church. The church in Iraq is under siege, yet
the world remains silent.

I found it strange that the United States has no base in Erbil to fight
the war on terror. The greatest success story in all of Iraq—a model
to inspire true democracy—is being completely ignored. Kurdistan is
where America needs to invest its money, rather than bleed money from
Kurdistan into the coffers of the regimes that consider America the
enemy. I also found it odd that four hundred billion dollars has been
spent in Iraq, yet the Kurds have no U.S. military equipment with which
to fight the war on terror. To see our allies using old Russian AK-47s is
an embarrassment.

In this book, I have given you a no-spin understanding of the problem,
but also of the solution. The first step is to begin by rewarding our allies
and to stop appeasing our enemies; what a novel approach.

As an example, I believe the United States needs to move a major
military base into Erbil and allow the Kurds to have 100 percent of the
money they were promised. This is not happening. The United States
needs to reward stable regimes economically. To do it, the United States
must stand up to Turkey and Iran, both of which hate the Kurds. The
Kirkuk oil fields should be turned over to the Kurds that have, in the past,

controlled the Kirkuk region. Saddam killed them to get them out and moved pro-Saddam regimes in to protect his investment.

The word in the United States is to redefine the war goals in Iraq. Yet it is clear that the United States has been 100 percent successful in the Kurdish region, which represents millions of people. I have proposed to the Iraqi Kurdish leaders that I would work with them to host an Iraq Study Group in the United States based on moral clarity, as opposed to an "appeasement study group."

The war in Iraq can be won; one only needs to go to Kurdistan to see one of the greatest success stories. Military moms and dads need to go to Kurdistan. When they do, they will be treated as heroes and will know that the sacrifice was not in vain. The Kurdish people run to kiss them and honor them in ways beyond America's ability to imagine. They love the families because they, too, have lost loved ones. They are filled with amazing compassion and gratitude.

The U.S. National Intelligence Agency declassified a report suggesting that President Bush's new strategy for controlling violence must show progress within twelve to eighteen months or risk further deterioration. Show progress? What a sick joke. You have one-fourth of Iraq living in stability; not one U.S. soldier has been killed there, ever. There has not been a terror attack in eighteen months. If that is not progress, what is?

Robert Gates, U.S. secretary of defense, says that the United States is planning to stop Iran from contributing to the violence in Iraq. If so, the border with Iran must be closed, the embassy and consulates must be closed, and the Iraqis that have proven their allegiance—meaning, the Kurds—must be given the tools to do the job. It is not about securing Baghdad; it is about isolating Iran. That will not happen unless the push is from the north to the south, with the Iraqi Kurds doing the pushing. The Turkish army has already pushed its way into Southern Kurdistan. If the United States does not move into the area quickly, the Turks and the Iranians will. The war must be fought north to south with allies, not south to north with enemies.

Over and over, I have been told that Iraqi ministries in Baghdad are helping the terrorists. The Shiites and Sunnis will not end their conflict; it is being fueled and fed by Arab countries. The only hope to save Iraq is by enlisting the Iraqi Kurds.

Winning the war in Iraq will not happen by fighting in central or southern Iraq. America is not going to win over corrupt theocracies by distorting their reality. Getting in bed with the enemy is not the solution; it is the problem.

It is so obvious to me that Iraq is headed over the cliff of an Islamic revolution that is being birthed between the Shiites and Sunnis.

WEDNESDAY, JANUARY 31, 2007

My first meeting today was in the State House with the minister of state, Karim Sinjari, at 9:00 a.m. I had two more high-level intelligence meetings with Iraqi diplomatic leaders. I cannot attribute any quotes from them for security reasons. I do not want an Iranian agent to put a bullet in their heads.

Karim is a very humble man; we sipped tea as he told me the story of three attempts on his life—the first two by terrorists and a third by Saddam, who poisoned him. He almost died. He repeated a story I had been told earlier:

"Saddam disappeared 191,000 men between the ages of ten and sixty years so the women could not remarry. They would have no proof that their husbands were dead."

Saddam used the Quran to back his claim that he had permission to kill the enemy and confiscate everything they owned. He secured a fatwah, a legal decree from an imam to give the legal, theocratic right to wipe out the Kurds.

I have been told that Iranian agents by the tens of thousands are everywhere in Iraq and that Iranian proxies number in the hundreds of thousands. I can honestly say I really don't like that, knowing I speak out strongly against Iran on network shows and that I wrote *Showdown With Nuclear Iran*. I feel a bit like a canary in a mine shaft. I am so thankful for my faith; it strengthens me in the darkness.

Karim told me that the biggest problem they have is the influx of Iranian agents into the whole of Iraq. Iran is working with Syria, a Sunni state, to kill Iraqis, and with the Shiites to pit one group against the other.

According to Karim, Paul Bremer (head of the Coalition Provisional Authority in Iraq) opened the borders, forcing the removal of all security checkpoints in Iraq. Bremer was warned that this would create terror, but he wanted to show the world he was tolerant of everyone. Iran is now running one of the biggest employment services in all of Iraq. For a few dollars, they put unemployed Iraqis on the terror payroll. It is also one of the biggest intelligence agencies operating through the Iraqi government. It makes no difference if you wear a police or military uniform; the vetting process does not work, and the fruit is that secrets are being shared with Iran, which now is aware of every move.

Said Karim, "Your army is in a holy war with jihadists worldwide. Thousands of Iraqi fanatics lived in Iran and returned home as agents with the full support of Iran. Remember, the Iranian revolution was planned in al Najaf by Ayatollah Khomeini. Al Najaf knows well how to plan Islamic revolutions. The only reason they are not attacking you in America is because you invited them to attack you in Iraq."

I think about the words of Nuri al-Maliki, the Iraqi prime minister, saying that the United States should not use Iraq for a confrontation with Iran. This is another sick joke. Al Qaeda has between four thousand and five thousand terrorists in Iraq. If we leave, the danger will be a thousand times greater—but in the United States, not in Iraq. The terrorists will take the battle to the streets of America. The only restraining factor is the U.S. troops. We keep the terrorists occupied by fighting them in Iraq. I was told that if we leave Iraq, all of the Arab countries will run away from the experiment in democracy and that the entire region will explode.

Karim further opined, "Saudi Arabia is so convinced that Iran is coming, they are building a four-hundred-mile wall at the cost of thirteen billion dollars to keep them out. Saudi is panicking because 50 percent of their population is Shiite and the oil region is in the Shiite area of Saudi. They know a nuclear Iran could mean their end. They pray that the U.S. or Israel will stop them."

I have been told that over five hundred thousand Shiite "missionaries" are gathered in Saudi Arabia with one goal: converting Sunnis.

This conversation with Karim was taped as one of the last segments of the prime-time special based on this book. Later on, at the studios of the state television station, our team (I'm traveling with a U.S. military officer, security, and a camera crew) was given classified footage never shown on U.S. television or anywhere else. I saw images of Saddam's flag being planted in each village after the gas canisters were dropped.

At first, gas that stayed low to the ground was used. When the people fled to the mountains, canisters containing poison gas that rose in the air was dropped in order to kill those fleeing. Later, I was shown footage of Saddam's death squads exterminating multitudes, including Islamic Fascists beheading Americans. It was the most unspeakably horrific sight I have ever seen.

It was a shock to see the face of Ali Hassan al-Majid on Iraqi television. He was standing trial for genocidal crimes against humanity. "I am not apologizing," he said. "I did not make mistakes. I am the one who gave the orders to the army to use WMDs against one hundred thousand Iraqi Kurds."

We were cleared by the government to see and have access to the footage. Some of it will be incorporated into the television special *The Final Move Beyond Iraq.*

THURSDAY, FEBRUARY 1, 2007

At 5:30 a.m., we began the drive northeastward toward Iran and the torture chamber of Chemical Ali. The road was dangerous. An Iranian terror organization inhabits that mountainous region; I had been up most of the night to do some serious praying for safety.

Kurdistan encompasses over one-third of the populated area of Iraq. It has the largest oil field in the world, Kirkuk. It reaches from Khanaqin in the east and stretches along the Iranian border to Sinjar in the west, taking in the Valley of Nineveh. Our first destination was Sulaymaniyah. I learned that the Iranians are smuggling heroin, opium, and hashish into Iraq. The border is open for more than four hundred miles and is controlled by the Mahdi army and the Bader Brigade, both pro-Iranian Shiite organizations.

Our first meeting in Sulaymaniyah was with Gen. Sheikh Ja'affra, a small man with a large black mustache who happens to be the minister of Peshmerga affairs. (Peshmerga are armed Kurdish fighters.) He was so thankful to the Americans for liberating his people. "If you withdraw now," he said, "you can be sure the terrorists will come to America. It's quite simple; you asked them to fight you in Iraq, and they did. If you leave, they will consider that you have been defeated and will take the fight to you.

"The Mahdi army is trained in Iran and is modeled after Hezbollah. Their terror equipment comes from Iran. And yes, it was responsible for the attack in al Najaf as well as all the attacks in the south. The suicide bombers are coming from Al Qaeda camps in Iraq and are being replenished from Afghanistan. They are moving Afghan drugs into Lebanon to sell throughout Europe. Iran is behind all the attacks in Iraq in one way or another."

He continued, "To win the war, the borders must be closed and monitored by troops that are not loyal to Iran—troops that can be monitored. Most of Iraq is controlled by the Shiites, and for that to change, a new Iraq must be built from Kurdistan southward. Our region is a model of democracy and stability. It is not necessary for U.S. troops to die here; we can stop the terror in these cities if you will let us. So far, your government has said, 'No.'"

Over lunch we met with Vice President Kosrat Rasul Ali. He invited me to come back and meet with him and President Barzani and Abdul Abdulbari Alzebari, a member of the Iraqi Congress. Mr. Ali said to me, "We have two hundred thousand soldiers; you have three hundred thousand. You don't need military in harm's way; work with us, and we will control all of the ground in Iraq. If you will let us, we will shut down Iran. Now 60 percent of Iraq is controlled by Iran; we will see that the number is 0 percent."

Following lunch, we visited the Red House, Saddam Hussein's headquarters in Sulaymaniyah, and the site of his torture chambers. A precious man, Kiowa, took us to the torture chambers where he was victimized. He was hanged from meat hooks from his chest while his arms were tied behind his back. At the same time, electrical shocks were applied to his body parts. I could see the terrible pain in his eyes as he repeated his story.

I was stunned to learn that Iranians are buying property in Iraq and pouring a fortune into the fundamentalist mosques. Most who escaped to Iran during Saddam's regime are back in Iraq and strongly support Iran. They have made trade agreements and are pouring money into Iraq. There is an embassy in Baghdad and consulates in almost every region. Tourism agreements allow millions of pilgrims to visit Karbala and al Najaf. This is a boon for terrorists who enter the country, along with the pilgrims.

Iran's goal of achieving instability in Iraq is succeeding. The Holy Grail of understanding is that the U.S. battle in Iraq is between stupidity and stability. America's liberal, antiwar Left is giving aid and comfort to the enemy. The cries of "We're losing the war; they're winning" emboldens an enemy that has a 9/11 ideology. As I looked at footage of terrorist attacks on U.S. troops, I became angry. To think that 9/11 terrorists have come to Iraq from around the world to fight us, while the liberals in the United States scream, "Get out!" This is insane. How can you make Iraq the central front on the war on terrorism and not have a mess on your hands?

To have uncapped the genie of Shiite fundamentalism in Iraq with a Shiite superstate next door was a prescription for disaster. One cannot find one Arab out of one thousand that does not believe the United States invaded Iraq over oil. To try to convince them otherwise is an exercise in futility.

While we outwardly threaten Iran for their interference in Iraq, we close our eyes to the fact that there are Iranian agents behind virtually every rock. The embassy and consulates of this member of the axis of evil are nothing more than war rooms to fund and plan the battles against U.S. troops.

I am certain that if the United States provided the tools for the Iraqi Kurds to fight the war and simply controlled the skies and provided backup, U.S. deaths would drop and victory would come in time. The liberal media, however, will have to be put into press pools and monitored; they are doing more to undermine a victory in Iraq than the enemy.

"Ali Baghdad" and his forty thieves that pillaged the banks in Iraq are out of their cage like a wild bird. They have migrated to the Middle East, their souls filled with hatred and their pockets filled with U.S. dollars. If an Iranian-style Islamic revolution happens in Iraq, the fire could jump across the Middle East.

FRIDAY, FEBRUARY 2, 2007

While waiting in the airport this morning for our flight out of Iraq, I have just watched a news report about a Black Hawk helicopter that was shot down in al Najaf last Sunday, the fourth in two weeks. Intelligence officers told me that the helicopter attacks are carried out with Iranian missiles. Nine more U.S. soldiers have been killed just in the past forty-eight hours.

I was just told by three different airport agents that our flight will not leave for Jordan this morning. Why? There is no jet fuel. Iranian proxies are blowing up the oil trucks as they head toward Kurdistan, and the Turks will not allow oil to be transported into Iraq.

Without morality, democracy is one of the worst forms of government. The world found it to be so during the French Revolution and during Hitler's day. No power on earth can ignore the Kurdish dilemma indefinitely. Thirty million living Kurds and the blood of a multitude of the dead cry out for justice.

Democracy literally means "rule by the people." The only people group supporting democracy is the Iraqi Kurdish people. It's a fantastic success. Everything President Bush wanted to see in Iraq is present in Kurdistan. Erbil is the fourth largest city in Iraq, with Baghdad first, Kirkuk second, and Mosul third.

The headlines today are gut-wrenching. A suicide bomber driving a truck loaded with explosives killed 135 in Iraq's deadliest bombing since 2003. Shiite Prime Minister al-Maliki blamed Saddam Hussein supporters. An Iraq-born Israeli official tells me that it was Sunni Al Qaeda members. The problem lies with al-Maliki and his political ally, Moqtada al-Sadr and his Mahdi army of over sixty thousand terrorists.

I am so glad I came to Iraq, and especially Kurdistan, in order to tell the world the story of democracy at work in at least a region of Iraq.

Maybe President Bush is right about fighting the global war from Iraq. If he does that, he must surely fight the war with America's allies—meaning, the 200,000-strong Kurdish army, not with those who would be enemies of America. The words of Christopher Columbus may very well describe the President's war on terror with Iraq as the central front:

> All who heard of my project rejected it with laughter, ridiculing me. There is no question that the inspiration was from the Holy Spirit because he comforted me with rays of marvelous inspiration from the Holy Scriptures.[1]

Appendix A

IRANIAN PRESIDENT DR. MAHMOUD AHMADINEJAD'S LETTER TO U.S. PRESIDENT GEORGE W. BUSH

May 9, 2006

In the Name of God, the Compassionate, the Merciful,

Mr George Bush,

President of the United States of America,

For sometime now I have been thinking, how one can justify the undeniable contradictions that exist in the international arena—which are being constantly debated, especially in political forums and amongst university students. Many questions remain unanswered. These have prompted me to discuss some of the contradictions and questions, in the hope that it might bring about an opportunity to redress them.

Can one be a follower of Jesus Christ (PBUH) [Peace Be Upon Him], the great Messenger of God, feel obliged to respect human rights, present liberalism as a civilization model, announce one's opposition to the proliferation of nuclear weapons and WMDs, make "War on Terror" his slogan, and finally, work towards the establishment of a unified international community—a community which Christ and the virtuous of the Earth will one day govern, but at the same time, have countries attacked. The lives, reputations and possessions of people destroyed and on the slight chance of the presence of a few criminals in a village, city, or convoy for example, the entire village, city or convoy (are) set ablaze.

Or because of the possibility of the existence of WMDs in one country, it is occupied, around one hundred thousand people killed, its water sources, agriculture and industry destroyed, close to 180,000 foreign troops put on the ground, sanctity of private homes of citizens broken, and the country pushed back perhaps 50 years. At what price? Hundreds of billions of dollars spent from the treasury of one country and certain other countries and tens of thousands of young men and women—as occupation troops—put in harms way, taken away from family and loved ones, their hands stained with the blood of others, subjected to so much psychological pressure that everyday some commit suicide and those returning home suffer depression, become sickly and grapple with all sorts of ailments; while some are killed and their bodies handed to their families.

On the pretext of the existence of WMDs, this great tragedy came to engulf both the peoples of the occupied and the occupying country. Later it was revealed that no WMDs existed to begin with.

Of course Saddam was a murderous dictator. But the war was not waged to topple him, the announced goal of the war was to find and destroy weapons of mass destruction. He was toppled along the way towards another goal; nevertheless the people of the region are happy about it. I point out that throughout the many years of the imposed war on Iran Saddam was supported by the West.

Mr. President,

You might know that I am a teacher. My students ask me how can these actions be reconciled with the values outlined at the beginning of this letter and duty to the tradition of Jesus Christ (PBUH), the Messenger of peace and forgiveness?

There are prisoners in Guantanamo Bay that have not been tried, have no legal representation, their families cannot see them and are obviously kept in a strange land outside their own country. There is no international monitoring of their conditions and fate. No one knows whether they are prisoners, POWs, accused or criminals.

European investigators have confirmed the existence of secret prisons in Europe too. I could not correlate the abduction of a person, and him or her being kept in secret prisons, with the provisions of any judicial system. For that matter, I fail to understand how such actions correspond to the values outlined in the beginning of this letter, i.e. the teachings of Jesus Christ (PBUH), human rights and liberal values.

Young people, university students, and ordinary people have many questions about the phenomenon of Israel. I am sure you are familiar with some of them.

Throughout history many countries have been occupied, but I think the establishment of a new country with a new people, is a new phenomenon that is exclusive to our times. Students are saying that sixty years ago such a country did not exist. They show old documents and globes and say try as we have, we have not been able to find a country named Israel. I tell them to study the history of WWI and II. One of my students told me that during WWII, which more than tens of millions of people perished in, news about the war, was quickly disseminated by the warring parties. Each touted their victories and the most recent battlefront defeat of the other party. After the war they claimed that six million Jews had been killed. Six million people that were surely related to at least two million families. Again let us assume that these events are true. Does that logically translate into the establishment of the state of Israel in the Middle East or support for such a state? How can this phenomenon be rationalized or explained?

Mr. President,

I am sure you know how—and at what cost—Israel was established:

—Many thousands were killed in the process.

—Millions of indigenous people were made refugees.

—Hundreds of thousands of hectares of farmland, olive plantations, towns and villages were destroyed.

This tragedy is not exclusive to the time of establishment; unfortunately it has been ongoing for sixty years now. A regime has been established which does not show mercy even to kids, destroys houses while the occupants are still in them, announces beforehand its list and plans to assassinate Palestinian figures, and keeps thousands of Palestinians in prison. Such a phenomenon is unique—or at the very least extremely rare—in recent memory.

Another big question asked by the people is "why is this regime being supported?" Is support for this regime in line with the teachings of Jesus Christ (PBUH) or Moses (PBUH) or liberal values? Or are we to understand that allowing the original inhabitants of these lands—inside and outside Palestine—whether they are Christian, Moslem or Jew, to determine their fate, runs contrary to principles of democracy, human rights and the teachings of prophets? If not, why is there so much opposition to a referendum?

The newly elected Palestinian administration recently took office. All independent observers have confirmed that this government represents the electorate. Unbelievingly, they have put the elected government under pressure and have advised it to recognize the Israeli regime, abandon the struggle and follow the programs of the previous government. If the current Palestinian government had run on the above platform, would the Palestinian people have voted for it? Again, can such position taken in opposition to the Palestinian government be reconciled with the values outlined earlier? The people are also asking "Why are all UNSC resolutions in condemnation of Israel vetoed?"

Mr. President,

As you are well aware, I live amongst the people and am in constant contact with them—many people from around the Middle East manage to contact me as well. They do not have faith in these dubious policies either. There is evidence that the people of the region are becoming increasingly angry with such policies.

It is not my intention to pose too many questions, but I need to refer to other points as well.

Why is it that any technological and scientific achievement reached in the Middle East region is translated into and portrayed as a threat to the Zionist regime? Is not scientific R&D one of the basic rights of nations?

You are familiar with history. Aside from the Middle Ages, in what other point in history has scientific and technical progress been a crime? Can the possibility of scientific achievements being utilized for military purposes be reason enough to oppose science and technology altogether? If such a supposition is true, then all scientific disciplines, including physics, chemistry, mathematics, medicine, engineering, etc., must be opposed.

Lies were told in the Iraqi matter. What was the result? I have no doubt that telling lies is reprehensible in any culture, and you do not like to be lied to.

Mr. President,

Don't Latin Americans have the right to ask why their elected governments are being opposed and coup leaders supported? Or, Why must they constantly be threatened and live in fear?

The people of Africa are hardworking, creative and talented. They can play an important and valuable role in providing for the needs of humanity and contribute to its material and spiritual progress. Poverty and hardship in large parts of Africa are preventing this from happening. Don't they have the right to ask why their enormous wealth—including minerals—is being looted, despite the fact that they need it more than others?

Again, do such actions correspond to the teachings of Christ and the tenets of human rights?

The brave and faithful people of Iran too have many questions and grievances, including: the coup d'etat of 1953 and the subsequent toppling of the legal government of the day, opposition to the Islamic revolution, transformation of an Embassy into a headquarters supporting the activities of those opposing the Islamic Republic (many thousands of pages of documents corroborate this claim), support for Saddam in the war waged against Iran, the shooting down of the Iranian passenger plane, freezing the assets of the Iranian nation, increasing threats, anger and displeasure vis-à-vis the scientific and nuclear progress of the Iranian nation (just when all Iranians are jubilant and celebrating their country's progress), and many other grievances that I will not refer to in this letter.

Mr. President,

September Eleven was a horrendous incident. The killing of innocents is deplorable and appalling in any part of the world. Our government immediately declared its disgust with the perpetrators and offered its condolences to the bereaved and expressed its sympathies.

All governments have a duty to protect the lives, property and good standing of their citizens. Reportedly your government employs extensive security, protection and intelligence systems—and even hunts its opponents abroad. September eleven was not a simple operation. Could it be planned and executed without coordination with intelligence and security services—or their extensive infiltration? Of course this is just an educated guess. Why have the various aspects of the attacks been kept secret? Why are we not told who botched their responsibilities? And, why aren't those responsible and the guilty parties identified and put on trial?

All governments have a duty to provide security and peace of mind for their citizens. For some years now, the people of your country and neighbors of world trouble spots do not have peace of mind. After 9.11, instead of healing and tending to the emotional wounds of the survivors and the American people—who had been immensely traumatized by the attacks—some Western media only intensified the climate of fear and insecurity—some constantly talked about the possibility of new terror attacks and kept the people in fear. Is that service to the American people? Is it possible to calculate the damages incurred from fear and panic?

American citizens lived in constant fear of fresh attacks that could come at any moment and in any place. They felt insecure in the streets, in their place of work and at home. Who would be happy with this situation? Why was the media, instead of conveying a feeling of security and providing peace of mind, giving rise to a feeling of insecurity?

Some believe that the hype paved the way—and was the justification—for an attack on Afghanistan. Again I need to refer to the role of media.

In media charters, correct dissemination of information and honest reporting of a story are established tenets. I express my deep regret about the disregard shown by certain Western media for these principles. The main pretext for an attack on Iraq was the existence of WMDs. This was repeated incessantly—for the public to finally believe—and the ground set for an attack on Iraq.

Will the truth not be lost in a contrived and deceptive climate?

Again, if the truth is allowed to be lost, how can that be reconciled with the earlier mentioned values? Is the truth known to the Almighty lost as well?

Mr. President,

In countries around the world, citizens provide for the expenses of governments so that their governments in turn are able to serve them.

The question here is "what has the hundreds of billions of dollars, spent every year to pay for the Iraqi campaign, produced for the citizens?"

As Your Excellency is aware, in some states of your country, people are living in poverty. Many thousands are homeless and unemployment is a huge problem. Of course these problems exist—to a larger or lesser extent—in other countries as well. With these conditions in mind, can the gargantuan expenses of the campaign—paid from the public treasury—be explained and be consistent with the aforementioned principles?

What has been said, are some of the grievances of the people around the world, in our region and in your country. But my main contention—which I am hoping you will agree to some of it—is:

Those in power have a specific time in office and do not rule indefinitely, but their names will be recorded in history and will be constantly judged in the immediate and distant futures.

The people will scrutinize our presidencies.

Did we manage to bring peace, security and prosperity for the people or insecurity and unemployment?

Did we intend to establish justice or just supported especial interest groups, and by forcing many people to live in poverty and hardship, made a few people rich and powerful—thus trading the approval of the people and the Almighty with theirs?

Did we defend the rights of the underprivileged or ignore them?

Did we defend the rights of all people around the world or imposed wars on them, interfered illegally in their affairs, established hellish prisons and incarcerated some of them?

Did we bring the world peace and security or raised the specter of intimidation and threats?

Did we tell the truth to our nation and others around the world or presented an inverted version of it?

Were we on the side of people or the occupiers and oppressors?

Did our administrations set out to promote rational behavior, logic, ethics, peace, fulfilling obligations, justice, service to the people, prosperity, progress and respect for human dignity or the force of guns, intimidation, insecurity, disregard for the people, delaying the progress and excellence of other nations, and trample on people's rights?

And finally, they will judge us on whether we remained true to our oath of office—to serve the people, which is our main task, and the traditions of the prophets—or not?

Mr. President,

How much longer can the world tolerate this situation?

Where will this trend lead the world to?

How long must the people of the world pay for the incorrect decisions of some rulers?

How much longer will the specter of insecurity—raised from the stockpiles of weapons of mass destruction—hunt the people of the world?

How much longer will the blood of the innocent men, women and children be spilled on the streets, and people's houses destroyed over their heads?

Are you pleased with the current condition of the world?

Do you think present policies can continue?

If billions of dollars spent on security, military campaigns and troop movement were instead spent on investment and assistance for poor countries, promotion of health, combating different diseases, education and improvement of mental and physical fitness, assistance to the victims of natural disasters, creation of employment opportunities and production, development projects and poverty alleviation, establishment of peace, mediation between disputing states, and extinguishing the flames of racial, ethnic and other conflicts, where would the world be today? Would not your government and people be justifiably proud?

Would not your administration's political and economic standing have been stronger? And I am most sorry to say, would there have been an ever increasing global hatred of the American government?

Mr. President,

It is not my intention to distress anyone.

If Prophet Abraham, Isaac, Jacob, Ishmael, Joseph, or Jesus Christ (PBUH) were with us today, how would they have judged such behavior? Will we be given a role to play in the promised world, where justice will become universal and Jesus Christ (PBUH) will be present? Will they even accept us?

My basic question is this: Is there no better way to interact with the rest of the world? Today there are hundreds of millions of Christians, hundreds of millions of Muslims and millions of people who follow the teachings of Moses (PBUH). All divine religions share and respect one word and that is "monotheism" or belief in a single God and no other in the world.

The Holy Koran stresses this common word and calls on all followers of divine religions and says: [3.64] Say: O followers of the Book! Come to an equitable proposition between us and you that we shall not serve any but Allah and (that) we shall not associate aught with Him, and (that) some of us shall not take others for lords besides Allah; but if they turn back, then say: Bear witness that we are Muslims. (The Family of Imran)

Mr. President,

According to divine verses, we have all been called upon to worship one God and follow the teachings of divine Prophets.

"To worship a God which is above all powers in the world and can do all He pleases." "The Lord which knows that which is hidden and visible, the past and the future, knows what goes on in the Hearts of His servants and records their deeds."

"The Lord who is the possessor of the heavens and the earth and all universe is His court." "Planning for the universe is done by His hands, and gives His servants the glad tidings of mercy and forgiveness of sins." "He is the companion of the oppressed and the enemy of oppressors." "He is the Compassionate, the Merciful." "He is the recourse of the faithful and guides them towards the light from darkness." "He is witness to the actions of His servants." "He calls on servants to be faithful and do good deeds, and asks them to stay on the path of righteousness and remain steadfast." "Calls on servants to heed His prophets and He is a witness to their deeds." "A bad ending belongs only to those who have chosen the life of this world and disobey Him and oppress His servants," and "A good end and eternal paradise belong to those servants who fear His majesty and do not follow their lascivious selves."

We believe a return to the teachings of the divine prophets is the only road leading to salvation. I have been told that Your Excellency follows the teachings of Jesus (PBUH) and believes in the divine promise of the rule of the righteous on Earth.

We also believe that Jesus Christ (PBUH) was one of the great prophets of the Almighty. He has been repeatedly praised in the Koran. Jesus (PBUH) has been quoted in Koran as well: [19.36] And surely Allah is my Lord and your Lord, therefore serve Him; this is the right path. Marium

Service to and obedience of the Almighty is the credo of all divine messengers.

The God of all people in Europe, Asia, Africa, America, the Pacific and the rest of the world is one. He is the Almighty who wants to guide and give dignity to all His servants. He has given greatness to Humans.

We again read in the Holy Book: "The Almighty God sent His prophets with miracles and clear signs to guide the people and show them divine signs and purify them from sins and pollutions. And He sent the Book and the balance so that the people display justice and avoid the rebellious."

All of the above verses can be seen, one way or the other, in the Good Book as well.

Divine prophets have promised:

The day will come when all humans will congregate before the court of the Almighty, so that their deeds are examined. The good will be directed towards Heaven and evildoers will meet divine retribution. I trust both of us believe in such a day, but it will not be easy to calculate the actions of rulers, because we must be answerable to our nations and all others whose lives have been directly or indirectly affected by our actions.

All prophets, speak of peace and tranquility for man—based on monotheism, justice and respect for human dignity.

Do you not think that if all of us come to believe in and abide by these principles, that is, monotheism, worship of God, justice, respect for the dignity of man, belief in the Last Day, we can overcome the present problems of the world—that are the result of disobedience to the Almighty and the teachings of prophets—and improve our performance?

Do you not think that belief in these principles promotes and guarantees peace, friendship and justice?

Do you not think that the aforementioned written or unwritten principles are universally represented?

Will you not accept this invitation? That is, a genuine return to the teachings of prophets, to monotheism and justice, to preserve human dignity and obedience to the Almighty and His prophets?

Mr. President,

History tells us that repressive and cruel governments do not survive. God has entrusted the fate of men to them. The Almighty has not left the universe and humanity to their own devices.

Many things have happened contrary to the wishes and plans of governments. These tell us that there is a higher power at work and all events are determined by Him.

Can one deny the signs of change in the world today?

Is the situation of the world today comparable to that of ten years ago? Changes happen fast and come at a furious pace.

The people of the world are not happy with the status quo and pay little heed to the promises and comments made by a number of influential world leaders. Many people around the world feel insecure and oppose the spreading of insecurity and war and do not approve of and accept dubious policies.

The people are protesting the increasing gap between the haves and the have-nots and the rich and poor countries.

The people are disgusted with increasing corruption.

The people of many countries are angry about the attacks on their cultural foundations and the disintegration of families. They are equally dismayed with the fading of care and compassion. The people of the world have no faith in international organizations, because their rights are not advocated by these organizations.

Liberalism and Western style democracy have not been able to help realize the ideals of humanity. Today these two concepts have failed. Those with insight can already hear the sounds of the shattering and fall of the ideology and thoughts of the Liberal democratic systems.

We increasingly see that people around the world are flocking towards a main focal point—that is the Almighty God. Undoubtedly through faith in God and the teachings of the prophets, the people will conquer their problems. My question for you is: "Do you not want to join them?"

Mr. President,

Whether we like it or not, the world is gravitating towards faith in the Almighty and justice and the will of God will prevail over all things.[1]

Appendix B

IRANIAN PRESIDENT DR. MAHMOUD AHMADINEJAD'S LETTER TO THE AMERICAN PEOPLE

November 29, 2006

Message of H.E. Dr. Mahmoud Ahmadinejad
President of the Islamic Republic of Iran
To the American People

In the name of God, the Compassionate, the Merciful

O, Almighty God, bestow upon humanity the perfect human being promised to all by You, and make us among his followers.

Noble Americans,

Were we not faced with the activities of the US administration in this part of the world and the negative ramifications of those activities on the daily lives of our peoples, coupled with the many wars and calamities caused by the US administration as well as the tragic consequences of US interference in other countries;

Were the American people not God-fearing, truth-loving, and justice-seeking, while the US administration actively conceals the truth and impedes any objective portrayal of current realities;

And if we did not share a common responsibility to promote and protect freedom and human dignity and integrity;

Then, there would have been little urgency to have a dialogue with you.

While Divine providence has placed Iran and the United States geographically far apart, we should be cognizant that human values and our common human spirit, which proclaim the dignity and exalted worth of all human beings, have brought our two great nations of Iran and the United States closer together.

Both our nations are God-fearing, truth-loving and justice-seeking, and both seek dignity, respect and perfection.

Both greatly value and readily embrace the promotion of human ideals such as compassion, empathy, respect for the rights of human beings, securing justice and equity, and defending the innocent and the weak against oppressors and bullies.

We are all inclined towards the good, and towards extending a helping hand to one another, particularly to those in need.

We all deplore injustice, the trampling of peoples' rights and the intimidation and humiliation of human beings.

We all detest darkness, deceit, lies and distortion, and seek and admire salvation, enlightenment, sincerity and honesty.

The pure human essence of the two great nations of Iran and the United States testify to the veracity of these statements.

Noble Americans,

Our nation has always extended its hand of friendship to all other nations of the world.

Hundreds of thousands of my Iranian compatriots are living amongst you in friendship and peace, and are contributing positively to your society. Our people have been in contact with you over the past many years and have maintained these contacts despite the unnecessary restrictions of US authorities.

As mentioned, we have common concerns, face similar challenges, and are pained by the sufferings and afflictions in the world.

We, like you, are aggrieved by the ever-worsening pain and misery of the Palestinian people. Persistent aggressions by the Zionists are making life more and more difficult for the rightful owners of the land of Palestine. In broad daylight, in front of cameras and before the eyes of the world, they are bombarding innocent defenseless civilians, bulldozing houses, firing machine guns at students in the streets and alleys, and subjecting their families to endless grief.

No day goes by without a new crime.

Palestinian mothers, just like Iranian and American mothers, love their children, and are painfully bereaved by the imprisonment, wounding and murder of their children. What mother wouldn't?

For 60 years, the Zionist regime has driven millions of the inhabitants of Palestine out of their homes. Many of these refugees have died in the Diaspora and in refugee camps. Their children have spent their youth in these camps and are aging while still in the hope of returning to homeland.

You know well that the US administration has persistently provided blind and blanket support to the Zionist regime, has emboldened it to continue its crimes, and has prevented the UN Security Council from condemning it.

Who can deny such broken promises and grave injustices towards humanity by the US administration?

Governments are there to serve their own people. No people wants to side with or support any oppressors. But regrettably, the US administration disregards even its own public opinion and remains in the forefront of supporting the trampling of the rights of the Palestinian people.

Let's take a look at Iraq. Since the commencement of the US military presence in Iraq, hundreds of thousands of Iraqis have been killed, maimed or displaced. Terrorism in Iraq has grown exponentially. With the presence of the US military in Iraq, nothing has been done to rebuild the ruins, to restore the infrastructure or to alleviate poverty. The US Government used the pretext of the existence of weapons of mass destruction in Iraq, but later it became clear that that was just a lie and a deception.

Although Saddam was overthrown and people are happy about his departure, the pain and suffering of the Iraqi people has persisted and has even been aggravated.

In Iraq, about one hundred and fifty thousand American soldiers, separated from their families and loved ones, are operating under the command of the current US administration. A substantial number of them have been killed or wounded and their presence in Iraq has tarnished the image of the American people and government.

Their mothers and relatives have, on numerous occasions, displayed their discontent with the presence of their sons and daughters in a land thousands of miles away from US shores. American soldiers often wonder why they have been sent to Iraq.

I consider it extremely unlikely that you, the American people, consent to the billions of dollars of annual expenditure from your treasury for this military misadventure.

Noble Americans,

You have heard that the US administration is kidnapping its presumed opponents from across the globe and arbitrarily holding them without trial or any international supervision in horrendous prisons that it has established in various parts of the world. God knows who these detainees actually are, and what terrible fate awaits them.

You have certainly heard the sad stories of the Guantanamo and Abu Ghraib prisons. The US administration attempts to justify them through its proclaimed "war on terror." But everyone knows that such behavior, in fact, offends global public opinion, exacerbates resentment and thereby spreads terrorism, and tarnishes the US image and its credibility among nations.

The US administration's illegal and immoral behavior is not even confined to outside its borders. You are witnessing daily that under the pretext of "the war on terror," civil liberties in the United States are being increasingly curtailed. Even the privacy of individuals is fast losing its meaning. Judicial due process and fundamental rights are trampled upon. Private phones are tapped, suspects are arbitrarily arrested, sometimes beaten in the streets, or even shot to death.

I have no doubt that the American people do not approve of this behavior and indeed deplore it.

The US administration does not accept accountability before any organization, institution or council. The US administration has undermined the credibility of international organizations, particularly the United Nations and its Security Council. But, I do not intend to address all the challenges and calamities in this message.

The legitimacy, power and influence of a government do not emanate from its arsenals of tanks, fighter aircrafts, missiles or nuclear weapons. Legitimacy and influence reside in sound logic, quest for justice and compassion and empathy for all humanity. The global position of the United States is in all probability weakened because the administration has continued to resort to force, to conceal the truth, and to mislead the American people about its policies and practices.

Undoubtedly, the American people are not satisfied with this behavior and they showed their discontent in the recent elections. I hope that in the wake of the mid-term elections, the administration of President Bush will have heard and will heed the message of the American people.

My questions are the following:

Is there not a better approach to governance?

Is it not possible to put wealth and power in the service of peace, stability, prosperity and the happiness of all peoples through a commitment to justice and respect for the rights of all nations, instead of aggression and war?

We all condemn terrorism, because its victims are the innocent.

But, can terrorism be contained and eradicated through war, destruction and the killing of hundreds of thousands of innocents?

If that were possible, then why has the problem not been resolved?

The sad experience of invading Iraq is before us all.

What has blind support for the Zionists by the US administration brought for the American people? It is regrettable that for the US administration, the interests of these occupiers supersedes the interests of the American people and of the other nations of the world.

What have the Zionists done for the American people that the US administration considers itself obliged to blindly support these infamous aggressors? Is it not because they have imposed themselves on a substantial portion of the banking, financial, cultural and media sectors?

I recommend that in a demonstration of respect for the American people and for humanity, the right of Palestinians to live in their own homeland should be recognized so that millions of Palestinian refugees can return to their homes and the future of all of Palestine and its form of government be determined in a referendum. This will benefit everyone.

Now that Iraq has a Constitution and an independent Assembly and Government, would it not be more beneficial to bring the US officers and soldiers home, and to spend the astronomical US military expenditures in Iraq for the welfare and prosperity of the American people? As you know very well, many victims of Katrina continue to suffer, and countless Americans continue to live in poverty and homelessness.

I'd also like to say a word to the winners of the recent elections in the US:

The United States has had many administrations; some who have left a positive legacy, and others that are neither remembered fondly by the American people nor by other nations.

Now that you control an important branch of the US Government, you will also be held to account by the people and by history.

If the US Government meets the current domestic and external challenges with an approach based on truth and Justice, it can remedy some of the past afflictions and alleviate some of the global resentment and hatred of America. But if the approach remains the same, it would not be unexpected that the American people would similarly reject the new electoral winners, although the recent elections, rather than reflecting a victory, in reality point to the failure of the current administration's policies. These issues had been extensively dealt with in my letter to President Bush earlier this year.

To sum up:

It is possible to govern based on an approach that is distinctly different from one of coercion, force and injustice.

It is possible to sincerely serve and promote common human values, and honesty and compassion.

It is possible to provide welfare and prosperity without tension, threats, imposition or war.

It is possible to lead the world towards the aspired perfection by adhering to unity, monotheism, morality and spirituality and drawing upon the teachings of the Divine Prophets.

Then, the American people, who are God-fearing and followers of Divine religions, will overcome every difficulty.

What I stated represents some of my anxieties and concerns.

I am confident that you, the American people, will play an instrumental role in the establishment of justice and spirituality throughout the world. The promises of the Almighty and His prophets will certainly be realized; Justice and Truth will prevail and all nations will live a true life in a climate replete with love, compassion and fraternity.

The US governing establishment, the authorities and the powerful should not choose irreversible paths. As all prophets have taught us, injustice and transgression will eventually bring about decline and demise. Today, the path of return to faith and spirituality is open and unimpeded.

We should all heed the Divine Word of the Holy Qur'an:

"But those who repent, have faith and do good may receive Salvation. Your Lord, alone, creates and chooses as He will, and

others have no part in His choice; Glorified is God and Exalted above any partners they ascribe to Him." (28:67–68)

I pray to the Almighty to bless the Iranian and American nations and indeed all nations of the world with dignity and success.[1]

Appendix C

EXCERPTS FROM AN INTERVIEW WITH
BENJAMIN NETANYAHU

Benjamin Netanyahu was prime minister of Israel from 1996–1999 and has been a good friend since before he was appointed as the deputy chief of mission in the Israeli embassy in Washington in 1982. More recently, in 2002, he served as Israel's foreign minister and was appointed finance minister in 2003, where he served until he resigned in protest of the withdrawals from Gaza in 2005.

MDE: **Talk to me about Iran's involvement with the recent outbreak of fighting in southern Lebanon.**

Mr. Netanyahu: I think there is no question that Hezbollah would not last a day without Iranian support—and, of course, Syrian support. They have been funding them, directing them, arming them, inspiring them, and there is no question that of the two, Iran is the more serious threat. It is guided now by a mad Shiite militancy that wants to throw the world back one thousand years—I was going to say to medieval times, but it is almost premedieval times—and to do this with an apocalyptic slaughter of millions. They have this creed, which you think would already have passed from the world. After all, three hundred years ago was the end of the religious wars, but they want to reconstruct it.

     The danger is, as you can see, we've been given a wake-up call here. Using their proxies in Lebanon, and coincidentally in Gaza, the Hamas—they are rocketing Israeli cities with these weapons they have now. Imagine what would happen later if Iran were to have missiles that would reach into every European capital within a decade, into the eastern coast of the U.S., and would be armed not with explosives but with nuclear weapons. I think that is a very grim possibility for the world. I think this has to be stopped. I think it has to be stopped today by a division of labor. Israel will deal with Hezbollah, cutting its military force and dismantling its missile arsenal, and the

U.S. should deal with Syria and especially with Iran by applying massive international pressure on them. Down the line, I think the most important statement is the one President Bush and Vice President Cheney have made, that Iran must not be allowed to acquire nuclear weapons. And when you see Israel's cities being hurled by Iran's proxies, to understand that we are just the forward position. They are really after you, not after us. We are just the front position of the West.

MDE: **We have proxies that are attacking your country, and no one is using the word "Iran" any longer. Is it possible that if America sleeps that America could be experiencing proxies coming across our borders?**

Mr. Netanyahu: Yes, but the more likely thing you would experience is a world we don't even want to contemplate. Up until now, nuclear weapons have been in the hands of responsible regimes. You have one regime, one bizarre regime, that apparently has them now in North Korea. There aren't a billion North Koreans that people seek to inspire into a religious war. That's what Iran could do. It could inspire the two hundred million Shiites. That's what they intend to do—inspire them into a religious war, first against other Muslims, then against the West.

The reason they despise us so much, the reason they want to eradicate us, is that they don't hate you because of us; they hate us because of you. They say we are the "Small Satan" and that America is the "Great Satan." Europe is the "Middle-Sized Satan," although they don't know it. It is important to understand that they could impose a direct threat to Europe and to the United States—and to Israel, obviously. They don't hide it. They don't even hide the fact that they intend to take on the West.

The only thing they are hiding is their nuclear program, which is being exposed by the international community. Many think that what they've done in Lebanon was merely a decoy strategy to deflect attention to growing pressure to their nuclear program. So we have to have our eyes fixed on the two objectives: one, dispatch Iran's proxy in Lebanon and give Lebanon a hope for the future, and give Israel security; but equally, deal with Iran's nuclear and missile program while there is still time, while that regime has not armed itself with weapons of mass death.

MDE: **On 9/11 you spoke to the nation and you described 9/11 as a "wake-up call from hell." What would America look like and what could happen to our nation if Iran goes nuclear?**

Mr. Netanyahu: Iran has said in unequivocal terms that, first of all, its target is Israel, and they do it with a particular brand of malevolence because they deny that the Holocaust took place—the murder of six million Jews—while they're openly declaring their intention to create another holocaust to destroy the six million Jews of Israel. Number one, Israel could be in great jeopardy. Number two, so will everybody else. That is, in short order, the Western-oriented regimes of the Middle East would fall by the wayside. That is why you see the Arab countries are siding against Iran, against Hezbollah, because they understand what I am saying. So, the Middle East could be taken over, and that means the oil fields—the oil spigot of the world—would be in Iranian hands. If you are worried about oil prices today, and what that does to the Western economy, just think about tomorrow. And number three, of course, is the ability of Iran to use its nuclear arsenal and its missile arsenal to threaten Europe and the U.S. directly.

Make no mistake about it: their mad, apocalyptic vision would be perfectly possible for them to do. This is not the Soviet Union; this is not China. These are not rational forces. Whatever you could say about the Soviet Union, it acted fairly carefully on the world scene. Every time their ideology of world domination conflicted with their survival, they always backed off...in Cuba, in Berlin. They always backed off; they were very rational in that regard. But you can't count on the ayatollahs of the world, armed with nuclear weapons, to back off. They often prefer their zeal over their survival. Have you ever heard of a Communist suicide bomber? No. But militant Islam produces battalions of them, and they smash into buildings in Manhattan, and they smash into the Pentagon, into U.S. warships, into buses, schools—you name it. So, this is a different ideology; it is a different threat. It must not be allowed to be armed.

It is the new barbarians who are seeking the weapons of mass death, and we have all been forewarned. This is another wake-up call. That's all it is.

MDE: **What was going through the minds of the nineteen who attacked America on 9/11, and what is in the minds of the Islamic Fascists in Iran? Is it any different?**

Mr. Netanyahu: It is a particular creed, and the creed that guides Iran is a particular brand of Shiism. Shiism dates back to the early years of Islam and the battle for the inheritance of Muhammad's legacy. It was a splinter group that lost out from the main trajectory of Islam that went to the Sunnis. It had a kind of mystical leader, the Mahdi, who was a great religious leader that disappeared about a thousand years ago. This Mahdi will come back in a great apocalyptic war that will claim the lives of millions. It almost mandates this kind of conflagration, and you really don't want the only country in the world with 90 percent Shiites, Iran among them, the most extreme part of this religious sect, to acquire the horrific weapons of atomic bombs and missiles to carry out their twisted ideology. It is very dangerous; people don't realize.

MDE: **Do they think they can usher him in with an apocalypse?**

Mr. Netanyahu: That's what they think.

MDE: **A Christian thinks of the coming of Jesus Christ as the blessed hope. So, you are saying there is an Islamic faction that would prefer a mushroom cloud in Israel and America, a world without Zionism and America, and that somehow they think we are all going to submit to Islam?**

Mr. Netanyahu: Prefer, no! That's what they want; it's not a preference. It's like they are ordered to do it. This is the danger of this creed. It's not a choice; it is almost like an order from Allah. That's why these people are willing to commit suicide. The question is: do we have suicidal regimes? Do we have regimes that will actually go the distance for this mad apocalyptic vision, believing they will somehow inherit paradise while they sow hell for everybody else and for their people as well? The answer is that this is probably the first time that such a mad militancy on a global scale would seek to acquire weapons of mass death. There was, sixty years ago, another mad militancy, Hitlerism, that was racing to produce the bomb but happily was defeated before this happened. Imagine a world in which Hitler had atomic bombs. That's pretty much the world you could have if the ayatollahs have atomic bombs.

MDE: **Having served as the prime minister of Israel and also the ambassador of Israel to the UN, this president of Iran spoke to the UN about the second coming of the Twelfth Mahdi, and he wrote an eighteen-page letter to the president of the United States, challenging him to convert to Islam. As a world leader, what in the world would cause a president of a country to write the president of the United States such a bizarre letter?**

Mr. Netanyahu: It is precisely this mad ideology that people underrate. They think that this is a normal country with a normal susceptibility to the calculation of cost and benefit—basically a country that operates on the world scene with a modicum of responsibility. That's not the case. Iran is an outlaw state. It fans terrorism and militancy worldwide. It is now organizing the rocketing of civilians in Israel because Hezbollah without Iran collapses in two seconds. And it is preparing to be able to launch atomic warheads into an enormous radius. It's not just targeting Israel. If they only wanted Israel, they would not build those long-range rockets that now can pretty much cover every European capital and soon will cover the U.S.

MDE: **Is it a coincidence that your soldiers were taken hostage, that Katyushas were fired at your nation during the same period of time that President Bush was going to the G8 to try to put pressure on Iran?**

Mr. Netanyahu: It has been said, not without reason, that Iran used this ploy of kidnapping and murdering our soldiers by two of its proxies, Hamas in the south and Hezbollah in the north of Israel, to deflect international attention from its nuclear program. I think this may work in the short-term, but I think it will backfire in the mid-term. I think right now people in America, not only the president of the U.S. and the American administration, but I think people in

America and in other countries can start asking themselves, "Wait a minute; is this what is in store for us?"

If they are willing to do this to Israel, which they openly say is merely a surrogate for the U.S.—that's the way they view it—then you know what they have in mind for America—and that's what underlines everything we are talking about. This is undoubtedly in their view a skirmish in a larger war, and the larger war is not against Israel. It begins with Israel, but just as was the case with the Nazis, you begin with the Jews, then you proceed to everyone else.

MDE: **How important is Christian support for the State of Israel at this time?**

Mr. Netanyahu: I think it's fundamentally important. But the fact is that we are very lucky that in the U.S. there is a great body of citizenry that understands that we have a common heritage. It is a heritage of freedom, of respecting individual rights, of respecting individual conscience, of allowing choice, of protecting freedom and democracy—and that comes from many quarters in the U.S., and most especially from many in the evangelical community and others across the political spectrum. The U.S. in this regard is different. It's different from Europe because it has a core belief.

America, like Israel, was built as the Promised Land, almost the new Promised Land. It is a carrier of so many universal values of freedom and justice that the Jewish people gave the world. I think that this is one of the great blessings of our time, that the world in the beginning of the twenty-first century is being led by the U.S. The first half of the twentieth century, the world was not led by the U.S., and the consequences were horrible indeed—World War II and the Holocaust. I think we are fortunate that the U.S. today is leading the world because it has its moral sights very, very clear.

MDE: **When you were prime minister, we had a president in office that did not respond to you with moral clarity. At this present moment, we have a president in office that is responding to the State of Israel with moral clarity. How important is that?**

Mr. Netanyahu: I think it's all-important. I think in America everyone wanted to see, through a change in administration, peace for Israel and security for Israel. And that is not changing, but what is required is to identify the source of the threat. Leadership is charged with two great tasks: to identify the threat to a society or a country, or a civilization, and to see the opportunity to protect it and make it survive and thrive. And I think, right now, America has such leadership. I think the world right now has such leadership.

MDE: **How do you see the current Iranian nuclear situation?**

Mr. Netanyahu: Now, you have one regime, North Korea, that seeks to inspire a nuclear war. That's what Iran could do: inspire three hundred million Shia to a religious war—first against other Arabs, then against the West. They don't hate you because of us; they hate us because of you. They say we are the Small Satan; you are the Great Satan, America. It is important to understand that. They don't hide the fact that they intend to take on the West. The only thing they are hiding is their nuclear program. They face growing pressure from their nuclear program. They are using a decoy strategy to deflect attention.

Many think that what they have done in Lebanon is merely a decoy strategy to deflect the growing pressure from their nuclear program. We have to have our eyes on the two objectives: one, to take care of Iran, especially Iran's part in Lebanon; and two, deal with Iran's nuclear missile program. Iran must not arm itself with weapons of mass destruction.

Appendix D

EXCERPTS FROM AN INTERVIEW WITH
JAMES WOOLSEY

James Woolsey was director of the CIA from 1993–1995. During his career in Washington, he served as advisor (during his military service) on the U.S. Delegation to the Strategic Arms Limitation Talks (SALT 1), Helsinki and Vienna, 1969–1970; general counsel to the U.S. Senate Committee on Armed Services, 1970–1973; undersecretary of the Navy, 1977–1979; delegate-at-large to the U.S.-Soviet Strategic Arms Reduction Talks (START) and Nuclear and Space Arms Talks (NST), Geneva, 1983–1986; and ambassador to the Negotiation on Conventional Armed Forces in Europe (CFE), Vienna, 1989–1991.

He is currently a trustee at the Center for Strategic and International Studies, advisor of the Institute for the Analysis of Global Security, founding member of the Set America Free Coalition, and vice president at Booz Allen Hamilton for Global Strategic Security.

MDE: **In 2000, you spoke before the Congress on terrorism. You gave an almost apocalyptic message concerning the growing design of the terrorists to kill the maximum number of people. Is this precisely what is on the agenda with Iran's obsession?**

Mr. Woolsey: I think so. Around then we were reporting on our National Terrorism Commission Report. It may have been in that context. We had some twenty-five recommendations, some of which would have helped catch some of the 9/11 terrorists. They were completely ignored in the House of Representatives, completely ignored by the administration, and completely ignored in the Senate except for Senator Jon Kyl, who put in a bill to try to implement them and it went nowhere.

So that testimony was almost certainly in that context. And yes, I think 9/11—which came afterward—fits that model. And certainly some of the crazier things that Ahmadinejad has said would fit the model even more.

MDE: **Since 1979, an Islamic revolution has been going on, with America being in the crosshairs. And it appears that America has maintained silence. Fundamentally, at this present moment, we're not seeing a whole lot of response to Iran. Is this in fact the case, or does the United States have a plan, a robust plan, to deal—to confront Iran in light of its threats?**

Mr. Woolsey: I haven't seen any evidence of any robust plan. And although the Islamic revolution is over a quarter of a century old, we have only really seen it in recent years, since it was disclosed by one of the émigré opposition groups, that Iran has a substantial nuclear program. So it's been over the course of the last four years, I think, that people in the United States have concentrated on and focused on Iran in a way that they really had not before.

Now certainly we have had serious attacks on the United States by Iran. Almost everybody who has looked at it says Khobar Towers in Saudi Arabia was an Iranian-sponsored terrorist attack. And in 1983, our embassy and our marine barracks were blown up by Hezbollah, almost certainly at Iran's guidance. So it's not as if we have had no Americans die as a result of Iranian action.

But generally speaking, the administrations from Jimmy Carter through the first nine months of George W. Bush have treated terrorism as a law enforcement problem. They figured that if you could go catch some of the terrorists and put them in jail, then that would deter the others. Now, I think, there's not much to that at all. Certainly some types of law enforcement actions are useful if you can use it to stop terrorist attacks.

But terrorists aren't deterred by some of their number being arrested and imprisoned. These aren't burglars or white-collar criminals. They're fanatics. So I think that although there have probably been some steps undertaken in the last two or three or four years to take Iranian and Iranian-backed terrorism far more seriously than was the case before the nuclear program of Iran's was discovered, it's still probably not a very robust one.

MDE: **When Iran makes the threats that they've made such as "a world without Zionism or the West," or threatening**

to exterminate the State of Israel—all these constant, irrational threats—are these threats just rhetoric or should they be taken serious?

Mr. Woolsey: They should be taken seriously. The people who have the mentality that they're just rhetoric are the same types of people who, sixty to seventy years ago, in the late 1920s and early 1930s, said that Hitler's *Mein Kampf* was just rhetoric. Hitler laid out his program very clearly to establish a one-thousand-year Reich, and exterminate the Jews, and on and on in *Mein Kampf.*

With these crazy, highly ideological, totalitarian movements, whether they're religiously rooted like Ahmadinejad and those around him in Iran or secular like Communism or Nazism, one's best guide often to what they will really do if they get power is their statements that they issue in line with their ideology in order to rally their troops and to get them enthusiastic. It would be very foolish and really quite naïve, I think, for people to say that Ahmadinejad is just blowing smoke about wanting to destroy Israel, for example. I think he would certainly do it if he could.

MDE: **Ahmadinejad gave a speech at the United Nations in which he talked about a messianic figure coming on the scene—his belief that he was on some divine religious mission. How strongly do his religious beliefs play into his apocalyptic desires?**

Mr. Woolsey: I think his religious beliefs are at the heart of his fanaticism. He is a religious fanatic. He is not a Communist or a Nazi who also happens to be a religious man. He's a religious fanatic in a Shiite Muslim world in somewhat the same way as, say, Torquemada, who was running the Spanish Inquisition in the Christian world five centuries or so ago.

I think that Ahmadinejad believes that the Twelfth Imam, the Hidden Imam, the Mahdi, went into occlusion, as he would put it—disappeared in the eighth century—and is waiting to come back. And he believes that, I think, along with a lot of others. Not all Shia, but many Shia, who hold that belief are people for whom it does not produce a crazed view. They believe it very much the way Jews believe the Messiah will come or Christians believe Christ will return. It's not something that drives them to crazy behavior in daily undertakings.

But in Ahmadinejad's case, he goes off every week or two to sort of commune with the Hidden Imam and get his instructions, from his point of view. His mentor is an ayatollah named Mesbah Yazdi, who runs a school in Qom, in the holy city in Iran. The reason Mesbah Yazdi was exiled there in 1979 by the Ayatollah Khomeini was because Khomeini thought he was too radical. So Ahmadinejad's mentor was too radical for Khomeini.

The beliefs that surround their worldview have to do with working hard to get a lot of people killed as quickly as possible. So the prize of pain will summon the Mahdi. And then they also believe once the Mahdi comes, the world will only exist for a brief period of time. So Ahmadinejad is effectively on a campaign to see if he can't get the world to end.

That's why I somewhat tongue in cheek say that Al Qaeda and the Wahabists of Saudi Arabia are the moderates of the Islamists in the Middle East because they just want a worldwide caliphate in which we all are demi and subordinate citizens, and our wives and daughters have to dress in burqas, and so forth. But they at least want—are willing to have—people live, whereas Ahmadinejad is, I think, on the other side of that divide.

MDE: **As nuclear plants, how serious would a nuclear Iran be to the Middle East and to the world?**

Mr. Woolsey: Well, it would be very serious, as serious as anything I can imagine. Precisely because of his crazed, ideological, totalitarian, fanatic, and anti-Semitic genocidal views. If this were a country with a set of beliefs that one could deal with the way we dealt with the Soviets, that would be different. We contained the Soviets for close to fifty years and deterred them for close to fifty years from using their nuclear weapons, and even from attacking conventionally in Europe.

And the reason we were able to do that is that the Soviet ideology was effectively dead by the 1950s. By the time of Khrushchev's speech before the Twenty-second Party

Congress in 1956, laying out all of Stalin's crimes, there weren't very many believing Communists as part of the Soviet system. They were cynics. These were an establishment, the nomenclature. They didn't want to die. They wanted to keep their dachas and their limousines. So they could be deterred.

And also, one could negotiate with them. I did it five times. I used to, when we got into a real jam in the negotiations in Vienna in the late '80s, I'd take my Soviet counterpart, the Soviet ambassador, out to dinner and buy him a nice bottle of Chablis and lobster thermidor, and we'd start telling Russian and American jokes, which are very similar and have a similar sense of irony—very funny. And we'd kind of laugh it up for a while and then we'd talk about some of the things that were dividing us and we would cut a bit of a deal. Maybe not everything, but we fixed this problem and that problem.

Could you imagine doing something like that with a representative of Ahmadinejad? It's, I think, beyond belief, really.

MDE: **On *60 Minutes,* the statement was asked about fifty-four thousand suicide bombers and martyrs that would be sent into the United States. And he agreed that that was highly possible. Is there any concern about the possibility of that type of thing happening in the United States, either directly through Iran or through their proxies?**

Mr. Woolsey: I think it's unlikely that we in the U.S. would see a series of individual suicide bombers of the sort that came into Israel, say from the West Bank before the barrier was put up by the Israelis. Partially it's because our law enforcement is very good. Partially it's because immigrant groups, including Lebanese Shia, of whom there are a fair number, especially in Michigan, are loyal Americans. And they're integrated into American society. Not absolutely everybody, but most.

We've had good tips from Arab Americans, Muslim Americans, with respect to terrorist groups, whether in Florida, or in New York, or wherever. We don't have the same kind of situation that exists even in Britain, much less in some place like France, with our immigrant groups. So I think it would be difficult for any sustained terrorist set of actions—suicide bombers blowing themselves up in shopping centers—because I don't think they really have a base of operations.

But for a single attack like 9/11 in which people are infiltrated in and then kill themselves while doing something devastating, that's certainly possible. And we may be in a situation where we have to, as horrible as it sounds, look for children. Hezbollah has trained up something like two thousand ten- to fifteen-year-old children—boys—as suicide bombers. And Hezbollah basically does what Iran tells it to do.

So this is a very serious situation. But I don't think it's serious in the same way or with regard to the same type of threat that we've seen, say, in Israel. I think when Iran or Hezbollah or some combination chooses to attack in this country, they'll try to make their first effort devastating.

MDE: **What does the United States need to do to hold Iran accountable so they do not go nuclear?**

Mr. Woolsey: Well, I think it's been the case for some time, and we put this on our Web site at the Committee on the Present Danger that former secretary of state George Schultz and I cochaired many, many months ago. I think we needed a long time ago to bring a lot more pressure to bear on Iran than we have. I think there was no real chance after the year from the spring of '97 to the spring of '98 to see an expansion of the role and influence of Iranian reformers under President Khatami's protection, in a sense.

By the spring of '98, the mullahs were back fully in charge. They were killing the students. They were killing the brave newspaper editors and the brave reformers. So I don't really think there's been much of a chance since the spring of '98. But there was a window of time there, I think, perhaps from May or so of '97 to May or so of '98 in which it was plausible to believe that we might find some way to work something out with Khatami and the reformers who were around him.

Since '98 I don't think that's been the case, and it certainly hasn't been the case since Ahmadinejad has become president. So as soon as that happened, if not before, but at least as soon as that happened, we should have been moving to do everything we could multilaterally, unilaterally, however, to stop travel with senior Iranian officials, to tie up their personal finances in the Iranian government's finances, to sharply increase our broadcasting into Iran. And I think before now, but certainly by around now, we ought to have been working with the countries that export gasoline and refined petroleum products into Iran, because Iran doesn't have nearly enough refineries to refine its own petroleum. So it imports 40 percent or more of its gasoline and diesel fuel.

And that gives us an opportunity to find some way to work with India or some of the other countries that ship refined petroleum products to Iran. And given now their clear violation of the mandate to stop the reprocessing of nuclear fuel, I think we might well be able to get some of these countries to agree with us that, "OK, we'll buy your refined gasoline. We think it's pretty reasonable for you to break this long-term contract with Iran given what they're doing to stability in the Middle East by their nuclear weapons program." It's certainly at least worth a try.

It would be much better, since some of these countries are friends of the United States, like India, to try to do this as a business deal rather than as a blockade of imports for them. But I think that would be much more effective than trying to block their exports of oil, which the world rather needs in order to keep oil below one hundred dollars a barrel.

MDE: **Islamic Fascists. It's a new word for President Bush. We just heard it recently. There seems to be almost a conflict in moralities in Americans and what we're looking at regarding the war on terrorism—it's almost being defined as our involvement in Iraq. What precisely is the war on terrorism, and what precisely is Islamic Fascism?**

Mr. Woolsey: Well, to call Ahmadinejad and the Wahabists of Saudi Arabia and Al Qaeda Islamic Fascists is really quite an insult to Mussolini. Because the Italian Fascists were not explicitly genocidal. They were terrible dictators. They were extremely authoritarian. They helped the Germans with the Holocaust. But their doctrine and their beliefs were not genocidal. They were not in favor themselves, as a matter of doctrine, of, say, exterminating all the Jews the way the Nazis were.

So it would really be more accurate to call these three groups Islamic Nazis. I would say, for example, that Torquemada, in the late fifteenth, early sixteenth century, was a Christian Nazi. He was a totalitarian. I don't see any reason not to call a spade a spade.

MDE: **Nuclear Iran. The American people don't see that Iran could ever be a nuclear threat to the United States because they could never launch a missile at us. Are there other ways to get nuclear weapons—nuclear dirty bombs—into this country?**

Mr. Woolsey: Certainly. You could hide one, say, in a bale of marijuana. There are all sorts of ways to get across our borders with fairly large things—both our southern border and our northern border and our coasts. At least you have the Coast Guard patrolling in the mid-sea, but some parts of the Canadian border, the Mexican border, are very easy to get across.

The amount of nuclear material you need for a bomb is twenty-five to thirty-five pounds—about the size of a volleyball or maybe a basketball. But getting an Iranian set of fissionable material, and then assembling a bomb once you've got it into the country, could well be done once they have that kind of material. And they don't need to make it themselves in order to have it.

All these estimates that they won't have a bomb for five or ten years depend upon their doing the reprocessing of the plutonium or their doing the enrichment of the uranium to bring about the existence of the fissionable material, which is the long pole in the tent of a nuclear weapon. The bomb itself is fairly easy to do, unfortunately. If Iranian intelligence working with Hezbollah got a bomb—or fissionable material enough to assemble into a bomb—into the United States across one of our borders, that would be one way they could attack.

The other would be to utilize what's sometimes colloquially called "a Scud in a bucket." A Scud is a short-range ballistic missile—maybe a couple of hundred miles—thousands, tens of thousands of them all over the world. The Iranians have them. They have longer-range ones. They have their joint missile program, essentially, with North Korea, that creates a much longer-range missile than that.

So if you launch something like that from a tramp steamer the world doesn't patrol—even the United States Navy doesn't patrol the oceans and identify all the tramp steamers. And also, the Persians invented chess, so deception is certainly something that is part of their repertoire. I would expect that if they got to within one hundred miles of New York City and launched a Scud from an old tramp steamer, they'd do everything they could to make it look like Al Qaeda. Or if Al Qaeda did it, they'd probably try to make it look like it was Hezbollah.

Those are all plausible scenarios even before you get to the possibility of the Iranians buying or developing some nuclear weapon that they could put on one of their, say, diesel submarines. They have ship missiles on their diesel submarines that are launched from beneath the water. It's considerably more difficult to launch a ballistic missile and to do so accurately. But that's not impossible to think of, either.

And the number of years that would have to go by after one has an intermediate-range missile that can go many hundreds of miles, like the Shahab, before one can have an intercontinental ballistic missile that can go a few thousand miles is not that long. Look at the progress the North Koreans have made. Theirs blew up shortly after it was launched, but the design and overall capabilities are such that it could probably reach Hawaii or Alaska, possibly even the Pacific Northwest.

So anybody who takes that kind of attitude is just being irresponsible. I think one of the reasonable conclusions of this is that we do not have a nearly robust enough ballistic missile defense program. We should not just have a few ballistic missile defense missiles in Alaska and California focused exclusively on North Korea. We need to upgrade a lot of our Aegis cruisers and destroyers so they can protect our coasts. And we need to move promptly into space-based ballistic missile defense.

MDE: **What about the Katyusha missiles and other military supplies that Iran supplied against Israel? Iran seems to be completely obsessed with Israel and its destruction. Why?**

Mr. Woolsey: They're anti-Semitic fanatics. I have long believed that anti-Semitism is the first refuge of the really nasty scoundrel—that whether you're a Nazi, or you're Ahmadinejad, or Hamas, or the Wahabites in Saudi Arabia—the Jews' respect for law and the history of the law as part of their religion, and that being a demonstrable part of Jewish culture and life, is something that has drawn the ire of particularly totalitarians who don't believe there can be any concept of the law other than what they say it is.

Now what Ahmadinejad would say is the law isn't what he says it is; it's what Allah says it is. But he'll interpret it for you—he or his mentor. So the idea of the rule of law, what we think of the rule of law—justice—is completely alien to totalitarians. And much, I would have to admit not all, much of the history of the Jewish people has been centered around the sanctity of the notion of law. So I think the totalitarians probably hate them first and hate them the most.

MDE: **He sent a letter to the president of the United States— which was completely ignored fundamentally—in which he attempted to convert him, persuade him. And then he warned him. He used terms like, "I hear the glass shattering and the towers falling of your liberal democracy."[1] Was this a fluke, or was there more to this thing with that letter?**

Mr. Woolsey: Well, I think it echoes a warning Muhammad gave at one point to some enemy. And no, it's not a fluke. All this is tied up within his crazed belief system. He is not a cynic. He's not self-interested. He's a true fanatic. And we have a hard time in the United States these days figuring out how to deal with religiously motivated fanatics. We haven't had to do that in a long time.

If you look at the Cold War, as I mentioned a few minutes ago, the Soviets were not fanatics. They weren't even believers in Communism. They were cynics. So we didn't get into the idea of ideology all that much. Communist ideology was kind of, well, if you were really interested in them, you might take a course in undergraduate or graduate school on Marxist-Lenin theory or something. But generally speaking, nobody thought we had to get in there and refute, or undermine, or deal with Marxist-Leninist doctrine, at least in terms of dealing with the Soviets. They were cynics.

There's nothing cynical about Ahmadinejad, or Mesbah Yazdi, or members of Al Qaeda. They really believe they are implementing Allah's will in destroying the infidels, driving them out of the Middle East, and ultimately either bringing an end to the world or establishing a worldwide caliphate, depending on which set of views they have. And this makes it a lot harder for us to deal with.

Because in the United States, we're used to letting everybody believe what he wants to believe, no matter how crazy it may be. And to say that Wahabites and followers of Mesbah Yazdi and the Shiite side of Islam are crazed fanatics, but most Sufi Muslims are quite easy to work with and reasonable—which I think is true—sounds to a lot of Americans as if we're saying, "Well, the Episcopalians are nuts, but the Presbyterians are OK." We have a really hard time getting into people's religious belief if they say it's based on religion.

The question I always ask them is: if Torquemada—who killed about three hundred thousand people by burning them at the stake and stealing their money in the late fifteenth to early sixteenth century in the Spanish Inquisition—were around doing that today in some country, would you say, "Well, he says he's a representative of Christ on earth and there's no way we can challenge that, I guess"? No. You take the guy out. We cannot let these fanatics drive the future of the Middle East, much less the world.

MDE: **Israel boldly confronted Iran's proxy subcontractor in Lebanon. Then all of a sudden, something turned**

quickly. It almost looked as if they had strategically tested the numbers of bodies that America could tolerate before America was willing to be repulsed by the "innocent victims." So the United States told Israel fundamentally that they were going to have to deal with the UN. Israel was in a crisis. The troops were moving toward the Litani River. All of a sudden, everything stops. The UN becomes the new partner for Israel. Why?

Mr. Woolsey: Well, I think the reason we've partnered with Israel is because unless things go well in Iraq and turn around in Lebanon, it's the Middle East's only democracy—and it's a religiously tolerant place. Muslims practice and live freely in Israel.

And Israel, on top of that, has very much gone the extra mile to try to make peace with the Palestinians by pulling out of Lebanon, pulling out of Gaza, preparing to pull out of the West Bank. They are perfectly willing to have a reasonable two-state solution. Indeed, one was proposed. A very generous offer was made by Ehud Barak in the closing days of the Clinton administration to Arafat.

But the Palestinians, whether they're secular like Arafat or religious fanatics, have walked away from a two-state solution. And now Hamas and Hezbollah aren't even remotely interested in a two-state solution. When they say "occupied Palestine," they mean Tel Aviv. When they say that they are part of the resistance, they mean the resistance against the existence of Israel. So there's no basis for compromise with Hamas or Hezbollah.

I think the Israelis have done everything they possibly could have to work with a reasonable subset of secular and decent Palestinians. And certainly some of the Palestinian leadership, I think, would fit that description. But Hamas certainly doesn't. I don't think it's plausible for anybody to say, "If Israel just made some more concessions, they could work things out." That's not what Hamas wants. They want to destroy them.

MDE: **Then why didn't America let Israel finish the job in Lebanon?**

Mr. Woolsey: I don't know the answer to the diplomatic questions sur-
                 rounding that. I do think that the Israelis uncharacteris-
                 tically were quite hesitant and did not have a very good
                 strategy. They tried to do this all with bombing, and then
                 when that didn't work, they had a hesitant offensive. And
                 then they pulled back, and then they—two days before the
                 deadline—they went in more heavily and called up their
                 reserves and did what one would expect them to if they had
                 decided to follow this course.

                 So I can't fault too much the U.S. government becoming
                 uncertain that Israel was going to get the job done and get
                 it done in a sound way. But if they had gone in—with some
                 air support, certainly—but if they had gone in heavily, they
                 would have suffered some more casualties. But if they had
                 gone in heavily right at the beginning after Hezbollah,
                 there would have been some bitter fighting, but they would
                 have been to the Litani, I think, far before this month or so
                 of fighting that took place.

MDE: **How important is moral clarity in winning the war on
                 terrorism?**

Mr. Woolsey: I think it's quite important. We shouldn't get ourselves
                 all seized up in self-doubt. These people hate us for what
                 we are. As a cab driver in Washington DC said to me one
                 time—I was following President Clinton's speech a few
                 years ago about the things that we had done wrong in deal-
                 ing with the Middle East—he said, "These people don't hate
                 us for what we've done wrong. They hate us for what we do
                 right."

                 And he's exactly right. They hate us for making it pos-
                 sible for women to have a decent life instead of being sub-
                 servient, as they are in their cultures. They hate us for free-
                 dom of speech. They hate us for freedom of religion. They
                 hate everything about the good parts of America.

                 And a lot of people would say, "Well, they wouldn't hate
                 us if we hadn't supported Israel." But I don't see what Israel
                 could do more than it's done in trying to make peace with
                 the Palestinians. And certainly, their principal reason for
                 hating us—attacking us—was not the Iraq war. Al Qaeda
                 attacked us not only on 9/11, but also the *Cole* and East
                 African embassies and a facility in Saudi Arabia long before

the thought ever crossed George W. Bush's mind to move into Iraq.

And the Israelis and Palestinians weren't really even on bin Laden's original list. His first—well, I said the main problem is that the Americans are in Saudi Arabia. Well, after a year or so, for other reasons, we got out of Saudi Arabia, so that went away. But that didn't keep him from going on with his attacks or moving other things up the list. What bin Laden wants, I think what the Wahabites want, and certainly Ahmadinejad, is they want us out of the Middle East so they can dominate one or another of them in different ways as much as possible. And then ultimately, they want to get rid of us....

MDE: **America—does it have the will, if all diplomatic measures fail, does it have the will to have a preemptive strike upon Iran?**

Mr. Woolsey: Oh, I don't think a preemptive strike alone is going to get the job done of taking out either Iran's nuclear program or the instruments of power of the state. I think it would have to be an air campaign. This is not like 1981 when the Israelis attacked the Osirak reactor. They took out one reactor and they stopped the Iraqi nuclear program for years.

In moving against Iran, we would perhaps not have to go in on the ground, but I think we would have to have a sustained air campaign against their air defenses, their nuclear weapons program, the instruments of power of the state such as the Revolutionary Guard, and on and on. We can't just drop one set of bombs and think we're going to accomplish anything.

I hope it doesn't come to that. I hope we could bring about a regime change with lots of other types of pressure of the sort we've discussed. But if it does come to that, we shouldn't think we can just launch a strike and get anything particularly useful done.

MDE: **Can the State of Israel—if Israel reaches the point where they feel like they have no other options—are they capable of doing the job?**

| Mr. Woolsey: | It's much harder for them because if I'm right, and it requires an air campaign rather than just a strike, they are going to need a lot more tankers and air surveillance, and a lot more assets than they have. They're a superb air force, but they're a relatively small one. And Iran is a lot further away from them than Iraq. So fueling their aircraft and getting ordinates on target—one doesn't want to say they couldn't do it. The Israelis are remarkably effective soldiers and airmen. But it would be really a very difficult operation if they were trying to win a sustained air campaign. |

MDE: **You hear over and over from Iran that they believe that America isn't going to do a thing.**

Mr. Woolsey: Well, the Iranians have more reason than that to doubt our will. They seized our hostages in '79, and we had an ineffective rescue operation. And then we tied yellow ribbons around trees. In '83, through Hezbollah, they blew up our embassy and our marine barracks in Lebanon, and we left. The '80s, for various Iranian and terrorist attacks, we basically sent lawyers. We treated it as a matter of law enforcement. We prosecuted a few of them. President Reagan did attack Libya that one time.

Then in '91, President Bush, the forty-first president, had half a million troops in Iraq. We'd encouraged the Kurds and Shiites to rebel against Saddam. They were succeeding in fifteen of Iraq's eighteen provinces. And we stopped and stood aside and effectively invited Saddam to move against them and watched while they were massacred. And then we left—but not completely. We had an air-protected area in the north.

In '93, Saddam tries to kill former President Bush in Kuwait with a bomb. And President Clinton launches two-dozen cruise missiles against an Iraqi intelligence headquarters in the middle of the night so it would be empty, and has his secretary of state explain that we did it in the middle of the night so there wouldn't be anyone there. And I don't know what we had against Iraqi cleaning women and night watchmen, but I would not have called that an effective response.

In '93, we had Black Hawk Down in Mogadishu, and we left. And then the '90s, with a reserve facility in Saudi

Arabia and the East African embassies and Khobar Towers and the *Cole.* And up until 9/11, we basically did what we did in the '80s. We ran this as a law enforcement operation and tried to catch a few terrorists and put them in prison, which doesn't have much effect at all on religious fanatics who'd really just as soon either go to prison or die—best of all, die.

So if the Iranians or, for that matter, the Baathists in Iraq, look back at the history of the last quarter-of-a-century-plus, I think that it's understandable how they got themselves into the mode of thinking that we're paper tigers. The most dangerous thing in the world in dealing with these religious fanatic totalitarians is to talk big and then not follow through. Teddy Roosevelt had it right: "Speak softly and carry a big stick."

MDE: **Are we winning the war on terrorism? And if we're not winning it, what can we do to win it?**

Mr. Woolsey: John Lehman had an excellent piece recently in the *Washington Post* analyzing this question.[2] And I would say there are some huge gaps. We've done well with some aspects of law enforcement and working with our immigrant communities here in the U.S., but I don't think the reorganizations of intelligence or the FBI have done much to help us so far.

We achieved brilliant initial victories in both Afghanistan and Iraq with a minimum of military force, and then we didn't plan in either case adequately for the long haul. And we're having difficulties in Afghanistan and big difficulties in Iraq because of that: insufficient military police, insufficient nation-building, insufficient money for immediate projects to improve the water and sewage and electricity, and so forth.

And in this country, as the Lehman article points out, about 80 percent of the mosques and religious institutes are funded by the Saudis. They're Wahabists, essentially. Certainly that's not true of 80 percent of American Muslims. But the institutions are funded by the Wahabites, and they are fanatics.

So we've got a problem. We've got a serious problem. We have problems in our prisons. We've got problems with some of our Muslim chaplains in the armed forces. We have not figured out that we can't open the gates to the Wahabites and let them structure—either through the organizations they fund or their mosques or anything else—let them structure in the West what it means to be Muslim. This would be like turning over Christianity to Torquemada.

We have got to find some way to work with the hundreds of millions of good and decent Muslims in the world who don't want to be terrorists, don't even like terrorists—Sufis and others—and figure out a way to make common cause with them so they can't be frightened into silence the way the Wahabites and their allies—people like Al Qaeda—are. Now Wahabites and Al Qaeda hate each other. They kill each other. They're sort of like the Trotskyites and the Stalinists in the '20s and '30s. But their underlying views are effectively the same. They're essentially genocidal with respect to Shiites, Jews, homosexuals, and apostates, and terribly repressive of everybody else, including, in particular, women.

MDE:	**Many describe this as a potential World War. Some call it World War III or IV. Is this, in essence, a World War? And what do these individuals have in common?**
Mr. Woolsey:	Well, I borrowed a term from my friend Elliot Abrams, who wrote a piece right after 9/11 calling this war World War IV, saying that essentially World War III was the Cold War and this had some things in common with the Cold War. It was going to be very long, the ideological elements, and so forth. But I stopped talking about World War because when people hear World War, they tend to think of World War I and II—and they tend to think of Gallipoli, or Iwo Jima, or something that's quick and very, very violent. Newt Gingrich is now back pushing World War III.

There's no really great term to define this. A Global War on Terror, or Terrorism, is really, I think, a bad phrase. We didn't call World War II in the Pacific a Global War on Kamikazes. Terrorism is a tactic—it's a terrible tactic—but it's a tactic. We've got much bigger problems than terrorism. And I think we, in using a phrase like "Islamic Fascist," or "Islamic Fascists," I think the president was coming closer to an accurate description of what we're fighting. Like I say, I prefer "Islamic Nazis."

And what do they have in common? Ahmadinejad and Mesbah Yazdi on the one hand—on the Shiite side—and Wahabites and Al Qaeda on the other? What they have in common is a passionate belief that they are the instruments of Allah's will; that infidels deserve at best to be put into a subservient position and in many cases killed; that there is no reasonable justification at all. Wahabist fatwas are very clear about this in even working with, or dealing with, infidels at all—that in Ahmadinejad's and Mesbah Yazdi's case, they are working to get the Mahdi to return so they can hopefully, from their point of view, get the world to end as quickly as possible.

From the Wahabists' and Al Qaeda's point of view, they want to get the United States and all Western entities, including Israel, as they would see it, out of the Middle East. And then after they establish a caliphate—a union of mosque and state, a totalitarian structure, essentially a theocracy—to govern the Arab world, then the Muslim world, then the part of the world like Spain that was once Muslim but isn't anymore, and then finally the whole world. That's the way things should go from their point of view. So I'd say what they have in common is that they're theocratic, totalitarian, and anti-Semitic genocidal fanatics.

Appendix E

EXCERPTS FROM AN INTERVIEW WITH RETIRED ARMY GENERAL HUGH SHELTON

G en. Hugh Shelton spent thirty-seven years in the infantry, serving two combat tours in Vietnam—the first with the Fifth Special Forces Group, the second with the 173rd Airborne Brigade. He also commanded the Third Battalion, Sixtieth Infantry, in the Ninth Infantry Division at Fort Lewis, Washington; served as the Ninth Infantry Division's chief of staff for operations; commanded the First Brigade of the Eighty-second Airborne Division at Fort Bragg, North Carolina; and was the chief of staff of the Tenth Mountain Division at Fort Drum, New York.

Selected for promotion for brigadier general in 1988, Gen. Shelton served two years in the operations directorate of the Joint Staff. In 1989, he began a two-year assignment as the assistant division commander for operations of the 101st Airborne Division (Air Assault) at Fort Campbell, Kentucky, during which he participated in the liberation of Kuwait during Operation Desert Shield/Storm. After the Gulf War, Gen. Shelton was promoted to major general and assumed command of the Eighty-second Airborne Division, Fort Bragg, North Carolina. In 1993, he was promoted to lieutenant general and assumed command of the Eighteenth Airborne Corps. In 1994, during his tenure as Corps commander, Gen. Shelton led the United States Joint Task Force that restored democracy in Haiti. In March 1996, he was promoted to general and became commander in chief of the U.S. Special Operations Command.

From 1997 until 2001, he also served as the chairman to the Joint Chiefs of Staff.

MDE:	**Do you feel like we have an effective plan to win the war?**
Gen. Shelton:	I think we've got a good plan. Could it be better? Yes, it could be. I do not think that right now we are using as effectively as we could all the tools in our kitbag, so to speak, to go after the terrorists. We're using the political tools. We're using the diplomatic tools to a degree. We certainly

are using the military big-time right now. But when you look at the economic and, in particular, the informational tools, there's room for improvement—considerable room.

This is a war of ideas that we're in today. It's an ideological war as much as it is a shooting war—and I don't think our program is that effective and that we can do it alone. It would require an informational war that is carried out in concert with our friends and allies around the globe.

We do a lot of good around the world, but yet what, for the most part, gets attention in a lot of these third world countries, so to speak, undeveloped nations, are the bad things that are presented to them by the radicals and by the fundamentalists. So we really need a more effective campaign to show them the good things that are coming about as a result of not only America's efforts but also our friends and allies that are in this war with us.

MDE: **There are some that have said that we have begun to move away to some degree from our position of not negotiating with terrorists. Do you feel like in our relationship with Iran, the way that it's developing, that any of that has happened?**

Gen. Shelton: For sure. I am quite concerned that we seem to want it both ways with Iran. We have elements in Washington, as an example, who are convinced, I believe, that we need to handle them with kid gloves because there's such a large number of the Iranian people that really like the United States and would like to see the regime that's in power—the more fundamental or more radical regimes. But those are the people with guns and those are the people that are ruling the nation-state of Iran right now, and I do believe we've handled them with kid gloves.

For example, direct traces by the FBI to the Khobar Towers incident that killed and wounded hundreds of U.S. airmen—they've yet to pay a price for it. They should have. There's a linkage, I believe, to just about every terrorist activity that's gone on that can be—that you can show—goes back to Iran and their support—or their direct involvement, one of the two—with those efforts against America and against our friends and allies.

MDE: **In light of everything, where is the outrage? With the knowledge of how Iran has been tied to so many activities, terrorist activities, where is the outrage? Why are we opening doors in allowing Iranian leaders to come over and to speak at the UN, and to speak at Harvard, as Khatami did this last weekend?**

Gen. Shelton: Well, of course, when you talk about the UN, you're talking about all the nations that are members having a right to come to America and to visit the UN and participate in UN activities. And then you find more liberal universities in America that would invite the president of Iran to come over and make speeches at their university, et cetera, and I wouldn't say that that's all bad.

I'm not opposed to freedom of speech and opposing opinions, but what I am more concerned about is turning a blind eye as a government to the movements that are going on and the support of terrorism that is coming out of Iran in almost every aspect—almost every aspect—of violence that has been directed against the U.S. in recent times.

I mean, if you look back at Bosnia and Kosovo and you look at the Khobar Towers and Afghanistan, Iraq—there are ties into Iran that can't be denied, and we shouldn't let them off the hook. They are supporting terrorism to a large degree, and yet because we have a military that is committed very heavily right now, we seem to want to just kind of turn the other way, and so they get away with it.

MDE: **One could argue that the threats that Osama bin Laden made, which were happening long before 9/11, were maybe not taken as seriously as they should have been. How might you compare the threats of Osama bin Laden with that of the Iranian president, and how seriously should we be taking this?**

Gen. Shelton: I think you have to take any threat that is made against America and against America's citizens or against our friends and allies around the world—I think you've got to take them all serious. I think you treat them both the same and you deal with both of them the same. Now I would tell you that, you know, before 9/11, there was a considerable effort made to go after Osama bin Laden, to capture or kill—and I emphasize the word *kill*—this individual because of the ills that he had already perpetrated against America and against our men and women and against our warships, et cetera.

But in the same breath, I'd have to tell you the guy's pretty good at avoiding them. He does all the right things. He knows how to survive. He's a survivor, and it's because he does what he has to do in order to survive. The result of that is he's not nearly as effective as he would have been, but still, our efforts have to be, I think, to continue to go after him and all of his lieutenants—to more or less chop the head off of the snake and that outfit. Al Qaeda is a snake.

MDE: **James Woolsey has said that we've treated the war on terrorism to some degree over the years as more of a law enforcement problem. You know, what's your opinion of that?**

Gen. Shelton: Well, I think probably that analogy to law enforcement is the fact that they're not a good military target. They are more like a law enforcement target. Fighting terrorism is more akin to fighting organized crime. You want to decapitate them for sure. You want to deny them their sanctuaries for sure. But you also want to go after their economics, their base of support. You want to do everything politically and diplomatically that you can.

Unlike a military organization, they don't have tanks and airplanes and infrastructure that you can attack and bomb and whatever. So you've got to go after individuals, and in that regard it's more like fighting crime than it is going after military. But again, the military is an integral piece of it, and in support of the FBI or in support of the CIA, it's a very potent piece of it—but it's only a piece and, to some degree, a relatively small piece....

MDE: **In our current confrontation with Iran, who would you really say at this point is winning?**

Gen. Shelton: You know, the confrontation with Iran, I think to some degree, you'd have to say, since there is no open conflict between the two nations, that the Iranians are getting away with a lot more than they should be allowed to get away with. Their continuous pursuit of a nuclear weapon even in the face of an international community telling them to stop, their resistance to do that, their continuous support of terrorism as the world's largest exporter of terrorism resources, advisors, et cetera, tells me that they're getting away with a lot that they should not be getting away with, and therefore I have to put them in a "win column" because they're doing a lot more than they should be allowed to do against the international community and against America....

MDE: **You know, as far as talking about whether or not Iran is winning or losing in this confrontation, what do you think that their potential—what their mentality is or opinion—regarding who's winning or losing?**

Gen. Shelton: I'd say that's a good question. It's a tough question. I think from the Iranian standpoint right now in their minds, they think they're winning, and I think they feel like they're winning because they have been able to get away with attacks on Khobar Towers. They've been able to get away with support of the radicals and fundamentalists without—you know, through both resources as well as through advisors—without having their hand called at it.

They have continued to defy the UN as they pursue nuclear power, and they keep getting warnings, and it's somewhat reminiscent of the warnings that the Taliban were getting to stop supporting Al Qaeda or they were going to pay the price. But they didn't stop until 9/11, and we went in and took out the Taliban. So I think Iran is in the same seat right now, and in their minds they're doing very well.

MDE: **I think there are examples of where we have gone in and addressed it fully and completely, like taking out the Taliban. You can possibly come up with other examples where we have stepped out of the situation and maybe didn't respond as fully. Do you feel like Iran has a reason to believe that America doesn't have the will to act and to truly take military action against them?**

Gen. Shelton: Well, if I were sitting in Iran right now with my Iranian hat on and I had defied America, if I had defied the UN in my pursuit of a nuclear weapon—nuclear power for sure; potentially a nuclear weapon—if I had continued to provide the resources, the wherewithal, for a lot of the activities being directed against America around the world and was not having my hand called at it, I would think that I'm doing pretty well. I'm walking that fine line the way I've stayed just outside enough to, offering enough provocation to America to come at me directly, and yet I'm getting away with an awful lot in the process and I'm damaging, probably, their self-esteem. But I'm damaging their reputation for sure.

MDE: **When you look at the various alternatives that we have in relationship to Iran, compare the ease or difficulty with which we can potentially do an invasion versus actually make peace. You know, which do you think is potentially the easier road? Do you think that it's impossible to make peace, or do you think the invasion is sort of a hopeless route as well? Or—you know, compare the two.**

Gen. Shelton: I think when you look at Iran, you have to put it in the context of how would you go about either one. How would you go about waging war against them? How would you go about pursuing peace with the greatest degree of leverage in your favor? And in my opinion, that is in an international environment. It is either through a coalition of United Nations partners or United Nations efforts or a coalition of European partners that you pursue peace.

And certainly if you want to—if you are going to go in and take out their nuclear capability—if it's going to become an outright shooting war between Iran and whoever starts the invasion—it's in America's best interest to use the international community that is also being rebuffed by the Iranians, not just America, and form a coalition. Use those political and diplomatic tools that I talked about. Get that coalition put together just like we did in Desert Storm—Desert Shield/Desert Storm—and use that coalition either to bring pressure against them to settle peacefully and accept a UN supervision of their nuclear development, or use them to go in and take it and do whatever you feel you need to do militarily that the international community feels is necessary.

MDE: **If we actually do go in after Ahmadinejad, what would the first strike look like? What steps might actually have to be taken?**

Gen. Shelton: You know, I would not want to speculate on that. I am too knowledgeable, you might say, of what some of the plans for dealing with the Iranians are if we had to deal with them—in waging war. But I would only say that I would hope that unlike some of the plans that we've got, that for the most part have been operational plans that have been developed by America, that we would take the time to develop those same types of plans with partners, with a coalition. And I think, needless to say, it should be overwhelming. It should be fast and with a follow-up plan that says, "Here's how we're going to deal with it in Phase 4," so to speak, unlike what we did when we went into Iraq.

MDE: **Can you speak to the advantages or disadvantages of pursuing a regime change?**

Gen. Shelton: I don't think there's any question that if it came down to the decision that we're going to go into Iran and we're going to have a regime change, hopefully, we'd be able to do that in an international—with an international force. I think that's extremely important because of the perception throughout the Middle East that America is there just for the oil. We're not there just for the oil, as all of us know. We're there to try to provide a peaceful and stable environment in a part of the world in vital national interest to the United States.

And so if you've elected to go into Iran, you want to do it as part of an international force. After all, they're defying the international community now with their nuclear program—not just America but the international—the UN—and, therefore, it should be the UN that makes that decision. And then in terms of what you're going to do once you go in, I think you're going to replace the regime. They've got to come out. They've been uncooperative. They have resulted in you having to go to war.

So consequently, you need to think through right up-front, who have we got? Who's in the wings? Who are the moderates in the country right now that you could then reach out to once you had removed that regime—and re-establish them as the central government and a plan to follow on—to help them get back on their feet with the new leadership in that country?

Needless to say, it's always easier to get in than it is to get out. We've learned that time and time again. But it's a lot easier to get out if you've got a good plan going in for transitioning into the nation-building aspect of it, and from that a withdrawal plan to pull all of your forces out or remain— a small contingent that stays as part of an international force until the new government is fully stood up and ready to maintain peace and security themselves.

MDE: **With our open borders and ports, we have all kinds of cargo packages arriving in our ports every month. How serious is the threat of a dirty bomb, and then what kind of space would even be required for the components needed to assemble a dirty bomb?**

Gen. Shelton: Well, when you look at, you know, the same rights, privileges, and freedoms that make America the envy of the world in terms of the freedoms we enjoy as individuals are also, in the eyes of the Al Qaedas of the world—the terrorists—our greatest threat, our greatest weakness. It is the porous borders that we have, and no matter how hard we try to protect them, if you look at the miles and miles of Canadian border or even our own abilities to try to stop the infiltration along the southwest border, it's just—it's hard.

And therefore, I say it's not a matter of when we're attacked—I mean not a matter of if—it's a matter of when. And anyone that really puts their mind to it and has time on their side and has the resources can eventually get the stuff where they need it in the United States to carry out an attack. What's our greatest defense? Our greatest defense is the intelligence community, and it has to be done on a worldwide basis. It is tips that you pick up that are coming out of Germany or just recently out of the United Kingdom, or coming out of Australia.

I mean, if you look down in Indonesia, the fourth largest nation in the world, the largest Muslim nation in the world, it's in the process of disintegrating. It's an ideal breeding ground for terrorism, and it could be the next training ground for Al Qaeda. Well, just because it's in Indonesia doesn't mean it can't come here and attack New York City or Los Angeles or whatever. So intelligence is how we're going to do it, and that's going to have to be an international effort, not just a United States effort. And if we're good at it, if we really devote the attention that we need to and the resources, I think that's our best defense against terrorism....

MDE: **How do you think that the terrorists are using the media against us?**

Gen. Shelton: Well, in a war of ideas—in informational warfare—the media is a powerful tool, and I think that what we find here is the terrorists unfortunately are a lot more effective in some cases of using that to their advantage than we are using it to ours. A typical example is you have an *Al Jazeera* that is propagating their propaganda throughout the Middle East, and yet our ability to get in as an international community—not just the United States, but everyone—to show all the good things that are happening in a lot of these countries—whether it's Iraq and the numerous schools we've rebuilt, or the number of hospitals that have been reopened.

You just got to bombard them with this stuff, and some people would call it propaganda. It's not propaganda; it's information. And it's getting the right information back out to the people that need it, and those are people that are making the decision as to whether or not they're going to believe what the radicals are saying or if they're going to believe what their own eyes are telling them—that things are getting better. You know, things are better in their life today than they were under Saddam Hussein—or under whomever. We can do a lot better, and it needs to be a really focused effort for the United States to really win this war of ideas.

MDE: **What would you say are the basic triggers that could prompt military action against Iran?**

Gen. Shelton: Well, certainly, when it comes to Iran, I think any kind of an overt military action against America—whether it was shooting one of our warplanes or transport planes or shooting down, you know, sinking one of our warships, or just an overt action of any type against us. And I would like to think that any type of a terrorist attack that immediately had, you know, a smoking gun associated with it, that Iran would pay one heck of a price by our own national retaliatory policy against terrorists.

So that's what should happen. I think everyone understands that. That's a policy everyone understands. If you aid, support, help, or in any other way assist a terrorist outfit and your fingerprints are on it, you're going to be treated just like a terrorist yourself—and I think the Iranians are smart enough to understand that as well.

MDE: **Iran seems to have succeeded in utilizing four thousand missiles in its recent attack from Lebanon into Israel. They have boasted that they've got fifty-two thousand suicide bombers ready to attack the West, to go into America. How realistic is a scenario like that?**

Gen. Shelton: Well, I would not put anything past Iran as the world's largest supporter of terrorism, from having a large number of missiles, a large number of all types of chemical or biological weapons that they could have at their disposal. I mean, here's an outfit that sends missile technology that is illegal by the UN standards to the North Koreans, another member of the axis of evil. They'll do about anything where they think it's in their best interest or against America or our closest allies.

And so, you know, that's part of the war of ideas and, you know, it tends to make you fear someone. You think fifty-two thousand suicide bombers. You know, it's a great psychological weapon. I'll turn them loose on you if you—you know.

Well, you know, get ready. We got something even bigger than fifty-two suicide bombers. It's like someone who backs away because the Chinese have got 1.3 billion in population. You know, we say, well, we won't stand up to them because they're so big. We have a lot going for us in terms of our will to fight and the technology that we have, and we've got a heck of a lot of good allies around the world that, when push comes to shove, will show up and be there by our side.

MDE: **But nevertheless, you do feel like the threat of those kinds of things being thrown out has to be taken seriously?**

Gen. Shelton: When the president of a nation stands up and boasts that he's going to eliminate another nation from the face of the earth—when he boasts that he has large numbers of suicide bombers—when he talks about his missile technology or what he would plan to do to hurt other nations—I think that has to be taken very seriously, not only by America, but by the United Nations and our other allies and friends as well.

MDE: **Benjamin Netanyahu said that the issues with the Cold War, for example, are so much different than those today and the way we are having to deal with other countries like Iran. Can you compare the way that we were maybe able to deter the Soviets with the way that we're having to address Iran? You know, I think essentially the ideology of the Soviets was pretty well dead by the mid-'50s, and so I think that our ability to negotiate with them was maybe a little bit different. Can you compare the two?**

Gen. Shelton: Well, I think that when you look at the Cold War versus the post–Cold War, the Cold War was considerably simpler. The reason I say that is because here you had two superpowers, the United States and Russia, which had the Soviet Union and all of its partners in the Warsaw Pact countries, et cetera, lined up against the United Nations and all of its partners. And no one stepped out of line without checking with the leader—and America being the leader of the free world; Russia being the leader—and when that wall came down and all those nations broke away from the Russians, it became a much more complicated world because you no longer had just the two superpowers talking.

You had independent actors now doing their thing and no one kind of a reign in power, and then you saw the outbreak of the ethnic, religious, and tribal wars around the world. And when you look at America, our commitment

of forces went up over 300 percent in the ten years following the wall coming down than it had been in the previous
twenty-five years. It's just a phenomenal number of things
that started to happen when this big coalition on each side
went away, and suddenly hatred in all these tribes and, you
know, it started breaking out.

And so it is more complicated in today's world for sure,
and we have to build new coalitions, and we have to build
new partnerships, and in some cases they're small groups
that are united against specific threats. In others, they can
be large like against the Iranian nuclear threat. There could
be a rather large—like the United Nations coalition against
the Iranians—but it is considerably more complicated, for
sure.

MDE: **What would you consider our greatest obstacles in
establishing the coalition that we need?**

Gen. Shelton: I think today the biggest obstacle that America has is
the fact that we went into Iraq for the most part alone.
Consequently, a lot of people are seeing the commitments
that we've had to make for that—both in terms of troops
as well as our national resources—and they're starting to
question whether or not they want to become a part of
anything like that—and they, you know, start to drain their
economy or start to deploy. A lot of these countries have
really reduced the size of their militaries as a result of the
Cold War going away, to where they have very little left
and not a lot of forces to contribute to major war-fighting
efforts.

And so I believe today that probably there's a lot of resistance to joining any kind of a coalition that might get them
involved in something like we're involved in, in Iraq—and
that's something we're going to have to overcome. We're
going to have to work hard at it to convince all of them
again that, you know, you've got to stand for what's right,
and it may mean sacrifice by your people. It may mean
using a military that's relatively small and giving them
some fatigue like our armed forces are experiencing right
now. But in the end, it's doing what's right for peace and
security throughout the world—not just worrying about
their own little piece of it.

MDE: **Let's talk about Israel for a moment. If Israel were to notify the United States that they were going to take a preemptive strike on Iran—first of all, do you think that they would be able to effectively accomplish that, and then, second, what do you think the U.S. response would be?**

Gen. Shelton: That's a hypothetical question for which I don't even have a good hypothetical answer. First of all, I'm not sure the Israelis would notify us if they were getting ready to take a preemptive strike, and I think there's precedent for that— and, secondly, I'm not sure what they'd expect out of us if they elected to do that. That's a pretty bold move and, you know, I would go back to my original point that any action taken against the Iranians right now should only be taken after every effort had been made to build an international coalition to go after the Iranians.

I don't think there's any nation out there that wants to see Iran running around with nuclear weapons, particularly given the importance of the Middle East region to the rest of the world, and if we can't build a coalition to protect against or to provide for greater peace and stability in the Middle East now—particularly with a potential nuclear threat that could be used against any of the Middle East countries out there—we'll never be able to build one. And so that should be the first attempt—and I think the Israelis understand that as well. I would think that would be a last resort. Only after all else had failed would they ever consider going in with a preemptive strike.

MDE: **In your opinion, if Iran was actually able to obtain a nuclear weapon, do you think that they're insane enough to use it on us or on Israel?**

Gen. Shelton: I think with the Iranians, you know, you never know what to expect from a madman. I mean, who would have ever anticipated that Saddam Hussein, idiot that he was, would ever invade Kuwait and think he could get away with it when the United States already had fifty thousand troops in the area and had been pretty clear in its intention to make sure that that remained a peaceful and secure, stable environment?

So guys like the North Korean leader and the Iranian president—I don't think you can ever take for granted anything with it. I don't think you can assume they're necessarily logical. I think in terms of using a nuclear weapon, they'd give that a lot of long and hard thought because they know what the consequences could turn out to be—and that could be that the nation of Iran was nothing more than a glass factory—and so they have to take that into consideration whether or not it's worth it.

MDE: **In your opinion, which do you feel is the greater threat to the United States—Iran or North Korea?**

Gen. Shelton: Well, I don't think you can treat it either/or. I think you've got to assume both of them are threats to the United States. You've got Kim Jong-il [chairman of the National Defense Committee of North Korea] sitting there with basically a quarter of a million Americans—our military service members, our foreign service people, our Americans that live in Korea—that if he decided he wanted to take over South Korea poses a significant threat to America and our ability to stop him.

On the other hand, the Iranians with their threats and their nuclear weapons potential capability—I think we got to deal with both of them almost as equal threats. One is more stable right now—although he's far from having a stable mind, in my opinion: the North Korean.

But on the other hand, you've got the Iranian president who's being almost confrontational today with America, and so I think both of them are threats and have to be treated accordingly. You have to make sure that you've got the military forces to deal with both of these threats, should the requirement be there.

MDE: **OK. One could argue that you're one of the most knowledgeable men on U.S. security right now. You know, rather than maybe the $50,000 question, you know, it's the 50,000 lives question. How would you really say that we have to take action right now in creating the most robust plan possible to win the war on terror?**

Gen. Shelton: Well, I think, first and foremost, we have to recognize, as President Bush has, I believe, that this is a global war that we're facing. It is a war that we've got to win. It is a war that we can win as we demonstrated back in the '70s when we had an outfit known as the Abu Nidal Organization headed up by Abu Nidal—specifically threatening Americans all over the world and carrying out those plans of killing Americans—and we put our resources to it and we leaned into it and now that's an extinct organization, and it was a few years after we went after it.

Today's threat is very similar—except even greater—because of 9/11, because of the World Trade Center, we have a chance to build this international coalition and it doesn't have to be all America's resources that are going after it. It's the world's resources that we can turn against the terrorist threat, and I believe that's what we have to do and devote whatever resources are necessary to make sure that our intelligence agencies—that our counterterrorism forces—are trained and ready and leaning into it, and that priority remains fixed, in spite of all the other challenges that we have around the world—and we have significant other challenges. We've talked about a few like North Korea, Iran, and potential developments with China, if that doesn't turn out the way we'd all like for it to turn out.

MDE: **Can you address the danger or the impact of talking big but not following through?**

Gen. Shelton: Well, I think anyone has to be concerned that if you talk big, if you make it sound like you're going to go after, for example, terrorists groups and after nation-states, and that you don't follow through—whenever you don't do that, you embolden the terrorists. It takes away from that threat that you gave them. A good example is if we knew that Iran attacked Khobar Towers—and we do—why did they not pay a big price for that? That emboldens terrorists.

If you know that Al Qaeda attacked the USS *Cole*, one of our warships, and almost sank it, why did we wait till 9/11 to go after the Taliban? You have to go after them, and you have to go after them the minute that you can have a definitive link and can show the rest of the world that you've got the smoking gun.

Now I think, for example, after 9/11, to have attacked Saddam because he was a bad guy and he was shooting at us all the time and we wanted him out of there—we didn't have the smoking gun. There was nothing that linked Saddam to terrorism in the true sense of the word, nothing that said he was a part of the Al Qaeda organization or was supporting them. It just wasn't there.

So not going after him under that pretext of the World Trade Center was also the right decision. So you have to make sure that you have that definitive proof, but once you get it, whether it's the day after or whether it's two years, three years later—the outfit that does it to you and that kills your citizens has got to pay a price—and it's going to be a lot worse than what they did to you.

Appendix F

EXCERPTS FROM AN INTERVIEW WITH
RETIRED U.S. NAVY CAPTAIN CHARLES NASH

Capt. Charles Nash retired from the navy in 1998 after serving more than twenty-five years as a pilot. During that time he accumulated more than 4,300 hours of flight time and 965 carrier landings. During his time in the service, Nash served as head of the Strike/Anti-Surface Unit Warfare and Air to Air/Strike Support sections on the staff of the Chief of Naval Operations in the Pentagon; executive assistant to the deputy commander in chief, U.S. Naval Forces Europe, London, Great Britain; commanding officer, Strike Fighter Squadron 137; and operations officer, Commander Carrier Airwing Thirteen.

Nash is founder and president of Emerging Technologies International, Inc., and also serves as a military analyst for FOX News.

MDE: **Is America at war?**

Capt. Nash: I think the American military is at war. I don't think the entirety of the American government [is at war], and the reason why I can say that is in my trip to Baghdad I spoke with U.S. military leadership over there. They could really use the help of the Treasury Department, the Agriculture Department, [and others] to help [create]...the ministries that they need to run a successful government. So by and large I would say the Department of Defense is at war, the Central Intelligence Agency and some of our other intelligence agencies are at war—supporting the military— but the vast majority of the American people are not at war. I don't believe the vast majority of the federal government is even at war.

MDE: **Why?**

Capt. Nash: I think because when people think of the war they think of Iraq only, or Iraq and Afghanistan [at best]. What they don't come to grips with is that those are battles in a real war—and the real war is against Islamic Fascism. The president was very clear on that matter. I think up until this point we've tended to see each individual battle as [a war]—the war in Afghanistan, the war in Iraq—but they're not. We would more accurately say the current *battle* in Afghanistan, and the *battle* in Iraq.

MDE: **You use the term "Islamofascism." Please explain.**

Capt. Nash: Islamofascism is a sliver of belief that is driven by a twisted version of religion where you cherry-pick certain parts of a religion, [then] you magnify those way out of proportion so that you have a tremendously unbalanced view. You then take people who, by and large, are disaffected from their society, have grievances against the government or the situation in their country, and then you tell them that it's not really their fault that they live that way—it's really the fault of the Jews and the Americans. Therefore, what you need to do to correct all these ills is not fix your own society; it's to go kill them.

The hard part about dealing with this as we have up until this point is that many people think of a war as a war for land or war for wealth, when the fact of the matter is these people do not want what we have—they just don't want us to have it. The option that they're presenting is to either do it their way or they kill us.

In World War II, we negotiated from one point: unconditional surrender. Essentially that's what they're telling us. This is a war, and the only [acceptable] outcome is unconditional surrender. So we have to want our way of life more than they want us to live under theirs, and if we don't, we're in for a very long and painful trip.

MDE: **In 1979, Iran made the decision they were going to humiliate the United States with 444 days of hostage crisis that ended with President Carter losing his second term. That seems quite obvious because they released the hostages the day of the inauguration of Ronald Reagan. With the fall midterm elections coming up, do you think that Iran is looking at the polls? And do you think that they're intending to use their insurgent activities and improvised explosive devices in Iraq to try to take Congress away from the president and the Republicans?**

Capt. Nash: I believe that the Iranians are a very politically aware group of folks—as are the folks that are running Al Qaeda, who are the Sunni extremists. All of these people at the top leadership of these countries and these organizations understand that the center of gravity in the war against them is the will of the American people to fight. Right now, you have a president in George W. Bush who is saying, "We are not going to back away from this fight. We're staying in Afghanistan until we fix this. We're staying in Iraq until we fix this."

[These groups are] trying to shake the will of the American people to sustain that effort, because if we back away from Iraq and Afghanistan there will be such a vacuum that they will implode and our grandchildren will be fighting this war as we never have.

MDE: **So if, in fact, they're trying to humiliate the president, they're trying to prove that he was wrong in Iraq—if they achieve that objective, what condition is this country going to be in with the president?**

Capt. Nash: I'm concerned that if the House flips in November of 2006 that more of this short-term political gamesmanship will occur, and that we will have totally stalemate in Washington with the House locked down, the Senate not able to sway because of thin majority there, and everyone just kind of holding their breath until the 2008 elections. If we weren't seeing such partisanship when the country is at war, I wouldn't be concerned. But I am seeing a side of partisanship that works for itself and not in the best interest of the country, and it's very troublesome.

MDE: **On *60 Minutes,* Ahmadinejad inferred that the president was in trouble. He said he had been noticing his dropping popularity in the polls. Do you believe that Iran is accelerating this war for the fall to try to intentionally affect the polls?**

Capt. Nash: I believe the Iranians, Al Qaeda, and a lot of the other terrorists groups have been significantly better in their information operations than we have. They are very good at their form of getting out the story, and the story that they're getting out is trying to shake the will of the

American people. It's propaganda. Do I think it's an orchestrated campaign working [toward] the fall elections? I think they are politically aware and astute enough to make such a move—yes.

It's very much like a major coffee chain in this country. Before that major coffee chain took off and became a household word, designer coffee shops in this country really didn't exist. They were few and far between. Everyone went to the doughnut shop, the little corner stores, or somewhere like that to get a cup of coffee. But once this nationally known chain became popular, all these mom-and-pop designer coffee shops starting popping up all over the place.

I liken that very much to the success of the 1979 Islamic revolution in spurring these groups [of] Islamic fundamentalists that have popped up all over the place—not necessarily with direct support, logistics, and guidance from Iran. It was the success of the big one that led the little ones to realize there was a market.

That's why when I traced things back [and ask], "Where is that front of Islamic revolution? Where is the front for Islamic radicalism?" It is coming out of Shia, Iran, and it started in 1979 when they took our embassy down. They have been fighting us and have been at war with us ever since. We have yet to truly realize the magnitude of that.

We are at war. We have been at war. We've been denying it through several administrations. Now here we are. We are where we are, and if we don't get serious about this soon, they're going to have nukes, and when they have nuclear weapons, a lot of options that we have today are going to evaporate. It's like we used to say in the navy: "Bad news does not get better with age."

MDE: **If the United States goes to war, what exactly could the United States do militarily? What are the steps we would need to take to stop Iran's nuclear program?**

Capt. Nash: The U.S. has an overwhelming military force. We are the strongest power on the planet right now. To stop the nuclear program in Iran would call for, in some cases, potentially a fairly significant loss of life because the Iranians—like their Hezbollah puppets—have built a lot of their nuclear research infrastructure underneath civilian neighborhoods. Now their reactor sites like Natanz and several of the other major nuclear installations are pretty much out in the open, but the research facilities are, unfortunately, literally under civilian neighborhoods. So to go out and blow up the reactors or take out the key elements, and to do what they call "nodal targeting"—take out the key points—that could be done very easily.

But that's only [taking out] one part—the ability for the Iranians to produce their own nuclear warheads. There are some observers who believe that the Iranians already have nuclear warheads, that they got them from China, Pakistan, or some of the former Soviet Union.

You don't take on Iranians directly with military force, but do it by air—that's what the Israelis did in Lebanon, tried to do it by air. What we're finding out is a lesson relearned, which is, if you're going to take land and you're going to try to win, that war is about people and you can't do it neatly. It takes people on the ground going in and saying there's a new sheriff in town. Until you're willing to do that—until you have the political will to do that—all you do is poke and prod. A savvy enemy like the Iranians will be very quick to pick that up.

MDE: **Where's the funding for terrorists coming from?**

Capt. Nash: It's being funded through Iran mostly on the Shia side, and it's coming from $75 a barrel for oil. Iran is a major oil producer, and their coffers are full right now. They're taking that money and they're using it to subsidize their political activities. They have, in fact, incorporated Hezbollah as part of their foreign policy. It's actually run through the Islamic revolutionary Guard Corp.

[They are also] funding groups that they hope one day will rise to the status of Hezbollah. They're at work in Africa and all over the rest of the world. In the Islamic world, they're trying to create the funding and the nurturing for these groups so that they'll grow.

Even the Arabs are starting to pay attention to this now, because the last time the Persian Empire stretched from modern-day Iran to modern-day Lebanon was in the seventh century. You have a lot of the existing regimes on the southern part of the Gulf starting all the way over in Pakistan and Indonesia and running west to Morocco [that are all Sunni]—that's the Sunni belt. And if there's only one thing that the Sunni extremists hate more than Jews and Christians, that's Shia—because they consider them the ultimate blasphemers. When you get into the differences between Al Qaeda and Hezbollah, you see the difference between Sunni extremists and the Shia extremists. You would think they would be fighting each other when in fact what you're seeing is Iran [Shia] supporting Hamas [Sunni] and supporting Al Qaeda [Sunni Wahabist] by giving them refuge from Afghanistan, as well as supporting [Hezbollah and other] Shia terrorists. This is more about winning a war, and they'll sort their grievances out later. Right now they have a common enemy, and that's Western civilization.

MDE: **If Iran went nuclear as a Shia state, would it precipitate a nuclear arms race among the Sunni states with Russia?**

Capt. Nash: I don't know if the Russians would be the supplier, but if Iranians were to have nuclear weapons capability, the Saudis would want it. Everybody along that Sunni belt—especially those right around Iran and within missile range of Iran—would want nuclear weapons. When you think of the instability of that region, then arm people with nuclear weapons, then throw in one of the most troubling aspects of the current Iranian regime—which is this Shia Twelvers or apocalyptic vision of the return in the Twelfth Imam—it's more than scary. It's something that has to be dealt with before they get those nuclear weapons.

MDE: **How much time do we have?**

Capt. Nash: That depends on who you talk to. If you talk to our Central Intelligence Agency, I think they are on record as saying about ten years. If you talk to the Russians, there are reports in the press where the Russians say they are eight months to a year [away]—and the Russians should know because they've been supplying and working with the Iranians. The CIA has missed a couple of rather large things in our recent past, so I don't know how good CIA intelligence is. I don't know how good our "on-the-ground" intelligence in Iran is, even though we've been at war with Iran since 1979. I don't know the status of our intelligence networks, but I'm afraid that it's probably not as good as we would like.

The threat from a nuclear Iran is that their nuclear weapons [would be] insulated from conventional attack if they can reach interests of the United States with nuclear weapons. In other words, with nuclear weapons they can shield their current way of doing business. They could step up direct support for terrorism around the world—be much more blatant about it than they are now—knowing that if they were ever struck, they would launch nukes [against U.S. allies].

So now, all the options are off the table except doing a massive preemptive strike on Iran to try to avoid that. That's the problem with this. Once they get nukes, the whole calculus changes—not just in the region—but they're also working on their rocket programs, their missile programs, and they're working on those harder almost than they are on their nuclear program, because they know once they get the range of those missiles [where they want it], then they can reach out and touch anybody once they put nuclear warheads on those missiles. [Then] they're not going to be worried about people coming after them to stop them from flipping the world upside down with terrorism.

MDE:	**Does this threaten Israel—our greatest allies in the fight against terrorism—or what we're doing in the war against terrorism?**
Capt. Nash:	I think Israel is definitely an ally in fighting terrorism. I don't know whether the UK or Israel would rank as our top—personally I think it's the UK because of the steps that the United Kingdom has taken in the war on terrorism and the support against the odds of world opinion. The rest of the world has pretty much cowered from this threat. They're afraid of it. They have large, indigenous populations of immigrant Muslim communities. They have not acclimated them well—and because of that you wind up with these conclaves of an immigrant population that is not being assimilated. That's a difference we've seen here in the United States. People who come to the United States

are assimilated into the culture and they get along and we have tolerance.

In a lot of European countries are very homogenous societies—you know, France, Belgium, Germany. They're trying to keep peace at home. They're playing to domestic politics as well as international politics.

The Israelis are unallied because they're personally threatened. They're surrounded, and you've got the head of the Iranian government publicly stating on multiple occasions that we need to wipe Israel off the map. So they're in the war on terrorism and have been in the war on terrorism because they've been at ground zero up until this point. Well that ground zero changed on 9/11, and it actually changed back in the 1980s when our embassies [in Africa] were being bombed, and when our embassy in Beirut was taken down. When we had U.S. people captured, held prisoner, and then executed by Iranian-backed terrorists organizations in Beirut. This has been going on for a long time. So, yes, we're at war. The UK is our best ally, and the Israelis are in it [as well].

MDE: **Talk to me about Iran's involvement in Iraq. Are they killing American soldiers?**

Capt. Nash: As U.S. forces swept north from Kuwait up the Mesopotamia and into Baghdad, Iranian intelligence was flooding operatives into southeastern Iraq. So right behind as our forces went up, their forces were coming in. They set themselves up like nongovernmental organizations providing food, medical supplies, blankets, [and medical] care when actually they were Iranian intelligence organizations. They fell right in on a lot of the Shia mosques. They had supporters in there undercover for some time, and they started taking over a lot of the communities in southern Iraq. What followed—and we have definite proof of this, because we have captured people in Iraq that have had Iranian training—the Iraqis have captured Iranian fighters, and we've captured a lot of Iranian weapons.

When I was in Baghdad, I actually held one of those explosive devices—IEDs—in my hand. At the time it was the latest threat—a brand-new generation. It actually forms a projectile when it blows up that pierces armor plate. You have to manufacture these things. It's not rocket science, but somebody has to know how to do it to make them effective.

Iranians have been doing that. We know they've been doing that. The Iraqi defense minister has called Iran "the number one threat to Iraq," because he can look down and see that is what's happening.

On one side you had the Iraqi Shia, who are Arab, across a political border from the Iranian Shia, who are Persian. The difference—even though they are in a similar religion and ethnicity—was a barrier. It is not just the political border.

But [at the same time] there was family that was going back and forth. In fact, there were a lot of the Arab Shia who fled Iraq and went to Iran because they were being persecuted by Saddam Hussein—so these communities have some tie-ins.

On either side of the border you had disaffected Diaspora willing to go back and fight the government from which they came. You had Iranians in the MEK [People's Mujahedin of Iran] willing to do that in Iran, and you had Iraqis in Iran willing to go back and fight in Iraq.

If Iran can get control of the southern oil fields in Iraq, this is more than just uniting the Shia. This is more than an Adolf Hitler view of reuniting the German people. Now that we've been in Iraq and we've done the mineral exploration, our forces are convinced that Iraq—not Saudi Arabia—has the largest oil resource on the planet. The vast majority of those oil reserves are in the Ramallah field, which is in the southeast part of Iraq. In other words, it's right under the Shia territory. So the Iranians are looking at uniting Shia and becoming the world's largest holder of oil. Then add being on the border of Kuwait and Saudi Arabia—that's a powerful inducement for them.

MDE: **Syria obviously has an agreement now with Iran. They are saying that there's even talk about the possibility of a future Syria having the Sunni area of Iraq.**

Capt. Nash: One of the biggest problems that we face right now is keeping Iraq together. There are three main divisions. The vast majority of the population—about 60 percent—is Shia, and they're in the south. They're sitting on all that oil—and they're sitting on some of the most beautiful agricultural land in the world.

You have the Kurds up in the north, a smaller percentage of the population, we'll say 5 to 10 percent—then you have to throw in a lot of other races, but a very small portion—they're all up in the north. Plenty of rainfall, good land, and that's where the rest of the oil is. So you have about 10 to 15 percent of Iraq's known reserves up in the north. The key city there is the refining and drilling city of Kirkuk. Kirkuk is just outside the area that belongs to the Kurds, but the Kurds claim that city. The rest of the neighbors, Iran, Syria, and Turkey, loathe seeing the Kurds get control of Kirkuk, because if they do, they will then have the economic engine that could sustain and empower a free Kurdistan.

And if you look at the Kurdish minorities in Syria, Turkey, and Iran, they're afraid that they would then, as they have in the past, claim a greater Kurdistan. The neighbors in that northern reach would not want to see an independent Kurdistan. The Shia in the south are not necessarily overjoyed with the fact that they too could fall under this religious monocracy in Tehran. They're scared to death of that—they really are.

The Sunnis [are] the other 30 percent of the population. They don't have oil, and they're not sitting on great agricultural land. What have they got? Look at the courses of the Tigris and the Euphrates Rivers. They flow through Sunni territory. They've got all the water. And it flows down into the southern part.

So when you look at this—and our people have—we've sent university agricultural experts over to Iraq to look at the soil samples, and they're convinced that Iraq doesn't need to pump a drop of oil to be a rich nation because they've got more water than anywhere else in the region. They could be the breadbasket [of the entire region]. So when the neighbors look at Iraq, they not only see chaos, they also see opportunity. The Iranians see the oil, the neighbors see keeping the Kurds down, and the Syrians see access to all that water in [and around] Baghdad.

That's why, to keep the neighbors from preying upon the carcass of Iraq, the Iraqis have to realize that their future lies in a sustainable political body called Iraq—as a unified country with defensible borders.

MDE: **Are we safer in America because of the war in Iraq?**

Capt. Nash: We are safer in America than we were before, but I think 9/11 should have disabused everyone of this notion of "Fortress America." The bad guys came once. There are probably sleeper cells here in this country, right now, and they're going to keep coming.

You see, that's just it. That's the thing we have to get in our heads. They are at war with us. They don't want to negotiate. They're trying to kill us. Pretty soon we're going to wake up to that fact—and we're going to realize that trying to get into the Middle East and set up shop, if you will, with a democracy—or at least a participatory government—to try to change that mind-set [and] change those basic conditions [is] an idea very far ahead of it's time.

MDE: **Is this World War III?**

Capt. Nash: I think it is World War III, and it's not World War III—not in the traditional sense that we think of with World War I and World War II, where you had uniformed armies fighting each other. We're going to see more and more of these state-sponsored but stateless terrorists group. If you look at Hezbollah—it's not just in Al Qaeda—when you look at Hezbollah, you see a terrorist group that has metastasized and actually taken on attributes of a fully trained army. Very properly provisioned, very well trained, and they also have a political arm that gives them the support of their local population who give them shelter. So they train, and they're supported by Iran, but they operate in an area that's their own, and they're part of the host government—they hold seats in the Lebanese parliament.

Lebanon is very much like the other places where these terrorist groups spring up. They're places where there's a weak body politic—where these kinds of organizations can grow and intimidate the local government. In the case of Hezbollah, they were offering support. They were taking Iranian money and building houses and putting the population back to work in southern Lebanon, building schools, hospitals, and clinics. They were using Iranian money to do that to gain the allegiance of the people in the south.

This is very well thought out. The reason the Iranians wanted Hezbollah right on Israel's northern border is because at the time Iran did not have weapons that could reach Israel. They knew that as soon as they started a nuclear weapons program and that got out, that Israel would not be able to tolerate that, so to protect themselves preemptively from an Israeli strike—knowing they couldn't reach back—they put weapons and forces right on Israel's northern border so they could operate them whenever they wanted to. They could use them to poke them in the ribs, or they could use them for a strategic retaliation or strike if they wanted to, anytime they wanted to.

MDE: **Knowing the risk that Israel took fighting this war, could it be that Israel had a phased plan for a preemptive strike on Iran attempting to break one of its proxies?**

Capt. Nash: That's a good point. I think Israel reacted to the events of July 12 because they had to. And let's go back to that July 12 period and look at what was going on. The IAEA [International Atomic Energy Agency] was about to make the final determination of what they were going to do— whether they were going to refer Iran to the UN Security Council [or some other action in response to continued refinement of uranium]. The chief negotiator from Iran flew to meet with [an IAEA representative]. [The representative] told him that Iran was going to be sent to the National Security Council for disposition. At that point, Iran's chief negotiator got back in the airplane and did not fly to Tehran—he flew to Damascus. That was the evening of [July] 11. He held meetings with Syrian military and political officials and Hezbollah officials. [The next morning the two Israeli soldiers were kidnapped and Hezbollah launched the rocket attacks on northern Israel.]

Appendix G

EXCERPTS FROM AN INTERVIEW WITH RETIRED ISRAEL DEFENSE FORCES LIEUTENANT GENERAL MOSHE YA'ALON

L t. Gen. Moshe Ya'alon served as the chief of staff for the Israeli Defense Forces from 2002 until 2005. He is currently a distinguished fellow at the Shalem Center Institute for International and Middle East Studies.

MDE: **General, can you tell us on how Iran intends to defeat the West?**

Lt. Gen. Ya'alon: Western like-minded people should understand the Iranian ideology to impose new caliphate over all the world. They call it Nation of Islam. They perceive the West is a threat to their ideology, to their culture, and they believe that they'll be able to defeat the West from the cultural point of view and to impose this new government by use of terrorism. Today the Iranian regime is determined to acquire military nuclear capability—first of all to use it as an umbrella for their terror activities. They prefer to use proxies to deal with the West and with Israel—to undermine our moderate regime, and then to dominate the Middle East. Of course to dominate the oil by undermining those regimes who are linked to the West and later on to try to export what they call the Iranian revolution—the Iranian ideology to Europe and to other Western countries using proxies with terrorism—exporting the ideology by force.

MDE: **What is the foundational theology that drives this?**

Lt. Gen. Ya'alon: It is interesting what we are facing today—we are facing different Islamic ideologies. In the Iranian case it is a Shiite ideology, but today the Al Qaeda ideology, which is very different but shares the same agenda and the same strategy. This is the case of the Muslim Brotherhood coming from this different ideology, calling to impose the Nation of Islam all over the world. The Iranian ideology actually is to dominate the Islamic world and to dominate the world by imposing Islam. The ideology is [ultimately] to reach peace and tranquility all over the world.

All the people all over the world should be Muslims—this is the idea. They use this idea of what they call the Mahdi—like their messiah—in order to encourage [people] to be proactive—to [perform] terror activities. By acquiring nuclear military capabilities [they hope] to convince by force those infidels who do not believe in Islam to become Muslims in order to reach peace and tranquility all over the world.

MDE: **Do they believe that an apocalypse would usher him in?**

Lt. Gen. Ya'alon: I'm not sure the idea is apocalypse—they are trying to convince people to convert themselves; like [when] President Ahmadinejad in his eighteen-page letter to President Bush actually recommended he be converted to Islam—not by force, but he tried try to convince him. He really believes in it. For westerners it might seem ridiculous, but he says what he means and he means what he says. In the letter—in calling to wipe Israel off the map and so forth—he means what he says. He really believes in it, so they prefer to convince the westerners.

This is the idea of Hamas. Hamas is part of the Muslim Brotherhood. We have it in a speech in Damascus. Last February, after they won the elections, he was talking about the Nation of Islam, and he recommended the westerners to be converted or not to support Israel, otherwise they will be full of remorse. They speak the same language although they do not share the same ideology—but the most tenuous force today regarding this kind of ideology is no doubt Iran.

MDE: **Talk to us about Iran's nuclear program.**

Lt. Gen. Ya'alon: No doubt today there is not any dispute in the Western intelligence community that Iran is determined to acquire military nuclear capability. This is not just a civilian project. We have information in the last decade that there is a clandestine Iranian military nuclear project. They will try to overcome the problems in the enrichment process, but they're on their way to overcoming it—they're on their way to acquiring it. And according to the experts, it's a question of a couple of months—I'm not sure how many months—to reach what they need to have—[that is] the indigenous know-how to be able to enrich the materials and to be able to produce a bomb. Then they will have a couple of years to build—to actually produce—the bomb, but no doubt they are determined to acquire the military nuclear capability. What we [have] faced in the last couple of years—especially since 2004 when the IAEA exposed their clandestine project—[is Iran] trying to gain time in order to go ahead with the process. Unfortunately, they feel like they are succeeding to manipulate—to deceive—the West and to go on with the project.

MDE: **How big is their project, and are the Russians involved?**

Lt. Gen. Ya'alon: You know, I was the head of the intelligence of the Israeli Defense Force in the years '95–'98, and actually I personally met Russian officials and introduced them to the information that we had about Russian experts involved in the missiles project—and of course a nuclear project at that time. Russian administration at the time denied it, but we had evidence of Russian involvement at the time. So no doubt when we are talking about the missile project it was even before the Shahab-6, which is already operational today. We had all evidence about Russian involvement in this project.

MDE: **How many sites are we talking about?**

Lt. Gen. Ya'alon: This is not one site like it was in Iraq. We are talking about dozens of facilities dealing with this project.

MDE: **And what is the difference between their sites now and the Iraq site?**

Lt. Gen. Ya'alon: In the Iraqi case, it was one reactor, Osirak, that was destroyed by the Israeli air strike in 1981. Today the Iranian regime has learned a lesson from the Iraqi case and they have many facilities—[they] know it's a challenge for intelligence, but we can cope with it.

MDE: **Are they built underground?**

Lt. Gen. Ya'alon: Yes. They're built underground; they're built in well-protected facilities.

MDE: **And do they face the Gulf? Are they lined up on the Gulf?**

Lt. Gen. Ya'alon: The Iranian intention strategically is to dominate the Gulf—to become a hegemony regarding all sources, which is the Gulf States of the Middle East. So this is a combination of religious ideology and political strategy. This is a combination in which they are trying—this regime—to dominate the religion and of course, to harm or [control] Western interest regarding oil in the Gulf.

MDE: **What kind of threats has the president of Iran made against the state of Israel?**

Lt. Gen. Ya'alon: President Ahmadinejad declared that Israel should be wiped off the map. He referred to it at a conference with the title "The World Without Zionism." They had another conference about "The World Without America." So they see Israel as a spearhead of Western culture—Western civilization— and believe that on the way to defeat the West, Israel should be defeated, and this is the reason that he supports all the terror organizations that operate against the State of Israel—like the Hezbollah in Lebanon, the Palestinian Islamic Jihad, the Hamas, Fata activists—on an individual basis. He believes that this is a step on the way to defeating the West. In this stage, Israel should be wiped off the map—and he really believes in it—and he believes that he's able to implement it.

Unfortunately, he's encouraged from our decisions like the fighting in Lebanon and in the Gaza Strip. We did it especially because of Israeli internal considerations. It was perceived—and is still perceived—by the Iranian regime as weakness—and he is encouraged by Israel like he is encouraged by the U.S. difficulties of the coalition—the difficulties in Iraq. Of course he's accountable for it as well because he does his best not to allow any political stability in Iraq behind the scene, and he provides the know-how— the terror know-how—he provides it to the insurgencies like the IEDs, improvised explosive devices, Iranian-made. And of course he does his best to undermine those moderate regimes who are linked to the West, like in Jordan, in Egypt, in Persian Gulf states, and unfortunately, he feels like he's winning because he doesn't face any determination from the West and he goes on with his policy using the proxies and acquiring the military nuclear capability for his benefit.

MDE: **You're saying that many of our troops that are blown up are actually blown up by military devices that are coming from Iran?**

Lt. Gen. Ya'alon: No doubt about it. The coalition troops—the Americans, the Brits, the Italians—who are blown up today in Iraq are blown up by Iranian-made improvised explosive devices. We faced the same devices in Lebanon used by the Hezbollah—Iranian-made devices—the same. We intercepted these kind of devices on the *Karine-A*—the ship that came from Iran—and we intercepted [it in the Red Sea] trying to smuggle these kind of devices to the Palestinian terrorists—so no doubt this is Iranian-made.

MDE: **When Iran uses the term "The Great Satan" referring to America, what do they mean?**

Lt. Gen. Ya'alon: Israel is perceived by this regime as a small Satan. The Great Satan is America—and actually the Iranian regime is challenging the United States as the leader of the Western culture. Israel is a marginal issue on the way to defeating the United States. Today the Iranian regime is concentrating on dealing with the American interest in the region—like in Iraq, in the Persian Gulf state, and in Israel. [They see America] as a spearhead of Western culture and religion. But the strategic goal is to defeat the United States—to defeat the Western culture—to defeat the Western values— and to impose the new caliphate and the Nation of Islam.

In the end, I believe that if they are successful in the Middle East, they will approach Europe, and of course the United States—and actually the Iranian regime has the terror infrastructure even today—a sleeping terror infrastructure everywhere. Like they did it in Argentina in '92 and '94 against the Jewish communities, like they did it in Europe against their opponents in Germany, and elsewhere—in Asher. Everywhere they have the sleeping terror infrastructure to be used on the day to come.

MDE: **If Iran gave the nod for those with the infrastructure to harm us that are living within our country, what are they capable of doing?**

Lt. Gen. Ya'alon: You can look to what happened in Germany toward assassinations, and you can look back to what happened in Argentina, which was blowing up huge buildings—the Israeli embassy and the Jewish community center—so they have the capability to send a truck loaded with explosives to blow any building in the United States or anywhere in the world.

MDE: **Israel has dealt with—in the last six years—over twenty thousand attempted suicide attacks. Obviously it has worked for them to achieve their objectives with Israel. Crime has paid for them in many ways, from their perspective. Is there any possibility that they could try that in the United States?**

Lt. Gen. Ya'alon: Why not? Using homicide bombers—I don't call them suicide bombers but homicide bombers—it becomes very effective from their perspective. From their perception, it becomes very effective. They believe that Israel retreated from Lebanon because of these kinds of terror attacks. Talking about the radical Islamists, they believe—all of them—Al Qaeda, Muslim Brotherhood, and the Iranian regime—they believe that they defeated Russia as a superpower—why [would they not believe they are] able to defeat the second superpower, or the first one—the United States—by using their determination or their will?

Not all of the West has the power, but actually I'm not sure that the West has an understanding, the awareness, the will, and the determination, and [Islamofascists] have the will and the determination and believe that they will win by their advantage of will and determination and that we just have to listen to them—to Osama bin Laden, to Ahmadinejad, to Khaled Mashaal [leader of Hamas]—and of course to the main generator today for any terror activities all over the world: the Iranian regime.

MDE: **When you said that they believed they defeated the Russian Soviet Union, were you referring to the Afghan war?**

Lt. Gen. Ya'alon: Yes, of course. The radical Islamists today, they feel like they are winning. They feel like they are winning although they do not have the power—but they believe they have the will and the determination.

Why do they feel that they are winning? First of all, they believe [that if] they defeated the Soviet Union in Afghanistan, then [they] will be able to defeat the United States. Secondly, they believe the Hezbollah defeated Israel in Lebanon. It was a victory for terror, according to their perception. They believe that they changed the Spanish policy because of the devastating attack in Madrid in 2004. They believe that Israelis withdrew from Gaza because of the Hamas terror attacks, and of course they are encouraged from the Hamas political victory in the [Palestinian] elections.

They're encouraged by the Muslim Brotherhood gaining power in Egypt. They're encouraged today from what's happening in Mogadishu in Somalia, and of course they're encouraged from the coalition troops' difficulties in Iraq, and from the political difficulties here in Washington for the president—for the administration. So they feel like they are winning and they are very self-confident today that they are on the way to defeating the West.

MDE: **How important is the support of Americans who have moral clarity in this battle?**

Lt. Gen. Ya'alon: In order to win this kind of war, we need the awareness of westerners. Then we need moral clarity, and then a clear strategy. We sleep. We in the West are sleeping, and we need a wake-up call to understand this threat is imminent. It's not a theoretical threat, and as long as [Islamofascists] feel like they are winning—as long as they do not witness Western determination to deal with this politically, economically and militarily, they will go on with it. They will use, first of all, the proxies against Western targets anywhere—not just Israel, but Western moderate regimes in the Middle East—and they will go on with it from the Middle East to Europe to the United States.

MDE: **If nothing is done, if the world continues to sleep—if the West continues to sleep—and we wake up a decade from**

now and nothing has been done, can you describe what America could be like in comparison to your nation when you were chief of staff as it relates to terrorism and the threat—what it could be like in the streets of America?

Lt. Gen. Ya'alon: It will be more difficult to any administration or government in the West to deal with nuclear Iran because of the nuclear umbrella. Cane said recently that the only worse option—rather than exercising the military option regarding the military nuclear project in Iran—is to have a nuclear Iran. I agree with him because to have a nuclear Iran with this kind of nonconventional regime—with these nonconventional capabilities—this is not even rational. We're not talking about a Soviet Union–type of leadership. They were rational. This regime is not rational. They have a strong religious belief—and they are driving this strong religious belief to defeat the West.

So first of all, they will use terror like we faced in Lebanon from the Palestinian Authority. They will oppose other countries by undermining them, blackmailing them, by terror activities—a combination of terror activities under a nuclear umbrella—and they will approach Europe and the United States with the use of proxies—not to use missiles, [they will] use proxies—and they have many proxies: Hezbollah, Palestinian terror organizations, and of course [those] run by the Iranian intelligence who were responsible for the devastating attacks in Argentina—special Iranian intelligence used covertly to launch terror attacks against Western targets. So it might come to the United States as well.

MDE: **What part did Iran play in 9/11?**

Lt. Gen. Ya'alon: Al Qaeda elements used Iran as a safe haven. [We] can't say that the Iranian regime was involved directly or in any other way with 9/11, but no doubt Al Qaeda elements used Iran for a certain period of time as a safe haven.

MDE: **I'd like to be able to describe to the American people a visual thing. What visually would they be seeing and hearing if homicide bombers began this strategy in the**

United States? What would it be like? What would be the particulars?

Lt. Gen. Ya'alon: There is a sleeping infrastructure—terror infrastructure—today all over the world like we have not seen—not simply in Canada—and this is the case everywhere because we are talking about ideology, which is spread by many radical Islamists. In many cases it's the Iranian regime talking with Shia elements, and in other cases the Al Qaeda organization—which is an umbrella—an ideology to encourage radical Islamists. I'm not talking about all Muslims. I'm talking about radical Islamists who become terrorists and are ready to sacrifice their lives by becoming homicide bombers, killing infidels, as they call us—Christians, Jews, Buddhists, whatever other than Muslims are infidels—to kill them, and in this way to convince them to be converted to Islam. All over the world there are radical Islamists who are ready to be become homicide bombers. It might be Osama bin Laden or others. They are ready, so if the Iranian regime decided to implement it here in the United States, they will have the capabilities to do it.

MDE: **Explain what it would be like practically if it happened in New York or DC.**

Lt. Gen. Ya'alon: I think, practically, today in Israel we assume that any minute a homicide bomber might try to approach any public facility, so we have a guard in the entrance of any public facility, which is any mall, any restaurant, any café, any public transportation to defend the civilians from homicide bombers. So it might happen even here.

MDE: **But the American people have never really experienced that type of terror. I know that when they do this, sometimes they work in pairs of twos. They strategically plan it. Describe for us what it would be like if it actually happened here in Washington DC or New York. What would it be like?**

Lt. Gen. Ya'alon: Of course people will not feel secure because of the idea of being blown up in a public facility—in the Metro, or in the restaurant, or in the concert hall, or in the theater, or anywhere—to lose your personal feeling of security on a daily basis and to be aware of any suspicious movement—not to trust anyone who goes with a suitcase or with any other bag—which might be an explosive bag—it changes the whole way of life when you face it.

MDE: **You mentioned that this president had the audacity to write a letter to try to convert the president of the United States. If you would attempt to convert the president of the United States, obviously he would certainly want to attempt to convert the American people.**

Lt. Gen. Ya'alon: Oh, of course.

MDE: **Could you talk about that for a minute? Start with the letter.**

Lt. Gen. Ya'alon: Actually, President Ahmadinejad recommended that the president of the United States be converted to Islam. Of course, this recommendation is for all the American people to be [converted] to avoid the conflict—to avoid the war that he declares on the West. Actually, he declares war against Western culture, and yes, he recommends—like any other radical Islamist today, like Osama bin Laden and Khaled Mashaal, who also talks about not supporting Israel and adopting Islam, otherwise you will be full of remorse, you will regret it in the end. Yes, this is the proposal: to be converted.

MDE: **The American people have a tendency to think this is just one person who believes this.**

Lt. Gen. Ya'alon: Actually, in Iran we should distinguish between the Iranian regime and the Iranian people, but when we are talking about the regime we should talk about the ayatollahs, the conservatives—the conservatives who do not allow any reforms and are trying to manage Iran using the Islamic law—who do not allow democracy or democratic values. So we should distinguish between the regime and the people. I believe that most of the Iranian people do not like the ayatollahs—but the problem is not with one man. The problem is with the system—with this ideology of the ayatollahs.

MDE: **How many are we approximately talking about, and how long has this ideology been fed to them?**

Lt. Gen. Ya'alon: We are talking about the Iranian revolution that emerged in 1979 quite successfully in Iran. Although they are not able as a regime to convince all the Iranians to believe in this ideology, they have succeeded in running the country successfully, and actually they succeeded in strengthening their grip in governing—building the intelligence, intimidation, discrimination, pressure against the people—and they are quite successful in their way. So we have to talk about the Iranian regime, not just the Iranian people, like we have to talk about the radical Islamists—not all the Muslims—and the Iranian regime is radical Islamist regime.

MDE: **Most people think of nuclear bombs as missiles, fired through missiles—but could there be a period of time where a nuclear bomb could be put in a cargo container or even brought across a border?**

Lt. Gen. Ya'alon: Actually, the bomb, according to my understanding, might be used by the Iranian regime as an umbrella, then by proxies—not by the regime itself, which means by aircraft or by missile—by proxies—the dirty bomb to be used by terror organizations as proxies. This is the best way to deny accountability and this is the way this regime is thinking about how to gain the benefits of these kinds of activities—like terror activities—and not to be considered accountable. That's what they are doing now in Iraq, in Lebanon, in the Palestinian Authority, and all over the Middle East against moderate regimes—denying accountability but no doubt generating, financing, equipping, supporting, and encouraging these kinds of proxies. So the idea of using proxies is the most probable scenario, even when it comes to nuclear capability.

MDE: **Would you describe what a dirty bomb is and what kind of damage that could do in a high-population area?**

Lt. Gen. Ya'alon: You can bring a dirty bomb to any city using maritime cargo or air cargo or ground cargo. It doesn't matter. It might be brought by ship, by airplane, or by truck to be used in a very highly populated urban area like a city anywhere. It might be Tel Aviv, it might be Berlin, it might be New York. And, of course, to cause devastating collateral damage—to kill as many civilians as they can—but to contain it to a certain area like a big city.

MDE: **Our worst horror was 9/11—and we know the number of deaths. Just approximately what would be a rough number [of casualties] if a dirty bomb went off in a highly populated city?**

Lt. Gen. Ya'alon: It might be dozens of thousands; it might be hundreds of thousands of casualties. It depends on the quantity of the materials in a dirty bomb.

MDE: **If Iran is not stopped and they go nuclear, then are you saying that they cannot be stopped—or, if they were stopped, what consequences would that take?**

Lt. Gen. Ya'alon: I believe that in one way or another they should be stopped. They shouldn't have nuclear capability. I prefer that a military option would be the last resort. We haven't experienced yet the political and economic option. It should be used early on—and I prefer that by not using the political and economic option—which means political isolation and economic sanctions—we will have to use the military option. I'm talking about the West—like my people—and no doubt Iran will respond to any option. They even might respond to economic sanctions, not talking about military option. They might respond using proxies, terror organizations—special Iranian apparatus—to execute terror attacks against certain targets.

Appendix H

EXCERPTS FROM AN INTERVIEW WITH ALAN DERSHOWITZ

Alan Dershowitz is Felix Frankfurter Professor of Law at Harvard Law School and has been called "the nation's most peripatetic civil liberties lawyer" and one of its "most distinguished defenders of individual rights," "the best-known criminal lawyer in the world," "the top lawyer of last resort," and "America's most public Jewish defender." He is also a prolific writer whose editorials and commentaries appear in a variety of magazines, newspapers, and online. He is also the author of twenty works of fiction and nonfiction, including six best sellers, among them *The Case for Israel* and *Why Terrorism Works.*

MDE: **Israel is in a great crisis, and you've read many books that relate to this subject. One of them has to do with preemption. Talk to me about the Iran crisis—as Israel is faced with it—and the consequences of it as it relates to Israel and the United States.**

Prof. Dershowitz: Iran is the big winner of the most recent crisis in the Middle East. Israel lost many civilians and soldiers. The Lebanese lost civilians, and Hezbollah lost soldiers. Iran lost no one. They gained power, they gained influence, and I think they tried very hard to send a message to the United States and to Israel that their nuclear facilities are invulnerable to attack because they have figured out a strategy for how to fight moral democracies. You hide behind your own civilians. You build a nuclear facility and then you put a hospital on top of it. You build a nuclear facility and you build a school on top of it, and you challenge the democracies. Either kill our children, our weak, our elderly, and get condemned by the United Nations, or leave us alone. What Israel tried to do in Lebanon is get to the Hezbollah fighters without killing civilians, but inevitably some civilians die in the process. In every war civilians die.

Our greatest generation in the Second World War killed hundreds of thousands of civilians in Germany and in other parts of the world where we were fighting in Japan— but Israel is held to a very different standard. Every time Israel kills a single civilian it becomes a first page story, a UN issue, and the blame is not put on those who deserve the blame, namely Hezbollah or Hamas, who hide behind civilians and basically induce Israel to kill them. The blame falls on Israel. So this is the beginning essentially of a new one-hundred-year war that will go beyond my children and my grandchildren's lives—a war between terrorist tyrannies and moral democracies.

This method of fighting couldn't work with an immoral democracy. If anybody ever tried this with Russia, Russia would simply do what they're doing in Chechnya. They would carpetbomb the cities and kill as many civilians as necessary to get at the one military target. It never would've worked with Stalin. It never would've worked with Hitler. It wouldn't work with China today. It wouldn't work with many of the nations in the world. It only works with a moral democracy like Israel and the United States.

MDE: **Now in light of that, how serious of a threat is Iran to the United States?**

Prof. Dershowitz: Iran is a major, major threat to the United States. Iran, if it's not stopped, will get a nuclear bomb, and it will use that nuclear bomb to blackmail America and other countries. Imagine if Iraq had a nuclear bomb when they went into Kuwait. They'd be in Kuwait today and they'd still be in power—Saddam Hussein and his sons. A nuclear weapon, whether used or hung, is the sword of Damocles—it changes the entire structure and balance of power—and an Iran with a nuclear bomb—especially an Iran more than North Korea, because North Korea's leaders don't want to die; they are secularists, and you can deter people who don't want to die—but many of Iran's leaders welcome death. They are part of the culture of death. They see life on Earth as only a segue to paradise with their seventy-two virgins—or whatever the rewards are going to be—and it's very hard to deter a culture that welcomes death. So Iran would be a great threat to the United States.

As Tom Friedman once said, "If terrorists are not stopped in the Middle East, they're coming to a theater near you"—and they're coming to the United States, to Europe, selectively in Europe. The French make their own deals, but most other Western European countries are vulnerable to an Iranian nuclear threat.

MDE: **In the latest crisis in Lebanon, it was obvious that they were subcontractors—Hezbollah were subcontractors, the right arm of Iran—but the media by and large exploited that to the advantage of Iran and did not have any sense of moral clarity and didn't see Jews suffering. Why? Why is that propensity?**

Prof. Dershowitz: The president of Iran is a clever man. He recently had an interview with Mike Wallace where he in many respects bested Mike Wallace—came across as a reasonable, charming person. He is, of course, the new Adolf Hitler without the means currently to do what Adolf Hitler did, but he and his surrogates have basically said their goal is to destroy Israel.

The head of Hezbollah said a couple of years ago that he hopes that all the Jews come to Israel—that will make Hezbollah's job easier in the sense that they can destroy all the Jews in Israel. They won't have to chase them around the world the way Hitler had to do.

The goal of Hezbollah, the goal of Hamas, the goal of Iran is not a two-state solution. It's not peace in the Middle East. It's the end of Israel and the end of all Western influences in the Middle East—and indeed in the world. This is an apocalyptic war between reason and democracy on the one hand, and between Islamic extremism and tyranny on the other hand—and it's a battle that will be fought to the death certainly by the Islamic extremists now headed by Iran.

MDE: **When the president of Iran says, "I see the world without Zionism and without America"—does he mean it?**

Prof. Dershowitz: He means it as much as Adolf Hitler meant it. The president of Iran would like to see a world without Zionism—without a crusader mentality—without Western values over which he is the dictator of a fourth Reich. That is what he would like to see. Can he accomplish it? Not without a nuclear weapon—but with a nuclear weapon there are almost no limits to what he could do because he will hide his nuclear weapons among civilians. We in the West, because of our moral code, will not bomb hospitals. We will not bomb day centers for children. We will not bomb schools. They will bomb anything, and it's very hard to fight an asymmetrical battle. You always hear about asymmetrical battles between Western armies that are more powerful and terrorist armies that are less powerful. There's a new form of asymmetry in warfare that is much more powerful, and that is the asymmetry of morality.

If you have an amoral and an immoral society willing to sacrifice their own children and their own hospital patients, their own aged people to the war, and you have another culture, Western democracy, that will not willfully kill children, will not willfully kill the elderly, will not willfully kill uninvolved civilians—that's asymmetrical.

When Israel was threatened with an Iraqi nuclear reactor, they said very clearly, "We are not at war with the children of Baghdad. We will not bomb Baghdad. We will not destroy a nuclear reactor if it means killing the children of Baghdad." And Golda Meir put it also very, very well when she said, "We can perhaps forgive the terrorists for killing our children but we can never forgive them for making us kill their children." Countries like Israel and the United States will do anything to avoid killing children, whereas the tyrannical regimes of terrorism will do anything to kill children—they figured out this cruel arithmetic of death.

Every time the terrorists kill a civilian, they win. Every time the terrorists get the democracies to kill a child, they win. It's a win/win for the terrorists, it's a lose/lose for the democracies, and it's all because of the asymmetry of morality.

MDE: **Who is winning the bigger battle in the media as far as Iraq?**

Prof. Dershowitz: Well, there's no question that Iran and its terrorist surrogates are winning the media war. They're winning the media war because today, unlike in the Second World War, every civilian casualty is featured on the evening news—the picture of the dead child, the picture of the weeping woman. Imagine if those media images had existed during the Second World War. Every time the United States bombed a facility, a nuclear facility as the British and United States did in Norway to prevent the development of nuclear bombs—every time we bombed a military facility anywhere in Germany, there would be pictures of dead German children and weeping German mothers. It would be almost impossible for the United States to carry out its military activities.

The Iranians, Hezbollah, and Hamas have learned how to use the media and how to use the United Nations—which is a democracy of tyrannies. Namely, every tyranny gets one vote at the General Assembly, and as Abba Eban once put it, "If the Algerians introduced a resolution to the General Assembly that the earth was flat and that Israel had flattened it, it would win 124/22 with thirty-six abstentions," and you could figure out which countries would be on which side. When the case involving the Israeli security fence went before the General Assembly, virtually every country that voted to send the matter to the International Court of Justice was a tyranny, and virtually every country that voted against the court having jurisdiction was a democracy—and yet the tyrannies outvoted the majorities.

And so the combination of the United Nations—the democracy of tyrannies—coupled with the media, which focuses always on the pictures of the civilian casualties, coupled with the fact that Israel is an open society and allows the media full reign, whereas Iran is a closed society, Hezbollah is a closed society, Hamas is a closed society. So the media images are always going to be more powerfully used against Israel than against its terrorist enemies.

MDE: **In your book *The Case for Israel,* you talk about why terrorism works and you use the analogy about how Arafat did it. There seems to be an enormous similarity between what's happening now and what happened then.**

Prof. Dershowitz: Yasser Arafat is the godfather of modern terrorism. He figured out how to use terrorism to his advantage. I didn't say to the advantage of the Palestinian people, because

I don't think in the end it worked to the advantage of the Palestinian people, but it certainly worked to Arafat's personal advantage and allowed him to accumulate billions of dollars in payments, basically extortion payments, made by Europe into his own bank accounts—but Arafat figured out how to use terrorism to gain publicity.

The destruction of the Israeli Olympic team in Munich was not the first but perhaps the most publicized. The destruction of airplanes in flight—the blowing up of the Swiss airliner, the attempt to blow up El Al planes, the destruction of four planes on the tarmac in Jordan—all of that brought tremendous attention to the situation of the Palestinians—much more than, for example, to the situation of the Kurds who never use this kind of international terrorism, or the Tibetans who never use terrorism at all—and the Kurds and the Tibetans' situation in the world today is ignored, whereas the Palestinian situation is highlighted because of their use of terrorism. So they figured out how to use terrorism, and they also figured out how to hide behind civilians and make it difficult for democracies with their high moral standards to get at the terrorists—and that paradigm continues to haunt Western democracies today.

MDE: **In your book *Preemption*, you talk about how the United States tends to look toward its experience. What are the American people thinking when they see the Iran crisis in its present form, as opposed to how you've explained how Iran is thinking?**

Prof. Dershowitz: For Iran, this has been a great victory. It's been muscle flexing; it's been thumbing a nose at the West—but for Americans, Iran is very far away. Most Americans don't understand why Iran poses this great threat. After all, they're so many thousands of miles away. We don't have soldiers in Iran since the hostages were released twenty-five years ago. We've never really lost anybody to Iran, so it's very hard to create an interest in a problem that's so distant.

It reminds me again of what was going on in Nazi Germany in the early 1930s, when Americans were not concerned and isolationist candidates were winning and it was very hard for President Roosevelt to energize the American people to get them concerned about what was going on in Europe at the time—and we better learn the lesson of having ignored Nazism.

The preventative war that was in the middle 1930s—before Hitler became the most powerful figure with the most powerful army in the world—he could've been prevented. Winston Churchill said he could've been prevented—and most interestingly, so did many of the Nazis themselves. They were shocked that the West, that France, that England, that the United States didn't attack them when they violated the Versailles Treaty and when they threatened to kill the Jews of the world. We didn't take them seriously. We didn't take them at face value—and the potential need for a preventive strike against Iran if they were on the verge of developing a nuclear weapon is also, I think, today being widely ignored in the West.

One of the reasons I personally was against the war in Iraq—for me it was a very close question, but I came out against it—was because I thought it would divert attention away from Iran, which posed a much more serious threat because religious extremism is always more dangerous than secular extremism. I also worried about the rule of unintended consequences—that the tyranny of Saddam Hussein would be replaced by a tyranny of radical Islamists—and unfortunately those fears have come to fruition and the United States probably today does not have the resources—or the incentive—to take as seriously Iran as we would've been able to had we not been bogged down today in Iraq. So I think there is a real crisis ahead of us.

MDE: **The generals in Israel see the military action as a success as it relates to long-range missiles, medium-range missiles, destroying Iran's infrastructure, military infrastructure, and retaliating. From that aspect they consider it a success. But before Ehud Olmert was able to get anywhere near the Litani River, the United States rushed to the UN to pressure Israel into a quick ceasefire with Hezbollah. Why?**

Prof. Dershowitz: I think that the United States expected Israel to be able to disarm Hezbollah more quickly and more effectively, and

Israel was caught between a rock and a hard place. In fact, the world today is divided in its criticism of Israel. Everybody is critical of Israel, but many people say Israel didn't do enough and many people say Israel did too much. Nobody thinks—except perhaps some of the generals in Israel—that Israel did just about the right thing. I think the United States in some respects thought it did too little in the beginning of the war and then, with all the civilian casualties, too much by the end of the war, and it felt the necessity to finally bring it to a halt. I think there were a lot of disappointed people in the American Pentagon—in the American State Department—that Israel was not able to disarm Hezbollah, but the only way Israel could've disarmed Hezbollah would've been by inflicting more civilian casualties.

Now let's remember that the total number of real civilian casualties inflicted by Israel during the fight in Lebanon was probably less than five hundred. The number being given by the Lebanese is over one thousand—but when you include among those Hezbollah fighters, active Hezbollah collaborators, active volunteer human shields who stayed behind, people who were prevented from leaving because of Hezbollah, the number of actual civilians for whom Israel bears any, any degree of responsibility—and I don't think they do deserve moral responsibility; it was Hezbollah's fault—is probably below five hundred.

That many civilians are killed every day by Muslims in the Sudan, in Iraq, in Afghanistan, and yet the media focus was obsessively on every Muslim killed by the bomb of an Israeli rather than on Muslims killed by Muslims or Arabs killed by Arabs in many other parts of the world—and that's the albatross that's always going to be around Israel's neck. So it was impossible to accomplish its military goals within the constraints of not killing civilians. In that respect, Hezbollah figured out a new way of using the morality of Israel as both a shield and a sword to be able to fire rockets and to be able to protect itself from counterfire by Israel.

MDE: **Do you think it's inevitable that either Israel or the United States is going to have to take out Iran's nuclear program?**

Prof. Dershowitz: I think the constant has to be that Iran will never be permitted to develop a nuclear program. And I think it is inevitable that if Iran is on the verge of developing a nuclear bomb, which they have said they would use against Israel, and if the United States did not preempt or preventively attack that nuclear facility, I think Israel would have no choice. Would any democracy allow its enemy to develop a nuclear bomb that it has already said it would use against its capital? Remember that the former liberal president, Rafsanjani, proudly boasted that if Iran got a nuclear bomb they would use it against Israel and they would kill three to five million Israelis and Israel would retaliate and kill ten to twenty million Muslims in Tehran—and said the tradeoff would be worth it because there are more Muslims than Jews.

No democracy, and certainly not one whose citizens are comprised largely of Holocaust survivors—and every Jew is a Holocaust survivor in that respect, because Hitler's goal was to kill every Jew—no country could permit its enemies sworn to its destruction to develop a nuclear bomb. So Israel will have no choice ultimately but to take some preemptive or preventative action if the United States fails in its diplomatic efforts—or if the United States does not engage in a military attack on Iranian nuclear facilities.

MDE: **In America's diplomatic efforts, the Atomic Energy Commission in Israel told me that thirty cents on the dollar of American money goes to the IAEA, which Iran is a member of, and that the United States is fundamentally doing nothing against Russia's full-blown intent of building these reactors. Why?**

Prof. Dershowitz: I think Russia is acting in a very shortsighted way. I think an armed Iran poses a great danger to Russia as well because a nuclear armed Iran has the potential for leakage and the leakage will result in Chechen rebels potentially having access to some kind of nuclear ability. And I think every country that's in any kind of a war with Islamic extremists would be the losers if Iran ever developed a nuclear bomb, particularly since the Iranian military is notorious for its corruption and for the ability of others to buy some facilities. They would not be able to control the facilities to the degree that the United States can today, or Israel can and has over the past thirty years, and it's a scandal that the international community, through various agencies, has not been able to prevent Iran from developing a bomb. The only countries that should be permitted to have nuclear bombs are countries that won't use them or countries that have them purely for deterrent purposes. Iran does not fit into that category. If it got a nuclear weapon, the risks are simply too high that it would use them. When the risks are catastrophic, the likelihood doesn't have to be very high in order for it to be morally and legally justified for the potential victims of a nuclear attack to take preemptive actions.

MDE: **Was the Lebanon war a test for the West?**

Prof. Dershowitz: The Lebanon war was a test for the West, and the West failed it. The Lebanon war was a challenge by terrorists—and tyrannical regimes—to the morality of the West. The message was, "We're going to kill your civilians and we're going to challenge you to kill our civilians, and unless you're willing to kill our civilians we will continue with impunity to kill your civilians." This moral asymmetry is a test that we haven't figured out a way around. We can't compromise our morality. We can't be in the business of killing children. We can't lower ourselves to the level of the Iranians or Hezbollah or Hamas, and yet we have to figure out a more effective way of being able to take out their military command structure—their ability to fire rockets, whether they be conventional rockets or in the future chemical, biological, and nuclear rockets—without killing their civilians, or we have to change international law and international perception that every civilian killed when tyrannical regimes—terrorist regimes—hide behind civilians—that all those civilian deaths are not attributable to the democracies that are acting in self defense, but to those who are using these civilians as human shields. Unless—and until—that perception changes, the tyrannical terrorists have an enormous advantage over the democracies—and that's what the Lebanese war proved.

MDE: **President Bush was on a fast track to G8 and all of a sudden, just about the time he was getting in the plane to head to St. Petersburg, hostages were taken**

and bombs were fired at the State of Israel. Was that a coincidence?

Prof. Dershowitz: I don't think you can ever assume that timing is a coincidence. Whenever events occur, you have to look at who gained some advantage from doing what they did at the time they did it. The timing of Hezbollah or Iran or whoever determined the timing—and I believe it was coordinated between Hezbollah, Hamas, and Iran—I think Iran sent a message: "Heat things up. Turn the heat on. Attack Israel in whatever way you think is the most effective for you—kidnap soldiers, kill soldiers, cross the border, build tunnels, send rockets."

I don't think that Iran necessarily micromanaged every aspect of it. I think it's enough that it turns on and off the spigot, and that's what happened, and Iran did it for it's advantage—whether it be to divert attention from its own nuclear ambitions, whether it be because it was fearful that there might be a peace between the Israelis and the Palestinians in the Middle East, which is the worst thing for Iran.

The best thing that could happen to thwart Iranian ambitions would be for Israel and the Palestinians to finally arrive at a peace based on the model that President Clinton and Ehud Barak tried to set forth in Camp David and in Taba in 2000 and 2001. The big losers for that failed peace process were the Palestinians, who could've been celebrating the fourth or fifth anniversary of an economically viable, successful Palestinian state (instead they continue to live in misery), and the Israelis, who I think would be living in a more secure neighborhood if there were a more peaceful resolution. And the big winners are Iran, Hezbollah, and Hamas, who don't want a two-state solution. They want the same solution the Nazis wanted in the 1930s.

The Nazis wanted a one-state solution for Europe. They wanted the Third Reich extending from Ireland to the end of the Soviet Union. They wanted a one-state solution—and Iran, Hezbollah, and Hamas want a one-state solution. They want one Islamic fundamentalist state living under the principles of the Sharia, living under the principles of the most extreme form of Islamic fundamentalism. They're not going to get it, but they're going to make life for the rest of the world miserable.

MDE: **When the Lebanese war took place, the word *Iran* was completely removed from the world screen and it became a proxy war with no sense of moral obligation to Iran. Is Iran capable of utilizing the same proxy tactics against the United States vis-à-vis Palestinian asymmetrical suicide bombers if they feel like it's to their advantage?**

Prof. Dershowitz: The way Iran used Lebanon, Hezbollah, and, to a lesser degree, Hamas as surrogates in the first battle of this one-hundred-year war—which I think they're engaged in—reminds me of the way Nazi Germany used the Spanish Civil War as a surrogate fight just prior to the beginning of the Second World War. The Nazi German army wasn't directly involved in the Spanish Civil War, but the Spanish Civil War was a surrogate, and when the democracies lost in the Spanish Civil War, it was the green light to Nazi Germany to move forward. And I think that the Hezbollah fight in Lebanon has been to the current crisis what the Spanish Civil War was in leading up to the Second World War. That's why we have to take it so seriously and why it's impossible to allow Hezbollah, Hamas, and Iran any further victories.

MDE: **Why should the United States continue to support Israel?**

Prof. Dershowitz: The United States should continue to support the interests of the United States globally, and the interests of the United States coincide with the interests of Israel. Israel is the only reliable ally the United States has ever had in the Middle East. Israel provided the United States with some of its most important intelligence and military information and resources during the Cold War, and Israel continues to provide the United States with some of its most important intelligence and military resources during this war with Islamic fundamentalism.

If Israel were to, God forbid, disappear off the face of the earth, that would not strengthen America's position in the world. It would weaken America's position in the world considerably. There would still be an Islamic campaign against America, but it would have to be fought without a reliable ally in the Middle East. So it's clearly in America's interest to see a strong and viable Israel.

It's also in America's interest to see an Israel at peace, if that's at all possible, and I think the United States should continue to play a constructive role in supporting Israel. But let there be no mistake about this—Israel can and would and will survive with or without the support of the United States. Israel has a formidable military capacity. It has nuclear capacities, which it never wants to use. It is economically a secure country because it doesn't have oil. That's been one of the great blessings. Because Israel doesn't have oil, it has to develop high technology. High technology is the wave of the future; oil is the resource of the past. And so Israel will remain a very important strategic ally of the United States in years to come, and that's, by the way, one of the reasons why the French have turned so anti-Israel. The French do not have an interest in the strength of the United States. The French have an interest in a weakened United States, and I think one of the reasons the French have turned against Israel is because they see Israel as a strategic ally of the United States in its global position in the world today.

MDE: **I spoke with Benjamin Netanyahu at the Press Club, and I noticed him speaking on his admiration for Ronald Reagan and he hissed like a snake. Is that similar to what you're discussing—a lack of moral clarity?**

Prof. Dershowitz: Well, for Americans who support Israel and who support social justice, admiration for Ronald Reagan has to be very, very mixed. I did not vote for Ronald Reagan. I would not vote for Ronald Reagan today if he were alive and well and running for office because I thoroughly disapprove of his domestic social programs. I believe in a much fairer distribution of wealth in America. I believe in a very high wall of separation between church and state. I believe in science and reason dominating the criteria for stem cell research. I believe very strongly in gay rights and in women's rights— so for me, the Republican platform has always been a non-starter. I'm a liberal Democrat and will continue to support liberal Democrats primarily for reasons of American domestic concern.

On the other hand, I had some admiration for the way in which Ronald Reagan stood up to the evils of Soviet Communism. I think that the fall of Communism was not solely attributable in any way to Ronald Reagan. I think the pope played a very significant role. I think the changing economics in the world played a significant role. Gorbachev played a significant role, and the Russian people played a significant role. So I think it is a mistake to attribute the success of American policy vis-à-vis the Soviet Union to one person or one policy.

I have the same feelings today toward the Bush administration. I'm a strong opponent of the Bush administration on domestic policies, and I also think it made a dreadful mistake in getting us into the war in Iraq, both from an American perspective and a pro-Israel perspective. I think it was a mistake from the point of view of Israel's security for America to get bogged down in a war in Iraq. So I think, as with many liberal Americans who support Israel, we have to look critically and skeptically at both parties and all candidates and always ask first the question, "What's best for America?" And I do believe that American support for Israel is best for America.

MDE: **Why is it that you seldom hear the word *Islamofascist* among liberal Democrats?**

Prof. Dershowitz: You certainly hear it from me. I'm a liberal Democrat and I strongly believe that "Islamofascist" is an appropriate term to describe one small group of Islamic radicals. I think one of the reasons why you have some hesitation is you don't want to have a word that has a religious context being used broadly. I have many, many, many associates, friends, colleagues—people who I admire and respect enormously— who are Muslims by their religious faith and background. They're a wonderful people and a peace-loving people, and they would love to see a two-state solution. So I don't want to ever generalize about Muslims—members of the Islamic faith—but there is an element within the Islamic faith that has hijacked the faith, and I think they are aptly called Islamofascists. They are Fascists without any doubt. Hezbollah is a Fascist movement and has all the elements of a Fascist movement, including educating youth and providing social services.

People forget that the reason Germans voted for the Nazi Party the first time the Nazis were up for office was not because of their anti-Semitism, but often despite their anti-Semitism. They voted for the Nazis because the Nazis had youth programs, because they had social welfare programs, because they had approaches to unemployment—and by the way, they were also anti-Semites. And Hezbollah has managed to use the same approach. Many people in Lebanon support Hezbollah because of their social programs, because of their educational programs—and by the way, they're also anti-Semites. They hate Jews and they hate Israel, but we can live with that as long as they're providing the social services.

So one has to look beyond the social services at the core—at the core of Hamas and Hezbollah—who will use these social services to seduce people to get them to join their mission, and the core of the mission is the destruction of Israel, the destruction of the Jewish people, the destruction of Western values, the destruction of Christianity, and the destruction of everything other than radical Islam.

MDE: **In your book *Why Terrorism Works,* you've laid out some strategic principles relating to how it could also be stopped. Can you speak on that subject?**

Prof. Dershowitz: Terrorism can be stopped. Terrorism succeeds because it succeeds—that is, it's self-perpetuating. The way to make terrorism stop is never to reward it and always to hold the terrorists responsible, but we don't do that. The UN doesn't do that, the international community doesn't do that, even the United States and Israel don't always do that. Every country in the world submits to terrorism. The old joke that I love to tell—because my mother is ninety-three years old—is, "What's the difference between a Jewish mother and a terrorist?" The answer is, "With a terrorist you can sometimes negotiate." And tragically, I think too many democracies have negotiated with terrorism and have strengthened the hands of terrorism.

Were I a national leader, I would take a no-negotiation posture—would've from the beginning of time—a no-reward posture. Terrorism has to be dealt with the way piracy was dealt with in the nineteenth and eighteenth centuries. Finally we were able to abolish piracy for the most part because pirates were regarded as international criminals that no country would give quarter to. If terrorism were treated that way—if we never would've permitted Yasser Arafat to set foot at the United Nations, if we would never have considered giving him a Nobel Prize, if we would never have recognized terrorists' organizations—I think terrorism would've disappeared of its own force.

Terrorism doesn't work against tyrannies because tyrannies don't in any way tolerate terrorists and they turn off their sources for support and they don't allow the media to be used by the terrorists. It's easy for tyrannies to defeat terrorism. It's much harder for democracies because democracies have to preserve our values, our morals, and our civil liberties—so it's a real challenge, but it's doable.

MDE: **What is the worst-case scenario for the West if a decade goes by and the West sleeps—if Iran gets the bomb? What are we faced with?**

Prof. Dershowitz: Well the worst-case scenario would be Iran getting a bomb and proving their strength by dropping it on Israel and counting on Israel's morality—counting on the fact that even if a bomb were dropped on Israel, the Israelis would be very reluctant to counterattack by bombing the city of Tehran and killing ten million people. The fact that Israel has such a higher morality than Iran and the terrorist enemies it faces is one of the great weapons that the tyrannies and the terrorists have. That wasn't true in the Second World War. In the Second World War, the United States was willing to drop a nuclear bomb on Hiroshima and Nagasaki. They were willing to, with Great Britain, firebomb Dresden. They were willing to firebomb Tokyo. Israel is not prepared to do that, and the United States today is probably not prepared to do that, and with the elevated morality that some countries have and other countries don't have, the combination of the elevated morality of the United States and Israel with the reduction in morality by terrorists and tyrannical organizations creates an asymmetry, which is going to be very, very hard to deal with when we face nuclear annihilation.

MDE: **What can we do to protect the United States in light of this crisis?**

Prof. Dershowitz: The United States has to look much further into the future. It has to have a long-term strategy for dealing with a potentially nuclearized terrorist state like Iran, which has surrogates. It has to be ready to act proactively, preemptively, preventively when necessary. It has to be ready to act with powerful deterrent force when necessary. It has to use all of its resources available to it—diplomatic, economic, political, moral, military—and it has to understand that this is a long-term war, which will not be won in my lifetime, maybe even in my children's lifetime, and it has to be ready to change the rules of engagement and adapt them to the new threats that it faces. In the end I'm not an optimist. I'm not a pessimist.

I'd like to be an optimist, but I was born in 1938—and had I been born in Europe, I would be dead today and I wouldn't have children and grandchildren. The world stood by idly while the Jewish communities of Europe were totally destroyed. So nobody who has lived through the years of the Holocaust can ever be a complete optimist. I have to be a pragmatist. I have to be somebody who is willing to look hard at the options that are available to prevent ultimate destruction.

Benjamin Franklin was wrong when he said, "Those who are willing to compromise a little bit of liberty to obtain a little bit of security deserve neither." I don't believe that. I think the most important and fundamental right that a human being has is the right to live, the right to have children, the right to be free of threats of tyranny, and sometimes compromises in other values and other liberties have to be made in order to secure that ultimate liberty. We have to be prepared to make economic and material sacrifices, but also sacrifices of other natures in order to prevent the bringing about of a cataclysmic event—which is not beyond the realm of human possibility, because we've seen it once—and the motto of "never again" has to clearly resonate with all of us. And it can't be just a motto. It has to be a pragmatic, realistic approach to the threat of cataclysmic destruction, which is a realistic possibility for the future.

MDE: **One more question. The Israeli ambassador yesterday referred to this cult of death—this Islamofascist crisis, as he called it—World War III. Do you see it that way?**

Prof. Dershowitz: I see the threat posed to the United States and Israel as the beginning of a one-hundred-year war. You can call it World War III. You can call it the beginning of a new type of warfare. I wouldn't want to call it World War III because there are no analogies to World War I and World War II. This war has to be fought very, very differently, and we have to be creative. It was Santayana who said, "Those who forget the lessons of the past are destined to relive them," but those who focus only on the past are destined to miss what the future holds. I think the past has a vote but it doesn't have a veto, and we have to look at the future and what threats are posed to us in the future. So I would rather not use analogies to World War I and World War II and just think of this as a new kind of warfare that the West is clearly disadvantaged by. The asymmetry of morality makes it very hard for us to fight groups that have no morality.

Appendix I

EXCERPTS FROM AN INTERVIEW WITH MORT ZUCKERMAN

M ort Zuckerman is the current editor-in-chief of *U.S. News & World Report* and has been the publisher/owner of the *New York Daily News* since 1993. His columns appear regularly in his publications, and he occasionally appears on *The McLaughlin Group*.

MDE: **Please talk to me about how the terrorists use the media.**

Mr. Zuckerman: Well, in the first place, they understand how important the media is. For example, Zawahiri, who was the number-two guy to Osama Bin Laden, wrote a famous letter to al-Zarqawi when he was still alive in Iraq and pointed out to him that this is a battle in the media, and that's more than half the battle.

And he was talking to him in those terms because al-Zarqawi was attacking the Shia, and he said, "You're losing public support, and the media gave you a bad coverage on that," so understand how important the media is.

Now, it's also understood because there was a cable network, like *al Jazeera*, as a platform from which they can propagate their various ideologies and the way they present the facts. The war between Hezbollah and Israel is an example.

A number of the pictures are doctored. They control the access of even the correspondence from CNN, never-mind *al Jazeera*, to those particular scenes with their own statistics. They would never, for example, indicate in their stories that Hezbollah was using various sites as launching pads for the rockets against the Israelis, putting the Israelis in the quandary as to what to do, because if they go after the rockets—they were deliberately building these and hiding these in the homes of civilians—and so there were innocent civilians whose lives were at risk.

They would never mention, for example, that the Israelis called these people—or gave notice by dropping leaflets—which eliminated the issue of surprise, which is an important element in these things. So they understand that the media is a way of shaping political opinion, and they use the media with the idea of arousing world opinion to go against Israel, for example.

So they're very much aware of that—frankly, much more than even the Israelis and the U.S. government—which is always astonishing to me.

MDE: **When you look at the media and you see Muslims, and they call them dead civilians, there almost seems to me a litmus number of the count that creates a repulsion of the world. Is that all planned?**

Mr. Zuckerman: Well, I don't know that it's all planned, but, for example, they sent the pictures, where they deliberately doctored the pictures to make them darker and look more menacing, as if this was a Dresden in World War II. So they try and create and maximize the sense that these are innocent civilians, when, in fact, this wasn't the war between Israel and Lebanon or innocent civilians—it was a war between Israel and Hezbollah, and Hezbollah was using women and children as shields. One of the great dilemmas of the modern world is how do you find some way to prevent people from using innocent women and children as shields. There is a principle for civilized countries that you always separate the combatants from the noncombatants, but generally that requires a uniform.

When you have a group that deliberately hides themselves and their efforts behind civilians, that's when you have the problems and the complications coming up. And when the pictures, therefore, become pictures that, while in one sense, they may tell the truth in fundamental terms, they distort the truth because they leave out the fact that these people are deliberately hiding in the civilian areas in order to deter them from being attacked.

MDE: **The American people are hearing a lot of threats coming out about Iran wanting to go nuclear, and many**

of them think that this is no threat to America. Is this a threat to America?

Mr. Zuckerman: Well, if they think this is no threat to America, it is only because they do not hear or have access to the speeches and to the writings of the leadership of Iran. Iran is the most radical, extremist, religious, religiously motivated group in that part of the world. They have been since 1979, when the Ayatollah Khomeini took over that country.

They were the founders of Hezbollah, and they positioned Hezbollah not just in Lebanon but also in Europe to kill Iranian dissidents. In fact, there are twenty members of Hezbollah in European jails that are there for attacking and assassinating Iranian dissidents.

They are totally hostile to the West. They really do believe it is their mission to reinstate the caliphate to have a return of what they call the Mahdi, or their version of the messiah, which requires a battle between the believers and the infidels, which they are literally trying to provoke.

This is a religious extreme that we have never encountered, and it is compounded by the fact that they do not have a culture of life as we do, but, if anything, it's a culture of death. The president of Iran, Ahmadinejad, is a part of a group called the Basige. The Basige were a group of people that the Ayatollah Khomeini inspired to, in a sense, become martyrs, as they call them, in the war between Iran and Iraq.

He had them literally walking across minefields—they were human landmine discoverers—and they would literally blow up. He had them throwing themselves with grenades and explosives on their bodies against tanks. There are now ten to twelve million of them in Iran, and this is the power base of Ahmadinejad. We have never been up against a group of people who believe that there is a higher calling by dying for their religion, not for living for it.

MDE: **What do they hope to achieve in all of this?**

Mr. Zuckerman: What they hope to achieve—and I have been exposed to them, really, for fifteen or twenty years—they literally hope to achieve what they believe is a part of what, in the covenant of Hamas, is called the Muslim WAQF, or the Muslim endowment.

What is the Muslim endowment? It is that every bit of land, which at one point was controlled by the world of Islam, should return to the world of Islam, going all the way to Spain and Andalusia and Spain to India. In 1990, I met with the leaders of the Islamist party in the Jordanian parliament, and they told me that back in 1990. So this goes back a long, long time, and for various reasons this kind of belief system has been spread (a) by Iran on one part, and (b) by the Wahabi sect in Saudi Arabia.

After Iran was taken over by Khomeini, the Saudis, for various reasons, got very worried about the support from their own religious extremists, and so they began providing huge funding to them, and those are Sunni and Shia who are both spreading the same message—that the world of Islam must become ascended once again. The caliph—the caliph means the successor to Muhammad—must come back. We must reestablish a Muslim world, a world of Islam, all of one country, all controlled by the caliph—and that is what they believe in, and it is an extraordinarily powerful force in their lives.

MDE: **New York City, and obviously 9/11, is very close to you. Could you talk about where you were the day of 9/11, and could you also talk to the American people about the possibility of nuclear material ending up in this country and endangering the city or any other city?**

Mr. Zuckerman: That is certainly the greatest danger because it would literally, if it exploded in a city like New York or any major city, render the city uninhabitable in huge portions, and for twenty or thirty years, before the radiation, in this sense, would have gone away. But, to my mind, that's not the only risk.

I just ask you to think about the possibility that the Islamists from England, who were just recently found attempting to blow up nine or ten airplanes flying over the Atlantic—if they had succeeded, it would have changed our whole way of life.

If you were to have two or three attacks on the United States—and in the United States we are such an open society; our whole tradition is being an open society, such that it is impossible for us to foreclose every possible source of danger—it will change our way of life. The pressure of the American public to be protected, the pressure on the American government to protect the American public is going to be so acute, the government will be forced to institute all kinds of changes in our lifestyle that could literally change what America has been all about.

That, to me, is the greatest [threat]—it doesn't have to be an atomic bomb. It doesn't have to be a chemical or biological agent. It could be something, for example, as what happened—almost happened—with these airplanes— anything that really made it clear that we were still under great attack. And sooner or later, because we're such an open society, this may very well happen. And therefore it is critical that we all appreciate that this is a danger and why it is we must go after them before they come after us—because there's no way in a world as open as we have in this country that we can find a way to protect ourselves totally and hermetically against them.

MDE: **The concept of proxies was completely hidden from the world during the Lebanese war, even in spite of the fact that people like you spoke very loudly about the connection between Hezbollah and Iran. Iran suffered nothing from it. Is America in danger of proxies— Palestinian or any kind of proxies—in this country?**

Mr. Zuckerman: Absolutely. That is one of the great unknowns of the danger that we face: the ability of a country like Iran, which has always operated through proxies. They set up Hezbollah. They set up Hamas. They set up the Palestinian Islamic Jihad. They are the principal funder [and] the principal supplier of weapons, the principal trainer of these people— I mean literally thousands of Hezbollah people went to Iran from Lebanon to be trained in terrorist activities.

And, through Syria, they were not only trained, but they were rearmed as Iran used Syria as a gateway to rearm them. So these are all proxies whom they use in order to put, in effect, something in between them and the perpetrator of the crime—but they are the puppeteers in all of this—and these are the groups, and in effect, are the puppets.

And you see this when Hamas was elected. The first place they went to was Iran, and Iran promised them money, and Iran promised them support in addition to what they had already been giving them. Iran, after all, you recall, was the supplier of a huge boatload of weapons [aboard the] *Karine-A*, even to the Palestinian Authority, but that's a secondary source of proxy for them.

The Iranians have said in a speech, including Ahmadinejad, "Hezbollah is Iran and Iran is Hezbollah, and we will stand by them, and they will be for us and we will be for them." So there is no question about who they are, who they represent, and what they are about. They're both—Hezbollah's Shia, and so is Iran—their purpose is a desire to literally obliterate Western values and Western civilization—and for them, Israel, in a sense, is at the cutting edge of Western civilization.

MDE: **The president of Iran wrote President Bush an eighteen-page letter, and what he said in it, "Those with insight can already hear the sounds of the shattering and fall of the ideology and thoughts of the Liberal democratic systems," as if referring to the World Trade Center towers attack. Should the president of Iran be taken seriously when he makes statements like this?**

Mr. Zuckerman: Without question. I mean, you know, it is for us, who have a different sense of civil values that permeates not only our lives, but our religions—to hear somebody speaking like that, it almost sounds as if this is sort of almost a cartoon, that it's something you can't take seriously.

But in fact, these people are absolutely serious, and we have never encountered people like this is our lifetimes. A level of extremism that is motivated by their version of their God, which is Muhammad, to literally go out and destroy the West and to demolish their civilizations and to reassert the ascendancy of the world of Islam against the world of, in their minds, "the unbelievers," "the faithful versus the unbelievers."

The Christians and Jews are referred to as the "immies." These are second-rate citizens who, by the sufferance of the world of Islam, can live in their community, but not as equal citizens. That's their vision of the world and their version of the world, and, for various reasons, a whole complex number of reasons, it has become ascendant in more and more parts of the world of Islam.

There are many, many millions and tens of millions of people who are not that extreme and are much more moderate and want to, in a sense, improve their own lives, but these are people who don't care about life as we understand it, as I said. It is a culture of death, and we have yet to figure out how to deal with it. But that threat is absolutely fundamental to the possibility that we all can continue to live the kind of life that we have been blessed with in this country and in many other liberal democracies.

MDE: **The Israeli ambassador to the United Nations described Islamofascists, and he used that term, and he used the term that this is a World War. Do you agree with him, and, if so, can you explain?**

Mr. Zuckerman: Well, without question, it is a World War. I mean, if you think about it in terms of where the violence has taken place, it hasn't only taken place in the United States, although we suffered 9/11. It has taken place in Bali, it is taking place in Indonesia, it is taking place in India. They just blew up a couple of trains in India, and, I don't know, 202 people died and hundreds were injured.

They blew up a train in Spain. The cartoons, which I might add were not even cartoons—all of which were published—were spread throughout the Muslim world and caused riots all around the Muslim world against Scandinavia. You've had these terrorist attacks in England. So there are [attacks in] country after country after country.

All over Africa, you've had these attacks, so what you are dealing with is a huge worldwide community, and not just the Muslim world, but there are Muslims all over Europe and all over England. And as we can see, even second- and third-generation Muslims—some of the youth never get connected into the countries that they are living in, and they only connect through the Internet, I might add, with these radical Muslim ideas and ideologies—they get caught up in it, and they too become willing to lose their own lives, to sacrifice their own lives, to become martyrs in the service of this vision of destroying and demolishing and

MDE: **Why is the United Nations running to their rescue?**

Mr. Zuckerman: Well, you know, that's a very sad story. There's no doubt but that the United Nations has become a platform for them because the United Nations works—the General Assembly works—on the basis of one vote for one country. And there are literally dozens and dozens of countries like this, who either are part of the Muslim world or, alternatively, the world of Islam or, alternatively, do not want to incur their wrath. And so they, in a sense, tend to support this kind of view, or at least tolerate it if they don't support it.

And it's a huge issue. The UN has become a dysfunctional organization in terms of its abilities to service the kinds of values it was originally founded to represent. Secondly, the UN was an organization that was based on states, and what we are dealing with are not just states but networks of individuals who do not wear military uniforms, who, in a sense, are caught up in this credo of violence and extremism and who have at their beck and call weapons that have a destructive power once reserved for the States.

So we now face a lethal threat from these people, and, as you say, it's not only the actual destruction that they can do, but it's the way they can affect our whole way of life. Just think: 9/11 was the first time that the United States was attacked on its homeland since 1812. And how were we attacked? We were attacked by a group of people who lived in some mountain ranges in Afghanistan, thousands upon thousands of miles away, and they were able to literally change life in America.

We're up against people who are willing to die, and therefore it's very difficult to deter them rationally—people who are willing to die in the process of killing as many civilians as possible. And the reason they want to maximize the number of deaths is to have the greatest possible impact on the countries where they are carrying out these terrorist acts.

And so we are faced with an unprecedented threat and are working to figure out how to cope with it, and nobody has all the answers. But one thing we have to be appreciative of is that this threat is for real, and we are going to have to deal with it, and we can't ignore it, and it's not a question of one government or another government in power in this country. We are simply going to have to deal with it.

MDE: **How important is Israel in winning the war on terror?**

Mr. Zuckerman: Well, there is no doubt that Israel is the canary in the coal mine. This is where you have Israel as an island surrounded by a sea of Islam, some of which are of the most extreme nature. These extremist groups—I mean it's Hamas, it's Islamic Jihad, it's Hezbollah—these are the main groups that are, in a sense, using terrorist attacks and using Israel as a practice ground, as a training ground in which to stage them.

Now, I'll give you an example of something that I was directly involved in to indicate how intolerant they are. In the basilica in Nazareth, which is one of the great sites of Christianity, the mayor of Nazareth who was elected there was a much more extreme individual. This was six or seven years ago approximately.

He decided to build a mosque literally in the parking lot outside the basilica. The mosque would have been higher than the basilica, and they would have had these prayers five times a day, and, in effect, it would have, as a practical matter, intimidated and made impossible the visits of a lot of Christians who wished to go visit one of their great holy sites.

And it took an enormous effort working with the Israeli government, which I did, and working with the churches here. The Israeli government finally stopped it, but this was an attempt—a deliberate attempt, in a sense—to intimidate the Christian population as they did in Bethlehem. So they are not just against the Jewish world but against even the symbols of the Christian world that are seen as a threat to the return of the world of Islam. They believe that Muhammad, after all, was the successor to both Moses and Jesus, and therefore, why doesn't the rest of the world follow Muhammad?

And so we are having a struggle, which is not just about the ascendancy of Muslims but against the ascendancy of

Islam as a religious imperative—and that is something that we are just going to have. There's no way of compromising with their gods.

MDE: **How is the media being exploited by the terrorists for recruitment, for fund-raising, for glorification of martyrs, for political concessions. How do they use the media?**

Mr. Zuckerman: Well, the principal media that they use is the Internet. There are thousands of Internet sites that are devoted to this attempt to proselytize and to attract young people and others into this world of religious extremism and violence, and they provide all kinds of training—not just religious instruction, but instruction in terrorism—on these various sites.

So, in effect, you have a new technology that has made it possible to spread this message and to spread the way to make this message operational, in terrorist terms, all around the world. And the people in England, for example, picked that up, or the people in France or the people in Spain. It is true some of them went back to Pakistan, where there were training camps, but not all of them did, and a lot of them get this through that form of media, and, of course, to the extent that they can, they also get it through the more conventional media, which is television, primarily, where they try and organize pictures of events.

The response to the cartoons in Denmark is an example of where they used the media as a vehicle and a platform to arouse a whole sector of the Muslim population. This wasn't such a big issue until they literally showed these cartoons—some of which were never published—and they showed them all over the Muslim world, as if this represented something which was an attack on their religion.

And, of course, they're using, in a sense, the alienation that they feel from the Western world—from Western values and from Western religions—as a way of provoking a people, who literally for three hundred or four hundred years have felt humiliated by the fact that they were at the apex of civilization in the sixteenth century and are now fallen so dramatically behind. Not only the Western world, but the world of the Far East, where countries like Taiwan and South Korea and even China have really done so well and developed themselves.

And it is the Muslim world that has had the greatest difficulty in making this adjustment.

MDE: **How serious is Iran's nuclear program, and what does the United States need to do about it?**

Mr. Zuckerman: Well, there is no question that this is going to be an extraordinary danger to the Western world if Iran is able to develop nuclear weapons out of their own capabilities—that is, with their own technologies—as they are now able to develop the rocketry to deliver it.

And since you have a people there who believe that there has to be this great violent moment between the faithful and the unfaithful—between the believers and the infidels, that they literally believe—and Ahmadinejad, the president of Iran, actually says this—that he is waiting for the return of the man whom they call the Twelfth Imam, the Twelfth. This is their messiah. But the return of this messiah can only happen after this cataclysmic struggle between the infidels and the believers.

And he wants to provoke it. He believes it'll happen within a matter of years, and when I say a matter of years, I'm not talking ten years—less than ten years. In fact, he refurbished the well into which they believe the Twelfth Imam disappeared, in the hopes that he will rise again.

And this is what you have to cope with. This is a level of fanaticism that is willing to endure the murder and the assassination and the killing of all kinds of innocent people in order to find some way to bring back what they believe will be the symbol of their reascendancy in the world.

So it is deadly dangerous, and you will never know if they are willing, as they have been in the past, to use proxies—to use your phrase—to use the Hezbollah, or the Islamic Jihad, which are literally subsidiaries of Iran—to drop some kind of weapon of mass destruction. As I say it won't even take that, but if they had that, if they had the so-called suitcase bombs that they could bring into a country, where their fingerprints wouldn't be as easily detected as they would if it were a missile.

That danger is overwhelming, and it is a threat. You know, there is an old principle in business: never take a risk with something that you can't afford to lose. This, unfortunately, is something we can't afford to lose, so we don't know how high the risk is. But whatever the risk is, we can't afford to lose it, so we have to find a way to deal with it.

MDE: **God forbid, if Iran goes nuclear, what is the world going to look like a decade from now?**

Mr. Zuckerman: Well, I'm going to remain an optimist. I cannot help but be an optimist. I have had a wonderful life in this country—and somebody once said the difference between an optimist and a pessimist is that an optimist believes this is the best of all possible worlds and a pessimist fears he may be right.

But I do believe that we will find a way to cope with it, that there are enough countries in the world who understand how serious this threat is and that nobody escapes it. I mean, if there were an atomic weapon or a weapon of mass destruction, some kind of chemical or some kind of biological agent that was dropped anywhere—whether it was in a city in Europe, whether it was a city in the United States, whether it was in Israel, whether it was in Russia—it will affect everybody around the world. So I have to believe that, at some point, the parochial interest of individual countries and individual leaders will somehow or another be transcended by this understanding of this common threat, and we will find a way to cope with it.

MDE: **The president of Iran keeps talking about oil—the price of oil—and about the polls. There was something interesting that happened in the fall of the Reagan and Carter election at the polls. The [oil prices] kept dropping and dropping and dropping; then all of a sudden, the very day Ronald Reagan was elected, the hostages were released.**

Mr. Zuckerman: That was the first victory of Ronald Reagan because everybody knew that if he came into office, he would be much, much more tough-minded in dealing with the Iranians than Jimmy Carter.

MDE: **Do the Iranians look at the American polls, and are they tactical enough to try to affect American polls?**

Mr. Zuckerman: Without question. If you think about the fact that just before the last election, Osama bin Laden delivered another video four days before—on the Friday before—the Tuesday election. And that video really, once again, took over the whole political dialogue. That was not by accident. They didn't do it by accident, and I can tell you that our intelligence services believe it was done deliberately to affect our election.

And so they understand what the polls are, and they follow them carefully. We're a very open society. It's not hard to figure out where they are. I'm sure they even do their own polling. So I think this is something they are quite well informed of.

I believe, by the way, that there are a lot of people in Iran who are opposed to this regime. There's a huge unemployment rate. A lot of the younger people there are fairly well educated. It's a great culture, the Persian culture, and they have superimposed upon this a religious extreme, which a lot of people are uncomfortable with and hostile to.

Nevertheless, because they are not a democracy in the real sense of that word, we have a disadvantage in the short run because they can find out much more easily what's happening in our society. But in the long run, our freedoms basically provide the very strength that I hope will see us through to the other side.

MDE: **Israelis—many of the generals that I met with a few weeks ago—they talked to me about improvised explosive devices. They were using numbers like 85 percent of all of them in Iraq are coming from Iran. And they also talked about the number of terrorists that are killing the troops. They said the majority of the troops are being killed by Iranian terrorists. If, in fact, that's so, why are we not hearing about that in the media in America?**

Mr. Zuckerman: Well, I don't know what the answer to that is because it is difficult to get proof of that. What you have ongoing now, you had somebody like Zarqawi, who was perhaps the leading figure in that world of terrorism and violence—and he was a

Sunni, not a Shiite—but the Iranians, in part, were responsible when he blew up the Golden Mosque of Samara. That really has triggered off a sectarian war there, and I think there is no question but that the Iranians have been feeding weapons, money, and all sorts of other things to the Shiites because they want to at least have some base of extension of their own security and their own control in Iraq.

Iraq, after all, was the great countervailing balance to Iran for many, many years. So there is no question but they are involved, but it is very difficult to get any real proof of that, and to the extent that we, the United States, have proof of that, we don't want to release how we got that because sources and methods will then expose the very sources of intelligence that we need.

MDE: **In the letter the president of Iran brought to President Bush—most of it was a preaching letter—it seemed he was trying to convert him. Does he really have a goal or an intention of trying somehow to convert Christians to his beliefs?**

Mr. Zuckerman: Well, it's hard for me to understand the way that man thinks, but there was an interview with him on *60 Minutes.* I mean, I'm always amazed that we provide a platform for these people to preach their message; in a way that is kind of dismaying, but that's the nature of our system.

And, basically, what he was clearly trying to do there—and considering where he was coming from and what his views are, he did, I thought, quite well—he was basically trying to say, "Oh, we're not such bad guys. We just want the same things as you do, and blah, blah, blah, blah, blah." But, in fact, they do wish to eject us from huge parts of the world, and they will use whatever weapons they have at their fingertips to do that.

And, as I have said, they have almost an unlimited supply of people who are willing to die as what they call martyrs in the service of whatever that vision is. They believe they will have a permanent life in heaven—in their version of heaven—and so will their families, if they do that, and they're willing to do that—and, as I have said, it is not absolutely clear how we are going to cope with that. We certainly are going to have to do a lot more than we are doing today.

MDE: **How influential are the forces of bigotry and oil economics in this battle?**

Mr. Zuckerman: Well, you know, this is the thing that I have to say is one of the most upsetting issues that I think this country has to face. With oil prices going up the way they have, we are funding the very people who are our enemies. We are funding Iran. We are funding the Saudis. We are funding even the Russians, who are sort of very, very strange friends.

All of these countries who possess this oil are using it in one form or another—I mean, certainly Iran—in effect, to support exactly the kinds of activities. They're funding all these terrorist groups, they give money to Hezbollah, they give weapons to Hezbollah, they buy weapons, training, whatever it takes—and where did it come from?

I can assure you that Russia would have been much more amenable supporting us when oil was at twenty dollars a barrel, and they had a huge international debt, than it is at seventy-five dollars a barrel, when they have one hundred billion in the bank. The same thing is true of Iran. Iran had a huge international debt. Saudi Arabia had a huge international debt. Now, they have—Iran has—who knows? Forty-five to fifty billion in the bank? Saudi Arabia has a couple of hundred billion dollars in the bank.

And, at this point, they think the world is their oyster and they don't have to really accommodate the kinds of things that we need them to accommodate in terms of having a civil world in which people live and let live.

MDE: **This is the last question. With the Iran crisis, we appear to be heading for a showdown. If, God forbid, this country does not comply with economic and diplomatic concessions, do you think that the United States—exhausting all other remedies—would have to use the military option?**

Mr. Zuckerman: The military option could never be taken off the table because if it is taken off the table, we're going to have to go in stages. The UN resolution, which has been passed by the

Security Council, calls for economic sanctions, and that may be the first step to show them that we mean what we say.

But, ultimately, at some point, if they continue to threaten the civilized world and the Western world and they do not wish to take into account how critical it is that they not have this capacity for nuclear weapons, that is going to become a major decision that's going to be on the table of some—on the desk of some president of the United States, either this one or the next one.

In my judgment, it'll be this one because within the next two and a half years, there's no doubt, they will deliver the capacity internally to develop nuclear weapons, as did, in fact, a country like North Korea, which doesn't have nearly the population, the intellectual sophistication, or the education of a lot of people that you have in Iran.

It's not impossible to do. We've seen North Korea do it. North Korea is a country that is much more easily containable. They are selling their nuclear technologies and their missile technology. They sold a lot of their missile technologies to Iran, and Iran then used that to develop their own domestic missile technologies. Now they're using whatever they have been able to buy from A. Q. Khan of Pakistan—who is selling this all over the world—or North Korea. They're using that to develop their own domestic nuclear capabilities. This is a disaster.

I interviewed Putin in Russia when we had just gone to war in Iraq, and he said, "Why Iraq?" He said, "Iran is the real danger." Well, we're going to find out whether Russia supports us, and for a long time they were in a very ambiguous position. I think they finally realized how dangerous this is for them.

China, I think, also understands it—but the only forum in which we can make progress in these areas, unfortunately, is the United Nations—and the United Nations gives all these countries vetoes. We must get them to join us, and that's just a basic fact of life.

Appendix J

A 21-DAY STUDY OF IRAN (PERSIA), IRAQ (BABYLON), AND ISRAEL IN BIBLICAL PROPHECY

WEEK 1		
Day 1	Daniel's prayer and the seventy weeks	Daniel 9
Day 2	Daniel's vision of the man	Daniel 10
Day 3	The kings of the north and south	Daniel 11
Day 4	The End of Days	Daniel 12
Day 5	Israel reborn	Ezekiel 36:1–11, 22–36
Day 6	Nations shall rise against Israel	Ezekiel 38
Day 7	Those nations are judged	Ezekiel 39
WEEK 2		
Day 8	Jesus on the End Times in Matthew	Matthew 24
Day 9	Jesus on the End Times in Mark	Mark 13
Day 10	Jesus on the End Times in Luke	Luke 21
Day 11	John before the throne of God	Revelation 4–5
Day 12	The seven seals	Revelation 6–8:5
Day 13	The seven trumpets	Revelation 8:6–11:19
Day 14	The beasts and the great harvest	Revelation 12–14
WEEK 3		
Day 15	The seven plagues and the seven bowls	Revelation 15–16
Day 16	Babylon rises	Revelation 17
Day 17	Babylon falls	Revelation 18–19:5
Day 18	The marriage supper of the Lamb and the coming of He who is faithful and true	Revelation 19:6–21
Day 19	The defeat of Satan	Revelation 20
Day 20	The new heaven and earth	Revelation 21
Day 21	"Surely, I am coming"	Revelation 22

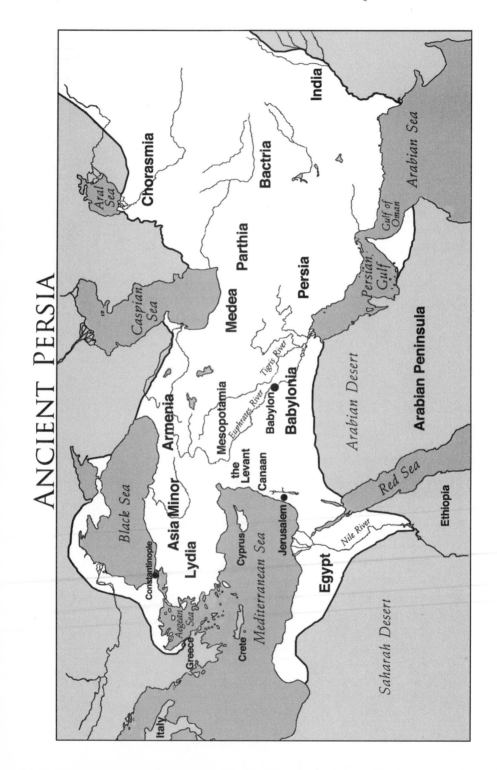

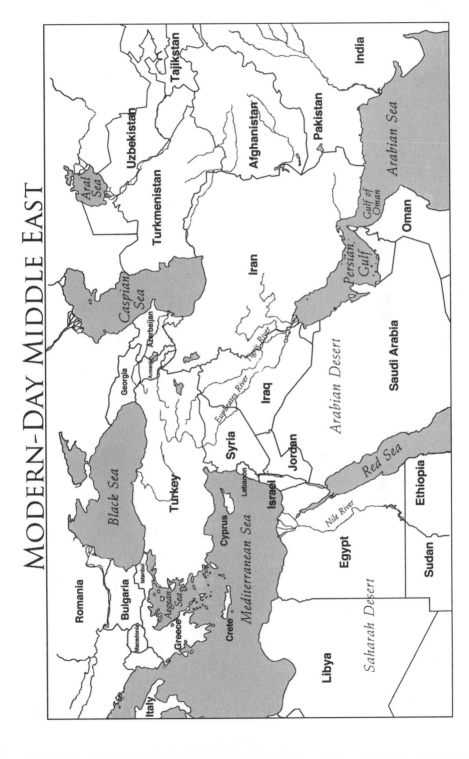

Notes

INTRODUCTION

1. CNN.com, "Giuliani Rejects $10 Million From Saudi Prince," October 12, 2001, http://archives.cnn.com/2001/US/10/11/rec.giuliani.prince/index .html (accessed January 22, 2007).

2. George W. Bush, "Address to the Nation," January 10, 2007, as quoted by the *New York Times,* http://www.nytimes.com/2007/01/10/world/ middleeast/10cnd-ptext.html?ex=1169701200&en=9e8ad4c46b84713e&ei =5070 (accessed January 23, 2007).

3. We will look at this again in chapter three, where the exact quote appears.

4. Joseph Farah, "U.S., Israel to Attack Iran Nukes 'Before April,'" G2 Bulletin at WorldNetDaily.com, January 23, 2006, http://www.worldnetdaily .com/news/article.asp?ARTICLE_ID=48430 (accessed January 21, 2007).

5. Daniel Pipes, "How the West Could Lose," *Jerusalem Post,* December 27, 2006, http://www.jpost.com/servlet/Satellite?cid=1164881991915&pagena me=JPost/JPArticle/ShowFull (accessed January 23, 2007).

6. Winston Churchill, "We Shall Fight on the Beaches" speech before the House of Commons, June 4, 1940, as quoted by the Churchill Centre, http://www.winstonchurchill.org/i4a/pages/index.cfm?pageid=393 (accessed January 22, 2007).

7. Winston Churchill, "The Years the Locusts Have Eaten," in *The Second World War,* vol. 1, as quoted in a speech by Newt Gingrich, printed in the *Atlanta-Journal Constitution,* as posted on the Newt.org e-Community forum "How to Deal With Iran?" http://www.newt.org/forum/topic.asp?fi =20000001&catId=30000001&ti=400000369 (accessed January 23, 2007).

8. Abraham Lincoln, "Proclamation Appointing a National Fast Day," March 30, 1863, as quoted by Abraham Lincoln Online, "Speeches and Writings," http://showcase.netins.net/web/creative/lincoln/speeches/fast.htm (accessed January 21, 2007).

CHAPTER ONE: A PROPHETIC STORM GATHERS

1. Walid Shoebat, personal interview with Mike Evans, August 26, 2006.

2. Iran Chamber Society, "Cyrus the Great," Historic Personalities, http:// www.iranchamber.com/history/cyrus/cyrus.php (accessed January 23, 2007).

3. *The Encyclopedia Britannica,* vol. 6 (1958), 940; as quoted by Wayne Jackson, "Cyrus the Great in Biblical Prophecy," ChristianCourier.com, September 28, 2000, http://www.christiancourier.com/articles/read/cyrus _the_great_in_biblical_prophecy (accessed December 19, 2006).

4. Wikipedia.org, s.v. "History of Iran," http://en.wikipedia.org/wiki/
History_of_Iran (accessed December 8, 2006); and Ehsan Yarshater, "Persia
or Iran," *Iranian Studies,* vol. 12, no. 1 (1989), as excerpted by the Circle of
Ancient Iranian Studies in "Persia or Iran? When 'Persia' Became 'Iran,'"
trans. Abbas Ferzamfar, 1998, http://www.cais-soas.com/CAIS/Iran/persia_
or_iran.htm (accessed December 8, 2006).

CHAPTER TWO: RECALIBRATING AMERICA'S
MORAL COMPASS

1. Alan Dershowitz, personal interview with Mike Evans, August 18,
2006. For more excerpts of this interview, see Appendix H.

2. Wikiquote.org, s.v. "Golda Meir," http://en.wikiquote.org/wiki/Golda_
Meir (accessed January 23, 2007).

3. George Washington, farewell address, as quoted by the Avalon Project,
"Washington's Farewell Address 1796," http://www.yale.edu/lawweb/avalon/
washing.htm (accessed February 2, 2007).

4. John Adams, letter to the officers of the First Brigade of the Third
Division of the militia of Massachusetts, October 11, 1798, as quoted by
Wikiquote.org, http://en.wikiquote.org/wiki/John_Adams (accessed January
23, 2007).

5. Natan Sharansky, *The Case for Democracy: The Power of Freedom to
Overcome Tyranny and Terror* (New York: PublicAffairs, 2004), 40–41.

6. See Proverbs 27:10.

7. Stephen Goode, "Bush Brings Faith Into Full View," *Insight on the News,*
May 11, 2004, http://www.findarticles.com/p/articles/mi_m1571/is_2004_
May_11/ai_n6145022 (accessed January 23, 2007).

8. Scott Stearns, "Bush Calls for Greater Religious Tolerance in U.S.,"
Voice of America, February 7, 2002, http://www.voanews.com/english/
archive/2002-02/a-2002-02-07-1-Bush.cfm (accessed December 21, 2006).

9. Debbie Daniel, "Life Is Just One Grand Sweet Song, So Start the Music!"
American Daily, June 10, 2004, http://www.americandaily.com/article/779
(accessed January 23, 2007).

10. Ronald Reagan, inaugural address, January 20, 1981, as quoted in
Ronald Reagan Presidential Archives, University of Texas, http://www
.reagan.utexas.edu/archives/speeches/1981/12081a.htm (accessed December
21, 2006).

11. Dinesh D'Souza, "Purpose: What It Was All About," *National
Review Online,* June 8, 2004, http://www.nationalreview.com/comment/
dsouza200406080824.asp (accessed January 24, 2007).

12. Whittaker Chambers, "Letter to My Children," foreword to *Witness*, as quoted by University of Missouri-Kansas City School of Law, http://www .law.umkc.edu/faculty/projects/ftrials/hiss/chambersletter.html (accessed December 21, 2006).

13. Ibid.

14. Ibid.

15. Ronald Reagan, "The Evil Empire," remarks at the annual convention of the National Association of Evangelicals, March 8, 1983, as quoted by American Rhetoric, http://www.americanrhetoric.com/speeches/ ronaldreaganevilempire.htm (accessed December 21, 2006).

16. Ariel Sharon, personal interview with Mike Evans.

17. Ronald Reagan, remarks at an ecumenical prayer breakfast in Dallas, Texas, August 23, 1984, as quoted in Ronald Reagan Presidential Archives, University of Texas, http://www.reagan.utexas.edu/archives/speeches/1984/ 82384a.htm (accessed January 24, 2007).

18. The White House, "State of the Union Address of the President to the Joint Session of Congress," news release, January 29, 2002, http:// www.c-span.org/executive/transcript.asp?cat=current_event&code=bush_ admin&year=2002 (accessed November 13, 2006).

19. Joseph Goebbels, "The Jews Are Guilty!" *Das Reich*, November 16, 1941, as quoted by Calvin College, German Propaganda Archive, http://www .calvin.edu/academic/cas/gpa/goeb1.htm (accessed January 24, 2007).

20. Alexander Solzhenitsyn, "A World Split Apart," address at Harvard Class Day afternoon exercises, June 8, 1978, http://www.columbia.edu/cu/ augustine/arch/solzhenitsyn/harvard1978.html (accessed December 21, 2006).

21. Lee Edwards, "The Reagan Doctrine," the Heritage Foundation, http:// www.heritage.org/Research/reagan_edwards13.cfm (accessed December 28, 2006).

22. George W. Bush, remarks at the swearing-in ceremony for Tom Ridge as director of the Office of Homeland Security, October 8, 2001, as quoted in the American Presidency Project, http://www.presidency.ucsb.edu/ws/print .php?pid=62592 (accessed December 21, 2006).

CHAPTER THREE: WHAT THE FUTURE HOLDS

1. The White House, "President Discusses War on Terrorism," news release, November 8, 2001, http://www.whitehouse.gov/news/releases/2001/ 11/20011108-13.html (accessed December 20, 2006).

2. The White House, "Press Briefing by Tony Snow," news release, October 19, 2006, http://www.whitehouse.gov/news/releases/2006/10/20061019-1.html (accessed January 24, 2007).

3. James A. Baker III and Lee H. Hamilton, et al., *The Iraq Study Group Report*, December 6, 2006, http://www.usip.org/isg/iraq_study_group_report/report/1206/iraq_study_group_report.pdf (accessed January 24, 2007).

4. Aaron Klein, "Terrorists Rejoicing Over New Iraq 'Plan,'" WorldNetDaily.com, December 6, 2006, http://www.worldnetdaily.com/news/article.asp?ARTICLE_ID=53269 (accessed December 13, 2006).

5. Ibid.

6. Ibid.

7. Brietbart.com, "Ahmadinejad: Britain, Israel, US to 'Vanish Like the Pharaohs,'" December 20, 2006, http://www.breitbart.com/news/2006/12/20/061220094102.ixs3bo81.html (accessed December 26, 2006).

8. InsightMag.com, "Baker Wants Israel Excluded From Regional Conference," December 5, 2006, http://www.insightmag.com/Media/MediaManager/Baker_1.htm (accessed December 13, 2006).

9. Ibid.

10. Peter W. Galbraith, *The End of Iraq* (New York: Simon and Schuster, 2006), 206–207.

11. Numbers on these distributions vary with the source but stay in roughly this range. See, for example, Wikipedia.org, s.v. "Iraq," http://en.wikipedia.org/wiki/Iraq (accessed November 9, 2006); David Gritten, "Long Path to Iraq's Sectarian Split," *BBC News*, February 25, 2006, http://news.bbc.co.uk/2/hi/middle_east/4750320.stm#su (accessed November 10, 2006); and Central Intelligence Agency, "The World Fact Book: Iraq," https://www.cia.gov/cia/publications/factbook/geos/iz.html (accessed November 10, 2006).

12. Joshua Holland, "Bush's Petro-Cartel Almost Has Iraq's Oil," *AlterNet*, October 16, 2006, http://www.alternet.org/waroniraq/43045/ (accessed November 12, 2006).

13. Charles Nash, interview with Mike Evans, August 16, 2006. For more excerpts from this interview, see Appendix F.

14. Daniel Pipes, "In Iraq, Stay the Course—But Change It," *New York Sun*, October 24, 2006, http://www.danielpipes.org/article/4066 (accessed November 11, 2006).

15. The White House, "Press Conference by the President," news release, October 25, 2006, http://www.whitehouse.gov/news/releases/2006/10/20061025.html (accessed November 11, 2006).

16. *WashingtonPost.com*, "Ahmadinejad's Letter to Bush," May 9, 2006, http://www.washingtonpost.com/wp-dyn/content/article/2006/05/09/AR2006050900878_pf.html (accessed January 24, 2007). For the complete letter, see Appendix A.

17. The Online NewsHour, "Plan Floated to Divide Iraq Along Ethnic Lines," October 24, 2006, http://www.pbs.org/newshour/bb/middle_east/july-dec06/iraq_10-24.html (accessed November 12, 2006).

18. Christopher Bodeen, "Al Qaeda in Iraq Claims It's Winning War," Associated Press, November 10, 2006, http://www.breitbart.com/news/2006/11/10/D8LAC4OG1.html (accessed November 12, 2006).

CHAPTER FOUR: THE CENTERS OF GRAVITY

1. Moshe Ya'alon, keynote speech in Dallas, Texas, June 28, 2006.

2. Charles Nash, personal interview with Mike Evans, August 16, 2006. For more excerpts of this interview, see Appendix F.

3. The White House, "President Bush Announces Major Combat Operations in Iraq Have Ended," news release, May 1, 2003, http://www.whitehouse.gov/news/releases/2003/05/20030501-15.html (accessed January 25, 2007).

4. Con Coughlin, "How the 45-Minute Claim Got From Baghdad to No. 10," *Telegraph*, July 12, 2003, http://www.telegraph.co.uk/news/main.jhtml?xml=/news/2003/12/07/wirq107.xml (accessed January 25, 2007).

5. Ibid.

6. Thomas McInerney and Paul Vallely, *Endgame: The Blueprint for Victory in the War on Terror* (Washington DC: Regnery Publishing, Inc., 2004), 41.

7. Wikipedia.org, "Iraq Resolution," http://en.wikipedia.org/wiki/Joint_Resolution_to_Authorize_the_Use_of_United_States_Armed_Forces_Against_Iraq (accessed December 2, 2006).

8. Wikipedia.org, "American Popular Opinion on Invasion of Iraq," http://en.wikipedia.org/wiki/American_popular_opinion_on_invasion_of_Iraq (accessed January 25, 2007).

9. Ayman El-Amir, "Ensnaring Saddam," *Al-Ahram Weekly Online*, July 11, 2002, http://weekly.ahram.org.eg/2002/594/op2.htm (accessed December 3, 2006).

10. Robert Marquand and Peter Ford, "A New Doctrine and a Scud Bust," *Christian Science Monitor*, December 12, 2002, http://www.csmonitor.com/2002/1212/p01s03-woap.html (accessed December 3, 2006).

11. Alan Dershowitz, personal interview with Mike Evans, August 18, 2006. For more excerpts of this interview, see Appendix H.

12. CBSNews.com, "Hezbollah: 'A-Team of Terrorists,'" April 18, 2003, http://www.cbsnews.com/stories/2003/04/18/60minutes/printable550000 .shtml (accessed December 3, 2006).

13. Ibid.

14. Israel Defense Forces/Military Intelligence, "Iran and Syria as Strategic Support for Palestinian Terrorism," September 30, 2002, http://www.mfa.gov .il/MFA/MFAArchive/2000_2009/2002/9/Iran%20and%20Syria%20as%20 Strategic%20Support%20for%20Palestinia (accessed December 3, 2006).

15. DEBKA*file*, "Tehran Plots Second Anti-U.S. War Front Deploying Syria, Hizballah, Palestinians," September 3, 2002, http://www.debka.com/ article.php?aid=167 (accessed December 3, 2006).

16. Israel Ministry of Foreign Affairs, "Hizbullah Attacks Along Israel's Northern Border May 2000–June 2006," July 12, 2006, http://www.mfa .gov.il/NR/exeres/9EE216D7-82EF-4274-B80D-6BBD1803E8A7,frameless .htm?NRMODE=Published (accessed December 3, 2006).

17. Guy Dinmore, "Iraqi Opposition Leaders Meet in Tehran," IranReporter.com, December 9, 2002, http://www.iranreporter.com/story .asp?id=407 (accessed December 3, 2006).

18. Yossef Bodansky, *The Secret History of the Iraq War* (New York: Regan Books, 2004), 142.

19. Ibid.

20. Mark Hosenball, "Intelligence: A Double Game," *Newsweek*, May 10, 2006, http://www.msnbc.msn.com/id/4881157/ (accessed December 3, 2006).

21. John Diamond, "Israel Reportedly Helping With U.S. War Preparation," *USA Today*, November 3, 2002, http://www.usatoday.com/ news/world/2002-11-03-israel-usat_x.htm (accessed December 2006).

22. DEBKA*file*, "Arafat's New Terror Weapon: Exploding Toy Planes," January 14, 2003, http://www.debka.com/article.php?aid=239 (accessed December 3, 2006).

23. WorldTribune.com, "Israel Gets the Word: Won't Fight in Iraq War," December 22, 2002, http://www.worldtribune.com/worldtribune/ WTARC/2002/ss_israel_12_20.html (accessed December 3, 2006).

24. David Rudge, "North on Alert After Car Bomb, Hizbullah Attack," *Jerusalem Post*, January 22, 2003, http://pqasb.pqarchiver.com/jpost/ access/279406881.html?dids=279406881:279406881&FMT=FT&FMTS=ABS: FT&date=Jan+22%2C+2003&author=DAVID+RUDGE&pub=Jerusalem+ Post&desc=North+on+alert+after+car+bomb%2C+Hizbullah+attack.

25. Milton Viorst, "The Wisdom of Imagining the Worst-Case Scenario," *New York Times*, September 12, 2002, http://select.nytimes.com/search/

restricted/article?res=F50C1FF739550C718DDDA00894DA404482 (accessed December 3, 2006).

26. Associated Press, "Text of Bush Speech on Iraq: President Gives Saddam Hussein a 48-Hour Deadline," *CBS News Online,* March 17, 2003, http://www.cbsnews.com/stories/2003/03/17/iraq/main544377.shtml (accessed: October 31, 2006).

CHAPTER FIVE: THE REAL BATTLE FOR IRAQ BEGINS

1. Chris Hamilton, personal interview with Mike Evans, August 16, 2006.

2. Dani Yatom, personal interview with Mike Evans, July 23, 2006.

3. *World Tribune,* "Hussein Given Safe Haven in Belarus?" April 25, 2003, as quoted by Truth Seeker, http://www.thetruthseeker.co.uk/article .asp?id=729 (accessed December 3, 2006).

4. The Online NewsHour, "Officials Investigate Shooting Attack on Russian Convoy," April 7, 2003, http://www.pbs.org/newshour/updates/ convoy.html (accessed December 3, 2006).

5. Air Force Association special report, "Gulf War II: Air and Space Power Led the Way," (Arlington, VA: Aerospace Education Foundation, 2003), 20, viewed at http://www.afa.org/media/reports/GulfWar.pdf (accessed February 22, 2007).

6. Steven Stalinsky, "Leading Egyptian Islamic Clerics on Jihad Against U.S. Troops in Iraq: March–August 2003," Middle East Media Research Institute, Inquiry and Analysis series, August 14, 2003, no. 145, http:// memri.org/bin/articles.cgi?Page=archives&Area=ia&ID=IA14503 (accessed December 6, 2006).

7. Bodansky, *The Secret History of the Iraq War,* 250.

8. Nazila Fathi, "Aftereffects: Tehran; Iran Opposes U.S. Accord With Fighters Based in Iraq," *New York Times,* May 2, 2003, http://select.nytimes .com/search/restricted/article?res=F50D14FF3C580C718CDDAC0894DB40 4482.

9. Glenn Kessler and Dana Priest, "U.S. Planners Surprised by Strength of Iraqi Shiites," *Washington Post,* April 23, 2003, http://www.washingtonpost .com/ac2/wp-dyn/A17886-2003Apr22?language=printer (accessed January 26, 2007).

10. *WashingtonPost.com,* "Administration Comments on Saddam Hussein and the Sept. 11 Attacks," May 1, 2003, http://www.washingtonpost .com/wp-srv/politics/polls/9-11_saddam_quotes.html (accessed December 6, 2006).

11. Kathy Gannon, "Alleged Bin Laden Tape Calls for Jihad," *CBS News*, April 8, 2003, http://www.cbsnews.com/stories/2003/02/11/attack/main540168.shtml (accessed December 6, 2006).

12. Douglas Farah and Dana Priest, "Bin Laden Son Plays Key Role in Al Qaeda," *Washington Post*, October 14, 2003, A1.

13. IslamistWatch.org, "Al Qaeda Communique," attributed to Ayman al-Zawahiri, on or about May 20, 2003, http://www.islamistwatch.org/texts/comms/zawahiri05-20-03.html/ (accessed March 1, 2007).

14. *Washington Post*, "U.S. Soldiers, Civilians Held Overnight by Iranians," June 3, 2003, A18.

15. Donald H. Rumsfeld, "Core Principles for a Free Iraq," *Opinion Journal*, from *Wall Street Journal* editorial page, May 27, 2003, http://www.opinionjournal.com/editorial/feature.html?id=110003545 (accessed January 29, 2007).

16. The White House, "President Bush, Prime Minister Blair Hold Press Availability," news release, March 27, 2003, http://www.whitehouse.gov/news/releases/2003/03/20030327-3.html (accessed December 6, 2006).

17. Ibid.

18. Uzi Landau, "A Map to National Disaster," *Ha'aretz*, April 11, 2003, as quoted by Tom Gross, "The Road Map Is a Huge Prize for Terror," Mideast Dispatch Archive, April 24, 2003, http://www.tomgrossmedia.com/mideastdispatches/archives/000611.html (accessed December 6, 2006).

19. Harry de Quetteville, "Will Iraqis Stand By and Watch Their Country Be Hijacked, Too?" *Telegraph* (UK), online version, December 31, 2003, http://www.telegraph.co.uk/opinion/main.jhtml?xml=/opinion/2003/12/31/do3101.xml (accessed December 17, 2006).

CHAPTER SIX: THE WORLD WAR AGAINST TERRORISM

1. Alan Dershowitz, personal interview with Mike Evans, August 18, 2006. For more excerpts of this interview, see Appendix H.

2. Associated Press, "Al-Qaida in Iraq: 4,000 Foreign Fighters Killed: Attacked Urged During Ramadan in Tape Purportedly From Group's Leader," MSNBC.com, September 28, 2006, http://www.msnbc.msn.com/id/15044435/ (accessed December 1, 2006).

3. Bodansky, *The Secret History of the Iraq War*, 9.

4. Con Coughlin, "Saddam Killed Abu Nidal Over al-Qa'eda Row," *Telegraph* (UK), online version, August 25, 2002, http://www.telegraph.co.uk/news/main.jhtml?xml=/news/2002/08/25/wnidal25.xml (accessed January 26, 2007); also, see Bodansky, *The Secret History of the Iraq War*, 14–15.

5. Michael R. Gordon, "After the War: Falluja; U.S. Troops Put on a Show of Military Force in a Center of Hard-Core Resistance," *New York Times*, June 8, 2003, http://select.nytimes.com/search/restricted/article?res= F30A13FB3F5D0C7B8CDDAF0894DB404482 (accessed December 12, 2006).

6. Ellen Knickmeyer and Omar Fekeiki, "Iraqi Shiite Cleric Pledges to Defend Iran: Sadr, With Powerful Militia, Vows to Respond to Attack by West on Neighbor," *WashingtonPost.com*, January 24, 2006, http://www .washingtonpost.com/wp-dyn/content/article/2006/01/23/AR2006012301701 .html (accessed January 26, 2007); GlobalSecurity.org, "Al-Mahdi Army/ Active Religious Seminary/Al-Sadr's Group," http://www.globalsecurity.org/ military/world/para/al-Sadr.htm (accessed January 26, 2007); GlobalSecurity .org, "Muqtada al-Sadr," http://www.globalsecurity.org/military/world/iraq/ al-Sadr.htm (accessed January 26, 2007); and Bryan Bender, "US Believes Iran Is Aiding Iraqi Militias," *Boston Globe,* April 9, 2004, http://www.boston .com/news/nation/articles/2004/04/09/us_believes_iran_is_aiding_iraqi_ militias/ (accessed January 26, 2007).

7. Charles Nash, personal interview with Mike Evans, August 16, 2006. For more excerpts of this interview, see Appendix F.

8. Jane Arraf, "Iraq Insurgents' Bombmaking Gets More Lethal," *NBC News*, December 8, 2006, http://www.msnbc.msn.com/id/16110075/ (accessed December 12, 2006).

9. James Woolsey, personal interview with Mike Evans, August 16, 2006. For more excerpts of this interview, see Appendix D.

10. Liz Neisloss and Matthew Chance, "UN: Sanctions Loom, Iran Keeps Enriching," *CNN.com,* August 31, 2006, http://www.cnn.com/2006/WORLD/ meast/08/31/iran.deadline/index.html (accessed November 1, 2006).

11. Nasser Karimi, "Ahmadinejad: Iran's Nuke Capability Up," Breitbart .com, October 23, 2006, http://www.breitbart.com/news/2006/10/23/ D8KUD2EG2.html (accessed November 1, 2006).

12. Nasser Karimi, "Iran Doubles Nuke Enrichment Capacity," *ABC News International*, October 27, 2006, http://news.yahoo.com/s/ap/20061027/ap_ on_re_mi_ea/iran_nuclear (accessed November 2, 2006).

13. *BBCNews.com,* "Bush Condemns Iran Nuclear Move," October 27, 2006, http://news.bbc.co.uk/2/hi/middle_east/6092540.stm (accessed November 2, 2006).

14. Ehud Olmert, interview on *CNN Late Edition with Wolf Blitzer,* May 21, 2006, online transcript, http://transcripts.cnn.com/ TRANSCRIPTS/0605/21/le.01.html (accessed December 17, 2006).

15. *BBCNews.com*, "Iran Bomb 'Within Next 10 Years,'" June 2, 2006, http://news.bbc.co.uk/2/hi/middle_east/5039956.stm (accessed November 2, 2006).

16. Wikipedia.org, s.v. "1983 Beirut Barracks Bombing," http://en.wikipedia.org/wiki/Beirut_barracks_bombing (accessed November 12, 2006).

17. Alan Dershowitz, personal interview withMike Evans, August 18, 2006. For more excerpts of this interview, see Appendix H.

18. Walid Shoebat, personal interview with Mike Evans, August 26, 2006.

19. Hyscience.com, "Ahmadinejad and the Mahdi," May 5, 2005, http://www.hyscience.com/archives/2006/05/ahmadinejad_and.php (accessed December 14, 2006).

20. Moshe Ya'alon, personal interview with Mike Evans, June 2006.

CHAPTER SEVEN: FUMBLING OUR ALLY, IRAN

1. Gerald Warner, "High Time for Dubya to Take Hard Line With the Nuclear Mullahs," *Scotland on Sunday*, June 19, 2005, http://news.scotsman.com/opinion.cfm?id=674332005 (accessed January 24, 2007).

2. Gary Sick, *All Fall Down* (Lincoln, NE: Author's Guild, 2001), 193–194.

3. University of Tehran Web site, "UT Overview," http://www.ut.ac.ir/en/main-links/overview.htm (accessed December 8, 2006).

4. John Dumbrell, *The Carter Presidency: A Re-evaluation* (Manchester, England: Manchester University Press, 1993), 181.

5. Asadollah Alam, *The Shah and I: The Confidential Diary of Iran's Royal Court 1969–1977* (New York: St. Martin's Press, 1993), 500.

6. Cyrus Vance, *Hard Choices: Critical Years in America's Foreign Policy* (New York: Simon and Schuster, 1983), 318.

7. James A. Bill, *The Eagle and the Lion* (New Haven: University Press, 1988), 233.

8. Amir Taheri, *The Spirit of Allah: Khomeini and the Islamic Revolution* (Bethesda, MD: Adler and Adler, 1985), 194, 197, 199–200.

CHAPTER EIGHT: THE RISE OF ISLAMOFASCISM

1. Raymond Tanter, personal interview with Mike Evans, June 15, 2006.

2. Irwin Cotler, personal interview with Mike Evans, September 28, 2006.

3. Sick, *All Fall Down*, 193–194.

4. Ofira Seliktar, *Failing the Crystal Ball Test* (Westport, CT: Praeger Publishers, 2000), 133.

5. Robert E. Huyser, *Mission to Tehran* (New York: Harper and Row, 1986), 17.

6. Michael D. Evans, *Showdown With Nuclear Iran* (Nashville: Nelson Current, 2006), 3–4.

7. Huyser, *Mission to Tehran,* 292.

8. Ibid., 294.

9. Ibid., 293, 296.

10. George Shadroui, "America's Security: The Genesis of a Problem," IntellectualConservative.com, April 26, 2005, http://www .intellectualconservative.com/article4303.html (accessed December 10, 2006).

11. Baqer Moin, *Khomeini: Life of the Ayatollah* (New York: Thomas Dunne Books, 2000), 204.

12. Ibid., 206.

13. Mohammad Reza Pahlavi, *Answer to History* (New York: Stein and Day, 1980), 12.

14. Amir Taheri, *The Cauldron: The Middle East Behind the Headlines* (London: Hutchinson, 1988), 192.

15. Wikipedia.org, s.v. "Iranian Hostage Crisis," http://en.wikipedia.org/ wiki/Iran_hostage_crisis (accessed December 10, 2006).

16. Amir Taheri, *Holy Terror* (London: Sphere Books Ltd., 1987), 196.

17. Chuck Morse, "Carter Sold Out Iran 1977–1978," IranianVoice.org, http://www.iranianvoice.org/article774.html (accessed December 10, 2006).

18. Sick, *All Fall Down,* 377.

19. Ibid., 397–398.

20. PBS.org, "People & Events: The Iranian Hostage Crisis, November 1979–January 1981," http://www.pbs.org/wgbh/amex/carter/peopleevents/ e_hostage.html (accessed December 10, 2006).

21. Cormac O'Brian, *Secret Lives of the U.S. Presidents* (Philadelphia: Quirk Books, 2004), 238.

22. Michael Foust, "Mohler: Carter Has Been Estranged From SBC Mainstream for Decades," Baptist 2 Baptist, October 30, 2000, www .baptist2baptist.net/b2barticle.asp?ID=185 (accessed December 10, 2006).

23. Ned Rice, "Jimmy of Mayberry: A Brutal Contrast," *National Review Online,* April 14, 2005, http://article.nationalreview.com/ ?q=ZGJlZTk5MWI3MmMwYTI2ZGMwNjFiNzkwZGZiNjhhMjY= (accessed December 10, 2006).

24. Steven F. Hayward, *The Real Jimmy Carter* (Washington DC: Regnery Publishing, Inc., 2004), 107.

25. J. A. Rosati, *The Carter Administration's Quest for Global Community: Beliefs and Their Impact on Behavior* (Columbia: University of South Carolina Press, 1987), 42.

26. Steven Hayward, interview by Jamie Glazov, "The Worst Ex-President," *FrontPageMagazine.com,* May 6, 2004, http://www.frontpagemag.com/articles/printable.asp?ID=13265 (accessed December 10, 2006).

27. Wikiquote.org, s.v. "Theodore Roosevelt," http://en.wikiquote.org/wiki/Theodore_Roosevelt#.22Speak_softly_and_carry_a_big_stick.22_.281901.29 (accessed January 29, 2007).

28. Seliktar, *Failing the Crystal Ball Test,* 185.

29. Jimmy Carter, *Palestine: Peace Not Apartheid* (New York: Simon & Schuster, 2006), 63.

30. Lowell Ponte, "Carter's Appease Prize," *FrontPageMagazine.com,* October 16, 2002, http://frontpagemag.com/articles/ReadArticle.asp?ID=3843 (accessed January 26, 2007).

31. Hayward, *The Real Jimmy Carter,* 208.

32. Ibid., 201–202.

33. Ben Johnson, "A Failed Former President," *FrontPageMagazine.com,* November 18, 2005, www.frontpagemag.com/Articles/ReadArticle.asp?ID=20232 (accessed December 11, 2006).

34. Joel Mowbray, "Jimmy Carter's Election Fraud," *FrontPageMagazine.com,* September 29, 2004, http://www.frontpagemag.com/Articles/ReadArticle.asp?ID=15283 (accessed January 25, 2007).

35. Hayward, *The Real Jimmy Carter,* 224.

36. Alan M. Dershowitz, "The World According to Carter," *FrontPageMagazine.com,* November 24, 2006, http://www.frontpagemag.com/Articles/ReadArticle.asp?ID=25653 (accessed January 29, 2007).

37. FOX Facts, "Dr. Kenneth W. Stein's Letter," December 7, 2006, http://www.foxnews.com/story/0,2933,235283,00.html (accessed January 24, 2007).

38. Taken from the private papers of Mike Evans.

39. *Spiegel Online International,* "The U.S. and Israel Stand Alone," August 15, 2006, http://www.spiegel.de/international/spiegel/0,1518,431793,00.html (accessed December 11, 2006).

40. Ann Coulter, *Treason: Liberal Treachery From the Cold War to the War on Terrorism* (New York: Three Rivers Press, 2003), 9, 13.

41. Ibid., 5–6.

42. Gordon Haff, "American Politics: 1960 to 1985," in *The Last Word,* reproduced at http://home.comcast.net/~ghaff/lword/newpol.html (accessed December 11, 2006).

43. R. Emmett Tyrrell Jr., "Jimmy Carter Pens the Worst Book of 2005," CNN.com, May 25, 2006, http://www.cnn.com/2006/POLITICS/05/25/tyrrell.carter/index.html (accessed December 11, 2006).

44. Matthias Küntzel, "Ahmadinejad's Demons," *The New Republic Online*, April 24, 2006, http://www.tnr.com/doc.mhtml?i=20060424&s=kuntzel042406 (accessed January 24, 2007).

Chapter Nine: The Nuclear Bomb of Islam

1. Osama bin Laden, "The Nuclear Bomb of Islam," May 29, 1998, quoted in "Indictment: United States of America vs. Zacarias Moussaoui," Overt Acts #11, The United States District Court for the Eastern District of Virginia, Alexandria Division, December 2001, as quoted by *Jurist*, "Terrorism Law and Policy," University of Pittsburgh School of Law, http://jurist.law.pitt.edu/terrorism/terrorismindict.htm (accessed December 11, 2006).

2. Raymond Tanter, personal interview with Mike Evans, June 15, 2006.

3. James Woolsey, personal interview with Mike Evans, September 2006.

4. Uzi Mahnaimi and Tony Allen-Mills, "Focus: Taking Aim at Iran," *Times Online*, March 13, 2005, http://www.timesonline.co.uk/article/0,,2089-1522800,00.html (accessed December 1, 2006).

5. Ibid.

6. Ibid.

7. *Hiroshima Witness*, video produced by the Hiroshima Peace Cultural Center and NHK, as quoted by AtomicArchive.com, "Testimony of Takehiko Sakai," http://www.atomicarchive.com/Docs/Hibakusha/Takehiko.shtml (accessed January 30, 2007).

8. Ibid., "Testimony of Yoshito Matsushige," http://www.atomicarchive.com/Docs/Hibakusha/Yoshito.shtml (accessed January 30, 2007).

9. Richard Rhodes, *The Making of the Atomic Bomb* (New York: Touchstone, 1988), 717–718.

10. Ibid., 718.

11. William L. Laurence, "Eye Witness Account: Atomic Bomb Mission Over Nagasaki," from War Department press release, August 9, 1945, as quoted by AtomicArchive.com, "The Bombing of Hiroshima and Nagasaki," http://www.atomicarchive.com/Docs/Hiroshima/Nagasaki.shtml (accessed January 30, 2007).

12. Fujie Urata Matsumoto, as quoted in Takashi Nagai, *We of Nagasaki: The Story of Survivors in an Atomic Wasteland* (New York: Duell, Sloan and Pearce, 1964), 43.

13. Hideko Tamura Friedman, "Hiroshima Memories," *Bulletin of the Atomic Scientists*, vol. 51, no. 3 (May/June 1995), 6–22.

14. Rhodes, *The Making of the Atomic Bomb*, 742.

15. J. Robert Oppenheimer, "'Now I Am Become Death...,'" AtomicArchive.com, http://www.atomicarchive.com/Movies/Movie8.shtml (accessed December 11, 2006).

16. McInerney and Vallely, *Endgame*, 30–31.

17. James Woolsey, personal interview with Mike Evans, August 31, 2006.

18. Alan Dershowitz, personal interview with Mike Evans, August 18, 2006. For more excerpts of this interview, see Appendix H.

19. Benjamin Netanyahu, personal interview with Mike Evans, August 2006. For more excerpts of this interview, see Appendix C.

20. "'Why We Fight America': Al Qa'ida Spokesman Explains September 11 and Declares Intentions to Kill 4 Million Americans with Weapons of Mass Destruction," as quoted by the Middle East Media Research Institute, special dispatch, no. 388, June 12, 2002, http://memri.org/bin/articles .cgi?Page=archives&area=sd&ID=SP38802 (accessed December 12, 2006).

21. Graham Allison, *Nuclear Terrorism* (New York: Times Books, 2004), 6.

22. Yossi Peled, personal interview with Mike Evans, July 22, 2006.

23. Raymond Tanter, personal interview with Mike Evans, June 15, 2006.

24. Walid Shoebat, personal interview with Mike Evans, September 26, 2006.

25. John R. Bolton, "Iran's Continuing Pursuit of Weapons of Mass Destruction," testimony before the House International Relations Committee Subcommittee on the Middle East and Central Asia, June 24, 2004, http:// www.state.gov/t/us/rm/33909.htm (accessed December 14, 2006).

26. GlobalSecurity.org, "Full text of President Ahmadinejad's Speech at General Assembly," *Islamic Republic News Agency (IRNA)*, Sept 17 2005, http://www.globalsecurity.org/wmd/library/news/iran/2005/iran-050918 -irna02.htm (accessed September 20, 2005).

27. Irwin Cotler, personal interview with Mike Evans, September 28, 2006.

28. Associated Press, "Iran Hosts 'The World Without Zionism,'" *Jerusalem Post*, October 26, 2005, http://www.jpost.com/servlet/Satellite ?cid=1129540603434&pagename=JPost%2FJPArticle%2FShowFull (accessed November 1, 2006).

29. Ayatollah Khomeini, quoted from an 11th-grade Iranian schoolbook by Bernard Lewis, reprinted by Mike Rosen, "Maniacs Mean Business," *Rocky Mountain News*, August 25, 2005, http://www.rockymountainnews.com/ drmn/opinion_columnists/article/0,2777,DRMN_23972_4942689,00.html (accessed December 14, 2006).

30. Wikipedia.org, s.v. "Mohammad Taghi Mesbah Yazdi," http://en.wikipedia.org/wiki/Mohammad_Taghi_Mesbah_Yazdi (accessed December 14, 2006).

31. James Woolsey, personal interview with Mike Evans, September 2006.

32. Mike Evans and Robert Wise, *The Jerusalem Scroll* (Nashville: Thomas Nelson Publishers, 2005), 62–63.

33. Yossef Bodansky, presentation notes given at conference and personal conversation with author.

34. Paul L. Williams, *Osama's Revenge* (New York: Prometheus Books, 2004), 33.

35. Ibid., 41.

36. Benjamin Weiser, "U.S. Says Bin Laden Aide Tried to Get Nuclear Material," *New York Times*, September 26, 1998, http://select.nytimes.com/gst/abstract.html?res=F20F13FC395D0C758EDDA00894D0494D81 (accessed November 10, 2004).

37. Williams, *Osama's Revenge*, 41.

38. Scott Parish and John Lepingwell, "Are Suitcase Nukes on the Loose? The Story Behind the Controversy," Center for Nonproliferation Studies, November 1997, http://cns.miis.edu/pubs/reports/lebedst.htm (accessed January 31, 2007).

39. Steve Kroft, host, "The Perfect Terrorist Weapon," *60 Minutes*, September 7, 1997, Burrel's transcripts.

40. Dick Cheney, interview on *Meet the Press*, December 15, 1991, as quoted in Graham Allison, "Nuclear Terrorism: How Serious a Threat to Russia?" *Russia in Global Affairs* online edition, September/October 2004, viewed at Belfer Center for Science and International Affairs, John F. Kennedy School of Government, Harvard University, http://bcsia.ksg.harvard.edu/publication.cfm?program=CORE&ctype=article&item_id=1223#_ftn12 (accessed February 22, 2007).

41. Yossef Bodansky, quoted in "Bin Laden Has 20 Nuclear Bombs," WorldTribune.com, August 9, 1999, http://www.worldtribune.com/worldtribune/x180.html (accessed January 31, 2007).

42. Hamid Mir, "If U.S. Uses Nuclear Weapons, It Will Receive Same Response," interview with Osama bin Laden, *Dawn* (Pakistan), November 10, 2001.

43. Kimberly McCloud and Matthew Osborne, "WMD Terrorism and Usama bin Laden," Center for Nonproliferation Studies, March 7, 2001, http://cns.miis.edu/pubs/reports/binladen.htm (accessed January 24, 2007).

44. DEBKA*file*, "America's War on Terror—Part III: Bin Laden May Have Small Nuclear Bombs," October 13, 2001, http://www.debka.com/article .php?aid=319 (accessed January 24, 2007).

45. Peter Bergen, "Trees and Tapes May Hint at Bin Laden Location," CNN.com, August 28, 2006, http://www.cnn.com/2006/WORLD/ asiapcf/08/23/bergen.binladen/index.html (accessed January 31, 2007).

46. Gopalaswami Parthasarathy, "Pakistan Plays Nuclear Footsie; Does Anyone Care?" *Wall Street Journal*, January 2, 2004, http://online.wsj.com/ article/0,,SB107300266639911800,00.html (accessed November 9, 2004).

47. Mohamed El Baradei, interview during the World Economic Forum, Davos, January 22, 2004.

48. Massimo Calabresi and Romesh Ratnesar, "Can We Stop the Next Attack?" *TIME.com*, March 11, 2002, http://www.time.com/time/magazine/ article/0,9171,1001961,00.html (accessed December 11, 2006).

49. David Johnston and James Risen, "Traces of Terrorism: The Intelligence Reports; Series of Warnings," *New York Times*, May 17, 2002, http://select.nytimes.com/gst/abstract.html?res=F10B14FA345D0C748DDDA C0894DA404482 (accessed November 9, 2004).

50. Andy Serwer, "The Oracle of Everything," *Fortune*, November 11, 2002, http://money.cnn.com/magazines/fortune/fortune_archive/2002/11/11/ 331843/index.htm (accessed November 9, 2004).

CHAPTER TEN: THE BATTLE FOR
THE SOUL OF AMERICA

1. *Corruption Chronicles*, "Congress Gets Muslim," a *Judicial Watch* blog, November 8, 2006, http://www.corruptionchronicles.com/2006/11/congress_ gets_muslim.html (accessed November 10, 2006).

2. Mort Zuckerman, personal interview with Mike Evans, August 22, 2006. For more excerpts of this interview, see Appendix I.

3. Michael D. Evans, *The American Prophecies* (Nashville: Warner Faith, 2004), 21.

4. First Amendment of the Constitution of the United States of America.

5. John T. Elson, "Toward a Hidden God," *TIME.com*, April 8, 1966, http://www.time.com/time/magazine/article/0,9171,835309,00.html (accessed November 10, 2006).

6. WorldNetDaily.com, "Dr. Dobson Urges: Head to Alabama," August 26, 2003, http://www.worldnetdaily.com/news/article.asp?ARTICLE_ID=34267 (accessed November 11, 2006).

7. Jerry Ropelato, "Internet Pornography Statistics," Internet Filter Review, http://internet-filter-review.toptenreviews.com/internet-pornography-statistics.html (accessed November 10, 2006).

8. *Washington Post*, "To Put it Another Way," October 7, 2001, B3.

9. Susan Sontag, "The Talk of the Town," *The New Yorker*, September 24, 2001, as quoted by the Highland Shepherd, http://www.msgr.ca/msgr-3/talk_of_the_town_susan_sontag.htm (accessed December 11, 2006).

10. Barbara Kingsolver, *Milwaukee Journal Sentinel*, September 27, 2001, as quoted by Right Wing News, http://www.rightwingnews.com/quotes/left.php (accessed November 11, 2006).

11. The White House, "Address to a Joint Session of Congress and the American People," news release, September 20, 2001, http://www.whitehouse.gov/news/releases/2001/09/20010920-8.html (accessed November 12, 2006).

12. Ibid.

13. The White House, "State of the Union Address of the President to the Joint Session of Congress," news release, January 29, 2002.

14. "Iraqi Liberation Act of 1998," as quoted by *Iraq Watch*, http://www.iraqwatch.org/government/US/Legislation/ILA.htm (accessed December 30, 2006).

15. Alan Colmes, *Red, White and Liberal* (New York: Regan, 2003), 53.

16. David Horowitz, "Moment of Truth (for the Anti-American Left)," *FrontPageMagazine.com*, March 31, 2003, http://www.frontpagemag.com/Articles/ReadArticle.asp?ID=6962 (accessed November 11, 2006).

17. Ibid.

18. Richard D. Heideman, "An Open Letter to all Jewish Community Leaders," September 3, 2001, as quoted by Jewis Ozzies Intern.Net, http://www.join.org.au/Releases/Durban_Open_Letter.htm (accessed November 13, 2006).

19. Herb Keinon, "Festival of Hate," *Jerusalem Post*, September 7, 2001.

20. David Horowitz, *Unholy Alliance: Radical Islam and the American Left* (Washington, DC: Regnery Publishing, Inc, 2004), 135–136.

21. James Woolsey, personal interview with Mike Evans, August 16, 2006. For more excerpts of this interview, see Appendix D.

22. CNN.com, "Saddam Hussein Is Losing Grip on Northern Cities in Iraq," transcript, April 10, 2003, http://transcripts.cnn.com/TRANSCRIPTS/0304/10/ip.00.html (accessed November 12, 2006).

23. George Barna, "A Biblical Worldview Has a Radical Effect on a Person's Life," The Barna Update, December 1, 2003, http://www.barna.org/FlexPage.aspx?Page=BarnaUpdate&BarnaUpdateID=154 (accessed November 12, 2006).

24. WorldNetDaily.com, "New Bible Translation Promotes Fornication," June 24, 2004, http://www.worldnetdaily.com/news/article.asp?ARTICLE_ID=39114 (accessed November 13, 2006).

25. Ibid.

26. Jacob Laksin, "The Church of the Latter-Day Leftists," *FrontPageMagazine.com*, January 13, 2005, http://www.frontpagemag.com/Articles/ReadArticle.asp?ID=16625 (accessed November 13, 2006).

27. John W. Chalfant, *Abandonment Theology: The Clergy and the Decline of American Christianity* (Winter Park, FL: Hartline Marketing, 1997), 8.

28. Francis A. Schaeffer, *The Great Evangelical Disaster* (Westchester, IL: Crossway Books, 1984), 37.

EPILOGUE

1. Christopher Columbus, *Book of Prophecies*, as quoted in Stephen Mansfield and Douglas Layton, *Searching for Democracy* (Nashville, TN: Servant Group International, 1997), 83.

APPENDIX A

1. United Nations, "Letter from President Ahmadi-Nejad to President Bush," news release, May 9, 2006, http://www.un.int/iran/pressaffairs/pressreleases/2006/articles/1.html# (accessed February 26, 2007).

APPENDIX B

1. United Nations, "Message of H. E. Dr. Mahmoud Ahmadinejad, President of the Islamic Republic of Iran to the American People," news release, November 29, 2006, http://www.un.int/iran/pressaffairs/pressreleases/2006/articles/13.htm (accessed February 26, 2007).

APPENDIX D

1. Author's paraphrase. See page 210.

2. John Lehman, "We're Not Winning This War: Despite Some Notable Achievements, New Thinking Is Needed on the Home Front and Abroad," *Washington Post*, August 31, 2006, http://www.washingtonpost.com/wp-dyn/content/article/2006/08/30/AR2006083002730.html (accessed February 1, 2007).

Index

About the Author

Mike Evans is one of America's top experts on the Middle East. For decades he has been a personal confidant to most of Israel's top leaders. Mr. Evans is an award-winning journalist and has been published in the *Wall Street Journal, Newsweek, USA Today, Washington Times, Jerusalem Post,* and numerous publications in America and the world. He is a member of the National Press Club and has covered world events for more than two decades.

He is the author of the *New York Times* best sellers *Beyond Iraq: The Next Move, Showdown With Nuclear Iran,* and *The American Prophecies.* Millions throughout the world have seen the television specials he has hosted. Mr. Evans's prime-time television specials have received national awards on thirteen different occasions.

Mr. Evans is a top-network Middle East analyst and is in constant demand. He has appeared on hundreds of network radio and television shows, such as *Fox and Friends,* MSNBC, *Nightline, Good Morning America, Crossfire, CNN World News,* BBC, *The Rush Limbaugh Show,* and others.

This book, *The Final Move Beyond Iraq,* has been translated into a major television documentary.

As a public speaker, Mike Evans has spoken to more than 4,000 audiences worldwide. In the last decade alone, he has addressed more than 10 million people around the globe, with more than 110,000 leaders in attendance at his conferences. He has spoken at the Kremlin Palace in Moscow, the Kennedy School of Law at Harvard University, and the World Summit on Terrorism in Jerusalem.

Mr. Evans's wife, Carolyn, is the chairwoman and founder of the Christian Woman of the Year Association. Ruth Graham, Elizabeth Dole, Mother Teresa, and other distinguished women are among the recipients who have been honored over the past fifteen years. The executive committee is comprised of a number of prominent women, including Dr. Cory SerVaas, owner of the *Saturday Evening Post.*

To contact Mr. Evans to speak at your event or to obtain a DVD of the documentary based on *The Final Move Beyond Iraq,* please write Dr. Mike Evans, P. O. Box 210489, Bedford, TX 76095.

Dear Reader,

In 2003, I wrote *Beyond Iraq: The Next Move*, which became a *New York Times* best seller and, in fact, toppled *Living History* by Hillary Clinton from its number-one spot on Amazon.com. Rush Limbaugh broke this story. The book became a *New York Times* best seller just weeks after its release.

In the book, I wrote that the greatest threat to American troops would come after the war for Baghdad had been won, that Iraq would become the new ground zero for terrorism, that an army of suicide bombers would spread out across Iraq in an attempt to weaken the resolve of the American people, and that Iran and Syria would play the diplomatic card but would clandestinely support terrorism in Iraq. All of these things have come to pass. Should the events outlined in *The Final Move Beyond Iraq* come to pass, it would be infinitely more catastrophic than the events of 9/11. The stakes are grave, indeed. The information in *Beyond Iraq: The Next Move* lays out the biblical and strategic basis for the battle in Iraq.

In chapter three of the book you have just read, I mentioned a petition to the president for a strong and safe America. It is a statement of moral clarity in a world of shifting and declining values. This urgent petition declares that patriotic Americans everywhere are against amnesty for the killers and murderers of our troops.

Over three thousand of our men and women have been killed and over twenty-one thousand wounded. There must be justice; the terrorists must not be allowed to go free. Israel should not have to pay the price of appeasement by giving away biblical lands, forcing them to divide Jerusalem and give away Judea, Samaria, and the Golan Heights to terrorist regimes. Iran must not gain nuclear superiority that could turn it into a deadly nuclear power. Iran and Syria, both terror states, must not be allowed to participate in the determination of the future of Iraq. Iran and Syria are not the solution; they are the problem.

The United Nations must not be permitted to determine the future of Iran's nuclear power—Iran is a nation that wants a world without Israel and the United States. Iran's president, Mahmoud Ahmadinejad, has stated, "The U.S., Britain, and Israel will eventually disappear from the world like the pharaohs. It's a divine promise."

If you would like a copy of the petition to the president, please write today to:

Petition to the President
Dr. Mike Evans
P. O. Box 210489
Bedford, TX 76095

If you would like to receive copies of my weekly Middle East alerts, please mention that when you write for your copy of the petition. My book *Beyond Iraq: The Next Move* may be ordered at the above address for $11.00 (includes postage and handling). You may also visit our Web site at www.beyondiraq.com to sign the petition, sign up for Middle East alerts, and order *Beyond Iraq: The Next Move*.